S0-DJY-612

# CHILTON BOOK COMPANY
## REPAIR & TUNE-UP GUIDE

# FORD/MERCURY FRONT WHEEL DRIVE 1981-87

All U.S. and Canadian models of FORD Escort, Escort GT, EXP, Tempo • MERCURY Lynx, LN7, Topaz

President LAWRENCE A. FORNASIERI
Vice President and General Manager JOHN P. KUSHNERICK
Editor-in-Chief KERRY A. FREEMAN, S.A.E.
Managing Editor DEAN F. MORGANTINI, S.A.E.
Senior Editor RICHARD J. RIVELE, S.A.E.
Senior Editor W. CALVIN SETTLE, JR., S.A.E.

CHILTON BOOK COMPANY
Radnor, Pennsylvania
19089

## SAFETY NOTICE

Proper service and repair procedures are vital to the safe, reliable operation of all motor vehicles, as well as the personal safety of those performing repairs. This book outlines procedures for servicing and repairing vehicles using safe, effective methods. The procedures contain many NOTES, CAUTIONS and WARNINGS which should be followed along with standard safety procedures to eliminate the possibility of personal injury or improper service which could damage the vehicle or compromise its safety.

It is important to note that repair procedures and techniques, tools and parts for servicing motor vehicles, as well as the skill and experience of the individual performing the work vary widely. It is not possible to anticipate all of the conceivable ways or conditions under which vehicles may be serviced, or to provide cautions as to all of the possible hazards that may result. Standard and accepted safety precautions and equipment should be used during cutting, grinding, chiseling, prying, or any other process that can cause material removal or projectiles.

Some procedures require the use of tools specially designed for a specific purpose. Before substituting another tool or procedure, you must be completely satisfied that neither your personal safety, nor the performance of the vehicle will be endangered.

Although the information in this guide is based on industry sources and is as complete as possible at the time of publication, the possibility exists that the manufacturer made later changes which could not be included here. While striving for total accuracy, Chilton Book Company cannot assume responsibility for any errors, changes, or omissions that may occur in the compilation of this data.

## PART NUMBERS

Part numbers listed in this reference are not recommendations by Chilton for any product by brand name. They are references that can be used with interchange manuals and aftermarket supplier catalogs to locate each brand supplier's discrete part number.

## SPECIAL TOOLS

Special tools are recommended by the vehicle manufacturer to perform their specific job. Use has been kept to a minimum, but where absolutely necessary, are they referred to in the text by the part number of the tool manufacturer. These tools can be purchased, under the appropriate part number, from Owatonna Tool Company, Owatonna, MN 55060 or an equivalent tool can be purchased locally from a tool supplier or parts outlet. Before substituting any tool for the one recommended, read the SAFETY NOTICE at the top of this page.

## ACKNOWLEDGMENTS

The Chilton Book Company expresses its appreciation to the Ford Motor Company, Dearborn, Michigan for their generous assistance.

Copyright © 1987 by Chilton Book Company
All Rights Reserved
Published in Radnor, Pennsylvania 19089 by Chilton Book Company

Manufactured in the United States of America
    4567890      654321098

Chilton's Repair & Tune-Up Guide: Ford/Mercury Front Wheel Drive 1981–87
ISBN: 0-8019-7748-7 pbk.
Library of Congress Catalog Card No. 86-47770

# CONTENTS

# Quick Reference Specifications For Your Vehicle

Fill in this chart with the most commonly used specifications for your vehicle. Specifications can be found in Chapters 1 through 3 or on the tune-up decal under the hood of the vehicle.

## Tune-Up

Firing Order_____

Spark Plugs:

    Type_____

    Gap (in.)_____

Torque (ft. lbs.)_____

Idle Speed (rpm)_____

Ignition Timing (°)_____

    Vacuum or Electronic Advance (Connected/Disconnected)_____

Valve Clearance (in.)

    Intake_____    Exhaust_____

## Capacities

Engine Oil Type (API Rating)_____

    With Filter Change (qts)_____

    Without Filter Change (qts)_____

Cooling System (qts)_____

Manual Transmission (pts)_____

    Type_____

Automatic Transmission (pts)_____

    Type_____

Front Differential (pts)_____

    Type_____

Rear Differential (pts)_____

    Type_____

Transfer Case (pts)_____

    Type_____

## FREQUENTLY REPLACED PARTS

Use these spaces to record the part numbers of frequently replaced parts.

| PCV VALVE | OIL FILTER | AIR FILTER | FUEL FILTER |
|---|---|---|---|
| Type_____ | Type_____ | Type_____ | Type_____ |
| Part No._____ | Part No._____ | Part No._____ | Part No._____ |

# General Information and Maintenance

## HOW TO USE THIS BOOK

Chilton's Repair & Tune-Up Guide for Ford/Mercury Front Wheel Drive models is intended to teach you more about the inner workings of your car and save you money on its upkeep. The first two chapters will be used the most, since they contain maintenance and tune-up information and procedures. The following chapters concern themselves with the more complex systems. Operating systems from engine through brakes are covered to the extent that we feel the average do-it-yourselfer should get involved. This book will not explain such things as rebuilding the differential for the simple reason that the expertise required and the investment in special tools make this task uneconomical. We will tell you how to change your own brake pads and shoes, replace spark plugs, perform routine maintenance, and many more jobs that will save you money, give you personal satisfactions, and help you avoid problems.

A secondary purpose of this book is as a reference for owners who want to understand their can and/or their mechanics better. In this case, no tools at all are required.

Before removing any parts, read through the entire procedure. This will give you the overall view of what tools and supplies will be required.

The sections begin with a brief discussion of the system and what it involves, followed by adjustments, maintenance, removal and installation procedures, and repair or overhaul procedures. When repair is not considered feasible, we tell you how to remove the part and then how to install the new or rebuilt replacement. In this way, you at least save the labor costs. Backyard repair of such components as the alternator is just not practical.

Two basic mechanic's rules should be mentioned here. One, whenever the left side of your car or engine is referred to, it is meant to specify the driver's side. Conversely, the right side means the passenger's side. Secondly, most screws and bolts are removed by turning counterclockwise, and tightened by turning clockwise. Safety is always the most important rule. Constantly be aware of the dangers involved in working on an automobile and take the proper precautions. Use jackstands when working under a raised vehicle. Don't smoke or allow an exposed flame to came near the battery or any part of the fuel system. Always use the proper tool and use it correctly; bruised knuckles and skinned fingers aren't a mechanic's standard equipment. Always take your time and have patience. Once you have some experience, working on your car will become an enjoyable hobby.

## TOOLS AND EQUIPMENT

I would be impossible to catalog each and every tool that you may need to perform all the operations included in this book. It would also not be wise for the amateur to rush out and buy an expensive set of tools on the theory that he may need one of them at some time. The best approach is to proceed slowly, gathering together a good quality set of those tools that are used most frequently. Don't be misled by the low cost of bargain tools. It is far better to spend a little more for quality, name brand tools. Forged wrenches, 10 or 12 point sockets and finetooth ratchets are by far preferable to their less expensive counterparts. As any good mechanic can tell you, there are few worse experiences than typing to work with bad tools. Your monetary savings will be far outweighed by frustration and mangled knuckles.

Begin accumulating those tools that are used most frequently; those associated with routine maintenance and tune-up. In addition

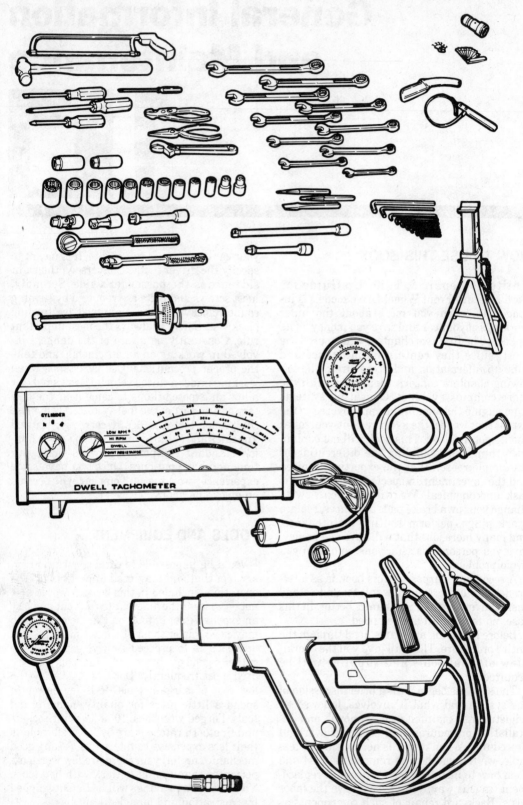

**You need only a basic assortment of hand tools for most maintenance and repair jobs**

to the normal assortment of screwdrivers and pliers, you should have the following tools for routine maintenance jobs.

1. SAE and metric wrenches, socket, and combination open end/box wrenches.
2. Jackstands, for support.
3. Oil filter wrench.
4. Oil filler spout or funnel.
5. Grease gun, for chassis lubrication.
6. Hydrometer, for checking the battery.
7. A low flat pan for draining oil.
8. Lots of rags for wiping up the inevitable mess.

In addition to the above items, there are several others that are not absolutely necessary, buy are handy to have around. These include oil drying compound, a transmission funnel, and the usual supply of lubricants, antifreeze and fluids, although these can be purchased as needed. This is a basic list for routine maintenance, but only your personal needs can accurately determine your list of tools.

The second list of tools is for tune-ups. While the tools involved here are slightly more sophisticated, they need not be outrageously expensive. There are several inexpensive tachometers on the market that are ever bit as good for the average mechanic as a $100.00 professional model. Just be sure that it goes to at least 1,200–1,500 rpm on the tach scale, and that it works on 4, 6, and 8 cylinder engines. A basic list of tune-up equipment could include:

1. Tachometer.
2. Spark plug wrench.
3. Timing light (preferably equipped with an inductive pickup).
4. A set of flat feeler gauges.
5. A set of round wire spark plug gauges.

In addition to these basic tools, there are several other tools and gauges you may find useful. These include:

1. A compression gauge. The screw-in type is slower to use, buy eliminates the possibility of a faulty reading due to escaping pressure.
2. A manifold vacuum gauge.
3. A test light.
4. An induction meter. This is used for determining whether or not there is current in a wire. These are handy for use if a wire is broken somewhere in a wiring harness. As a final note, you will probably find a torque wrench necessary for all buy the most basic work. The beam type models are perfectly adequate, although the newer click type are more precise.

## Special Tools

Normally, the use of special factory tools is avoided for repair procedures, since these are not readily available for the do-it-yourself mechanic. When it is possible to perform the job with more commonly available tools, it will be pointed out, but occasionally, a special tool was designed to perform a specific function and should be used. Before substituting another tool, you should be convinced that neither your safety nor the performance of the vehicle will be compromised.

Some special tools are available commercially from major tool manufacturers. Others for your car can be purchased from your dealer or from Owatonna Tool Co., Owatonna, Minnesota 55060.

## SERVICING YOUR CAR SAFELY

It is virtually impossible to anticipate all of the hazards involved with automotive maintenance and service but care and common sense will prevent most accidents.

The rules of safety for mechanics range from "don't smoke around gasoline," to "use the proper tool for the job." The trick to avoid injuries is to develop safe work habits and take every possible precaution.

### Do's

• Do keep a fire extinguisher and first aid kit within easy reach.
• Do wear safety glasses or goggles when cutting, drilling, grinding or prying. If you wear glasses for the sake of vision, then they should be made of hardened glass that can serve also as safety glasses, or wear safety goggles over your regular glasses.
• Do shield your eyes whenever you work around the battery. Batteries contain sulphuric acid. In case of contact with the eyes or skin, flush the area with water or a mixture of water and baking soda and get medical attention immediately.
• Do use safety stands for any under-car service. Jacks are for raising vehicles; safety stands are for making sure the vehicle stays raised until you want it to come down. Whenever the vehicle is raised, block the wheels remaining on the ground and set the parking brake.
• Do use adequate ventilation when working with any chemicals. Asbestos dust resulting from brake lining wear can cause cancer.
• Do disconnect the negative battery cable when working on the electrical system. The primary ignition system can contain up to 40,000 volts.
• Do follow manufacturer's directions whenever working with potentially hazardous materials. Both brake fluid and antifreeze are poisonous if taken internally.

• Do properly maintain your tools. Loose hammerheads, mushroomed punches and chisels, frayed or poorly grounded electrical cords, excessively worn screwdriver, spread wrenches (open end), cracked sockets can cause accidents.

• Do use the proper size and type of tool for the job being done.

• Do when possible, pull on a wrench handle rather than push on it, and adjust your stance to prevent a fall.

• Do be sure that adjustable wrenches are tightly adjusted on the nut or bolt and pulled so that the face is on the side of the fixed jaw.

• Do select a wrench or socket that fits the nut or bolt. The wrench or socket should sit straight, not cocked.

• Do strike squarely with a hammer to avoid glancing blows.

• Do set the parking brake and block the drive wheels if the work requires that the engine is running.

## Don'ts

• Don't run an engine in a garage or anywhere else without proper ventilation – EVER! Carbon monoxide is poisonous. It is absorbed by the body 400 times faster than oxygen. It takes a long time to leave the human body and you can build up a deadly supply of it in you system by simply breathing in a little every day. You may not realize you are slowly poisoning yourself. Always use power vents, windows, fans or open the garage doors.

• Don't work around moving parts while wearing a necktie or other loose clothing. Short sleeves are much safer than long, loose sleeves. Hard-toed shoes with neoprene soles protect your toes and give a better grip on slippery surfaces. Jewelry such as watches, fancy belt buckles, beads or body adornment of any kind is not safe working around a car. Long hair should be hidden under a hat or cap.

• Don't use pockets for toolboxes. A fall or bump can drive a screwdriver deep into you body. Even a wiping cloth hanging from the back pocket can wrap around a spinning shaft or fan.

• Don't smoke when working around gasoline, cleaning solvent or other flammable material.

• Don't smoke when working around the battery. When the battery is being charged, it gives off explosive hydrogen gas.

• Don't use gasoline to wash your hands. There are excellent soaps available. Gasoline may contain lead, and lead can enter the body through a cut, accumulating in the body until you are very ill. Gasoline also removes all the natural oils from the skin so that bone dry hands will suck up oil and grease.

• Don't service the air conditioning system unless you are equipped with the necessary tools and training. The refrigerant, R-12, is extremely cold and when exposed to the air, will instantly freeze any surface it comes in contact with, including your eyes. Although the refrigerant is normally nontoxic, R-12 becomes a deadly poisonous gas in the presence of an open flame. One good whiff of the vapors from burning refrigerant can be fatal.

## IDENTIFICATION

### Vehicle Identification Number (VIN)

The official vehicle identification (serial) number (used for title and registration purposes) is stamped on a metal tab fastened to the instrument panel and visible through the driver's side of the windshield from the outside. The vehicle identification (serial) number contains a 17 character number. The number is used for warranty identification of the vehicle and indicates: manufacturer, type of restraint system, line, series, body type, engine, model year, and consecutive unit number.

### Vehicle Certification Label

The Vehicle Certification Label is found on the left door lock face panel or door pillar. The upper half of the label contains the name of the manufacturer, month and year of manufacture, gross weight rating, gross axle weight, and the certification statements pertinent. The certification also repeats the VIN number and gives the color code and the accessories found on the car.

### Transaxle Codes

The transmission code is located on the bottom edge of the Vehicle Certification Label.

### Transaxle Codes

| Code | Year | Type |
|---|---|---|
| 4 | 81–82 | MTX 4 spd |
| 9 | 83–87 | MTX 4 spd |
| D | 84–87 | MTX 5 spd |
| B | 81–87 | ATX Batavia |
| O | 84–85 | ATX Toyo Kogyo |

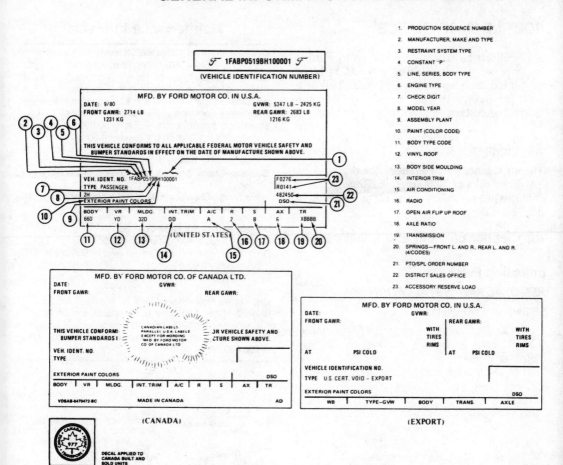

1. PRODUCTION SEQUENCE NUMBER
2. MANUFACTURER, MAKE AND TYPE
3. RESTRAINT SYSTEM TYPE
4. CONSTANT "P"
5. LINE, SERIES, BODY TYPE
6. ENGINE TYPE
7. CHECK DIGIT
8. MODEL YEAR
9. ASSEMBLY PLANT
10. PAINT (COLOR CODE)
11. BODY TYPE CODE
12. VINYL ROOF
13. BODY SIDE MOULDING
14. INTERIOR TRIM
15. AIR CONDITIONING
16. RADIO
17. OPEN AIR FLIP UP ROOF
18. AXLE RATIO
19. TRANSMISSION
20. SPRINGS—FRONT L. AND R., REAR L. AND R. (4/CODES)
21. PTO/SPL ORDER NUMBER
22. DISTRICT SALES OFFICE
23. ACCESSORY RESERVE LOAD

**Vehicle Identification and Certification Plates**

## Engine Codes

| Code | Year | Liters | CID | Fuel System |
|------|------|--------|-----|-------------|
| H | 84–87 | 2.0 | 122 | Diesel |
| J | 86–87 | 1.9 | 113.5 | EFI |
| R | 84–87 | 2.3 HSC | 140 | 1 bbl |
| S | 85–87 | 2.3 HSC HO | 140 | 1 bbl |
| X | 85–87 | 2.3 HSC | 140 | CFI |
| 1 | 81 | 1.3 | 79 | 2 bbl |
| 2 | 81–85 | 1.6 | 98 | 2 bbl |
| 4 | 83–85 | 1.6 HO | 98 | 2 bbl |
| 5 | 83–85 | 1.6 | 98 | EFI |
| 8 | 84–85 | 1.6 | 98 | EFI (Turbo) |
| 9 | 86–87 | 1.9 | 113.5 | 2 bbl |

NOTE: The engine code is indicated by the eighth digit of the vehicle identification number.

## ROUTINE MAINTENANCE

Major efforts have been undertaken by Ford to improve serviceability and provide reduced scheduled maintenance for our car. This is a built-in savings to you, the owner, in man hours and dollars.

## Air Cleaner

The air cleaner element should be replaced every 30 months or 30,000 miles. More frequent changes are necessary if the car is operated in dust conditions.

## Air Cleaner Element and Crankcase

## Emission Filter

### REMOVAL AND INSTALLATION

#### 1.6 Base and HO Engines

NOTE: *The crankcase emission filter should be changed each time you replace the air cleaner element.*

## Maintenance Intervals

### Gasoline Engines—Replace/Change
Engine Oil—Every 7500 miles/12 months
Oil Filter—Every other oil change, on turbo models, at every oil change. At least every 12 months
Air Cleaner Element—Every 30,000 miles, more frequently if operation under severe conditions
Crankcase Breather Filter—Every 30,000 miles, more frequently if operation under severe conditions
Spark Plugs—Every 30,000 miles, more frequently if operation under severe conditions
Coolant—Check condition and coolant protection every year
Drive Belts—Check condition and tension annually. Replace every 3 years

### Diesel Engine—Replace/Change
Valve Clearance—Adjust every 15,000 miles
Drive Belts—Inspect and adjust every 7500 miles. Replace every 3 years
Engine Oil, Oil Filter—Every 7500 miles/7 months
Oil By-Pass Filter—Every 15,000 miles
Drain Water Fuel Filter—Every 7500 miles/7 months
Coolant—Check annually for condition and protection. Change every 30,000 miles/2 years
Camshaft and Injection Pump Belts—Replace every 100,000 miles

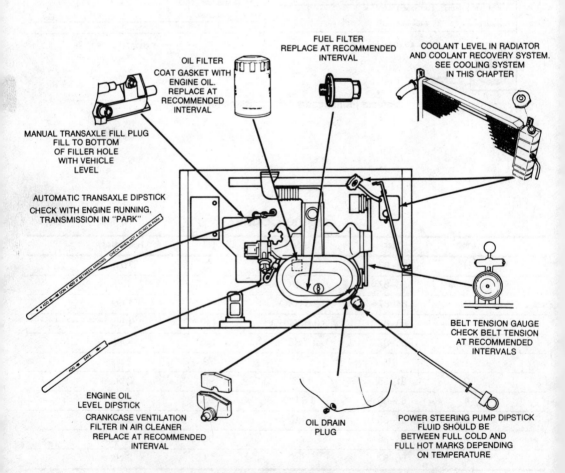

Lubrication and service points—1.3L, 1.6L and 1.9L non EFI engines

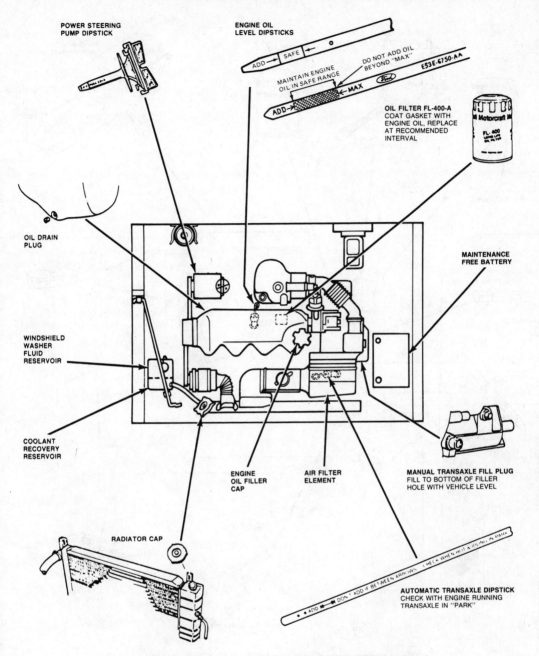

**POWER STEERING PUMP DIPSTICK**

**ENGINE OIL LEVEL DIPSTICKS**

ADD — SAFE ←

DO NOT ADD OIL BEYOND "MAX"

E53E-6750-AA

MAINTAIN ENGINE OIL IN SAFE RANGE

← MAX

ADD→

**OIL FILTER FL-400-A** COAT GASKET WITH ENGINE OIL, REPLACE AT RECOMMENDED INTERVAL

Motorcraft
FL-400

**OIL DRAIN PLUG**

**MAINTENANCE FREE BATTERY**

**WINDSHIELD WASHER FLUID RESERVOIR**

**COOLANT RECOVERY RESERVOIR**

**ENGINE OIL FILLER CAP**

**AIR FILTER ELEMENT**

**MANUAL TRANSAXLE FILL PLUG** FILL TO BOTTOM OF FILLER HOLE WITH VEHICLE LEVEL

**RADIATOR CAP**

ADD • DON'T ADD IF BETWEEN ARROWS CHECK WHEN HOT & RUNNING IN PARK

**AUTOMATIC TRANSAXLE DIPSTICK** CHECK WITH ENGINE RUNNING TRANSAXLE IN "PARK"

**Lubrication and service points—1.6L and 1.9L EFI engines**

1. Remove the wing nut that retains the air cleaner assembly to the carburetor. Remove any support bracket bolts (engine to air cleaner). Disconnect the air duct tubing, vacuum lines and heat tubes connected to the air cleaner.

2. Remove the air cleaner assembly from the car.

NOTE: *Removing the air cleaner as an assembly helps prevent dirt from falling into the carburetor.*

3. Remove the spring clips that hold the top of the air cleaner to the body. Remove the cover.

4. Remove the air cleaner element. Disconnect the spring clip that retains the emission filter to the air cleaner body, and remove the filter.

5. Clean the inside of the air cleaner body by wiping with a rag. Check the mounting gasket (gaskets, if the car is equipped with a spacer), replace any gasket(s) that show wear.

6. Install a new emission filter and a new air cleaner element.

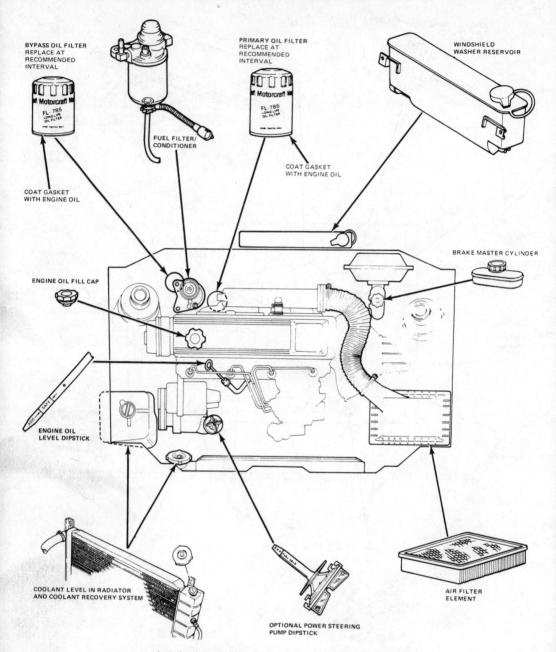

BYPASS OIL FILTER
REPLACE AT
RECOMMENDED
INTERVAL

PRIMARY OIL FILTER
REPLACE AT
RECOMMENDED
INTERVAL

WINDSHIELD
WASHER RESERVOIR

Motorcraft
FL-785
LONG LIFE
OIL FILTER

Motorcraft
FL-786
LONG LIFE
OIL FILTER

FUEL FILTER/
CONDITIONER

COAT GASKET
WITH ENGINE OIL

COAT GASKET
WITH ENGINE OIL

BRAKE MASTER CYLINDER

ENGINE OIL FILL CAP

ENGINE OIL
LEVEL DIPSTICK

COOLANT LEVEL IN RADIATOR
AND COOLANT RECOVERY SYSTEM

OPTIONAL POWER STEERING
PUMP DIPSTICK

AIR FILTER
ELEMENT

**Lubrication and service points—2.0L diesel engine**

7. Install the air cleaner element. Reconnect the spring clip that retains the emission filter to the air cleaner body, and install the filter.

8. Install the spring clips that hold the top of the air cleaner to the body. install the cover.

9. Install the air cleaner assembly from the car.

10. Install the wing nut that retains the air cleaner assembly to the carburetor. install any support bracket bolts (engine to air cleaner). reconnect the air duct tubing, vacuum lines and heat tubes connected to the air cleaner.

**1.6L and 1.9L EFI Engines**

1. Unclip the air intake tube and remove the tube from the air cleaner tray.

2. Unclip the air cleaner tray from the air cleaner assembly.

3. Pull the cleaner tray out to expose the air cleaner element.

4. Pull the air cleaner element from the tray. Visually inspect the air cleaner tray and cover for signs of dust or leaking holes in the filter or past the seals.

5. Assemble the air cleaner element to the tray making sure the element is installed in its

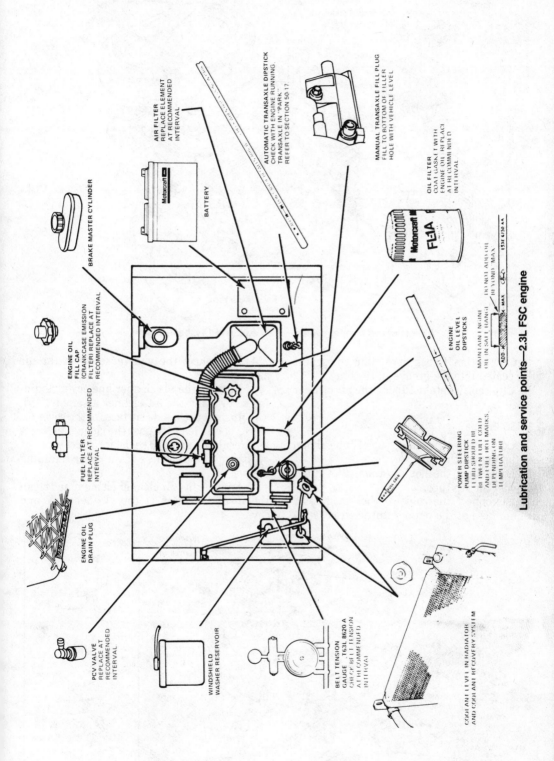

**AIR FILTER** REPLACE ELEMENT AT RECOMMENDED INTERVAL.

**AUTOMATIC TRANSAXLE DIPSTICK** CHECK WITH ENGINE RUNNING. TRANSAXLE IN "PARK". REFER TO SECTION 50 17.

**MANUAL TRANSAXLE FILL PLUG** FILL TO BOTTOM OF FILLER HOLE WITH VEHICLE LEVEL

**OIL FILTER** COAT GASKET WITH ENGINE OIL. REPLACE AT RECOMMENDED INTERVAL.

**BRAKE MASTER CYLINDER**

BATTERY

**ENGINE OIL FILL CAP** (CRANKCASE EMISSION FILTER) REPLACE AT RECOMMENDED INTERVAL

**FUEL FILTER** REPLACE AT RECOMMENDED INTERVAL

**ENGINE OIL DRAIN PLUG**

**ENGINE OIL LEVEL DIPSTICKS**

MAINTAIN ENGINE OIL IN SAFE RANGE

**POWER STEERING PUMP DIPSTICK** FLUID SHOULD BE BETWEEN FULL COLD AND FULL HOT MARKS, DEPENDING ON TEMPERATURE

**PCV VALVE** REPLACE AT RECOMMENDED INTERVAL

**WINDSHIELD WASHER RESERVOIR**

**BELT TENSION GAUGE    T63L 8620 A** CHECK BELT TENSION AT RECOMMENDED INTERVAL

COOLANT LEVEL IN RADIATOR AND COOLANT RECOVERY SYSTEM

**Lubrication and service points—2.3L FSC engine**

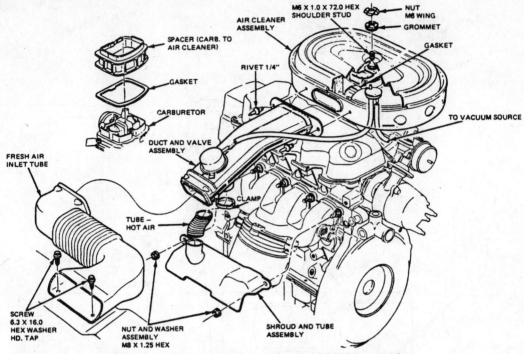

**Air intake and cleaner system—1.3L, 1.6L and 1.9L base engine**

original position. Check to see that the seal is fully seated into the groove in the tray.

6. Clip the air intake tube to the air cleaner tray.

### 2.3 HSC Engine

1. Loosen the air cleaner outlet tube clamp and disconnect the tube.

2. Disconnect the hot air tube, PCV inlet tube and the zip tube.

3. Disconnect the cold weather modulator vacuum hose at the temperature sensor.

4. Disconnect the vent hoses from the air cleaner cover.

5. Remove the air cleaner and cover retaining screws and the air cleaner assembly.

6. Inspect the inside surfaces of the cover for traces of dirt leakage past the cleaner element as a result of damaged seals, incorrect element or inadequate tightness of the cover retaining screws.

7. Remove the air cleaner element and clean the inside surfaces of the cleaner tray and cover.

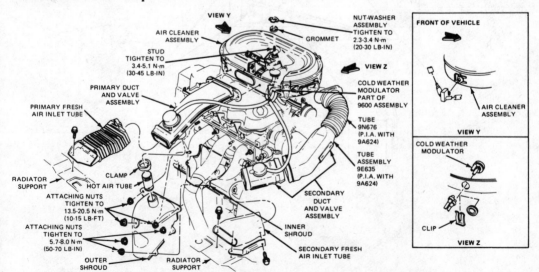

**1.6L HO air intake system**

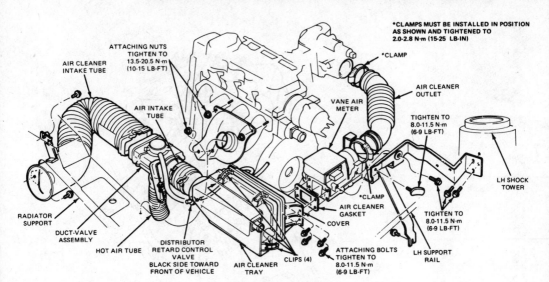

**1.6L EFI air intake system**

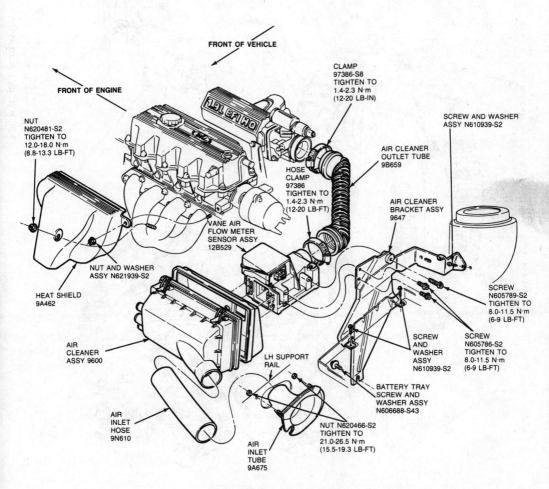

**1.9L EFI air intake system**

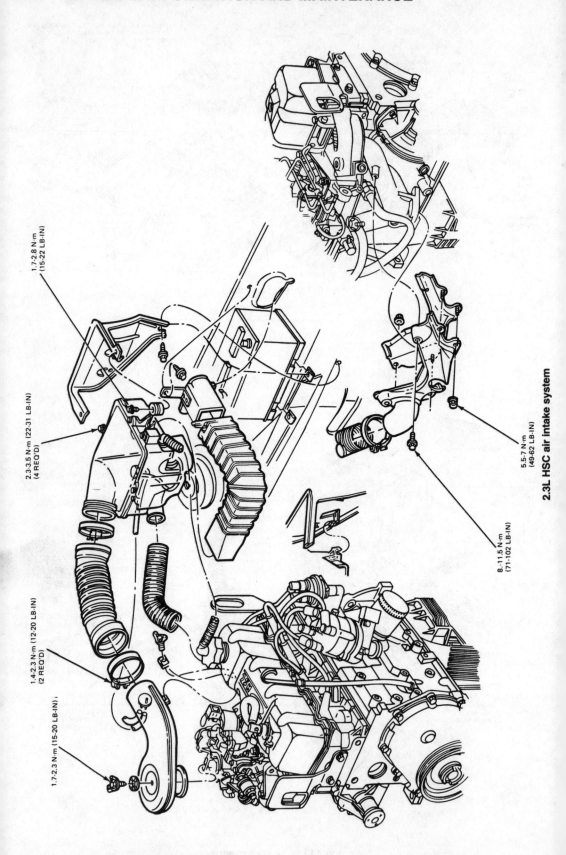

1.7-2.8 N·m
(15-22 LB-IN)

2.3-3.5 N·m (22-31 LB-IN)
(4 REQ'D)

1.4-2.3 N·m (12-20 LB-IN)
(2 REQ'D)

1.7-2.3 N·m (15-20 LB-IN)

5.5-7 N·m
(49-62 LB-IN)

8.-11.5 N·m
(71-102 LB-IN)

**2.3L HSC air intake system**

8. Install a new air cleaner element, install the cover and assembly. Tighten the retaining screws to 22–32 in.lb.

9. Reconnect all vacuum and air duct hoses and lines.

## PCV Valve

No PCV (positive crankcase ventilation) valve is used. Instead, an internal baffle and an orifice control the flow of crankcase gases. (See Chapter 4 for more details on emission controls).

## Fuel Filter

The fuel filter should be replaced, immediately, upon evidence of dirt in the fuel system. Regular replacement of the fuel filter should be every 30,000 miles. If the engine seems to be suffering from fuel starvation, remove the filter and blow through it to see if it is clogged. If air won't pass through the filter easily, or if dirt is visible in the inlet passage, replace the filter.

NOTE: *A backup wrench is an open end wrench of the proper size used to hold a fuel filter or fitting in position while a fuel line is removed. A flared wrench is a special hex wrench with a narrow open end allowing the fuel line nut to be gripped tightly. A regular open end wrench may be substituted if used carefully so the fitting is not rounded.*

The fuel filter on the non-EFI models contains a screen to minimize the amount of contaminants entering the carburetor via the fuel system. The fuel filter on the non-EFI models is located in the carburetor.

The EFI model fuel filter provides extremely fine filtration to protect the small metering orifices of the injector nozzles. The filter is a one-piece construction which cannot be cleaned. If the filter becomes clogged or restricted, it should be replaced with a new filter. The filter is located downstream of the electric pump, mounted on the dash panel extension in the right rear corner of the engine compartment on the Escort/Lynx. And on the Tempo/Topaz the filter is mounted on the right fender apron.

### REMOVAL AND INSTALLATION

#### Gasoline Engines

##### ESCORT/LYNX/EXP w/CARBURETOR

1. Remove the air cleaner assembly.
2. Use a backup wrench on the fuel filter (located in the carburetor inlet) inlet hex nut. Loosen the fuel line nut with a flare wrench. Remove the fuel line from the filter.
3. Unscrew the filter from the carburetor.

**To Install:**

4. Apply a drop of Loctite® Hydraulic Seal-

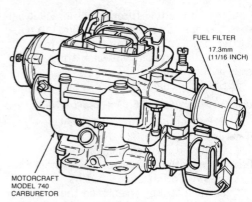

**Fuel filter mounting Escort/Lynx/EXP with carburetor**

ant No. 069 to the external threads of the fuel filter.

5. Hand start the new filter into the carburetor, then use a wrench to tighten the fuel filter to 6.5–8 ft.lb.

6. Apply a drop of engine oil to the fuel supply tube nut and flare, and hand start the nut into the filter inlet approximately two threads.

7. Use a backup wrench on the fuel filter to prevent the filter from rotating while tightening. Tighten the nut to 15–18 ft.lb.

8. Start the engine and check for fuel leaks.

9. Install the air cleaner assembly.

##### ESCORT/LYNX/EXP w/FUEL INJECTION

1. With the engine turned OFF, depressurize the fuel system on the EFI engines using special tool T80L-9974-A Fuel Pressure Gauge, or equivalent.

2. Remove the push connect fittings from both side of the fuel filter.

NOTE: *The fuel filter is located downstream of the electric fuel pump on the right rear corner of the engine compartment. Push connect fitting disconnection procedures are covered in Chapter 4 after Fuel Pumps.*

3. Remove the filter from the mounting bracket by loosening the retaining clamp enough to allow the filter to pass through.

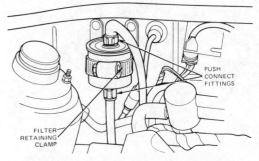

**Fuel filter mounting Escort/Lynx/EXP—EFI engines**

4. Install the fuel filter in the bracket, ensuring proper direction of the flow as noted earlier. Tighten the clamp to 15–25 in.lb.

5. Install the push connect fittings at both ends of the filter.

6. Start the engine and check for fuel leaks.

*TEMPO/TOPAZ w/CARBURETOR – CANADA ONLY*

1. Remove the air cleaner bonnet assembly if necessary.

2. Using a backup wrench on the return line fitting on the top of the fuel filter, remove the fuel line with a flare nut wrench.

3. Using a backup wrench on the fuel filter inlet fitting, remove the fuel line from the fuel filter with a flare nut wrench.

4. Using a backup wrench on the fuel filter outlet fitting, loosen the fuel lin and remove the fuel filter from the engine with a flare nut wrench.

**To Install:**

5. Apply engine oil the fuel line nuts and flared ends.

6. Position the fuel filter with flow arrow on the filter directed towards the fuel line to the carburetor.

7. Finger-tighten the fitting at the fuel filter outlet.

8. Finger-tighten the return line fitting into the top of the filter.

9. Finger-tighten the fitting at the fuel filter inlet.

10. Using a backup wrench on the fuel filter fittings, tighten the fuel lines in the following sequence:

    a. Tighten the return line nut to 6–9 ft.lb.

    b. Tighten the nut on the fuel line at the filter outlet to 15–18 ft.lb.

    c. Tighten the nut on the fuel line from the fuel pump to the fuel filter to 15–18 ft.lb.

11. Inspect the fuel line routings and install the fuel line clips if loosened or removed during disassembly. Adjust the fuel lines if they are interfering with the carburetor, air pump, or fuel filter housing.

12. Start the engine and check for fuel leaks at all the fuel line connections, fuel pump, fuel filter and the carburetor while the engine is idling for two minutes. Retighten if necessary.

13. If removed, install the air filter bonnet assembly to the carburetor.

*TEMPO/TOPAZ w/FUEL INJECTION*

1. Remove the air cleaner bonnet assembly for clearance if necessary.

2. Use a backup wrench on the return line fitting on the top of the fuel filter. Remove the fuel line using a flare wrench.

3. Use a backup wrench on the fuel filter inlet fitting. Remove the fuel line using a flare wrench.

4. Use a backup wrench on the fuel filter outlet fitting. Remove the fuel line using a flare wrench. Remove the fuel filter.

5. Position the fuel filter with the arrow on the filter pointing towards the fuel line to the carburetor.

6. Hand start all the fuel lines in their respective fittings.

7. Use a backup wrench and flare wrench to tighten all fuel lines. Tighten the return line first, the outlet line second and the inlet line last. Do not overtighten. Install the remaining parts in the reverse order of removal.

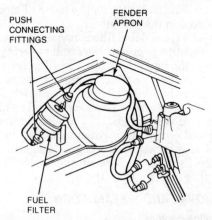

Fuel filter mounting Tempo/Topaz—CFI engines

**Diesel Engine**

The fuel filter/conditioner must be serviced (water purged) at each engine oil change (7500 miles) interval. To purge water from the system:

1. Make sure the engine and ignition switch are off.

2. Place a suitable container under the fuel

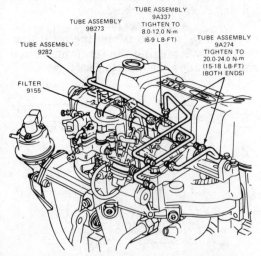

**Fuel filter mounting Tempo/Topaz—Canada Only**

filter/conditioner water drain tube under the car.

3. Open the water drain valve at the bottom of the filter/conditioner element 2 ½–3 turns.

4. Pump the prime pump at the top of the filter from 10 to 15 strokes, or until all of the water is purged from the filter, and clear diesel fuel is apparent.

NOTE: *If the water/fuel will not drain from the tube, open the drain valve one more turn or until the water/fuel starts to flow.*

5. Close the drain valve and tighten.

6. Start the engine and check for leaks.

### REMOVAL AND INSTALLAION

1. Make sure that the engine and ignition are off.

2. Disconnect the module connector from the water level sensor located at the bottom of the filter element.

3. Use an appropriate filter strap wrench and turn the filter element counterclockwise to loosen from the top mounting bracket. Remove the element from the mount adapter.

4. Remove the water drain valve/sensor probe from the bottom of the element. Wipe the probe with a clean dry cloth.

5. Unsnap the sensor probe pigtail from the bottom of the filter element and wipe with a clean dry rag.

6. Snap the probe onto the new filter element.

7. Lubricate the two O-rings on the water sensor probe with a light film of oil. Screw the probe into the bottom of the new filter element and tighten.

8. Clean the gasket mounting surface of the adapter mount.

9. Lubricate the sealing gasket of the filter element with oil. Screw the filter element onto the mount adapter. Hand tighten the element, then back off the filter to a point where the gasket is just touching the adapter. Retighten by hand and then an additional ½–⅝ turn.

10. Reconnect the water level sensor module connector.

11. Prime the fuel system by pumping the primer handle until pressure is felt when pumping.

12. Start the engine and check for fuel leaks.

## Evaporative Emission Canister

To prevent gasoline vapors from being vented into the atmosphere, an evaporative emission system captures the vapors and stores them in a charcoal filled canister.

### SERVICING THE EMISSION CANISTER

Since the canister is purged of fumes when the engine is operating, no real maintenance is re-

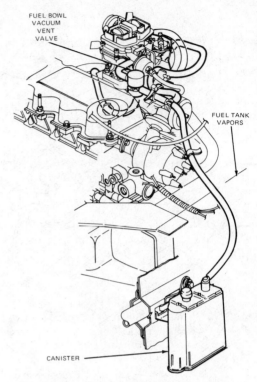

**Evaporative canister—Escort/Lynx**

quired. However, the canister should be visually inspected for cracks, loose connections, etc. Replacement is simply a matter of disconnecting the hoses, loosening the mount and replacing the canister.

## Battery

Your car is equipped with a maintenance free battery which eliminates the need for periodic checking and adding fluid.

NOTE: *If you replace your battery with a non-maintenance free battery see the following section.*

### FLUID LEVEL (EXCEPT MAINTENANCE FREE BATTERIES)

Check the battery electrolyte level at least once a month, or more often in hot weather or during periods of extended car operation. The level can be checked through the case on translucent polypropylene battery cases; the cell caps must be removed on other models. The electrolyte level in each cell should be kept filled to the split ring inside, or the line marked on the outside of the case.

If the level is low, add only distilled water, or colorless, odorless drinking water, through the opening until the level is correct. Each cell is completely separate from the others, so each must be checked and filled individually.

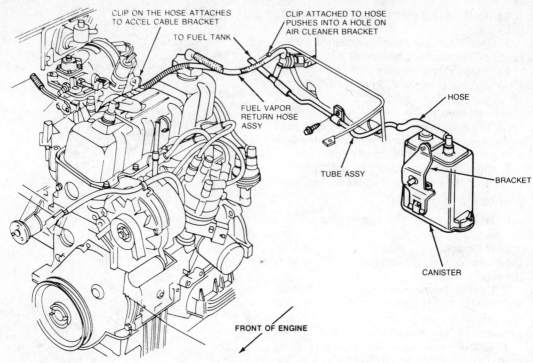

CLIP ON THE HOSE ATTACHES
TO ACCEL CABLE BRACKET

CLIP ATTACHED TO HOSE
PUSHES INTO A HOLE ON
AIR CLEANER BRACKET

TO FUEL TANK

FUEL VAPOR
RETURN HOSE
ASSY

HOSE

TUBE ASSY

BRACKET

CANISTER

FRONT OF ENGINE

**Evaporative canister—Tempo/Topaz**

If water is added in freezing weather, the car should be driven several miles to allow the water to mix with the electrolyte. Otherwise, the battery could freeze.

### SPECIFIC GRAVITY

At least once a year, check the specific gravity of the battery. It should be between 1.20 and 1.26 at room temperature.

The specific gravity can be checked with the use of an hydrometer, an inexpensive instrument available from many sources, including auto parts stores. The hydrometer has a squeeze bulb at one end and a nozzle at the oth-er. Battery electrolyte is sucked into the hydrometer until the float is lifted from its seat. The specific gravity is then read by noting the position of the float. Generally, if after charging, the specific gravity between any two cells

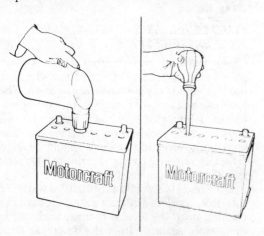

**Adjusting the battery fluid level**

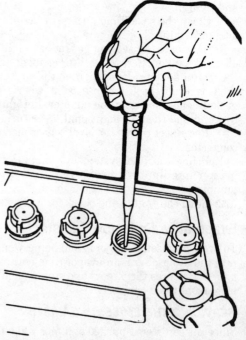

**Checking the battery with a battery hydrometer**

varies more than 50 points (.050), the battery is bad and should be replaced.

It is not possible to check the specific gravity in this manner on sealed maintenance free batteries. Instead, the indicator built into the top of the case (on some batteries) must be relied on to display any signs of battery deterioration. If the indicator is dark, the battery can be assumed to be OK. If the indicator is light the specific gravity is low, and the battery should be charged or replaced.

## CABLES AND CLAMPS

Once a year, the battery terminals and the cable clamps should be cleaned. Loosen the clamps and remove the cables, negative cable first. On batteries with posts on top, the use of a puller specially made for the purpose is recommended. These are inexpensive, and available in auto parts stores. Side terminal battery cables are secured with a bolt.

Clean the cable clamps and the battery terminal with a wire brush, until all corrosion, grease, etc. is removed and metal is shiny. It is especially important to clean the inside of the clamp thoroughly, since a small deposit of foreign material or oxidation there will prevent a sound electrical connection and inhibit either starting or charging. Special tools are available for cleaning these parts, one type of conventional batteries and another type for side terminal batteries.

Before installing the cable, loosen the battery holddown clamp or strap, remove the battery and check the battery tray. Clear it of any debris, and check it for soundness. Rust should be wire brushed away, and the metal given a coat of anti-rust paint. Replace the battery and tighten the holddown clamp or strap securely,

**Clean battery cable clamps with a wire brush**

but be careful not to overtighten, which will crack the battery case.

After the clamps and terminals are clean, reinstall the cables, negative cable last; do not hammer on the clamps to install. Tighten the clamps securely, but do not distort them. Give the clamps and terminals a thin external coat of grease after installation, to retard corrosion.

Check the cables at the same time that the terminals are cleaned. If the cable insulation is cracked or broken, or if the ends are frayed, the cable should be replace with a new cable of the same length and gauge.

NOTE: *Keep flame or sparks away from the battery; it gives off explosive hydrogen gas. Battery electrolyte contains sulphuric acid. If you should splash any on your skin or in your eyes, flush the affected areas with plenty of clear water; if it lands in your eyes, get medical help immediately.*

## REPLACEMENT

When it becomes necessary to replace the battery, select a battery with a rating equal to or greater than the battery originally installed. Deterioration, embrittlement and just plain aging of the battery cables, starter motor, and associated wires makes the battery's job harder in successive years. The slow increase in electrical resistance over time makes it prudent to install a new battery with a greater ca-

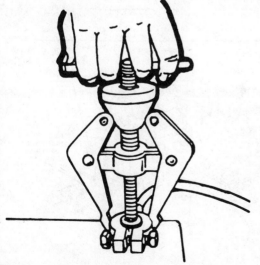

**Use a puller to remove the battery cable**

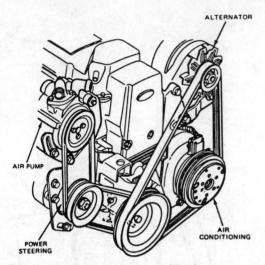

Drive belts, engine with air conditioning

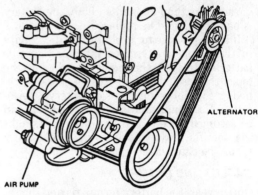

Drive belts, engine without air conditioning

pacity then the old. Details on battery removal and installation are covered in Chapter 3.

## Belts

NOTE: *Due to the compactness of the engine compartment, it may be necessary to disconnect some spark plug leads when* adjusting or replacing drive belts. If a spark plug lead is disconnected it is necessary to coat the terminal of the lead with silicone grease (Part number D7AZ19A331A or the equivalent).

Your car may be equipped with 4 rib, 5 rib, or a conventional ¼″ (6mm) V-belt depending on accessories.

CAUTION: *On models equipped with power steering, the air pump belt tension cannot be adjusted until the power steering belt has*

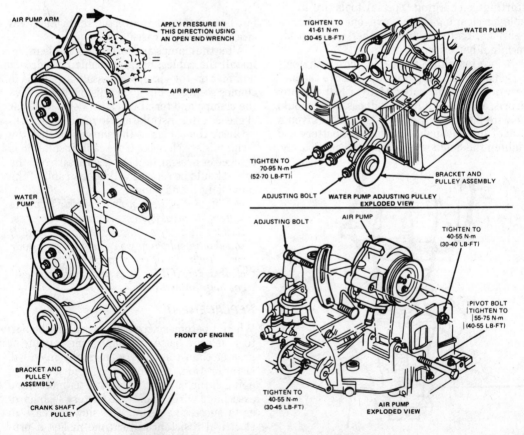

Belt tension adjustment—Air pump, Water pump

## HOW TO SPOT WORN V-BELTS

V-Belts are vital to efficient engine operation—they drive the fan, water pump and other accessories. They require little maintenance (occasional tightening) but they will not last forever. Slipping or failure of the V-belt will lead to overheating. If your V-belt looks like any of these, it should be replaced.

**Cracking or weathering**

This belt has deep cracks, which cause it to flex. Too much flexing leads to heat build-up and premature failure. These cracks can be caused by using the belt on a pulley that is too small. Notched belts are available for small diameter pulleys.

**Softening (grease and oil)**

Oil and grease on a belt can cause the belt's rubber compounds to soften and separate from the reinforcing cords that hold the belt together. The belt will first slip, then finally fail altogether.

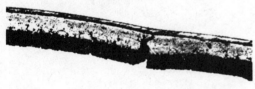

**Glazing**

Glazing is caused by a belt that is slipping. A slipping belt can cause a run-down battery, erratic power steering, overheating or poor accessory performance. The more the belt slips, the more glazing will be built up on the surface of the belt. The more the belt is glazed, the more it will slip. If the glazing is light, tighten the belt.

**Worn cover**

The cover of this belt is worn off and is peeling away. The reinforcing cords will begin to wear and the belt will shortly break. When the belt cover wears in spots or has a rough jagged appearance, check the pulley grooves for roughness.

**Separation**

This belt is on the verge of breaking and leaving you stranded. The layers of the belt are separating and the reinforcing cords are exposed. It's just a matter of time before it breaks completely.

*been replaced and adjusted (or just adjusted if an old belt).*

## INSPECTION

Inspect all drive belts for excessive wear, cracks, glazed condition and frayed or broken cords. Replace any drive belt showing the above condition(s).

NOTE: *If a drive belt continually gets cut, the crankshaft pulley might have a sharp* *projection on it. Have the pulley replaced if this condition exists.*

## REPLACEMENT

1. Loosen the pivot bolt and/or the adjustment bolt.

2. Move the driven unit (power steering pump, air pump, etc.) toward or away from the engine to loosen the belt. Remove the belt.

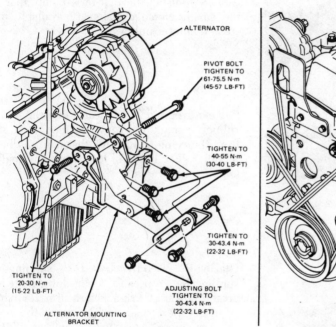

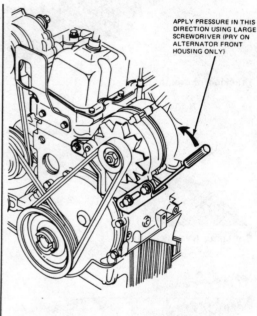

ALTERNATOR

PIVOT BOLT TIGHTEN TO 61-75.5 N·m (45-57 LB-FT)

TIGHTEN TO 40-55 N·m (30-40 LB-FT)

TIGHTEN TO 30-43.4 N·m (22-32 LB-FT)

TIGHTEN TO 20-30 N·m (15-22 LB-FT)

ADJUSTING BOLT TIGHTEN TO 30-43.4 N·m (22-32 LB-FT)

ALTERNATOR MOUNTING BRACKET

APPLY PRESSURE IN THIS DIRECTION USING LARGE SCREWDRIVER (PRY ON ALTERNATOR FRONT HOUSING ONLY)

**Belt tension adjustment—Alternator etc.**

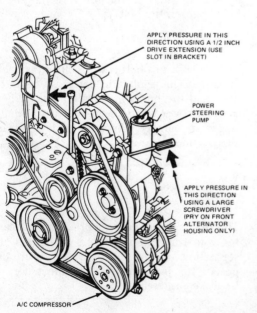

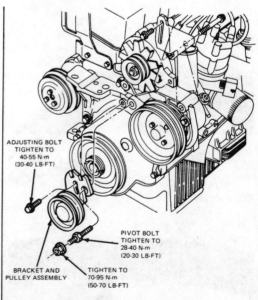

APPLY PRESSURE IN THIS DIRECTION USING A 1/2 INCH DRIVE EXTENSION (USE SLOT IN BRACKET)

POWER STEERING PUMP

APPLY PRESSURE IN THIS DIRECTION USING A LARGE SCREWDRIVER (PRY ON FRONT ALTERNATOR HOUSING ONLY)

A/C COMPRESSOR

ADJUSTING BOLT TIGHTEN TO 40-55 N·m (30-40 LB-FT)

PIVOT BOLT TIGHTEN TO 28-40 N·m (20-30 LB-FT)

TIGHTEN TO 70-95 N·m (50-70 LB-FT)

BRACKET AND PULLEY ASSEMBLY

**Belt tension adjustment—Power steering, etc.**

3. Install the new bolt on the driven unit and either move toward or away from the engine to put tension on the belt.

4. Snug up the mounting and/or adjusting bolt to hold the driven unit, but do not completely tighten.

5. See the following procedure for the deflection method of belt adjustment.

### ADJUSTMENT

NOTE: *Proper adjustment requires the use of the tension gauge. Since most people don't have the necessary gauge, a deflection method of adjustment is given.*

1. Locate a point on the belt midway between the two pulleys driven.

2. The deflection of the belt should be:
- For all belts with a distance of 12″ (305) between pulley: ⅛–¼″ (3–6mm).
- For all belts with a distance greater than 12″ (305mm) between pulleys: ⅛–⅜″ (3–6mm).

3. Correctly adjust the bolt deflection and tighten all mounting bolts. Start the engine and allow it to reach the normal operating temperature. Shut the engine OFF and recheck belt deflection. Readjust if necessary.

### ALTERNATOR BELT ADJUSTMENT

#### Modified Bracket

Some later models are equipped with a modified alternator bracket (high mount alternator). The bracket incorporates a slot that will accommodate a tapered pry bar, such as a lug wrench, to give a place to apply leverage.

Insert the tire lug wrench into the slot opening. Pry on the alternator until the correct belt tension is reached.

While maintaining belt tension, first tighten the ⅜″ adjusting bolt (24–30 ft.lb.), then tighten the pivot bolt (45–65 ft.lb.).

## Hoses

CAUTION: *The cooling fan motor is controlled by a temperature switch. The fan may come on when the engine is off. It will continue to run until the correct temperature is reached. Before working on or around the fan, disconnect the negative battery cable or the fan wiring connector.*

### HOSE REPLACEMENT

1. Open the hood and cover the fenders to protect them from scratches.

2. Disconnect the negative (ground) battery cable at the battery.

3. Place a suitable drain pan under the radiator and drain the cooling system.

NOTE: *Place a small hose on the end of the*

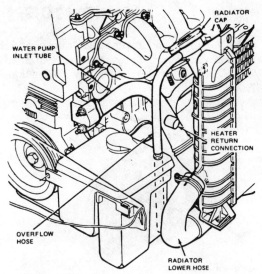

Hose locations

*radiator petcock, this will direct the coolant into the drain pan.*

4. After the radiator has drained, position the drain pan under the lower hose. Loosen the lower hose clamps, disconnect the hose from the water pump inlet pipe and allow to drain. Disconnect the other end of the hose from the radiator and remove the hose.

5. Loosen the clamps retaining the upper hose, disconnect and remove the hose.

NOTE: *If only the upper hose is to be replaced, drain off enough coolant so the level is below the hose.*

6. If heater hoses need replacement, drain the coolant, loosen the clamps and remove the hose(s).

7. Installation of new hose(s) is in the reverse order of removal.

8. Be sure the petcock is closed. Fill the cooling system with the required protection mixture of water and permanent coolant/antifreeze. Connect the negative battery cable.

9. Run the engine until normal operating temperature is reached. Shut off the engine and check for coolant leaks. When the engine cools, recheck the coolant level in the radiator, or reservoir container.

## Air Conditioning System

NOTE: *This book contains simple testing and charging procedures for your car's air conditioning system. More comprehensive testing, diagnosis and service procedures may be found in CHILTON'S GUIDE TO AIR CONDITIONING SERVICE AND REPAIR, book part number 7580, available at your local retailer.*

## HOW TO SPOT BAD HOSES

Both the upper and lower radiator hoses are called upon to perform difficult jobs in an inhospitable environment. They are subject to nearly 18 psi at under hood temperatures often over 280°F., and must circulate nearly 7500 gallons of coolant an hour—3 good reasons to have good hoses.

**Swollen hose**

A good test for any hose is to feel it for soft or spongy spots. Frequently these will appear as swollen areas of the hose. The most likely cause is oil soaking. This hose could burst at any time, when hot or under pressure.

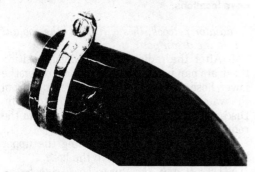

**Cracked hose**

Cracked hoses can usually be seen but feel the hoses to be sure they have not hardened; a prime cause of cracking. This hose has cracked down to the reinforcing cords and could split at any of the cracks.

**Frayed hose end (due to weak clamp)**

Weakened clamps frequently are the cause of hose and cooling system failure. The connection between the pipe and hose has deteriorated enough to allow coolant to escape when the engine is hot.

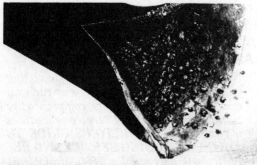

**Debris in cooling system**

Debris, rust and scale in the cooling system can cause the inside of a hose to weaken. This can usually be felt on the outside of the hose as soft or thinner areas.

A/C REFRIGERATING SYSTEM

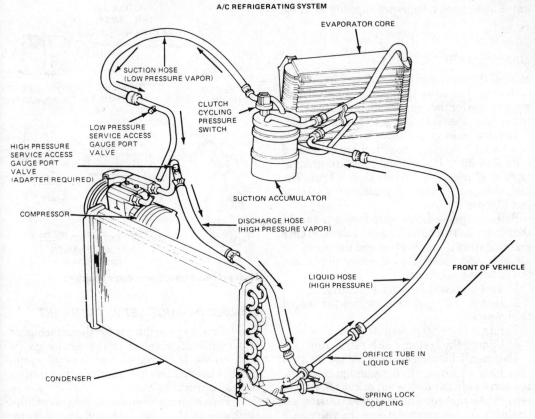

**Air conditioning component layout**

## SAFETY PRECAUTIONS

There are two particular hazards associated with air conditioning systems and they both relate to the refrigerant gas.

First, the refrigerant gas is an extremely cold substance. When exposed to air, it will instantly freeze any surface it comes in contact with, including you eyes. The other hazard relates to fire. Although normally nontoxic, refrigerant gas becomes highly poisonous in the presence of an open flame. One good whiff of the vapor formed by burning refrigerant can be fatal. Keep all forms of fire (including cigarettes) well clear of the air conditioning system.

## CHECKING FOR OIL LEAKS

Refrigerant leaks show up as oily areas on the various components because the compressor oil is transported around the entire system along with the refrigerant. Look for only spots on all the hoses and lines, and especially on the hose and tubing connections. If there are oily deposits, the system may have a leak, and you should have it checked by a qualified repairman.

NOTE: *A small area of oil on the front of the compressor is normal and no cause for alarm.*

## KEEP THE CONDENSER CLEAR

Periodically inspect the front of the condenser for bent fins or foreign material (dirt, bugs, leaves, etc.). If any cooling fins are bent, straighten them carefully with needlenosed pliers. You can remove any debris with a stiff bristle brush or hose.

## OPERATE THE A/C SYSTEM PERIODICALLY

A lot of A/C problems can be avoided by simply running the air conditioner at least once a week, regardless of the season. Let the system run for at least 5 minutes a week (even in the winter), and you'll keep the internal parts lubricated as well as preventing the hoses from hardening.

## REFRIGERANT LEVEL CHECK

The only way to accurately check the refrigerant level to measure the system evaporator pressures with a manifold gauge set, although rapid on/off cycling of the compressor clutch indicates that the A/C system is low on refrigerant. The normal refrigerant capacity is 41 oz. ± 1 oz.

### MANIFOLD TEST GAUGES

Most of the service work performed in air conditioning requires the use of a set of two gauges, one for the high (head) pressure side of the system, the other for the low (suction) side.

The low side gauge records both pressure and vacuum. Vacuum readings are calibrated from 0 to 30 in.Hg and the pressure graduations read from 0 to no less than 60 psi. The high side gauge measures pressure from 0 to at last 600 psi.

Both gauges are threaded into a manifold that contains two hand shut-off valves. Proper manipulation of these valves and the use of the attached test hoses allow the user to perform the following services:

1. Test high and low side pressures.
2. Remove air, moisture, and contaminated refrigerant.
3. Purge the system (of refrigerant).
4. Charge the system (with refrigerant).

The manifold valves are designed so that they have no direct effect on gauge readings, but serve only to provide for, or cut off, flow of refrigerant through the manifold. During all testing and hook-up operations, the valves are kept in a close position to avoid disturbing the refrigeration system. The valves are opened only to purge the system or refrigerant or to charge it.

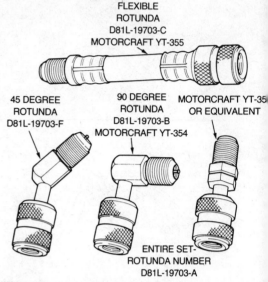

High pressure gauge port valve adapters

### MANIFOLD GAUGE SET ATTACHMENT

The following procedure is for the attachment of a manifold gauge set to the service gauge port valves. If charge station type of equipment is used, follow the equipment manufacturers instructions.

1. Turn both manifold gauge set valves fully clockwise to close the high and low pressure hoses at the gauge set refrigerant center outlet.

NOTE: *Rotunda high side adapter set D81L-19703-A or Motorcraft Tool YT-354 or 355 or equivalent is required to connect the manifold gauge set or a charging station to the high pressure service access gauge port valve.*

2. Remove the caps from the high and low pressure service gauge port valves.

3. If the manifold gauge set hoses do not have the valve depressing pins in them, install fitting adapters T71P-19703-S and R containing the pins on the manifold gauge hoses.

4. Connect the high and low pressure refrigerant hoses to their respective service ports, making sure they are hooked up correctly and fully seated. Tighten the fittings by hand and make sure they are not cross-threaded. Remember that an adapter is necessary to connect the manifold gauge hose to the high pressure fitting.

### CHARGING THE SYSTEM

If the system has been completely purged of refrigerant, it must be evacuated before charging. A vacuum pump should be connected to the center hose of the manifold gauge set, both valves should be opened, and the vacuum pump operated until the low pressure gauge

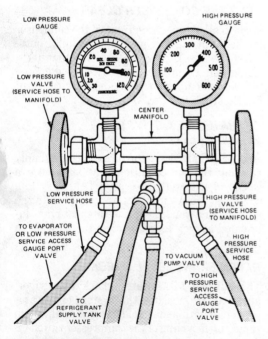

Air conditioning manifold gauge set

## Troubleshooting Basic Air Conditioning Problems

| Problem | Cause | Solution |
|---|---|---|
| There's little or no air coming from the vents (and you're sure it's on) | • The A/C fuse is blown<br>• Broken or loose wires or connections<br>• The on/off switch is defective | • Check and/or replace fuse<br>• Check and/or repair connections<br><br>• Replace switch |
| The air coming from the vents is not cool enough | • Windows and air vent wings open<br>• The compressor belt is slipping<br>• Heater is on<br>• Condenser is clogged with debris<br>• Refrigerant has escaped through a leak in the system<br>• Receiver/drier is plugged | • Close windows and vent wings<br>• Tighten or replace compressor belt<br>• Shut heater off<br>• Clean the condenser<br>• Check system<br><br>• Service system |
| The air has an odor | • Vacuum system is disrupted<br>• Odor producing substances on the evaporator case<br>• Condensation has collected in the bottom of the evaporator housing | • Have the system checked/repaired<br>• Clean the evaporator case<br><br>• Clean the evaporator housing drains |
| System is noisy or vibrating | • Compressor belt or mountings loose<br>• Air in the system | • Tighten or replace belt; tighten mounting bolts<br>• Have the system serviced |
| Sight glass condition<br>  Constant bubbles, foam or oil streaks<br>  Clear sight glass, but no cold air<br>  Clear sight glass, but air is cold<br>  Clouded with milky fluid | <br>• Undercharged system<br><br>• No refrigerant at all<br>• System is OK<br>• Receiver drier is leaking dessicant | <br>• Charge the system<br><br>• Check and charge the system<br><br>• Have system checked |
| Large difference in temperature of lines | • System undercharged | • Charge and leak test the system |
| Compressor noise | • Broken valves<br>• Overcharged<br><br>• Incorrect oil level<br><br><br>• Piston slap<br>• Broken rings<br>• Drive belt pulley bolts are loose | • Replace the valve plate<br>• Discharge, evacuate and install the correct charge<br>• Isolate the compressor and check the oil level. Correct as necessary.<br>• Replace the compressor<br>• Replace the compressor<br>• Tighten with the correct torque specification |
| Excessive vibration | • Incorrect belt tension<br>• Clutch loose<br>• Overcharged<br><br>• Pulley is misaligned | • Adjust the belt tension<br>• Tighten the clutch<br>• Discharge, evacuate and install the correct charge<br>• Align the pulley |
| Condensation dripping in the passenger compartment | • Drain hose plugged or improperly positioned<br>• Insulation removed or improperly installed | • Clean the drain hose and check for proper installation<br>• Replace the insulation on the expansion valve and hoses |
| Frozen evaporator coil | • Faulty thermostat<br>• Thermostat capillary tube improperly installed<br>• Thermostat not adjusted properly | • Replace the thermostat<br>• Install the capillary tube correctly<br><br>• Adjust the thermostat |
| Low side low—high side low | • System refrigerant is low<br><br>• Expansion valve is restricted | • Evacuate, leak test and charge the system<br>• Replace the expansion valve |
| Low side high—high side low | • Internal leak in the compressor—worn | • Remove the compressor cylinder head and inspect the compressor. Replace the valve plate assembly if necessary. If the compressor pistons, rings or |

## Troubleshooting Basic Air Conditioning Problems (cont.)

| Problem | Cause | Solution |
|---|---|---|
| Low side high—high side low (cont.) | | cylinders are excessively worn or scored replace the compressor |
| | • Cylinder head gasket is leaking | • Install a replacement cylinder head gasket |
| | • Expansion valve is defective | • Replace the expansion valve |
| | • Drive belt slipping | • Adjust the belt tension |
| Low side high—high side high | • Condenser fins obstructed | • Clean the condenser fins |
| | • Air in the system | • Evacuate, leak test and charge the system |
| | • Expansion valve is defective | • Replace the expansion valve |
| | • Loose or worn fan belts | • Adjust or replace the belts as necessary |
| Low side low—high side high | • Expansion valve is defective | • Replace the expansion valve |
| | • Restriction in the refrigerant hose | • Check the hose for kinks—replace if necessary |
| | • Restriction in the receiver/drier | • Replace the receiver/drier |
| | • Restriction in the condenser | • Replace the condenser |
| Low side and high side normal (inadequate cooling) | • Air in the system | • Evacuate, leak test and charge the system |
| | • Moisture in the system | • Evacuate, leak test and charge the system |

reads as close to 30 in.Hg as possible. If a part in the system has been replaced or excessive moisture is suspected, continue the vacuum pump operation for about 30 minutes.

Close the manifold gauge valves to the center hose, then disconnect the vacuum pump and connect the center hose to a charging cylinder, refrigerant drum or a small can refrigerant dispensing valve. Disconnect the wire harness from the clutch cycling pressure switch and install a jumper wire across the two terminals of the connector. Open the manifold gauge LOW side valve to allow refrigerant to enter the system, keeping the can(s) in an upright position to prevent liquid from entering the system.

When no more refrigerant is being drawn into the system, start the engine and move the function selector lever to the NORM A/C position and the blower switch to HI to draw the remaining refrigerant in. Continue to add refrigerant until the specified 3½ lbs. is reached. Close the manifold gauge low pressure valve and the refrigerant supply valve. Remove the jumper wire from the clutch cycling pressure switch connector and reconnect the pressure switch. Disconnect the manifold gauge set and install the service port caps.

### Charging From Small Containers

When using a single can A/C charging kit, such as is available at local retailers, make the connection at the low pressure service port, located on the accumulator/drier. This is very important as connecting the small can to the high pressure port will cause the can to explode. Once the can is connected, charge the system as described above. If a manifold gauge set is being used, the low pressure valve must be closed whenever another can is being connected to the center hose. Hold the cans upright to prevent liquid refrigerant from entering the system and possibly damaging the compressor.

## Windshield Wipers
### BLADE AND ARM REPLACEMENT

1. Cycle the wiper arm and blade assembly and stop at a position on the windshield where removal can be accomplished without difficulty.

2. To remove the blade: Pull the wiper arm out and away from the windshield. Grasp the wiper blade assembly and pull away from the mounting pin of the wiper arm (Trico® type). Or pull back on the spring lock, where the arm is connected to the blade, and pull the wiper blade assembly from the wiper arm (Tridon® type).

3. To remove the wiper arm: Pull the bade and arm assembly away from the windshield. Move the slide latch (located at base of wiper arm) away from the arm mounting pivot shaft. The arm is now unlocked. Lift the arm up and away from the pivot shaft.

4. Installation is in the reverse order of removal.

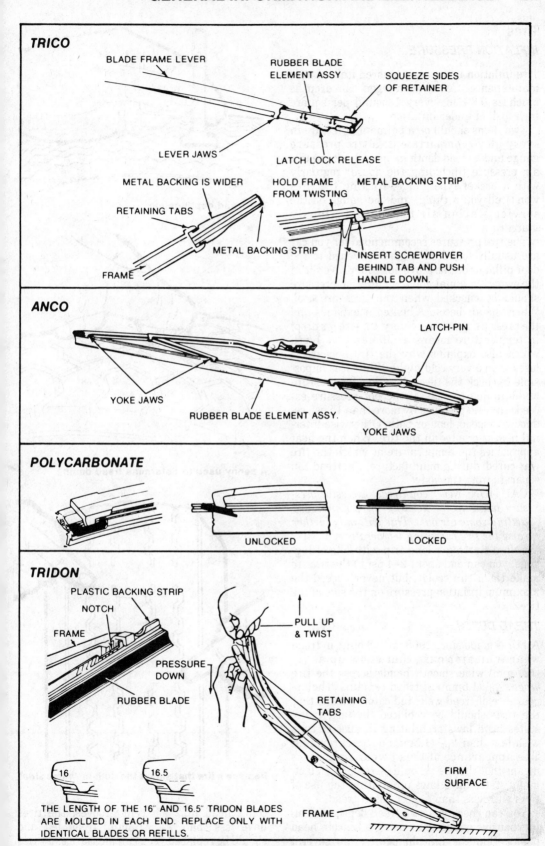

**TRICO**

BLADE FRAME LEVER

RUBBER BLADE ELEMENT ASSY

SQUEEZE SIDES OF RETAINER

LEVER JAWS

LATCH LOCK RELEASE

METAL BACKING IS WIDER

RETAINING TABS

METAL BACKING STRIP

FRAME

HOLD FRAME FROM TWISTING

METAL BACKING STRIP

INSERT SCREWDRIVER BEHIND TAB AND PUSH HANDLE DOWN.

**ANCO**

LATCH-PIN

YOKE JAWS

RUBBER BLADE ELEMENT ASSY.

YOKE JAWS

**POLYCARBONATE**

UNLOCKED

LOCKED

**TRIDON**

PLASTIC BACKING STRIP

NOTCH

FRAME

PULL UP & TWIST

PRESSURE DOWN

RUBBER BLADE

RETAINING TABS

16

16.5

THE LENGTH OF THE 16" AND 16.5" TRIDON BLADES ARE MOLDED IN EACH END. REPLACE ONLY WITH IDENTICAL BLADES OR REFILLS.

FIRM SURFACE

FRAME

**Wiper insert replacement**

# Tires

## INFLATION PRESSURE

Tire inflation is the most ignored item of auto maintenance. Gasoline mileage can drop as much as 0.8% for every 1 pound per square inch (psi) of under inflation.

Two items should be a permanent fixture in every glove compartment: a tire pressure gauge and a tread depth gauge. Check the tire air pressure (including the spare) regularly with a pocket type gauge. Kicking the tires won't tell you a thing, and the gauge on the service station air hose is notoriously inaccurate.

The tire pressures recommended for you car are usually found on a label attached to the door pillar or on the glove box inner cover or in the owner's manual. Ideally, inflation pressure should be checked when the tires are cool. When the air becomes heated it expands and the pressure increases. Every 10° rise (or drop) in temperature means a difference of 1 psi, which also explains why the tire appears to lose air on a very cold night. When it is impossible to check the ties cold, allow for pressure build-up due to heat. If the hot pressure exceeds the cold pressure by more than 15 psi, reduce you speed, lead or both. Otherwise internal heat is created in the tire. When the heat approaches the temperature at which the tire was cured, during manufacture, the tread can separate from the body.

CAUTION: *Never counteract excessive pressure build-up by bleeding off air pressure (letting some air out). This will only further raise the tire operating temperature.*

Before starting a long trip with lots of luggage, you can add about 2–4 psi to the tires to make them run cooler, but never exceed the maximum inflation pressure on the side of the tire.

## TREAD DEPTH

All tires made since 1968 have 8 built-in tread wear indicator bars that show up as ½" (12.7mm) wide smooth bands across the tire when $\frac{1}{16}$" (1.5mm) of tread remains. The appearance of tread wear indicators means that the tires should be replaced. In fact, many states have laws prohibiting the use of tires with less than $\frac{1}{16}$" (1.5mm) of tread remains. The appearance of tread wear indicators means that the tires should be replace. In fact, many states have laws prohibiting the use of tires with less than $\frac{1}{16}$" (1.5mm) tread.

You can check you own tread depth with an inexpensive gauge or by using a Lincoln head penny. Slip the Lincoln penny into several tread grooves. If you can see the top of Lin-

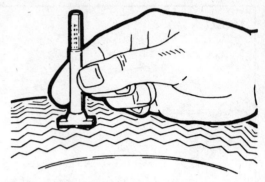
Tire tread depth gauge

A penny used to determine tread depth

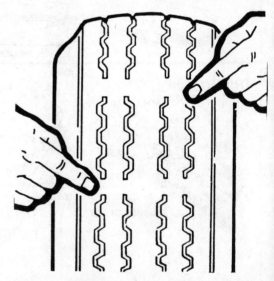
Replace a tire that shows the built-in "bump strip"

coln's head in 2 adjacent grooves, the tires have less than $\frac{1}{16}$" (1.5mm) tread left and should be replaced. You can measure snow ties in the same manner by using the tails side of

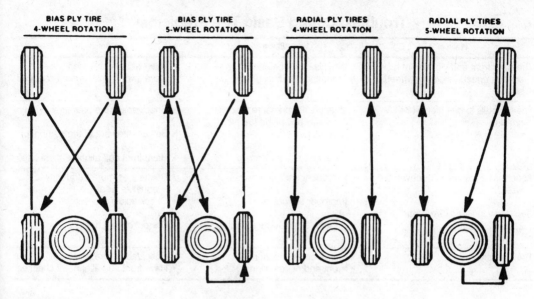

| BIAS PLY TIRE 4-WHEEL ROTATION | BIAS PLY TIRE 5-WHEEL ROTATION | RADIAL PLY TIRES 4-WHEEL ROTATION | RADIAL PLY TIRES 5-WHEEL ROTATION |

**Tire rotation patterns**

the Lincoln penny. If you see the top of the Lincoln memorial, it's time to replace the snow tires.

## TIRE ROTATION

NOTE: *Ford does not recommend tire rotation. They suggest that tires be replaced in pairs as needed without rotation.*

Tire wear can be equalized by switching the position of the tires about every 6,000 miles. Including a conventional spare in the rotation pattern can give up to 20% more tire life.

CAUTION: *Do not include the new SpaceSaver® of temporary spare tires in the rotation pattern.*

There are certain exceptions to tire rotation, however. Studded snow tires should not be rotated, and radials should be kept on the same side of the car (maintain the same direction of

## Troubleshooting Basic Wheel Problems

| Problem | Cause | Solution |
|---|---|---|
| The car's front end vibrates at high speed | · The wheels are out of balance<br>· Wheels are out of alignment | · Have wheels balanced<br>· Have wheel alignment checked/adjusted |
| Car pulls to either side | · Wheels are out of alignment<br><br>· Unequal tire pressure<br>· Different size tires or wheels | · Have wheel alignment checked/adjusted<br>· Check/adjust tire pressure<br>· Change tires or wheels to same size |
| The car's wheel(s) wobbles | · Loose wheel lug nuts<br>· Wheels out of balance<br>· Damaged wheel<br><br><br>· Wheels are out of alignment<br><br>· Worn or damaged ball joint<br>· Excessive play in the steering linkage (usually due to worn parts)<br>· Defective shock absorber | · Tighten wheel lug nuts<br>· Have tires balanced<br>· Raise car and spin the wheel. If the wheel is bent, it should be replaced<br>· Have wheel alignment checked/adjusted<br>· Check ball joints<br>· Check steering linkage<br><br>· Check shock absorbers |
| Tires wear unevenly or prematurely | · Incorrect wheel size<br><br>· Wheels are out of balance<br>· Wheels are out of alignment | · Check if wheel and tire size are compatible<br>· Have wheels balanced<br>· Have wheel alignment checked/adjusted |

## Troubleshooting Basic Tire Problems

| Problem | Cause | Solution |
|---|---|---|
| The car's front end vibrates at high speeds and the steering wheel shakes | • Wheels out of balance<br>• Front end needs aligning | • Have wheels balanced<br>• Have front end alignment checked |
| The car pulls to one side while cruising | • Unequal tire pressure (car will usually pull to the low side)<br>• Mismatched tires<br><br>• Front end needs aligning | • Check/adjust tire pressure<br><br>• Be sure tires are of the same type and size<br>• Have front end alignment checked |
| Abnormal, excessive or uneven tire wear<br><br>See "How to Read Tire Wear" | • Infrequent tire rotation<br><br>• Improper tire pressure<br><br>• Sudden stops/starts or high speed on curves | • Rotate tires more frequently to equalize wear<br>• Check/adjust pressure<br><br>• Correct driving habits |
| Tire squeals | • Improper tire pressure<br>• Front end needs aligning | • Check/adjust tire pressure<br>• Have front end alignment checked |

## Tire Size Comparison Chart

| "60 Series" | "70 Series" | "78 Series" | Inch Sizes 1965–77 | "60 Series" | "70 Series" | "80 Series" |
|---|---|---|---|---|---|---|
| "Letter" sizes | | | Inch Sizes | Metric-inch Sizes | | |
|  |  |  | 5.50-12, 5.60-12 | 165/60-12 | 165/70-12 | 155-12 |
|  | Y78-12 |  | 6.00-12 |  |  |  |
|  |  | W78-13 | 5.20-13 | 165/60-13 | 145/70-13 | 135-13 |
|  |  | Y78-13 | 5.60-13 | 175/60-13 | 155/70-13 | 145-13 |
|  |  |  | 6.15-13 | 185/60-13 | 165/70-13 | 155-13, P155/80-13 |
| A60-13 | A70-13 | A78-13 | 6.40-13 | 195/60-13 | 175/70-13 | 165-13 |
| B60-13 | B70-13 | B78-13 | 6.70-13 | 205/60-13 | 185/70-13 | 175-13 |
|  |  |  | 6.90-13 |  |  |  |
| C60-13 | C70-13 | C78-13 | 7.00-13 | 215/60-13 | 195/70-13 | 185-13 |
| D60-13 | D70-13 | D78-13 | 7.25-13 |  |  |  |
| E60-13 | E70-13 | E78-13 | 7.75-13 |  |  | 195-13 |
|  |  |  | 5.20-14 | 165/60-14 | 145/70-14 | 135-14 |
|  |  |  | 5.60-14 | 175/60-14 | 155/70-14 | 145-14 |
|  |  |  | 5.90-14 |  |  |  |
| A60-14 | A70-14 | A78-14 | 6.15-14 | 185/60-14 | 165/70-14 | 155-14 |
|  | B70-14 | B78-14 | 6.45-14 | 195/60-14 | 175/70-14 | 165-14 |
|  | C70-14 | C78-14 | 6.95-14 | 205/60-14 | 185/70-14 | 175-14 |
| D60-14 | D70-14 | D78-14 |  |  |  |  |
| E60-14 | E70-14 | E78-14 | 7.35-14 | 215/60-14 | 195/70-14 | 185-14 |
| F60-14 | F70-14 | F78-14, F83-14 | 7.75-14 | 225/60-14 | 200/70-14 | 195-14 |
| G60-14 | G70-14 | G77-14, G78-14 | 8.25-14 | 235/60-14 | 205/70-14 | 205-14 |
| H60-14 | H70-14 | H78-14 | 8.55-14 | 245/60-14 | 215/70-14 | 215-14 |
| J60-14 | J70-14 | J78-14 | 8.85-14 | 255/60-14 | 225/70-14 | 225-14 |
| L60-14 | L70-14 |  | 9.15-14 | 265/60-14 | 235/70-14 |  |
|  | A70-15 | A78-15 | 5.60-15 | 185/60-15 | 165/70-15 | 155-15 |
| B60-15 | B70-15 | B78-15 | 6.35-15 | 195/60-15 | 175/70-15 | 165-15 |
| C60-15 | C70-15 | C78-15 | 6.85-15 | 205/60-15 | 185/70-15 | 175-15 |
|  | D70-15 | D78-15 |  |  |  |  |
| E60-15 | E70-15 | E78-15 | 7.35-15 | 215/60-15 | 195/70-15 | 185-15 |
| F60-15 | F70-15 | F78-15 | 7.75-15 | 225/60-15 | 205/70-15 | 195-15 |
| G60-15 | G70-15 | G78-15 | 8.15-15/8.25-15 | 235/60-15 | 215/70-15 | 205-15 |
| H60-15 | H70-15 | H78-15 | 8.45-15/8.55-15 | 245/60-15 | 225/70-15 | 215-15 |
| J60-15 | J70-15 | J78-15 | 8.85-15/8.90-15 | 255/60-15 | 235/70-15 | 225-15 |
|  | K70-15 |  | 9.00-15 | 265/60-15 | 245/70-15 | 230-15 |
| L60-15 | L70-15 | L78-15, L84-15 | 9.15-15 |  |  | 235-15 |
|  | M70-15 | M78-15 |  |  |  | 255-15 |
|  |  | N78-15 |  |  |  |  |

Note: Every size tire is not listed and many size comparisons are approximate, based on load ratings. Wider tires than those supplied new with the vehicle, should always be checked for clearance.

rotation). The belts on radial tires get set in a pattern. If the direction of rotation is reversed, it can cause rough ride and vibration.

NOTE: *When radials or studded snows are taken off the car, mark them, so you can maintain the same direction of rotation.*

## TIRE STORAGE

Store the tires at proper inflation pressures if they are mounted on wheels. All tires should be kept in a cool, dry place. If they are stored in the garage or basement, do not let them stand on a concrete floor; set them on strips of wood.

## FLUIDS AND LUBRICANTS

### Engine

#### FUEL RECOMMENDATIONS

##### Gasoline Engine

Unleaded gasoline having a Research Octane Number (RON) of 91, or an Antiknock Index of 87 is recommended for your car. Leaded gasoline will quickly interfere with the operation of the catalytic converter and just a few tankfuls of leaded gasoline will render the converter useless. This will cause the emission of much greater amounts of hydrocarbons and carbon monoxide from the exhaust system, void you warranty and cost a considerable amount of money for converter replacement.

##### Diesel Engine

The 2.0L diesel engine is designed to use number 2-D diesel fuel. Use of number 1-D diesel fuel in temperatures +20°F is acceptable, but not necessary.

Do not use number 1-D diesel fuel in temperatures above +20°F as damage to the engine may result. Also fuel economy will be reduced with the use of number 1-D diesel fuel.

The 2.0L diesel engines are equipped with an electric fuel heater to prevent cold fuel problems. For best results in cold weather use winterized number 2-D diesel fuel which is blended to minimize cold weather operation problems.

CAUTION: *DO NOT add gasoline, gasohol, alcohol or cetane improvers to the diesel fuel. Also, DO NOT use fluids such as either in the diesel air intake system. The use of these liquids or fluids will cause damage to the engine and/or fuel system.*

#### OIL RECOMMENDATIONS

Oil meeting API classification SF or SF/CC or SF/CD is recommended for use in your vehicle.

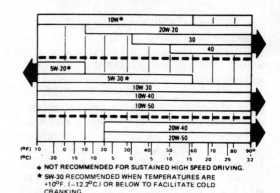

Engine oil viscosity recommendations—1981–83

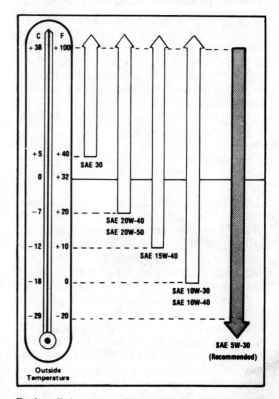

Engine oil viscosity recommendations—1984 and later

Viscosity grades 10W-30 or 10W-40 are recommended on models before 1984 and 5W-30 on models 1984 and later. See the viscosity to temperature chart in this section.

#### OIL LEVEL CHECK

It is a good idea to check the engine oil each time or at least every other time you fill your gas tank.

1. Be sure your car is on level ground. Shut off the engine and wait for a few minutes to allow the oil to drain back into the oil pan.

2. Remove the engine oil dipstick and wipe clean with a rag.

3. Reinsert the dipstick and push it down until it is fully seated in the tube.

4. Remove the stick and check the oil level shown. If the oil level is below the lower mark, add one quart.

5. If you wish, you may carefully fill the oil pan to the upper mark on the dipstick with less than a full quart. Do not, however, add a full quart when it would overfill the crankcase (level above the upper mark on the dipstick). The excess oil will generally be consumed at an excessive rate even if no damage to the engine seals occurs.

### CHANGING OIL AND FILTER

Change the engine oil and oil filter every 7 months or 7,500 miles. If the car is used in severe service or dusty conditions, change the engine oil and oil filter every 3 months or 3,000 miles. Following these recommended intervals will help keep you car engine in good condition.

1. Make sure the engine is at normal operating temperature (this promotes complete draining of the old oil).

2. Apply the parking brake and block the wheels or raise and support the car evenly on jackstands.

3. Place a drain pan of about a gallon and a half capacity under the engine oil pan drain plug. Use the proper size wrench, loosen and remove the plug. Allow all the old oil to drain. Wipe the pan and the drain plug with a clean rag. Inspect the drain plug gasket, replace if necessary.

4. Reinstall and tighten the drain plug. DO NOT OVERTIGHTEN.

5. Move the drain pan under the engine oil filter. Use a strap wrench and loosen the oil filter (do not remove), allow the oil to drain. Unscrew the filter the rest of the way by hand. Use a rag, if necessary, to keep from burning your fingers. When the filter comes loose from

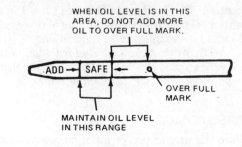

WHEN OIL LEVEL IS IN THIS AREA, DO NOT ADD MORE OIL TO OVER FULL MARK.

OVER FULL MARK

MAINTAIN OIL LEVEL IN THIS RANGE

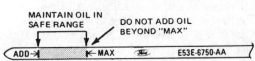

MAINTAIN OIL IN SAFE RANGE

DO NOT ADD OIL BEYOND "MAX"

**Engine oil level check recommendations**

the engine, turn the mounting base upward to avoid spilling the remaining oil.

6. Wipe the engine filter mount clean with a rag. Coat the rubber gasket on the new oil filter with clean engine oil, applying it with a finger. Carefully start the filter onto the threaded engine mount. Turn the filter until it touches the engine mounting surface. Tighten the filter, by hand, ½ turn more or as recommended by the filter manufacturer.

7. Lower the vehicle to the ground. Refill the crankcase with four quarts of engine oil. Replace the filler cap and start the engine. Allow the engine to idle and check for oil leaks. Shut off the engine, wait for several minutes, then check the oil level with the dipstick. Add oil if necessary.

## Transaxle
### SERVICE

Changing the fluid in either the automatic or manual transaxle is not necessary under normal operating conditions. However, the fluid levels should by checked at normal intervals as described previously in this chapter.

If your car is equipped with an automatic transaxle and the region in which you live has severe cold weather, a multi-viscosity automatic transaxle fluid should be used. Ask your dealer about the use of the MV Automatic Transaxle Fluid.

If you operate you car in very dusty conditions, tow a trailer, have extended idling or low speed operation, it may be necessary to change the ATX fluid at regular intervals (20 months, 20,000 miles or more often). Ask your dealer for his recommendations. A description of the fluid change procedure may be found in Chapter 6.

**Lubricate the gasket on the new filter with clean engine oil. A dry gasket may not make a good seal and will allow the filter to leak**

## FLUID LEVELS

### Manual Transaxle

Each time the engine oil is changed, the fluid level of the transaxle should be checked. The car must be resting on level ground or supported on jackstands (front and back) evenly. To check the fluid, remove the filler plug, located on the upper front (driver's side) of the transaxle with a $^9/_{16}"$ wrench.

CAUTION: *The filler plug has a hex-head, do not mistake any other bolts for the filler. Damage to the transaxle could occur if the wring plug is removed.*

The oil level should be even with the edge of the filler hole or within ¼" (6mm) of the hole. If the oil is low, add Type F or Dexron®II automatic fluid. Manual transmission type GL is NOT to be used.

NOTE: *A rubber bulb syringe will be helpful in adding the Type F or Dexron®II fluid to the manual transaxle.*

### Automatic Transaxle

A dipstick is provided in the engine compartment to check the level of the automatic transaxle. Be sure the car is on level ground and that the car's engine and transmission have reached normal operating temperatures. Start the engine, put the parking brake on the transmission selector lever in the PARK position. Move the selector lever through all the positions and return to the PARK position. DO NOT TURN OFF THE ENGINE DURING THE FLUID LEVEL CHECK. Clean all dirt from the dipstick cap before removing the dipstick. Remove the dipstick and wipe clean. Reinsert the dipstick making sure it is fully seated. Pull the dipstick out of the tube and check the fluid level. The fluid level should be between the FULL and ADD marks.

If necessary, add enough fluid through the dipstick tube/filler to bring the level to the FULL mark on the dipstick. Use only Dexron®II fluid.

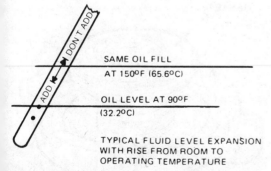

TYPICAL FLUID LEVEL EXPANSION WITH RISE FROM ROOM TO OPERATING TEMPERATURE

SAME OIL FILL AT 150°F (65.6°C)

OIL LEVEL AT 90°F (32.2°C)

**Dipstick markings showing typical fluid expansion from "room" to normal operating temperatures**

CAUTION: *Do not overfill. Make sure the dipstick is fully seated.*

### Differential

The differential is incorporated with the transmission, hence transaxle. The transmission fluid lubricates the differential so any checks or fluid changes can be done by following the procedures above, or in Chapter 6.

## Cooling System

### LEVEL CHECK

The cooling system of your car contains, among other items, a radiator and an expansion tank. When the engine is running heat is generated. The rise in temperature causes the coolant, in the radiator, to expand and builds up internal pressure. When a certain pressure is reached, a pressure relief valve in the radiator filler cap (pressure cap) is lifted from its seat and allows coolant to flow through the radiator filler neck, down a hose, and into the expansion reservoir.

When the system temperature and pressure are reduced in the radiator, the water in the expansion reservoir is syphoned back into the radiator.

Check the level in the coolant recovery reservoir at least one month. With the cold engine the level must be maintained at or above the ADD mark. At normal operating temperatures, the coolant level should be at the FULL HOT mark. If the level is below the recommended level a 50/50 mixture of coolant (antifreeze) and water should be added to the reservoir. If the reservoir is empty, add the coolant to the radiator and then fill the reservoir to the required level.

CAUTION: *The cooling fan motor is controlled by a temperature switch. The fan may come on and run when the engine is off. It will continue to run until the correct temperature is reached. Take care not to get your fingers, etc. caught in the fan blades.*

*Never remove the radiator cap under any circumstances when the engine is operating. Before removing the cap, switch off the engine and wait until it has cooled. Even then, use extreme care when removing the cap from a hot radiator. Wrap a thick cloth around the cap and turn it slowly to the first stop. Step back while the pressure is released from the cooling system. When you are sure all the pressure has been released, press down on the cap — still with a cloth — turn and remove it.*

### SERVICING

Check the freezing protection rating of the coolant at least once a year, just before winter.

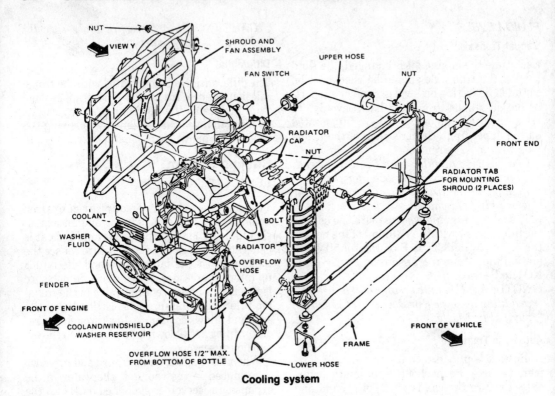

**Cooling system**

Maintain a protection rating of at least 20°F (–29°C) to prevent engine damage as a result of freezing and to assure proper engine operating temperature. Rust and corrosion inhibitors tend to deteriorate with time, changing the coolant every 3 years or 30,000 miles is recommended for proper protection of the cooling system.

Check the coolant level in the radiator at least once a month, only when the engine is cool. Whenever coolant checks are made, check the condition of the radiator cap rubber seal. Make sure it is clean and free of any dirt particles. Rinse off with water if necessary. When replacing cap on radiator, also make sure that the radiator filler neck seat is clean. Check that overflow hose in the reservoir is not kinked and is inserted to within ½″ (13mm) of bottom of the bottle.

### ADDING COOLANT

Anytime you add coolant to the radiator, use a 50/50 mixture of coolant and water. If you have to add coolant more than once a month, or if you have to add more than one quart at a time, have the cooling system checked for leaks.

### COOLANT SPECIFICATION

This engine has an aluminum cylinder head and requires a special unique corrosion inhibited coolant formulation to avoid radiator damage. Use only a permanent type coolant that meets Ford Specifications such as Ford Cooling System Fluid, Prestone® II or other approved coolants.

### DRAINING COOLANT

To drain the coolant, connect an 18″ (457mm) long, ⅜″ (9.5mm) inside diameter hose to the nipple on the drain valve located on the bottom of the radiator. With the engine cool, set the heater control to the maximum heat position, remove the radiator cap and open the drain valve or remove allen head plug (³⁄₁₆″) allowing the coolant to drain into a container. When all of the coolant is drained, remove the ⅜″ hose and close the drain valve.

### REPLACING COOLANT

If there is any evidence of rust or scaling in the cooling system the system should be flushed

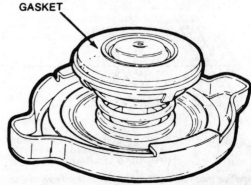

**Check the radiator cap gasket for cuts or cracks**

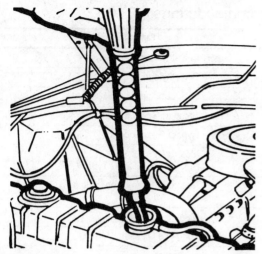

**Testing coolant protection with an antifreeze tester**

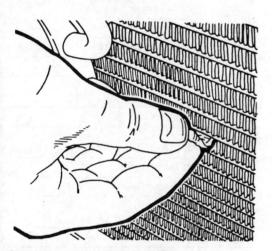

**Clean the radiator fins of debris**

thoroughly before refilling. With the engine OFF and COOL:

1. Add 50 percent of system's capacity of specified coolant to the radiator. Then add water until the radiator is full.

2. Reinstall the radiator cap to the pressure relief position by installing the cap to the fully installed position and then backing off to the first stop.

3. Start and idle the engine until the upper radiator hose is warm.

4. Immediately shut off engine. Cautiously remove radiator cap and add water until the radiator is full. Reinstall radiator cap securely.

5. Add coolant to the ADD mark on the reservoir, then fill to the FULL HOT mark with water.

6. Check system for leaks and return the heater temperature control to normal position.

## Brake Master Cylinder
### LEVEL CHECK

The brake master cylinder is located under the hood, on the left side firewall. Before removing the master cylinder reservoir cap, make sure the vehicle is resting on level ground and clean all the dirt away from the top of the master cylinder. Pry the retaining clip off to the side. Remove the master cylinder cover.

If the level of the brake fluid is within ¼" (6mm) of the top it is OK. If the level is less than half the volume of the reservoir, check the brake system for leaks. Leaks in the brake system most commonly occur at the rear wheel cylinders. or at the front calipers. Leaks at brake lines or the master cylinder can also be the cause of the loss of brake fluid.

There is a rubber diaphragm at the top of the master cylinder cap. As the fluid level lowers due to normal brake shoe wear or leakage, the diaphragm takes up the space. This is to prevent the loss of brake fluid out the vented cap and to help stop contamination by dirt. After filling the master cylinder to the proper level with brake fluid (Type DOT 3), but before replacing the cap, fold the rubber diaphragm up into the cap, then replace the cap on the reservoir and snap the retaining clip back in place.

## Manual Steering
No periodic lubrication is required unless the system is disassembled for service.

## Power Steering Pump Reservoir
### LEVEL CHECK

Run the engine until it reaches normal operating temperature. While the engine is idling, turn the steering wheel all the way to the right and then left several times. Shut OFF the engine. Open the hood and remove the power steering pump dipstick. Wipe the dipstick clean and reinstall into the pump reservoir. Withdraw the dipstick and note the fluid level shown. The level must show between the cold full mark and the hot full mark. Add fluid if necessary, buy do not overfill. Remove any excess fluid with a suction bulb or gun.

## Windshield Washer Reservoir
### LEVEL CHECK

You can fill the water tank with plain water in the summer time, but the pre-mixed solvents available help dissolve grime and dirt better and provide protection against freezing in the winter. Add fluid through the filler cover when

## Lubrication Recommendations

| Item | Part Name |
|---|---|
| Hinges, Hinge Checks and Pivots* | Polyethylene Grease |
| Hood Latch and Auxiliary Catch | Polyethylene Grease |
| Lock Cylinders | Lock Lubricant |
| Steering Gear Housing (Manual) | Steering Gear Grease |
| Steering Gear (Rack and Pinion) | Hypoid Gear Lube |
| Steering-Power (Pump Reservoir) | Motorcraft Auto. Trans. Fluid—Type F |
| Transmission (Automatic) | Motorcraft Auto. Trans. Fluid Dexron® II |
| Transmission (Manual) | Manual Trans. Lube |
| Engine Oil Filter | Long Life Oil Filter |
| Engine Oil | Motorcraft 10W40 Super Premium |
| | 10W30 Premium |
| | 20W40 Premium |
| | SAE 30 Single Weight |
| Speedometer Cable | Speedometer Cable Lube |
| Engine Coolant | Cooling System Fluid |
| Front Wheel Bearings and Hubs Front Wheel Bearing Seals | Long Life Lubricant |
| Brake Master Cylinder | H.D. Brake Fluid |
| Brake Master Cylinder Push Rod and Bushing | Motorcraft SAE 10W-30 Engine Oil |
| Drum Brake Shoe Ledges | High Temp. Grease |
| Parking Brake Cable | Polyethylene Grease |
| Brake Pedal Pivot Bushing | Motorcraft SAE 10W-30 Engine Oil |
| Tire Mounting Bead (of Tire) | Tire Mounting Lube |
| Clutch Pedal Pivot Bushing | Motorcraft SAE 10W-30 Engine Oil |

the level drops below the line on the side of the reservoir case.

## JACKING

Contact points for jacking with either the jack supplied with the car, or with a floor jack are located on the side rocker flanges. When using a floor jack, the front of the car may be raised by positioning the jack under the front body rail behind the suspension arm-to-body bracket. The rear of the car may be raised by positioning the jack forward of the rear suspension rod on the bracket.

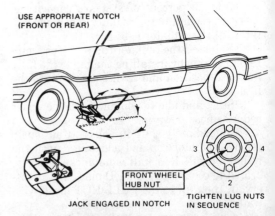

USE APPROPRIATE NOTCH (FRONT OR REAR)

FRONT WHEEL HUB NUT

JACK ENGAGED IN NOTCH

TIGHTEN LUG NUTS IN SEQUENCE

**Jack locations, using the jack equipped with your car**

## TRAILER TOWING

Towing a trailer puts additional load on your Ford FWD's engine, drivetrain, brakes, tires and suspension. For your safety and the care of your car, make sure the trailer towing equipment is properly matched to the trailer. All towing equipment should be safely attached to the vehicle and of the proper weight class.

The maximum trailer weight that your Ford FWD is 1000 lbs. gross trailer axle weight with a minium tongue load of 100 lbs. and must abide to the following qualifications:

• Any model equipped with a 2.85 manual transaxle final drive (green identification tag on the transaxle housing) should not be used to tow trailers of any size

• Auxiliary oil coolers are recommended for the power steering system and the automatic transaxle during long distance towing (greater than 50 miles, towing in hilly terrain or frequent towing).

• Vehicle speed no higher than 55 mph is recommended while towing a 1,000 lb. GVW trailer.

## Trailer Hitches

Choose a proper hitch and ball and make sure its location is compatible with that of the trailer. Use a good weight carrying hitch that uniformly distributes the trailer tongue loads through the underbody structure for towing trailers up to 1,000 lb.

Under no circumstances should a single or multiclamp type hitch be installed on your Ford FWD, damage to the bumper would result. Nor should any hitch which attaches to the axle be used. Underbody mounted hitches are acceptable if installed properly. Never attach safety chains to the bumper.

### TOWING TIPS

Before starting on a trip, practice turning, stopping and backing up in an area away from other traffic (such as a deserted shopping center parking lot) to gain experience in handling the extra weight and length of the trailer. Take enough time to get the feel of the vehicle/trailer combination under a variety of situations.

Skillful backing requires practice. Back up slowly with an assistant acting as a guide and watching for obstructions. Use both rear view mirrors. Place your hand at the bottom of the steering wheel and move it in the direction you want the rear of the trailer to swing. Make small corrections, instead of exaggerated ones, as a slight movement of the steering wheel will result in a much larger movement of the rear of the trailer.

Allow considerable more room for stopping when a trailer is attached to the vehicle. If you have a manual brake controller, lead with the trailer brakes when approaching a stop. Trailer brakes are also handy for correcting side sway. Just touch them for a moment without using your vehicle brakes and the trailer should settle down and track straight again.

To assist in obtaining good handling with the car/trailer combination, it is important that the trailer tongue load be maintained at approximately 10–15% of the loaded trailer weight.

Check everything before starting out on the road, then stop after you've traveled about 50 miles and double-check the trailer hitch and electrical connections to make sure everything is still OK. Listen for sounds like chains dragging on the ground (indicating that a safety chain has come loose) and check your rear view mirrors frequently to make sure the trailer is still there and tracking properly. Check the trailer wheel lug nuts to make sure they're tight and never attempt to tow the trailer with a space saver spare installed on the car.

Remember that a car/trailer combination is more sensitive to cross winds and slow down when crossing bridges or wide open expanses in gusty wind conditions. Exceeding the speed limit while towing a trailer is not only illegal, it is foolhardy and invites disaster. A strong gust of wind can send a speeding car/trailer combination out of control.

Because the trailer wheels are closer than the towing vehicle wheels to the inside of a turn, drive slightly beyond the normal turning point when negotiating a sharp turn at a corner. Allow extra distance for passing other vehicles and downshift if necessary for better acceleration. Allow at least the equivalent of one vehicle and trailer length combined for each 10 mph of road speed.

Finally, remember to check the height of the loaded car/trailer, allowing for luggage racks, antenna, etc. mounted on the roof and take note of low bridges or parking garage clearances.

## TOWING

Whenever you are towing another vehicle, or being towed, make sure the chain or strap is sufficiently long and strong. Attach the chain securely at a point on the frame, shipping tie-down slots are provided on the front and rear of you car and should be used. Never attach a chain or strap to any steering or suspen-

## JUMP STARTING A DEAD BATTERY

The chemical reaction in a battery produces explosive hydrogen gas. This is the safe way to jump start a dead battery, reducing the chances of an accidental spark that could cause an explosion.

### Jump Starting Precautions

1. Be sure both batteries are of the same voltage.
2. Be sure both batteries are of the same polarity (have the same grounded terminal).
3. Be sure the vehicles are not touching.
4. Be sure the vent cap holes are not obstructed.
5. Do not smoke or allow sparks around the battery.
6. In cold weather, check for frozen electrolyte in the battery.
7. Do not allow electrolyte on your skin or clothing.
8. Be sure the electrolyte is not frozen.

### Jump Starting Procedure

1. Determine voltages of the two batteries; they must be the same.
2. Bring the starting vehicle close (they must not touch) so that the batteries can be reached easily.
3. Turn off all accessories and both engines. Put both cars in Neutral or Park and set the handbrake.
4. Cover the cell caps with a rag—do not cover terminals.
5. If the terminals on the run-down battery are heavily corroded, clean them.
6. Identify the positive and negative posts on both batteries and connect the cables in the order shown.
7. Start the engine of the starting vehicle and run it at fast idle. Try to start the car with the dead battery. Crank it for no more than 10 seconds at a time and let it cool off for 20 seconds in between tries.
8. If it doesn't start in 3 tries, there is something else wrong.
9. Disconnect the cables in the reverse order.
10. Replace the cell covers and dispose of the rags.

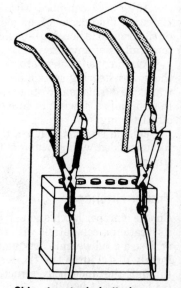

**Side terminal batteries occasionally pose a problem when connecting jumper cables. There frequently isn't enough room to clamp the cables without touching sheet metal. Side terminal adaptors are available to alleviate this problem and should be removed after use.**

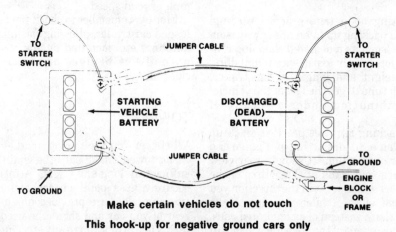

**Make certain vehicles do not touch**

**This hook-up for negative ground cars only**

# Capacities Chart

## Escort/Lynx

| Years | Engine Ltr. (CID) | Crankcase Includes Filter (qts) | Transmission (pts) | | | Drive Axle (pts) | Fuel Tank (gal) | Cooling System (qt) | |
|---|---|---|---|---|---|---|---|---|---|
| | | | 4-sp | 5-sp | Auto | | | w/AC | wo/AC |
| '81 | 1.3 (79) | 4.0 | 5.0 | — | ② | ③ | ④ | 6.3 | 6.3 |
| | 1.6 (98) | 4.0 | 5.0 | — | ② | ③ | ④ | 6.4 | 6.3 |
| '82 | 1.6 (98) | 4.0 | 5.0 | — | ② | ③ | ④ | 6.4 | 6.3 |
| '83 | 1.6 (98) | 4.0 | 5.0 | 6.1 | ② | ③ | ④ | 6.4 | 6.3 |
| '84 | 1.6 (98) | 4.0 | 5.0 | 6.1 | ② | ③ | ④ | 7.8 | 7.3 |
| | 2.0 (122) | 7.2 ⑤ | — | 6.1 | — | ③ | 13 | 9.2 | 9.2 |
| '85 | 1.6 (98) | 4.0 | 5.0 | 6.2 | ② | ③ | ④ | 7.1 | 6.6 |
| | 2.0 (122) | 7.2 ⑤ | — | 6.1 | — | ③ | 13 | 9.2 | 9.2 |
| '86–'87 | 1.9 (113.5) | 4.0 | 5.0 | 6.2 | ② | ③ | ④ | 7.3 ① | 7.9 |
| | 2.0 (122) | 7.2 ⑤ | — | 6.1 | — | ③ | 13 | 9.2 | 9.2 |

① Man. Trans.: 6.8 qts
② Total dry capacity-converter, cooler and sump drained.
    1981–82: 19.6 pts
    1985–86: 16.6 pts
    Partial fluid change (pan sump only), add 8 pts, start engine and check level. Add necessary fluid until correct level is reached.
③ Included in transmission capacity
④ 1981–82: 10 gal. Auto. Trans.
         9 gal. Manual Trans.
         11.3 gal. Extended range◢
    1983–87: 10 gal. FE models
         13 gal. Standard
         13 gal. EXP/LN7
⑤ Capacity for complete system—pan capacity is 5.3 qts.

## Tempo/Topaz

| Years | Engine Ltr. (CID) | Crankcase Includes Filter (qts) | Transmission (pts) | | | Drive Axle (pts) | Fuel Tank (gal) | Cooling System (qt) | |
|---|---|---|---|---|---|---|---|---|---|
| | | | 4-sp | 5-sp | Auto | | | w/AC | wo/AC |
| '84 | 2.0 (122) | 7.2 ④ | — | 6.1 | — | ③ | 15.2 | 9.2 | 9.2 |
| | 2.3 (140) | 4.5 ⑤ | 5.3 | 6.1 | ② | ③ | 15.2 | 8.4 | 8.4 |
| '85 | 2.0 (122) | 7.2 ④ | — | 6.1 | — | ③ | 15.2 | 9.2 | 9.2 |
| | 2.3 (140) | 4.5 ⑤ | 5.0 | 6.2 | ② | ③ | 15.2 | 7.7 | 7.1 |
| '86–'87 | 2.0 (122) | 7.2 ④ | — | 6.1 | — | ③ | 15.2 | 9.2 | 9.2 |
| | 2.3 (140) | 4.5 ⑤ | 5.0 | 6.2 | ② | ③ | 15.4 | 7.8 ① | 8.3 |

① Man. Trans.: 7.3 qts
② Total dry capacity-converter, cooler and sump drained 16.6 pts.
    Partial fluid change (pan sump only), add 8 pts, start engine and check level. Add necessary fluid until correct level is reached.
③ Included in transmission capacity.
④ Capacity for complete system—pan capacity is 5.3 qts.
⑤ After filter replacement, add 4 qts of oil and run engine. Shut engine off and check the oil level. Add ½ qt. if necessary.

sion part. Never try to start the vehicle when being towed, it might run into the back of the tow car. Do not allow too much slack in the tow line, the towed car could run over the line and damage to both cars could occur. If you car is being towed by a tow truck, the towing speed should be limited to 50 mph with the driving wheels off the ground. If it is necessary to tow the car with the drive wheels on the ground, speed should be limited to no more then 35 mph and the towing distance should not be greater than 50 miles. If towing distance is more than 50 miles the front of the car should be put on dollies.

NOTE: *If the car is being towed with the front (drive) wheels on the ground, never allow the steering lock to keep the wheels straight, damage to the steering could occur.*

## PUSHING

Push starting is not recommended on wheels with a catalytic converter. Gas accumulation in the converter will cause damage to the system.

## HOW TO BUY A USED CAR

Many people believe that a two or three year old used car is a better buy than a new car. This may be true. The new car suffers the heaviest depreciation in the first two year, but is not old enough to present a lot of costly repair problems. Whatever the age of the used car you might want to buy, this section and a little patience will help you select one that should be safe and dependable.

### TIPS

1. First decide what model you want, and how much you want to spend.

2. Check the used car lots and you local newspaper ads. Privately owned cars are usually less expensive, however you will not get a warranty that, in most cases, comes with a used car purchased from the lot.

3. Never shop at night. The glare of the lights make it easy to miss faults on the body caused by accident or rust repair.

4. Try to get the name and phone number of the previous owner. Contact him/her and ask about the car. If the owner of the lot refuses this information, look for a car somewhere else.

A private seller can tell you about the car and maintenance. Remember, however, there's no law requiring honesty from private citizens selling used cars. There is a law that forbids the tampering with or turning back the odometer mileage. This includes both the private citizen and the lot owner. The law also requires that the seller or anyone transferring ownership of the car must provide the buyer with a signed statement indicating the mileage on the odometer at the time of transfer.

5. Write down the year, model and serial number before you buy any used car. Then dial 1-800-424-9393, the toll free number of the National Highway Traffic Safety Administration, and ask if the car has ever been included in any manufacturer's recall list. If so, make sure the needed repairs were made.

6. Use the Used Car Checklist in this section and check all the items on the used car you are considering. Some items are more important than others. You know how much money you can afford for repairs, and, depending on the price of the car, may consider doing any needed work yourself. Beware, however, of trouble in areas that will affect operation, safety or emission. Problems in the Used Car Checklist break down as follows:

1–8: Two or more problems in these areas indicate a lack of maintenance. You should beware.

9–13: Indicates a lack of proper car, however, these can usually be corrected with a tune-up or relatively simple parts replacement.

14–17: Problems in the engine or transmission can be very expensive. Walk away from any car with problems in both of these areas.

7. If you are satisfied with the apparent condition of the car, take it to an independent diagnostic center or mechanic for a complete check. If you have a state inspection program, have it inspected immediately before purchase, or specify on the bill of sale that the sale is conditional on passing state inspection.

8. Road test the car – refer to the Road Test Checklist in this section. If your original evaluation and road test agree – the rest is up to you.

### USED CAR CHECKLIST

NOTE: *The numbers on the illustrations refer to the numbers on this checklist.*

1. *Mileage:* Average mileage is about 12,000 miles per year. More than average mileage may indicate hard usage. 1975 and later catalytic converter equipped models may need converter service at 50,000 miles.

2. *Paint:* Check around the tailpipe, molding and windows for overspray indicating that the car has been repaired.

3. *Rust:* Check fenders, doors, rocker panels, window moldings, wheelwells, floorboads,

under floormats, and in the trunk for signs of rust. Any rust at all will be a problem. There is no way to check the spread of rust, except to replace the part or panel.

4. *Body appearance:* Check the moldings, bumpers, grille, vinyl roof, glass, doors, trunk lid and body panels for general overall condition. Check for misalignment, loose holddown clips, ripples, scratches in glass, rips or patches in the top. Mismatched paint, welding in the trunk, severe misalignment of body panels or ripples may indicate crash work.

5. *Leaks:* Get down and look under the car. There are no normal leaks, other than water from the air conditioning condenser.

6. *Tires:* Check the tire air pressure. A common trick is to pump the tire pressure up to make the car roll easier. Check the tread wear, open the trunk and check the spare too. Uneven wear is a clue that the front end needs alignment. See the troubleshooting chapter for clues to the causes of tire wear.

7. *Shock absorbers:* Check the shock absorbers by forcing downward sharply on each corner of the car. Good shock will not allow the car to bounce more than twice after you let go.

8. *Interior:* Check the entire interior. You're looking for an interior condition that agrees with the overall condition of the car. Reasonable wear is expected, but be suspicious of new seatcovers on sagging seats, new pedal pads, and worn armrest. These indicate an attempt to cover up hard use. Pull back the carpets and look for evidence of water leaks or flooding. Look for missing hardware, door handles, control knobs etc. Check lights and signal opera-

tions. Make sure all accessories (air conditioner, heater, radio, etc.) work. Check windshield wiper operation.

9. *Belts and Hoses:* Open the hood and check all belts and hoses for wear, cracks or weak spots.

10. *Battery:* Low electrolyte level, corroded terminals and/or cracked case indicate a lack of maintenance.

11. *Radiator:* Look for corrosion or rust in the coolant indicating a lack of maintenance.

12. *Air filter:* A dirty air filter usually means a lack of maintenance.

13. *Ignition Wires:* Check the ignition wires for cracks, burned spots, or wear. Worn wires will have to be replaced.

14. *Oil level:* If the oil level is low, chances are the engine uses oil or leaks. Beware of water in the oil (cracked block), excessively thick oil (used to quiet a noisy engine), or thin, dirty oil with a distinct gasoline smell (internal engine problems).

15. *Automatic Transmission:* Pull the transmission dipstick out when the engine is running. The level should read Full, and the fluid should be clear or bright red. Dark brown or black fluid that has distinct burnt odor, signals a transmission in need of repair or overhaul.

16. *Exhaust:* Check the color of the exhaust smoke. Blue smoke indicates, among other problems, worn rings; black smoke can indicate burnt valves or carburetor problems. Check the exhaust system for leaks. It can be expensive to replace.

17. *Spark Plugs:* Remove one of the spark plugs (the most accessible will do). An engine

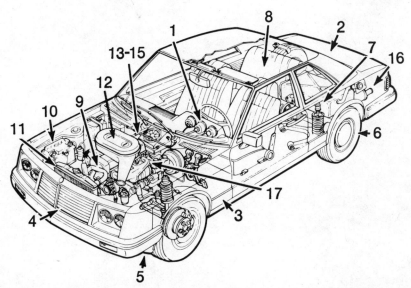

**You should check these points when buying a used car. The "Used Car Checklist" gives an explanation of the numbered items**

in good condition will show plugs with a light tan or gray deposit on the firing tip. See the color Tune-Up tips section for spark plug conditions.

## ROAD TEST CHECK LIST

1. *Engine Performance:* The car should be peppy whether cold or warm, with adequate power and good pickup. It should respond smoothly through the gears.

2. *Brakes:* They should provide quick, firm stops with no noise, pulling or brake fade.

3. *Steering:* Sure control with no binding, harshness, or looseness and no shimmy in the wheel should be expected. Noise or vibration from the steering wheel when turning the car means trouble.

4. *Clutch (Manual Transmission):* Clutch action should give quick, smooth response with easy shifting. The clutch pedal should have about 1–1½″ (25–38mm) of freeplay before it disengages the clutch. Start the engine, set the parking brake, put the transmission in first gear and slowly release the clutch pedal. The engine should begin to stall when the pedal is ½–¾ of the way up.

5. *Automatic Transmission:* The transmission should shift rapidly and smoothly, with no noise, hesitation, or slipping.

6. *Differential:* No noise or thumps should be present. Differentials have no normal leaks.

7. *Driveshaft, Universal Joints:* Vibration and noise could mean driveshaft problems. Clicking at low speed or coast conditions means worn U-Joints.

8. *Suspension:* Try hitting bumps at different speeds. A car that bounces has weak shock absorbers. Clunks mean worn bushings or ball joints.

9. *Frame:* Wet the tires and drive in a straight line. Tracks should show two straight lines, not four. Four tire tracks indicate a frame bent by collision damage. If the tires can't be wet for this purpose, have a friend drive along behind you and see if the car appears to be traveling in a straight line.

# Tune-Up and Performance Maintenance

# 2

## Gasoline Engine Tune-Up Specifications

| Years | Engine Ltr. (CID) | Spark Plug Type ④ | Gap (in.) | Ignition Timing (deg) Man. Trans. | Auto Trans. | Idle Speed Man. Trans. | Auto. Trans. | Valve Clearance In. | Exh. | Fuel Pump Pressure (psi) |
|---|---|---|---|---|---|---|---|---|---|---|
| '81 | 1.3 (79) | ① | .044 | 10B ① | 10B ① | ① | ① | Hyd. | Hyd. | 4–6 |
| | 1.6 (98) | AGSP-32 ④ | .044 | 10B ① | 10B ① | ① | ① | Hyd. | Hyd. | 4–6 |
| '82 | 1.6 (98) | AWSF-32 ④ | .044 | ① | ① | ① | ① | Hyd. | Hyd. | 4–6 |
| '83 | 1.6 (98) | AWSF-34 ② ④ | .044 | ① | ① | ① | ① | Hyd. | Hyd. | ③ |
| '84 | 1.6 (98) | AWSF-34 ② | .044 | ① | ① | ① | ① | Hyd. | Hyd. | ③ |
| | 2.3 (140) | AWSF-62 | .044 | 10B ① | 15B ① | ① | ① | Hyd. | Hyd. | 5 |
| '85 | 1.6 (98) | AWSF-34 ② | .044 | ① | ① | ① | ① | Hyd. | Hyd. | ③ |
| | 2.3 (140) | AWSF-62 | .044 | 10B ① | 15B ① | ① | ① | Hyd. | Hyd. | 5 |
| '86–'87 | 1.9(113.5) | AWSF-34C ⑤ | .044 | 10B ① | 10B ① | ① | ① | Hyd. | Hyd. | ③ |
| | 2.3 (140) | AWSF-44C ⑥ | .044 | 13B ① | 10B ① | ① | ① | Hyd. | Hyd. | ⑦ |

NOTE: The underhood specification sticker often reflects changes made in production. Stickers figures must be used if they disagree with those in the above chart.
① Calibration levels vary from model to model. Always refer to the underhood sticker for your car requirements.
② EFI Models: AWSF24
③ Carbureted system 4–6 psi, EFI system 35–45 psi
④ CAUTION: Two different plug designs are used on the 1.6L engines. The designs are: gasket equipped and tapered seat (no gasket). All 1981 Escort/Lynx models; and 1982 EXP/LN7 models built before 9/4/81 use gasket equipped plugs. All 1982 and later Escort/Lynx models; and EXP/LN7 models built after 9/4/81 are equipped with tapered seat plugs. DO NOT INTERCHANGE TYPES. Tighten gasket equipped plugs to 17–22 ft. lbs. Tapered seat plugs are tightened to 10–15 ft. lbs. DO NOT OVERTIGHTEN.
⑤ EFI Models: AWSF-24C
⑥ EFI Models: AWSF-32C
⑦ Carbureted system 5 psi, CFI system 15–16 psi.

## Diesel Engine Tune-Up Specifications

| Years | Engine Ltr. (CID) | Static Injection Timing | Compression Pressure (psi) | Injection Nozzle Opening Pressure (psi) | Idle Speed Man. Trans. | Auto. Trans. | Valve Clearance In. | Exh. |
|---|---|---|---|---|---|---|---|---|
| '84–'87 | 2.0 (122) | TDC | 427 @ 200 rpm | 1914 | 800–850 | 800–850 | 0.010 | 0.014 |

NOTE: The underhood specification sticker often reflects changes made in production. Stickers figures must be used if they disagree with those in the above chart.

## TUNE-UP PROCEDURES

### Spark Plugs

Spark plugs ignite the air and fuel mixture in the cylinder as the piston reaches the top of the compression stroke. The controlled explosion that results forces the piston down, turning the crankshaft and the rest of the drive train.

Ford recommends that spark plugs be changed every 30,000 miles (60,000 Calif.). Under severe driving conditions, those intervals should be halved. Severe driving conditions are:

1. Extended periods of idling or low speed operation, such as off-road or door-to-door delivery.

2. Driving short distances (less than 10 miles) when the average temperature is below 10°F (–12°C) for 60 days or more.

3. Excessive dust or blowing dirt conditions.

When you remove the spark plugs, check their condition. They are in good indicator of the condition of the engine. It is a good idea to remove the spark plugs at regular intervals, such as every 6,000 or so miles, just so you can keep an eye on the mechanical state of the engine.

A small deposit of light tan or gray material on a spark plug that has been used for any period of time is considered normal. Any other color, or abnormal amounts of deposit, indicate that there is something amiss in the engine.

The gap between the center electrode and the side or ground electrode can be expected to increase not more than 0.001″ (0.025mm) every 1,000 miles under normal conditions. When, and if, a plug fouls and begins to misfire, you will have to investigate, correct the cause of the fouling and either clean or replace the plug.

There are several reasons why a spark plug will foul and you can learn which reason is at fault by just looking at the plug. A few of the most common reasons for plug fouling and a description of fouled plug appearance are shown in the Four-Color section.

### SPARK PLUG HEAT RANGE

Spark plug heat range is the ability of the plug to dissipate heat. The longer the insulator (or the farther it extends into the engine), the hotter the plug will operate; the shorter the insulator the cooler it will operate. A plug that absorbs little heat and remains too cool will quickly accumulate deposits of oil and carbon since it is not hot enough to burn them off. This leads to plug fouling and consequently to misfiring. A plug that absorbs too much heat will have no deposits, but, due to the excessive heat, the electrodes will burn away quickly and in some instances, preignition may result. Preignition takes place when plug tips get so hot that they glow sufficiently to ignite the fuel/air mixture before the actual spark occurs. This early ignition will usually cause a pinging during low speeds and heavy loads.

The general rule of thumb of choosing the correct heat range when picking a spark plug is: if most of your driving is long distance, high speed travel, use a cooler plug; if most of your driving is stop and go, use a hotter plug. Original equipment plugs are compromise plugs, but most people never have occasion to change their plugs from the factory recommended heat range.

### REPLACING SPARK PLUGS

CAUTION: *Two different plug designs are used on early 1.6L engines. The designs are: gasket equipped and tapered seat (no gasket). All 1981 Escort/Lynx models, and 1982 EXP/LN7 models built before 9/4/81 use gasket equipped plugs. All 1982 and later Escort/Lynx and EXP/LN7 models built after 9/4/81 are equipped with tapered seat plugs. DO NOT INTERCHANGE TYPES. Tighten gasket equipped plugs to 17–22 ft.lb. Tapered plugs are tightened to 10–15 ft.lb. DO NOT OVERTIGHTEN.*

A Set of spark plugs usually requires replacement every 30,000 miles, depending on your style of driving. In normal operation, plug gap increases about 0.001″ (0.025mm) for every 1,000–2,500 miles. As the gap increases, the plug's voltage requirement also increases. It requires greater voltage to jump the wider gap and about two to three times as much voltage to fire a plug at higher speeds than at idle.

The spark plugs used in your car require a deep spark plug socket for removal and installation. A special designed pair of plug wire removal pliers is also a good tool to have. The special pliers have cupped jaws that grip the plug wire boot and make the job of twisting and pulling the wire from the plug easier.

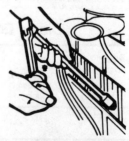

**Remove the spark plugs with a ratchet and long extension**

## REMOVAL AND INSTALLATION

NOTE: *The original spark plug wires are marked for cylinder location. If replacement wires have been installed, be sure to tag them for proper location. It is a good idea to remove the wires one at a time, service the spark plug, reinstall the wire and move onto the next cylinder.*

For easy access for servicing the spark plugs, remove the air cleaner assembly and air intake tube.

1. Twist the spark plug boot and gently pull it and the wire from the spark plug. This is where the special plug wire pliers come in handy.

CAUTION: *Never pull on the wire itself, damage to the inside conductor could occur.*

2. The plug wire boot has a cover which shields the plug cavity (in the head) against dirt. After removing the wire, blow out the cavity with air or clean it out with a small brush so dirt will not fall into the engine when the spark plug is removed.

3. Remove the spark plug with a plug socket. Turn the socket counterclockwise to remove the plug. Be sure to hold the socket straight on the plug to avoid breaking the insulator (a deep socket designed for spark plugs has a rubber cushion built-in to help prevent plug breakage).

4. Once the plug is out, compare it with the spark plug illustrations to determine the engine condition. This is crucial since spark plug readings are vital signs of engine condition and pending problems.

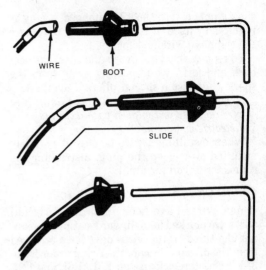

Use a bent "tool" to install new plug boots

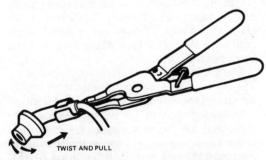

Special pliers used to remove the boots and wire from the spark plug

Check the spark plug gap with a wire feeler gauge

5. If the old plugs are to be reused, clean and regap them. If new spark plugs are to be installed, always check the gap. Use a round wire feeler gauge to check plug gap. The correct size gauge should pass through the electrode gap with a slight drag. If you're in doubt, try the next smaller and one size larger. The smaller gauge should go through easily and the larger should not go through at all. If adjustment is necessary use the bending tool on the end of the gauge. When adjusting the gap, always bend the side electrode. The center electrode is non-adjustable.

6. Squirt a drop of penetrating oil on the threads of the spark plug and install it. Don't oil the threads heavily. Turn the plug in clockwise by hand until it is snug.

7. When the plug is finger tight, tighten it to the proper torque 17–22 ft.lb. DO NOT OVERTIGHTEN.

8. Install the plug wire and boot firmly over the spark plug after coating the inside of the boot and terminal with a thin coat of dielectric compound (Motorcraft D7AZ19A331A or the equivalent).

9. Proceed to the next spark plug.

## CHECKING AND REPLACING SPARK PLUG CABLES

Your car is equipped with a electronic ignition system which utilizes 8mm wires to conduct the hotter spark produced. The boots on these wires are designed to cover the spark plug cavities on the cylinder head.

Inspect the wires without removing them from the spark plugs, distributor cap or coil. Look for visible damage such as cuts, pinches, cracks or torn boots. Replace any wires that show damage. If the boot is damaged, it may be replaced by itself. It is not necessary to replace the complete wire just for the boot.

To replace the wire, grasp and twist the boot back and forth while pulling away from the spark plug. Use a special pliers if available.

NOTE: *Always coat the terminals of any wire removed or replaced with a thin layer of dielectric compound.*

When installing a wire be sure it is firmly mounted over or on the plug, distributor cap connector or coil terminal.

### FIRING ORDER

If new wires have been installed (original wires are marked for cylinder location) and are not identified, or the wires have been removed from the distributor cap, the firing order is: 1–3–4–2 counterclockwise on 1.3L, 1.6L and 1.9L engines and clockwise on 2.3L HSC models.

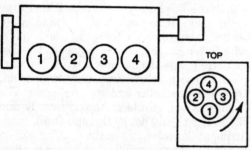

**Escort, Lynx 1.3L, 1.6L, 1.9L Engine Firing Order; 1–3–4–2 Distributor Rotation; Counterclockwise**

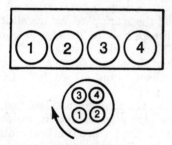

**Tempo, Topaz 2.3L Engine Firing Order; 1–3–4–2 Distributor Rotation; Clockwise**

## Electronic Ignition System

NOTE: *This book contains simple testing procedures for your Ford's electronic ignition. More comprehensive testing on this system and other electronic control systems on your Ford can be found in CHILTON'S GUIDE TO ELECTRONIC ENGINE CONTROLS, book part number 7535, available at your local retailer.*

Your car uses an electronic ignition system.

The purpose of using an electronic ignition system is: To eliminate the deterioration of spark quality which occur in the breaker point ignition system as the breaker points wore. To extend maintenance intervals. To provide a more intense and reliable spark at every firing impulse in order to ignite the leaner gas mixtures necessary to control emissions.

The breaker points, point actuating cam and the condenser have been eliminated in the solid state distributor. They are replace by an ignition module and a magnetic pulse-signal generator (pick-up).

The Dura Spark II is a pulse triggered, transistor controlled breakerless ignition system. With the ignition switch **ON**, the primary circuit is on and the ignition coil is energized. When the armature spokes approach the magnetic pick-up coil assembly, they induce a voltage which tells the amplifier to turn the coil primary current off. A timing circuit in the amplifier module will turn the current on again after the coil field has collapsed. When the current is on, it flows from the battery through the ignition switch, the primary windings of the ignition coil, and through the amplifier module circuits to ground. When the current is off, the magnetic field built up in the ignition coil is allowed to collapse, inducing a high voltage into the secondary windings of the coil. High voltage is produced each time the field is thus built up and collapsed.

A Universal Distributor equipped with either a TFI-I or TFI-IV system is used on some models, depending on year, engine option, and model. TFI stands for Thick Film Integrated which incorporates a molded thermoplastic module mounted on the distributor base. Models equipped with TFI also use an **E** coil which replaces the oil filled design used with Dura-Spark.

The Universal Distributor equipped with TFI-IV uses a vane switch stator assembly which replace the coil stator. The IV system incorporates provision for fixed octane adjustment and has no centrifugal or vacuum advance mechanisms. All necessary timing requirements are handled by the EEC-IV electronic engine control system.

## Ignition Timing

1. Timing marks on 1.3/1.6/1.9L engines consist of a notch on the crankshaft pulley and a graduated scale molded into the camshaft drive belt cover. The number of degrees before or after TDC (top dead center) represented by each mark can be interpreted according to the decal affixed to the top of the belt cover (emissions decal).

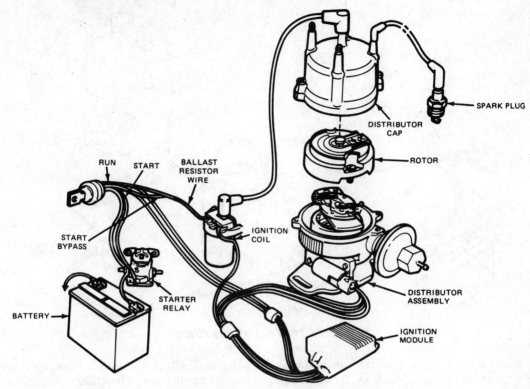

The Dura Spark ignition system

2. Timing marks on 2.3 HSC engines are located on the flywheel edge (manual transaxle or flywheel face (automatic transaxle) and are visible through a slot in the transaxle case at the back of the engine. A cover plate retained by two screws must be removed to view the timing marks on manual cars. Each mark (small graduation) equals 2°. Early automatic cars have timing marks punched on the flywheel, the marks are 5° apart. The required degree mark should align with the timing slot pointer. Unless the emission decal specifies

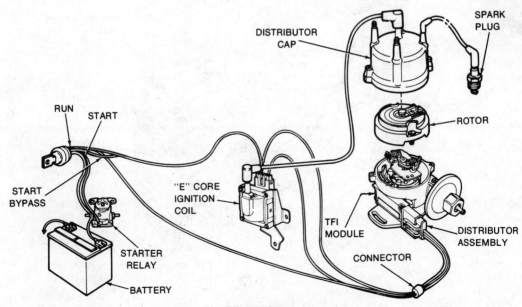

The TFI ignition system

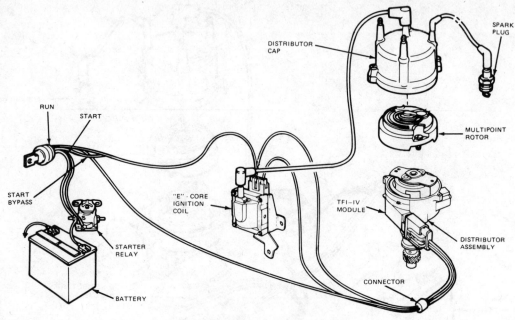

**2.3L HSC TFI-IV on the Tempo/Topaz**

otherwise, timing for manual transaxle models is 10° BTDC and 15° BTDC for automatic transaxle models.

3. Turn the engine until No. 1 piston is at TDC on the compression stroke. Apply white paint or chalk to the rotating timing mark (notch on pulley or flywheel) after cleaning the metal surface.

4. Refer to the emissions decal for timing, engine rpm and vacuum hose (if equipped) sta-

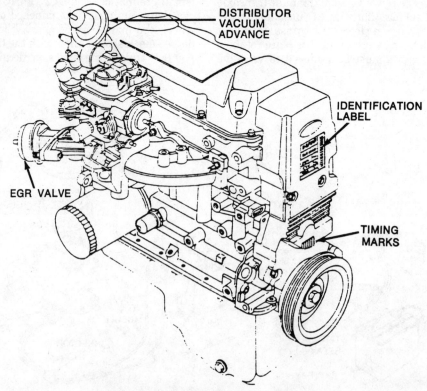

**1.6L, 1.9L timing marks on the front cover**

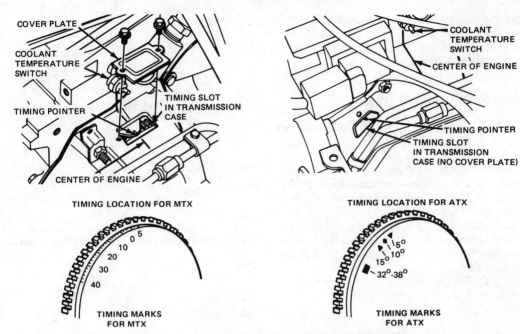

Timing marks and identification—2.3L HSC engine

tus information. Disconnect and plug the distributor vacuum line(s) if equipped and required. On models equipped with the EEC IV system engine, disconnect the ignition spout wire (circuit 36–yellow/light green dots or black) from the distributor connector. On 1.6/1.9L engines equipped with a 2-bbl carburetor, disconnect the barometric pressure switch and connect a jumper wire across the ignition module black and yellow wire connector pins.

5. Attach a timing light and tachometer to the engine. Start the engine and allow to idle until normal operating temperature is reached.

6. Be sure the parking brake is applied and wheels blocked. Place the transmission in gear specified on emissions decal. Check idle rpm and adjust if necessary.

7. Aim the flashing timing light at the timing marks. If the proper marks are not aligned, loosen the distributor holddown bolt/nut slightly and rotate the distributor body until the marks are aligned. Tighten the holddown.

8. Recheck the ignition timing, readjust if necessary. Shut off the engine and reconnect vacuum hoses or spout connector. Start engine and readjust idle rpm is necessary.

## TACHOMETER HOOKUP

Models equipped with a conventional type coil have an adapter on the top of the coil that provides a clip marked Tach Test. On models (TFI) equipped with an **E** type coil, the tach connection is made at the back of the wire har-

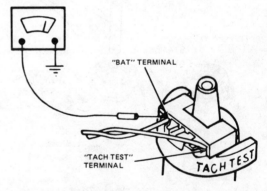

Hook up to test on coil "Bat" terminal

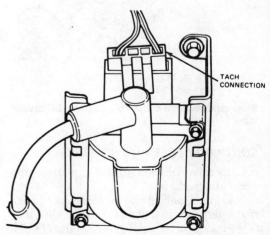

"E" coil tachometer connection

ness connector. A cutout is provided and the tachometer lead wire alligator clip can be connected to the dark green/yellow dotted wire of the electrical harness plug.

## Distributor Cap and Rotor

1. The distributor cap is held on by two cap screws. Release them with a screwdriver and lift the cap straight up and off, with the wires attached. Inspect the cap for cracks, carbon tracks, or a worn center contact. Replace it if necessary, transferring the wires one at a time from the old cap to the new.

2. Remove the screw retaining the ignition rotor and remove the rotor. Replace it if its contacts are worn, burned, or pitted. Do not file the contact.

NOTE: *Always coat the cap and rotor contacts with dielectric compound.*

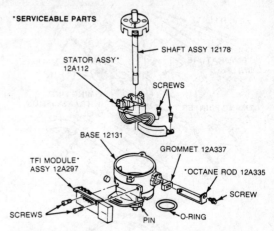

Semi-exploded view of the 1.6L, 1.9L EFI distributor

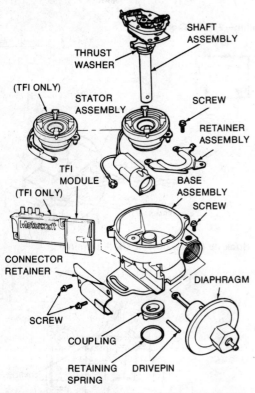

Semi-exploded view of the 1.6L, 1.9L non-EFI distributor

## CONTINUITY TEST – PLUG WIRES

1. Remove the distributor cap with plug wires attached.

2. Connect one end of an ohmmeter to the spark plug terminal end of the wire, the other to the inside corresponding terminal of the distributor cap.

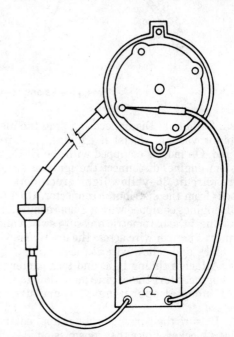

To check the spark plug wire resistance, measure from the cap terminal to the plug end of the wire with an ohmmeter. Resistance should be less than 5000 ohms per inch of plug wire length

3. Measure the resistance. If the reading is more than 5,000Ω per inch of cable, replace the wire.

## Ignition Coil

### PRIMARY RESISTANCE

1. Verify that the ignition switch is in the OFF position.

2. Remove the coil connector, clean and inspect for dirt or corrosion.

3. Measure the resistance between the positive and negative terminals of the coil with an ohmmeter. On TFI models, resistance should

```
 3567507055
981567               AD              7.99
 1857502085
613296               AD             13.99


LSTAX                                  .88
OTAL                              $22.86


ASH                              $23.00
HANGE                              $.14
TEMS             2
```

CLERK  508

```
634
002 0113-0002 7627  3:48PM  3-20-89  MON
```

THANK YOU
FOR SHOPPING
NATIONWISE
1183 BANKHEAD HIGHWAY, S.W.
MABELTON, GEORGIA 30059
404-944-2925, STORE# 113

1857502085

CLERK 508

234
802 0113-0003 7627  3:48PM 3-20-89 MON

measure 0.3–1.0Ω. On Dura-Spark models, the resistance should measure 0.8–1.6Ω.

4. Replace the coil if resistance is not within specifications.

## SECONDARY RESISTANCE

1. Follow Steps 1 and 2 of the Primary Resistance Test.

2. Measure resistance between the negative (BATT) and high tension lead terminal of the coil.

3. Resistance for Dura-Spark should be between 7,700–10,500Ω. TFI should be between 8000–11,500Ω.

4. Replace the coil if not within specifications.

## Dura Spark II Troubleshooting

The following procedures can be used to determine whether the ignition system is working or not. If these procedures fail to locate and correct the problem, full troubleshooting procedures should be performed by a qualified service department.

### PRELIMINARY CHECKS

1. Check the battery's state of charge and connections.

2. Inspect all wires and connections for breaks, cuts, abrasions, or burn spots. Repair as necessary.

3. Unplug all connectors one at a time and inspect for corroded or burned contacts. Repair and plug connectors back together. DO NOT remove the dielectric compound in the connectors.

4. Check for loose or damaged spark plug or coil wires. Check for excessive resistance. If the boots or nipples are removed on 8mm ignition wires, reline the inside of each with silicone dielectric compound (Motorcraft WA 10).

### Special Tools

To perform the following tests, two special tools are needed: the ignition test jumper

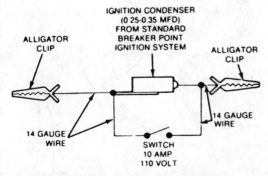

**Test jumper switch used for troubleshooting the Ford electronic ignition system**

shown in the illustration and a modified spark plug. Use the illustration to assemble the ignition test jumper. The test jumper must be used when performing the following tests. The modified spark plug is basically a spark plug with the side electrode removed. Ford makes a special tool called a Spark Tester for this purpose, which besides not having a side electrode is equipped with a spring clip so that it can be grounded to engine metal. It is recommended that the Spark Tester be used as there is less chance of being shocked.

### Run Mode Spark Test

NOTE: *The wire colors given here are the main color of the wires, not the dots or stripe marks.*

*STEP 1*

1. Remove the distributor cap and rotor from the distributor.

2. With the ignition off, turn the engine over by hand until one of the teeth on the distributor armature aligns with the magnet in the pick-up coil.

3. Remove the coil wire from the distributor cap. Install the modified spark plug (see Special Tools) in the coil wire terminal and using insulated pliers, hold the spark plug base against the engine block.

4. Turn the ignition to RUN (not START) and tap the distributor body with a screwdriver handle. There should be a spark at the modified spark plug or at the coil wire terminal.

5. If a good spark is evident, the primary circuit is OK, perform Start Mode Spark Test. If there is no spark, proceed to Step 2.

*STEP 2*

1. Unplug the module connector(s) which contain(s) the green and black module leads.

2. In the harness side of the connector(s), connect the special test jumper (see special tools) between the leads which connect the green and black leads of the module pig tails. Use paper clips on connector socket holes to make contact. Do not allow clips to ground.

3. Turn the ignition switch to RUN (not START) and close the test jumper switch. Leave closed for about one second, then open. Repeat several times. There should be a spark each time the switch is opened.

4. If there is NO spark, the problem is probably in the primary circuit through the ignition switch, the coil, the green lead or the black lead, or the ground connection in the distributor. Perform Step 3. If there IS a spark, the primary circuit wiring and coil are probably OK. The problem is probably in the distributor

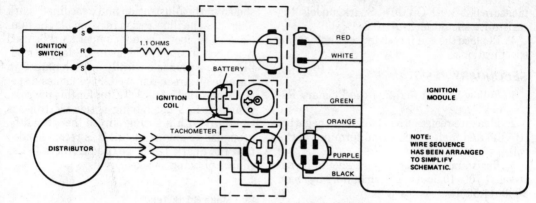

**Color codes for the Dura Spark module and harness**

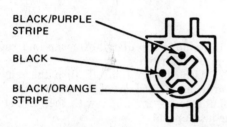

**Dura Spark distributor connector color codes**

pick-up, the module red wire, or the module. Perform Step 6.

**STEP 3**

1. Disconnect the test jumper lead from the black lead and connect it to a good ground. Turn the test jumper switch on and off several times as in Step 2.

2. If there is NO spark, the problem is probably in the green lead, the coil, or the coil feed circuit. Perform Step 5.

3. If there IS spark, the problem is probably in the black lead or the distributor ground connections. Perform Step 4.

**STEP 4**

1. Connect an ohmmeter between the black lead and ground. With the meter on its lowest scale, there should be NO measurable resistance in the circuit. If there is resistance, check the distributor ground connections and the black lead from the module. Repair as necessary, remove the ohmmeter, plug in all connections and repeat Step 1.

2. If there is NO resistance, the primary ground wiring is OK. Perform Step 6.

**STEP 5**

1. Disconnect the test jumper from the green lead and ground and connect it between the TACH-TEST terminal of the coil and a good ground on the engine.

2. With the ignition switch in the RUN posi-

tion, turn the jumper switch on. Hold it on for about one second then turn it off as in Step 2. Repeat several times. There should be a spark each time the switch is turned off. If there is NO spark, the problem is probably in the primary circuit running through the ignition switch to the coil BAT terminal, or in the coil itself. Check coil resistance (test given later in this section), and check the coil for internal shorts or opens. Check the coil feed circuit for opens, shorts or high resistance. Repair as necessary, reconnect all connectors and repeat Step 1. If there IS spark, the coil and its feed circuit are OK. The problem could be in the green lead between the coil and the module. Check for open or short, repair as necessary, reconnect all connectors and repeat Step 1.

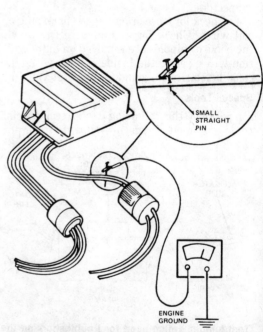

**Inserting straight pin to test a circuit**

*STEP 6*

To perform this step, a voltmeter which is not combined with a dwell meter is needed. The slight needle oscillations (0.5V) you'll be looking for may not be detectable on the combined voltmeter/dwell meter unit.

1. Connect a voltmeter between the orange and purple leads on the harness side of the module connectors.

CAUTION: *On catalytic converter equipped cars, disconnect the air supply line between the Thermactor by-pass valve and the manifold before cranking the engine with the ignition off. This will prevent damage to the catalytic converter. After testing, run the engine for at least 3 minutes before reconnecting the by-pass valve, to clear excess fuel from the exhaust system.*

2. Set the voltmeter on its lowest scale and crank the engine. The meter needle should oscillate slightly (about 0.5V). If the meter does not oscillate, check the circuit through the magnetic pick-up in the distributor for open shorts, shorts to ground and resistance. Resistance between the orange and purple leads should be 400–1,000Ω, and between each lead and ground should be more than 70,000Ω. Repair as necessary, reconnect all connectors and repeat Step 1.

3. If the meter oscillates, the problem is probably in the power feed to the module (red wire) or in the module itself. Proceed to Step 7.

*STEP 7*

1. Remove all meters and jumpers and plug in all connectors.

2. Turn the ignition switch to the RUN position and measure voltage between the battery positive terminal and engine ground. It should be 12 volts.

3. Next, measure voltage between the red lead of the module and engine ground. To make this measurement, it will be necessary to pierce the red wire with a straight pin and connect the voltmeter to the straight pin and to ground. DO NOT ALLOW THE STRAIGHT PIN TO GROUND ITSELF.

4. The two readings should be within one volts of each other. If not within one volt, the problem is in the power feed to the red lead. Check for shorts, open, or high resistance and correct as necessary. After repairs, repeat Step 1.

If the readings are within one volt, the problem is probably in the module. Replace with a good module and repeat Step 1. If this corrects the problem reconnect the old module and repeat Step 1. If the problem returns, replace the module.

**Start Mode Spark Test**

NOTE: *The wire colors given here are the main color of the wires, not the dots and stripe marks.*

1. Remove the coil wire from the distributor cap. Install the modified spark plug mentioned under Special Tools, above, in the coil wire and ground it to engine metal either by its spring clip (Spark Tester) or by holding the spark plug shell against the engine block with insulated pliers.

CAUTION: *See the Caution under Step 6 of Run Mode Spark Test.*

2. Have an assistant crank the engine using the ignition switch and check for spark. If there IS a good spark, the problem is most probably in the distributor cap, rotor, ignition cables or spark plugs. If there is NO spark, proceed to Step 3.

3. Measure the battery voltage. Next, measure the voltage at the white wire of the module while cranking the engine. To make this measurement, it will be necessary to pierce the white wire with a straight pin and connect the voltmeter to the straight pin and to ground.

NOTE: *DO NOT ALLOW THE STRAIGHT PIN TO GROUND ITSELF. The battery voltage and the voltage at the white wire should be within one volt of each other. If the readings are not within one volt of each other, check and repair the feed through the ignition switch to the white wire. Recheck for spark (Step 1). If the readings are within one volt of each other, or if there is still NO spark after power feed to white wire is repaired, proceed to Step 4.*

4. Measure the coil **BAT** terminal voltage while cranking the engine. The reading should be within one volt of battery voltage. If the readings are not within one volt of each other, check and repair the feed through the ignition switch to the coil. If the readings are within one volt of each other, the problem is probably in the ignition module. Substitute another module and repeat test for spark (Step 1).

## *BALLAST RESISTOR*

The ballast resistor wire is usually red with light green stripes. To check it you must disconnect it at the coil **BAT** connections and at the connector at the end of the wiring harness. The connector at the end of the wiring harness is a rectangular connector with eight terminals. Connect an ohmmeter to each end of the wire and set it to the **High** scale. The resistance of the wire should be between 1.05Ω and 1.15Ω. Any other reading merits replacement of the resistor wire with one of the correct service resistor wires.

## TFI Troubleshooting

NOTE: *Refer to the comments, preliminary checks and special tool paragraphs of the proceeding Dura-Spark Troubleshooting section. In addition to preliminary checks mentioned, check to be sure the TFI module is securely attached to the distributor.*

### VOLTAGE TEST

1. Disconnect the TFI module wire harness connector at the module. Check for battery voltage between each pin of the connector and ground. Use a straight pin the connector socket hole to make contact. Test as follows:

2. With the ignition switch in the Off position, check of 0 volts at each terminal. If voltage is present, check the ignition switch for problems.

3. Set the ignition switch to the RUN position. Check for battery voltage at the color/coded W/LBH and DG/YD wires. Check for 0 volts at the R/LB wire. If not as required, check the continuity of the ignition switch, coil and wires.

4. Disconnect the R/LB wire lug at the starter relay. Set the ignition switch to START. Check for battery voltage at all three wires. If voltage is not present, check the continuity of the ignition switch and R/LB wire. Reconnect the wire lug to the starter relay.

### RUN MODE TEST

1. Remove the coil wire from the distributor cap. Install the modified spark plug (see special tools in previous section) in the coil wire terminal.

2. Unplug the wire connector at the TFI module. In the harness side of the connector, connect the special jumper (see special tools in previous section) between the ground and the color coded DG/YD lead. Use a straight pin in the socket to make the connection.

CAUTION: *Do not leave the special jumper switch closed for more than a second at a time.*

3. Place the ignition switch in the RUN position. Quickly close (no more than one second) and open the jumper switch. Repeat the closing and opening several times. Spark should occur each time the jumper switch is opened.

4. If there is no spark the problem is in the primary circuit. Check the coil for internal shorts or opens, check primary and secondary resistance. Replace the coil if necessary.

5. If there is spark when the jumper switch is opened, the problem is in the distributor or TFI module.

## Valve Lash

Valve adjustment determines how far the valves enter the cylinder and how long they stay open and closed.

If the valve clearance is too large, part of the lift of the camshaft will be used in removing the excessive clearance. Consequently, the valve will not be opening as far as it should. This condition has two effects: the valve train components will emit a tapping sound as they take up the excessive clearance and the engine will perform poorly because the valves don't open fully and allow the proper amount of gases to flow into and out of the engine.

If the valve clearance is too small, the intake valve and the exhaust valves will open too far and they will not fully seat on the cylinder head when they close. When a valve seats itself on the cylinder head, it does two things: it seals the combustion chamber so that none of the gases in the cylinder escape and it cools itself by transferring some of the heat it absorbs from the combustion in the cylinder to the cylinder head and to the engine's cooling system. If the valve clearance is too small, the engine will run poorly because of the gases escaping from the combustion chamber. The valves will also become overheated and will warp, since they cannot transfer heat unless they are touching the valve seat in the cylinder head.

### VALVE LASH ADJUSTMENT

#### Gasoline Engines

The intake and exhaust valves are driven by the camshaft, working through hydraulic lash adjusters and stamped steel rocker arms. The lash adjusters eliminate the need for periodic valve lash adjustments.

#### Diesel Engine

1. Disconnect breather hose from the intake manifold and remove camshaft cover.

2. Rotate crankshaft until No. 1 piston is at TDC on the compression stroke.

3. Using a Go-No-Go feeler gauge, check the valve shim to cam lobe clearance for No. 1 and No. 2 intake valves, and No. 1 and No.3 exhaust valves.

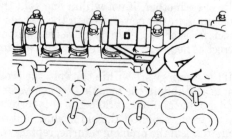

**Checking the diesel engine valve clearance**

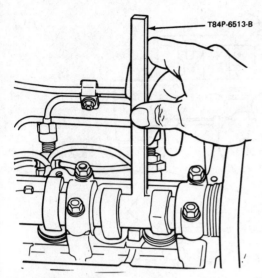

**Cam follower retainer**

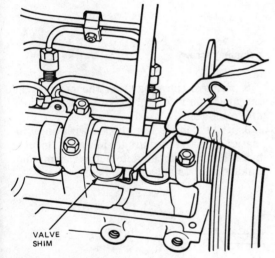

**Shim removal adjustment**

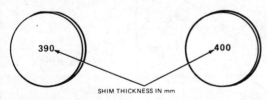

**Valve shims**

- Intake Valves: 0.20–0.30mm (0.008–0.011").
- Exhaust Valves: 0.30–0.40mm (0.011–0.015").

4. Rotate crankshaft one complete revolution. Measure valve clearance for No.3 and No. 4 intake valves, and No. 2 and No. 4 exhaust valves.

5. If a valve is out of specifications, adjust as follows:

- Rotate crankshaft until the lobe of the valve to be adjusted is down.
- Install cam follower retainer, T84P-6513-B.
- Rotate crankshaft until the cam lobe is on the base circle.
- Using O-ring pick tool T71P-19703-C or equivalent, pry the valve adjusting shim out of the cam follower.
- Valve shims are available in thicknesses ranging from 3.40mm to 4.60mm.
- If the valve was too tight, install a new shim, of the appropriate size.
- If the valve was too loose, install a new shim of the appropriate size.

NOTE: *Shim thickness is stamped on valve shim. Install new shim with numbers down, to avoid wearing the numbers off the shim. If numbers have been worn off, use a micrometer to measure shim thickness.*

6. Rotate crankshaft until cam lobe is down and remove cam follower retainer.

7. Recheck valve clearance.

8. Repeat Steps 4, 5 and 6 for each valve to be adjusted.

9. Make sure the camshaft cover gasket is fully seated in the camshaft cover and install valve cover. Tighten bolts to 5–7 ft.lb.

10. Connect breather hose.

## Idle Speed

NOTE: *A tachometer must be used while making any idle rpm adjustments. Refer to the preceding section for tach hook up instructions.*

Refer to emissions decal for idle speed and specific instructions. If the decal instructions differ from the following procedures, use the decal procedures. They reflect current production changes.

### CURB IDLE

#### 1.6L Engine w/740 Carb w/o Idle Speed Control

1. Place the transmission in Neutral or Park, set the parking brake and block the wheels. Connect tachometer.

2. Bring the engine to normal operating temperature.

3. Disconnect and plug the vacuum hose at the thermactor air control valve bypass sections.

4. Place the fast idle adjustment screw on the second highest step of the fast idle cam. Run engine until cooling fan comes on.

5. Slightly depress the throttle to allow the fast idle cam to rotate. Place the transmission in specified gear, and check/adjust the curb idle rpm to specification.

NOTE: *Engine cooling fan must be running*

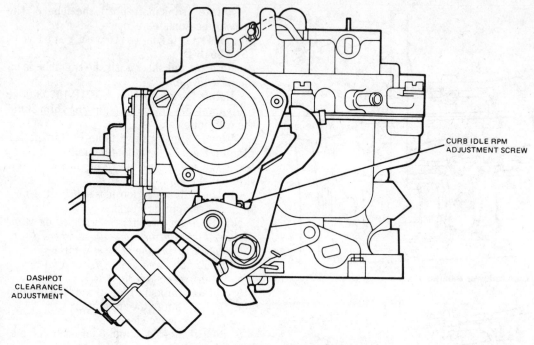

**Location of curb idle adjusting screw**

*when checking curb idle rpm. (Use a jumper wire is necessary).*

6. Place the transmission in Neutral or Park. Rev the engine momentarily. Place transmission in specified position and recheck curb idle rpm. Readjust if requires.

7. If the vehicle is equipped with a dashpot, check/adjust clearance to specification.

8. Remove the plug from the hose at the thermactor air control valve bypass sections and reconnect.

9. If the vehicle is equipped with an automatic transmission and curb idle adjustment is more than 50 rpm, an automatic transmission linkage adjustment may be necessary.

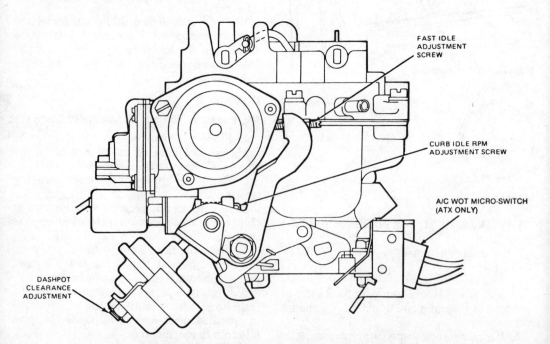

**740 carburetor—fast idle and curb idle rpm adjustments**

### 1.6L, 1.9L Engines w/740 & 5740 Carb — Mechanical Vacuum Idle Speed Control (ISC)

1. Place the transmission in Neutral or Park, set the parking brake and block the wheels. Connect tachometer.

2. Bring the engine to normal operating temperature.

3. Disconnect and plug the vacuum hose at the thermactor air control valve bypass section.

4. Place the fast idle adjustment screw on the second highest step of the fast idle cam. Run the engine until cooling fan comes on.

5. Slightly depress the throttle to allow fast idle cam to rotate. Place the transmission in Drive (fan on) and check curb idle rpm to specification.

NOTE: *Engine cooling fan must be running when checking curb idle rpm.*

6. If adjustment is required:

a. Place the transmission in Park, deactivate the ISC by removing the vacuum hose at the ISC and plugging the hose.

b. Turn ISC adjusting screw until ISC plunger is clear of the throttle lever.

c. Place the transmission in Drive position, if rpm is not at the ISC retracted speed (fan on), adjust rpm by turning the throttle stop adjusting screw.

d. Place the transmission in Park, remove plug from the ISC vacuum line and reconnect the ISC.

e. Place transmission in Drive if rpm is not at the curb idle speed (fan on), adjust by turning the ISC adjustment screw.

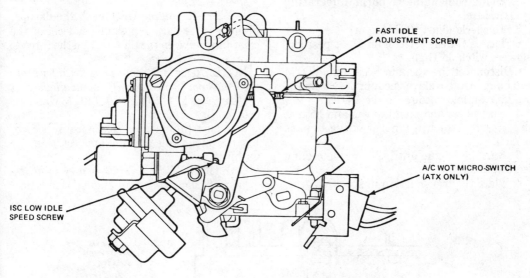

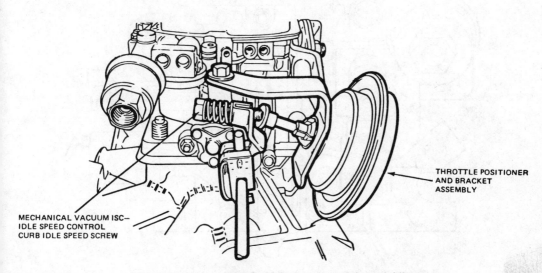

**740 carburetor—mechanical idle speed control—curb idle**

7. Place transmission in Neutral or Park. Rev the engine momentarily. Place the transmission in specified position and recheck curb idle rpm. Readjust if required.

8. Remove the plug from the thermactor air control valve bypass section hose and reconnect.

9. If the vehicle is equipped with an automatic transmission and curb idle adjustment is more than 50 rpm, an automatic transmission linkage adjustment may be necessary.

### 1.6L, 1.9L Engines w/740 & 5740 Carb — Vacuum Operated Throttle Modulator (VOTM)

1. Place the transmission in Neutral or Park, set the parking brake and block the wheels. Connect the tachometer.

2. Bring the engine to normal operating temperature.

3. To check/adjust VOTM rpm:
• Place A/C heat selector in Heat position, blower switch on High.
• Disconnect the vacuum hose from VOTM and plug, install a slave vacuum hose from the intake manifold vacuum to the VOTM.

4. Disconnect and plug the vacuum hose at the Thermactor air control valve bypass section.

5. Run the engine until the engine cooling fan comes on.

6. Place the transmission in specified gear, and check/adjust VOTM rpm to specification.

NOTE: *Engine cooling fan must be running when checking VOTM rpm. Adjust rpm by turning screw on VOTM.*

7. Remove the slave vacuum hose. Remove the plug from the VOTM vacuum hose and reconnect the hose to the VOTM.

8. Return the intake manifold vacuum supply source to original location.

9. Remove the plug from the vacuum hose at the Thermactor air control valve bypass section and reconnect.

### Dashpot Clearance Adjustment — 1.6, 1.9L Engines

NOTE: *If the carburetor is equipped with a dashpot, it must be adjusted if the curb idle speed is adjusted.*

1. With the engine OFF, push the dashpot plunger in as far as possible and check the clearance between the plunger and the throttle lever pad.

NOTE: *Refer to the emissions decal for proper dashpot clearance. If not available, set clearance to 0.138" ± 0.020" (3.5mm ± 0.5mm).*

2. Adjust the dashpot clearance by loosening the mounting locknut and rotating the dashpot.

CAUTION: *If the locknut is very tight, remove the mounting bracket, hold it in a suit-*

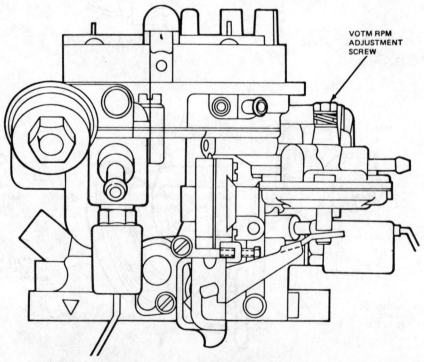

VOTM RPM
ADJUSTMENT
SCREW

**740 carburetor—VOTM adjustment**

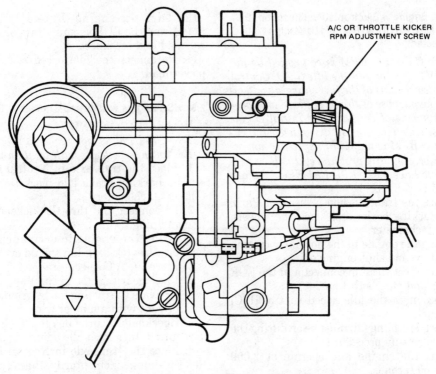

A/C OR THROTTLE KICKER
RPM ADJUSTMENT SCREW

**An adjustment is necessary, at times, if your car is equipped with air conditioning**

*able device, so that it will not bend, and loosen the locknut. Reinstall bracket and dashpot.*

3. After gaining the required clearance, tighten the locknut and recheck adjustment.

### Fast Idle RPM — 1.6L, 1.9L Engines

1. Place the transmission in Neutral or Park, set the parking brake and block the wheels. Connect tachometer.

2. Bring the engine to normal operating temperature.

3. Disconnect the vacuum hose at the EGR and plug.

4. Place the fast idle adjustment screw on the second highest step of the fast idle cam. Run engine until cooling fan comes on.

5. Check/adjust fast idle rpm to specification. If adjustment is required, loosen locknut, adjust and retighten.

NOTE: *Engine cooling fan must be running when checking fast idle rpm. (Use a jumper wire is necessary).*

6. Remove the plug from the EGR hose and reconnect.

### Air Conditioning/Throttle Kicker Adjustment — 1.6L, 1.9L Engine

1. Place the transmission in Neutral or Park.

2. Bring engine to normal operating temperature.

3. Identify vacuum source to air bypass section of air supply control valve. If vacuum hose is connected to carburetor, disconnect and plug hose at air supply control valve. Install slave vacuum hose between intake manifold and air bypass connection on air supply control valve.

4. To check/adjust A/C or throttle kicker rpm:

• If vehicle is equipped with A/C, place selector to maximum cooling, blower switch on High. Disconnect A/C compressor clutch wire.

• If vehicle is equipped with kicker and no A/C, disconnect vacuum hose from kicker and plug, install slave vacuum hose from intake manifold vacuum to kicker.

5. Run engine until engine cooling fan comes on.

6. Place transmission in specified gear and check/adjust A/C or throttle kicker rpm to specification.

NOTE: *Engine cooling fan must be running when checking A/C or throttle kicker rpm. Adjust rpm by turning screw on kicker.*

7. If slave vacuum hose was installed to check/adjust kicker rpm, remove slave vacuum hose. Remove plug from kicker vacuum hose and reconnect hose to kicker.

8. Remove slave vacuum hose. Return intake manifold supply source to original condition. Remove plug from carburetor vacuum hose and reconnect to air bypass valve.

**1.6L, 1.9L Engine w/Electronic Fuel Injection (EFI) – Initial Engine RPM Adjustment (ISC Disconnected)**

NOTE: *Curb idle RPM is controlled by the EEC IV processor and the Idle Speed Control (ISC) device (part of the fuel charging assembly). The purpose of this procedure is to provide a means of verifying the initial engine RPM setting with the ISC disconnected. If engine idle RPM is not within specification after performing this procedure, it will be necessary to have 1.6L, 1.9L EFI EEC IV diagnostics performed.*

1. Place the transmission Neutral or Park, set the parking brake and block the wheels. Connect tachometer.

2. Bring the engine to the normal operating temperature and shut engine off.

3. Disconnect vacuum connector at the EGR solenoids and plug both lines.

4. Disconnect the idle speed control (ISC) power lead.

5. Electric cooling fan must be on during the idle speed setting procedure.

6. Start the engine and operate at 2,000 RPM for 60 seconds.

7. Place transmission in Neutral for MT and Drive for AT, check/adjust initial engine RPM within 120 seconds by adjusting throttle plate screw.

8. If idle adjustment is not completed within 120 second time limit, shut engine Off, restart and repeat Steps 6 and 7.

9. If the vehicle is equipped with an automatic transmission and initial engine RPM adjustment increases or decreases by more than 50 RPM, an automatic transmission linkage adjustment may be necessary.

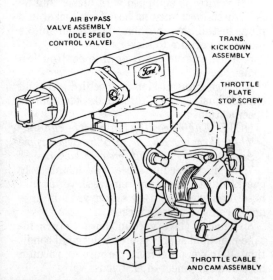

AIR BYPASS VALVE ASSEMBLY (IDLE SPEED CONTROL VALVE)

TRANS. KICK DOWN ASSEMBLY

THROTTLE PLATE STOP SCREW

THROTTLE CABLE AND CAM ASSEMBLY

**EFI—air intake throttle body assembly**

10. Turn the engine Off and remove the plugs from the EGR vacuum lines at the EGR solenoid and reconnect.

11. Reconnect the idle speed control (ISC) power lead.

**2.3L HSC Engine w/1949 and 6149 FB – Curb Idle**

NOTE: *A/C-On RPM is non-adjustable. TSP-Off RPM is not required. Verify that TSP plunger extends with ignition key On.*

1. Place the transaxle in Neutral or Park, set the parking brake and block the wheels. Connect tachometer.

2. Disconnect the throttle kicker vacuum line and plug.

3. Bring the engine to normal operating temperature. (Cooling fan should cycle).

4. Place the A/C selector in the Off position.

5. Place gear selector in specified position.

6. Activate the cooling fan by grounding the control wire with a jumper wire.

7. Check/adjust curb idle rpm. If adjustment is required, turn curb idle adjusting screw.

8. Place the transaxle in Neutral or Park. Rev the engine momentarily. Place the transaxle in specified position and recheck curb idle rpm. Readjust if required.

9. Reconnect the cooling fan wiring.

10. Turn the ignition key to the Off position.

11. Reconnect the vacuum line to the throttle kicker.

12. If the vehicle is equipped with an automatic transaxle and curb idle adjustment exceeds 50 rpm, an automatic transaxle linkage adjustment may be necessary.

13. Remove all test equipment and reinstall the air cleaner assembly.

**2.3L HSC Engine w/1949 and 6149 FB – TSP Off RPM**

NOTE: *This adjustment is not required as part of a normal engine idle RPM check/adjustment. Use if engine continues to run after ignition key is turned to OFF position.*

1. Place the transaxle in Neutral or Park, set the parking brake and block the wheels. Connect tachometer.

2. Bring the engine to normal operating temperature.

3. Disconnect the throttle kicker vacuum line and plug.

4. Place the A/C selector to Off position.

5. Disconnect the electrical lead to the TSP and verify that plunger collapses. Check/adjust engine RPM to specification (600 RPM).

6. Adjust the TSP Off RPM to specification.

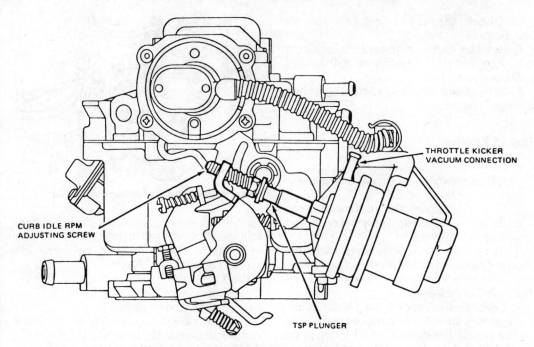

**THROTTLE KICKER VACUUM CONNECTION**

**CURB IDLE RPM ADJUSTING SCREW**

**TSP PLUNGER**

**1949/6149FB—Curb idle adjustment**

7. Shut the engine off, reconnect TSP electrical lead and throttle kicker vacuum line.

### 2.3L HSC Engine w/1949 and 6149 FB — Fast Idle RPM

1. Place the transaxle in Neutral or Park, set the parking brake and block the wheels.
2. Bring the engine to normal operating temperature with the carburetor set on second step of fast idle cam.
3. Return the throttle to normal idle position.
4. Place the A/C selector in the Off position.
5. Disconnect the vacuum hose at the EGR valve and plug.
6. Place the fast idle adjusting screw on the specific step of the fast idle cam.

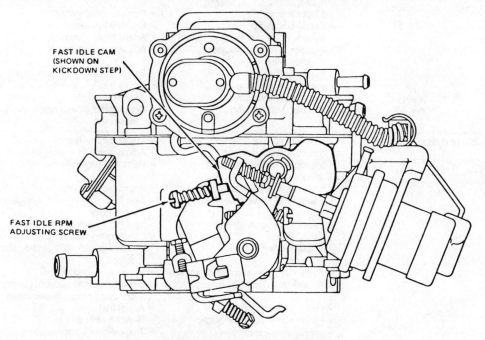

**FAST IDLE CAM (SHOWN ON KICKDOWN STEP)**

**FAST IDLE RPM ADJUSTING SCREW**

**1949/6149FB—Fast idle adjustment**

7. Check/adjust the fast idle rpm to specification.

8. Rev the engine momentarily, allowing engine to return to idle and turn ignition key to Off position.

9. Remove the plug from the EGR vacuum hose and reconnect.

### Diesel Engine

*CURB IDLE*

NOTE: *A special diesel engine tachometer is required for this procedure.*

1. Place the transmission in Neutral.

2. Bring the engine up to normal operating temperature. Stop engine.

3. Remove the timing hole cover. Clean the flywheel surface and install reflective tape.

4. Idle speed is measured with manual transmission in Neutral.

5. Check curb idle speed, using Rotunda 99–0001 or equivalent. Curb idle speed is specified on the vehicle Emissions Control Information decal (VECI). Adjust to specification by loosen-

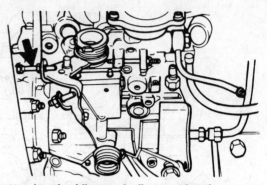

Diesel engine idle speed adjustment location

ing the locknut on the idle speed bolt. Turn the idle speed adjusting bolt clockwise to increase, or counterclockwise to decrease engine idle speed. Tighten the locknut.

6. Place transmission in Neutral. Rev engine momentarily and recheck the curb idle RPM. Readjust if necessary.

7. Turn A/C On. Check the idle speed. Adjust to specification by loosening the nut on the A/C throttle kicker and rotating the screw.

## Troubleshooting Engine Performance

| Problem | Cause | Solution |
|---|---|---|
| Hard starting (engine cranks normally) | • Binding linkage, choke valve or choke piston | • Repair as necessary |
| | • Restricted choke vacuum diaphragm | • Clean passages |
| | • Improper fuel level | • Adjust float level |
| | • Dirty, worn or faulty needle valve and seat | • Repair as necessary |
| | • Float sticking | • Repair as necessary |
| | • Faulty fuel pump | • Replace fuel pump |
| | • Incorrect choke cover adjustment | • Adjust choke cover |
| | • Inadequate choke unloader adjustment | • Adjust choke unloader |
| | • Faulty ignition coil | • Test and replace as necessary |
| | • Improper spark plug gap | • Adjust gap |
| | • Incorrect ignition timing | • Adjust timing |
| | • Incorrect valve timing | • Check valve timing; repair as necessary |
| Rough idle or stalling | • Incorrect curb or fast idle speed | • Adjust curb or fast idle speed |
| | • Incorrect ignition timing | • Adjust timing to specification |
| | • Improper feedback system operation | • Refer to Chapter 4 |
| | • Improper fast idle cam adjustment | • Adjust fast idle cam |
| | • Faulty EGR valve operation | • Test EGR system and replace as necessary |
| | • Faulty PCV valve air flow | • Test PCV valve and replace as necessary |
| | • Choke binding | • Locate and eliminate binding condition |
| | • Faulty TAC vacuum motor or valve | • Repair as necessary |
| | • Air leak into manifold vacuum | • Inspect manifold vacuum connections and repair as necessary |
| | • Improper fuel level | • Adjust fuel level |
| | • Faulty distributor rotor or cap | • Replace rotor or cap |
| | • Improperly seated valves | • Test cylinder compression, repair as necessary |

## Troubleshooting Engine Performance (cont.)

| Problem | Cause | Solution |
|---|---|---|
| Rough idle or stalling (cont.) | • Incorrect ignition wiring | • Inspect wiring and correct as necessary |
| | • Faulty ignition coil | • Test coil and replace as necessary |
| | • Restricted air vent or idle passages | • Clean passages |
| | • Restricted air cleaner | • Clean or replace air cleaner filler element |
| | • Faulty choke vacuum diaphragm | • Repair as necessary |
| Faulty low-speed operation | • Restricted idle transfer slots | • Clean transfer slots |
| | • Restricted idle air vents and passages | • Clean air vents and passages |
| | • Restricted air cleaner | • Clean or replace air cleaner filter element |
| | • Improper fuel level | • Adjust fuel level |
| | • Faulty spark plugs | • Clean or replace spark plugs |
| | • Dirty, corroded, or loose ignition secondary circuit wire connections | • Clean or tighten secondary circuit wire connections |
| | • Improper feedback system operation | • Refer to Chapter 4 |
| | • Faulty ignition coil high voltage wire | • Replace ignition coil high voltage wire |
| | • Faulty distributor cap | • Replace cap |
| Faulty acceleration | • Improper accelerator pump stroke | • Adjust accelerator pump stroke |
| | • Incorrect ignition timing | • Adjust timing |
| | • Inoperative pump discharge check ball or needle | • Clean or replace as necessary |
| | • Worn or damaged pump diaphragm or piston | • Replace diaphragm or piston |
| | • Leaking carburetor main body cover gasket | • Replace gasket |
| | • Engine cold and choke set too lean | • Adjust choke cover |
| | • Improper metering rod adjustment (BBD Model carburetor) | • Adjust metering rod |
| | • Faulty spark plug(s) | • Clean or replace spark plug(s) |
| | • Improperly seated valves | • Test cylinder compression, repair as necessary |
| | • Faulty ignition coil | • Test coil and replace as necessary |
| | • Improper feedback system operation | • Refer to Chapter 4 |
| Faulty high speed operation | • Incorrect ignition timing | • Adjust timing |
| | • Faulty distributor centrifugal advance mechanism | • Check centrifugal advance mechanism and repair as necessary |
| | • Faulty distributor vacuum advance mechanism | • Check vacuum advance mechanism and repair as necessary |
| | • Low fuel pump volume | • Replace fuel pump |
| | • Wrong spark plug air gap or wrong plug | • Adjust air gap or install correct plug |
| | • Faulty choke operation | • Adjust choke cover |
| | • Partially restricted exhaust manifold, exhaust pipe, catalytic converter, muffler, or tailpipe | • Eliminate restriction |
| | • Restricted vacuum passages | • Clean passages |
| | • Improper size or restricted main jet | • Clean or replace as necessary |
| | • Restricted air cleaner | • Clean or replace filter element as necessary |
| | • Faulty distributor rotor or cap | • Replace rotor or cap |
| | • Faulty ignition coil | • Test coil and replace as necessary |
| | • Improperly seated valve(s) | • Test cylinder compression, repair as necessary |
| | • Faulty valve spring(s) | • Inspect and test valve spring tension, replace as necessary |

## Troubleshooting Engine Performance (cont.)

| Problem | Cause | Solution |
|---|---|---|
| Faulty high speed operation (cont.) | • Incorrect valve timing | • Check valve timing and repair as necessary |
| | • Intake manifold restricted | • Remove restriction or replace manifold |
| | • Worn distributor shaft | • Replace shaft |
| | • Improper feedback system operation | • Refer to Chapter 4 |
| Misfire at all speeds | • Faulty spark plug(s) | • Clean or replace spark plug(s) |
| | • Faulty spark plug wire(s) | • Replace as necessary |
| | • Faulty distributor cap or rotor | • Replace cap or rotor |
| | • Faulty ignition coil | • Test coil and replace as necessary |
| | • Primary ignition circuit shorted or open intermittently | • Troubleshoot primary circuit and repair as necessary |
| | • Improperly seated valve(s) | • Test cylinder compression, repair as necessary |
| | • Faulty hydraulic tappet(s) | • Clean or replace tappet(s) |
| | • Improper feedback system operation | • Refer to Chapter 4 |
| | • Faulty valve spring(s) | • Inspect and test valve spring tension, repair as necessary |
| | • Worn camshaft lobes | • Replace camshaft |
| | • Air leak into manifold | • Check manifold vacuum and repair as necessary |
| | • Improper carburetor adjustment | • Adjust carburetor |
| | • Fuel pump volume or pressure low | • Replace fuel pump |
| | • Blown cylinder head gasket | • Replace gasket |
| | • Intake or exhaust manifold passage(s) restricted | • Pass chain through passage(s) and repair as necessary |
| | • Incorrect trigger wheel installed in distributor | • Install correct trigger wheel |
| Power not up to normal | • Incorrect ignition timing | • Adjust timing |
| | • Faulty distributor rotor | • Replace rotor |
| | • Trigger wheel loose on shaft | • Reposition or replace trigger wheel |
| | • Incorrect spark plug gap | • Adjust gap |
| | • Faulty fuel pump | • Replace fuel pump |
| | • Incorrect valve timing | • Check valve timing and repair as necessary |
| | • Faulty ignition coil | • Test coil and replace as necessary |
| | • Faulty ignition wires | • Test wires and replace as necessary |
| | • Improperly seated valves | • Test cylinder compression and repair as necessary |
| | • Blown cylinder head gasket | • Replace gasket |
| | • Leaking piston rings | • Test compression and repair as necessary |
| | • Worn distributor shaft | • Replace shaft |
| | • Improper feedback system operation | • Refer to Chapter 4 |
| Intake backfire | • Improper ignition timing | • Adjust timing |
| | • Faulty accelerator pump discharge | • Repair as necessary |
| | • Defective EGR CTO valve | • Replace EGR CTO valve |
| | • Defective TAC vacuum motor or valve | • Repair as necessary |
| | • Lean air/fuel mixture | • Check float level or manifold vacuum for air leak. Remove sediment from bowl |
| Exhaust backfire | • Air leak into manifold vacuum | • Check manifold vacuum and repair as necessary |
| | • Faulty air injection diverter valve | • Test diverter valve and replace as necessary |
| | • Exhaust leak | • Locate and eliminate leak |

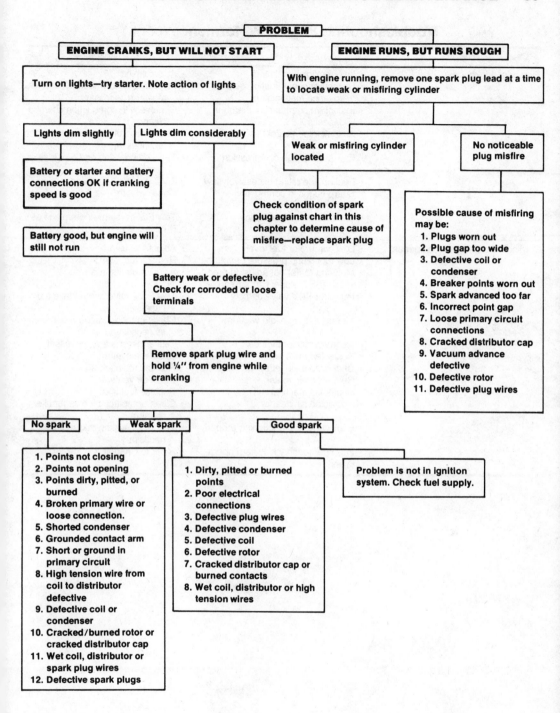

Troubleshooting basic point-type ignition system problems

## Troubleshooting Engine Performance (cont.)

| Problem | Cause | Solution |
|---|---|---|
| Ping or spark knock | • Incorrect ignition timing | • Adjust timing |
| | • Distributor centrifugal or vacuum advance malfunction | • Inspect advance mechanism and repair as necessary |
| | • Excessive combustion chamber deposits | • Remove with combustion chamber cleaner |
| | • Air leak into manifold vacuum | • Check manifold vacuum and repair as necessary |
| | • Excessively high compression | • Test compression and repair as necessary |
| | • Fuel octane rating excessively low | • Try alternate fuel source |
| | • Sharp edges in combustion chamber | • Grind smooth |
| | • EGR valve not functioning properly | • Test EGR system and replace as necessary |
| Surging (at cruising to top speeds) | • Low carburetor fuel level | • Adjust fuel level |
| | • Low fuel pump pressure or volume | • Replace fuel pump |
| | • Metering rod(s) not adjusted properly (BBD Model Carburetor) | • Adjust metering rod |
| | • Improper PCV valve air flow | • Test PCV valve and replace as necessary |
| | • Air leak into manifold vacuum | • Check manifold vacuum and repair as necessary |
| | • Incorrect spark advance | • Test and replace as necessary |
| | • Restricted main jet(s) | • Clean main jet(s) |
| | • Undersize main jet(s) | • Replace main jet(s) |
| | • Restricted air vents | • Clean air vents |
| | • Restricted fuel filter | • Replace fuel filter |
| | • Restricted air cleaner | • Clean or replace air cleaner filter element |
| | • EGR valve not functioning properly | • Test EGR system and replace as necessary |
| | • Improper feedback system operation | • Refer to Chapter 4 |

## ENGINE ELECTRICAL

### Understanding the Engine Electrical System

The engine electrical system can be broken down into three separate and distinct systems: (1) the starting system, (2) the charging system, and (3) the ignition system.

### BATTERY AND STARTING SYSTEM

#### Basic Operating Principles

The battery is the first link in the chain of mechanisms which work together to provide cranking of the automobile engine. In most modern cars, the battery is a lead/acid electrochemical device consisting of six two-volt (2 V) subsections connected in series so the unit is capable of producing approximately 12 V of electrical pressure. Each subsection, or cell, consists of a series of positive and negative plates held a short distance apart in a solution of sulfuric acid and water. The two types of plates are of dissimilar metals. This causes a chemical reaction to be set up, and it is this reaction which produces current flow from the battery when its positive and negative terminals are connected to an electrical appliance such as a lamp or motor. The continued transfer of electrons would eventually convert the sulfuric acid in the electrolyte to water, and make the two plates identical in chemical composition. As electrical energy is removed from the battery, its voltage output tends to drop. Thus, measuring battery voltage and battery electrolyte composition are two ways of checking the ability of the unit to supply power. During the starting of the engine, electrical energy is removed from the battery. However, if the charging circuit is in good condition and the operating conditions are normal, the power removed from the battery will be replaced by the generator (or alternator) which will force electrons back through the battery, reversing the normal flow, and restoring the battery to its original chemical state.

The battery and starting motor are linked by very heavy electrical cables designed to minimize resistance to the flow of current. Generally, the major power supply cable that leaves the battery goes directly to the starter, while other electrical system needs are supplied by a smaller cable. During starter operation, power flows from the battery to the starter and is grounded through the car's frame and the battery's negative ground strap.

The starting motor is a specially designed, direct current electric motor capable of producing a very great amount of power for its size. One thing that allows the motor to produce a great deal of power is its tremendous rotating speed. It drives the engine through a tiny pinion gear (attached to the starter's armature), which drives the very large flywheel ring gear at a greatly reduced speed. Another factor allowing it to produce so much power is that only intermittent operation is required of it. This, little allowance for air circulation is required, and the windings can be built into a very small space.

The starter solenoid is a magnetic device which employs the small current supplied by the starting switch circuit of the ignition switch. This magnetic action moves a plunger which mechanically engages the starter and electrically closes the heavy switch which connects it to the battery. The starting switch circuit consists of the starting switch contained within the ignition switch, a transmission neutral safety switch or clutch pedal switch, and the wiring necessary to connect these in series with the starter solenoid or relay.

A pinion, which is a small gear, is mounted to a one-way drive clutch. This clutch is splined to the starter armature shaft. When the ignition switch is moved to the **start** position, the solenoid plunger slides the pinion toward the flywheel ring gear via a collar and spring. If the teeth on the pinion and flywheel match properly, the pinion will engage the flywheel immediately. If the gear teeth butt one another, the spring will be compressed and will force the gears to mesh as soon as the starter turns far enough to allow them to do so. As the solenoid plunger reaches the end of its travel, it closes the contacts that connect the battery and starter and then the engine is cranked.

As soon as the engine starts, the flywheel ring gear begins turning fast enough to drive the pinion at an extremely high rate of speed. At this point, the one-way clutch begins allowing the pinion to spin faster than the starter shaft so that the starter will not operate at excessive speed. When the ignition switch is released from the starter position, the solenoid is de-engerized, and a spring contained within the solenoid assembly pulls the gear out of mesh and interrupts the current flow to the starter.

Some starter employ a separate relay, mounted away from the starter, to switch the motor and solenoid current on and off. The relay thus replaces the solenoid electrical switch, buy does not eliminate the need for a solenoid mounted on the starter used to mechanically engage the starter drive gears. The relay is used to reduce the amount of current the starting switch must carry.

## THE CHARGING SYSTEM

### Basic Operating Principles

The automobile charging system provides electrical power for operation of the vehicle's ignition and starting systems and all the electrical accessories. The battery services as an electrical surge or storage tank, storing (in chemical form) the energy originally produced by the engine driven generator. The system also provides a means of regulating generator output to protect the battery from being overcharged and to avoid excessive voltage to the accessories.

The storage battery is a chemical device incorporating parallel lead plates in a tank containing a sulfuric acid/water solution. Adjacent plates are slightly dissimilar, and the chemical reaction of the two dissimilar plates produces electrical energy when the battery is connected to a load such as the starter motor. The chemical reaction is reversible, so that when the generator is producing a voltage (electrical pressure) greater than that produced by the battery, electricity is forced into

the battery, and the battery is returned to its fully charged state.

The vehicle's generator is driven mechanically, through V belts, by the engine crankshaft. It consists of two coils of fine wire, one stationary (the stator), and one movable (the rotor). The rotor may also be known as the armature, and consists of fine wire wrapped around an iron core which is mounted on a shaft. The electricity which flows through the two coils of wire (provided initially by the battery in some cases) creates an intense magnetic field around both rotor and stator, and the interaction between the two fields creates voltage, allowing the generator to power the accessories and charge the battery.

There are two types of generators: the earlier is the direct current (DC) type. The current produced by the DC generator is generated in the armature and carried off the spinning armature by stationary brushes contacting the commutator. The commutator is a series of smooth metal contact plates on the end of the armature. The commutator is a series of smooth metal contact plates on the end of the armature. The commutator plates, which are separated from one another by a very short gap, are connected to the armature circuits so that current will flow in one directions only in the wires carrying the generator output. The generator stator consists of two stationary coils of wire which draw some of the output current of the generator to form a powerful magnetic field and create the interaction of fields which generates the voltage. The generator field is wired in series with the regulator.

Newer automobiles use alternating current generators or alternators, because they are more efficient, can be rotated at higher speeds, and have fewer brush problems. In an alternator, the field rotates while all the current produced passes only through the stator winding. The brushes bear against continuous slip rings rather than a commutator. This causes the current produced to periodically reverse the direction of its flow. Diodes (electrical one-way switches) block the flow of current from traveling in the wrong direction. A series of diodes is wired together to permit the alternating flow of the stator to be converted to a pulsating, but unidirectional flow at the alternator output. The alternator's field is wired in series with the voltage regulator.

The regulator consists of several circuits. Each circuit has a core, or magnetic coil of wire, which operates a switch. Each switch is connected to ground through one or more resistors. The coil of wire responds directly to system voltage. When the voltage reaches the required level, the magnetic field created by the winding of wire closes the switch and inserts a resistance into the generator field circuit, thus reducing the output. The contacts of the switch cycle open and close many times each second to precisely control voltage.

While alternators are self-limiting as far as maximum current is concerned, DC generators employ a current regulating circuit which responds directly to the total amount of current flowing through the generator circuit rather than to the output voltage. The current regulator is similar to the voltage regulator except that all system current must flow through the energizing coil on its way to the various accessories.

## Distributor

### REMOVAL AND INSTALLATION

#### 1.6L, 1.9L Engines

The camshaft driven distributor is located at the top left end of the cylinder head. It is retained by two holddown bolts at the base of the distributor shaft housing.

1. Turn engine to No. 1 piston at TDC of the compression stroke. Disconnect negative battery cable. Disconnect the vacuum hose(s) from the advance unit. Disconnect the wiring harness at the distributor.

2. Remove the capscrews and remove the distributor cap.

3. Scribe a mark on the distributor body, showing the position of the ignition rotor. Scribe another mark on the distributor body

and cylinder head, showing the position of the body in relation to the head. These marks can be used for reference when installing the distributor, as long as the engine remains undisturbed.

4. Remove the two distributor holddown bolts. Pull the distributor out of the head.

5. To install the distributor with the engine undisturbed, place the distributor in the cylinder head, seating the offset tang of the drive coupling into the groove on the end of the camshaft. Install the two distributor holddown screws and tighten them so that the distributor can just barely be moved. Install the rotor (if removed), the distributor cap and all wiring, then set the ignition timing.

6. If the crankshaft was rotated while the distributor was removed, the engine must be brought to TDC (Top Dead Center) on the compression stroke of the No. 1 cylinder. Remove the No. 1 spark plug. Place your finger over the hole and rotate the crankshaft slowly (use a wrench on the crankshaft pulley bolt) in the direction of normal engine rotation, until engine compression is felt.

CAUTION: *Turn the engine only in the direction of normal rotation. Backward rotation will cause the cam belt to slip or lose teeth, altering engine timing.*

When engine compression is felt at the spark plug hole, indicating that the piston is approaching TDC, continue to turn the crankshaft until the timing mark on the pulley is aligned with the **0** mark (timing mark) on the

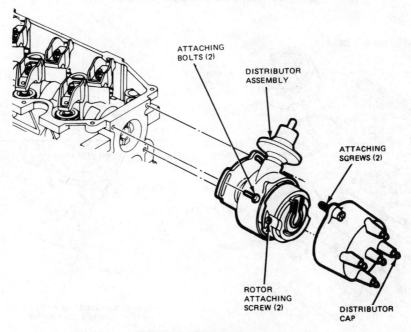

ATTACHING
BOLTS (2)

DISTRIBUTOR
ASSEMBLY

ATTACHING
SCREWS (2)

ROTOR
ATTACHING
SCREW (2)

DISTRIBUTOR
CAP

**1.6L, 1.9L distributor mounting**

engine front cover. Turn the distributor shaft until the ignition rotor is at the No. 1 firing position. Install the distributor into the cylinder head, as outlined in Step 5 of this procedure.

### 2.3L HSC Engine

The TFI-IV distributor is mounted on the side of the engine block. Some engines may be equipped with a security type distributor hold down bolt which requires a special wrench for removal. The TFI-IV distributor incorporates a Hall Effect advance switch stator assembly and an integrally mounted thick-film module. When the Hall Effect device is turned on and a pulse is produced, the EEC-IV electronics computes crankshaft position and engine demand to calibrate spark advance. Initial ignition timing adjustment/checking is necessary when the distributor has been removed. Repairs to the distributor are accomplished by distributor replacement.

1. Turn engine to No. 1 piston at TDC of the compression stroke. Disconnect the negative battery cable.

2. Disconnect the wiring harness at the distributor. Mark No. 1 spark plug wire cap terminal location on the distributor base. Remove the coil wire from the cap.

3. Remove he distributor cap with plug wires attached and position out of the way. Remove the rotor.

4. Remove the distributor base hold down bolt and clamp. Slowly remove the distributor from the engine. Be careful not to disturb the intermediate driveshaft.

5. Install in reverse order after aligning the center blade of the rotor with the reference mark made on the distributor base for No. 1 plug wire terminal location.

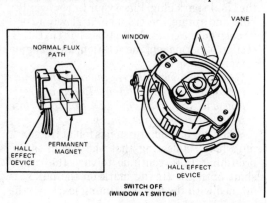 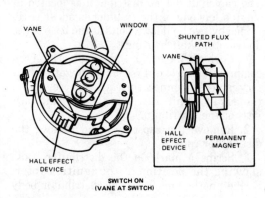

**2.3L HSC—Hall effect distributor operation**

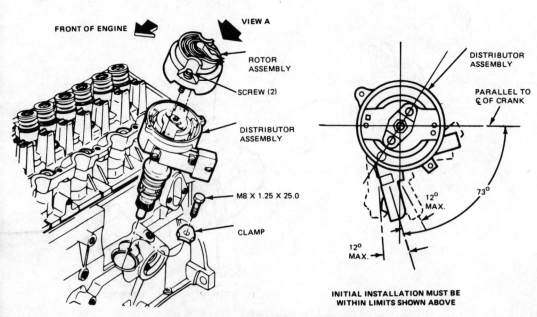

**Distributor installation, 2.3L HSC engine**

6. If the engine was disturbed (turned) while the distributor was out, the engine will have to reset at TDC before installation.

## Alternator

### ALTERNATOR PRECAUTIONS

To prevent damage to the alternator and regulator, the following precautionary measures must be taken when working with the electrical system.

1. Never reverse battery connections. Always check the battery polarity visually. This is to be done before any connections are made to ensure that all of the connections correspond to the battery ground polarity of the car.

2. Booster batteries must be connected properly. Make sure the positive cable of the booster battery is connected to the positive terminal of the battery which is getting the boost. Engines must be shut off before cables are connected.

3. Disconnect the battery cables before using a fast charger; the charger has a tendency

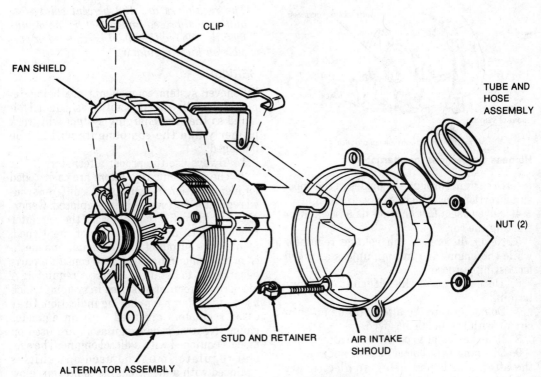

On air-conditioned cars, cool air shrouding is added

## Alternator Specifications

| Supplier | Stamp Color | Rating | | Field Current Amps @ 12V ① | Slip-Ring. Turning mm (Inches) | | Brush Length mm (Inches) | | Pulley Nut Torque N-m (lb.-ft.) |
|---|---|---|---|---|---|---|---|---|---|
| | | Amperes @ 15V | Watts @ 15V | | Min. Dia. | Max Runabout | New | Wear-Limit | |
| Ford | Orange | 40 | 600 | 4.0 | 31 (1.22) | .013 (0.0005) | 12.19 (.480) | 6.35 (1/4) | 82–135 (60–100) |
| Ford | Black | 65 | 975 | 4.0 | 31 (1.22) | .013 (0.0005) | 12.19 (.480) | 6.35 (1/4) | 82–135 (60–100) |
| Ford | Green | 60 | 900 | 4.0 | 31 (1.22) | .013 (0.0005) | 12.19 (.480) | 6.35 (1/4) | 82–135 (60–100) |
| Ford | Red | 40 HE | 600 | 4.0 | 31 (1.22) | .013 (0.0005) | 12.19 (.480) | 6.35 (1/4) | 82–135 (60–100) |

① A Field Current of 4 amps is used with solid state regulation.

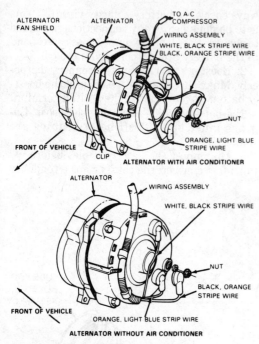

Harness connections for alternators

to force current through the diodes in the opposite directions for which they were designed.

4. Never use a fast charger as a booster for starting the car.

5. Never disconnect the voltage regulator while the engine is running, unless as noted for testing purposes.

6. Do not ground the alternator output terminal.

7. Do not operate the alternator on an open circuit with the field energized.

8. Do not attempt to polarize the alternator.

9. Disconnect the battery cables and remove the alternator before using an electric arc welder on the car.

10. Protect the alternator from excessive moisture. If the engine is to be steam cleaned, cover or remove the alternator.

### REMOVAL AND INSTALLATION

1. Disconnect the negative battery cable.

2. If equipped with a pulley cover shield, remove the shield at this time.

3. Loosen the alternator pivot bolt. Remove the adjustment bracket to alternator bolt (and nut, if equipped). Pivot the alternator to gain slack in the drive belt and remove the belt.

4. Disconnect and label (for correct installation) the alternator wiring.

NOTE: *Some models use a push-on wiring connector on the field and stator connections. Pull or push straight when removing or installing, or damage to the connectors may occur.*

5. Remove the pivot bolt and the alternator.

6. Install in the reverse order of removal. Adjust the drive belt tension so that there is approx. ¼–½″ (6–13mm) deflection on the longest span between the pulleys. Reinstall the pulley shield, if equipped and connect the negative battery cable.

### Regulator

NOTE: *Three different types of regulators are used, depending on models, engine, alternator output and type of dash mounted charging indicator used (light or ammeter). The regulators are 100 percent solid state and are calibrated and preset by the manufacturer. No readjustment is required or possible on these regulators.*

### SERVICE

Whenever system components are being replaced the following precautions should be followed so that the charging system will work properly and the components will not be damaged.

1. Always use the proper alternator.

2. The electronic regulators are color coded for identification. Never install a different coded regulator for the one being replaced. General coding identification follows, if the regulator removed does not have the color mentioned, identify the output of the alternator and method of charging indication, then consult a parts department to obtain the correct regulator. A black coded regulator is used in systems which use a signal lamp for charing indication. Gray coded regulators are used with an ammeter gauge. Neutral coded regulators are used on models equipped with a diesel engine. The special regulator must be used on vehicles equipped with a diesel engine to prevent glow plug failure.

3. Models using a charging lamp indicator are equipped with a 500Ω resistor on the back of the instrument panel.

### REMOVAL AND INSTALLATION

1. Disconnect the negative battery cable.

2. Unplug the wiring harness from the regulator.

3. Remove the regulator mounting bolts.

4. Install in the reverse order.

### Fuse Link

The fuse link is a short length of insulated wire contained in the alternator wiring harness, between the alternator and the starter relay. The fuse link is several wire gauge sizes smaller than the other wires in the harness. If a booster battery is connected incorrectly in the car battery or if some component of the charging system is shorted to ground, the fuse link melts and protects the alternator. The fuse link is attached to the starter relay. The insulation on the wire reads: Fuse Link. A melted fuse link can usually be identified by cracked or bubbled insulation. If it is difficult to determine if the fuse link is melted, connect a test light to both ends of the wire. If the fuse link is not melted, the test light will light showing that an open circuit does not exist in the wire.

### REPLACEMENT

NOTE: *Also refer to the end of Chapter 3 for procedures.*

1. Disconnect the negative battery cable.
2. Disconnect the eyelet end of the link from the starter relay.
3. Cut the other end of the link from the wiring harness at the splice.
4. Connect the eyelet end of the new fuse link to the starter relay.

NOTE: *Use only an original equipment type fuse link. Do not replace with standard wire.*

5. Splice the open end of the new fuse link into the wiring harness.
6. Solder the splice with rosin core solder and wrap the splice in electrical tape. This splice must be soldered.
7. Connect the negative battery cable.

## Starter

### REMOVAL AND INSTALLATION

#### Gasoline Engines

1. Disconnect the negative battery cable.
2. Raise and safely support the front of the vehicle on jackstands. Disconnect the starter cable from the starter motor.
3. On models that are equipped with a manual transaxle, remove the three nuts that attach the roll restrictor brace to the starter mounting studs at the transaxle. Remove the brace.

On models that are equipped with an automatic transaxle, remove the nose bracket mounted on the starter studs.

4. Remove the two bolts attaching the rear starter support bracket, remove the retaining nut from the rear of the starter motor and remove the support bracket.
5. On models equipped with a manual transaxle, remove the three starter mounting studs and the starter motor.

On models equipped with a automatic transaxle, remove the two starter mounting studs and the starter motor.

6. Position the starter motor on the transaxle housing and install in the reverse order of

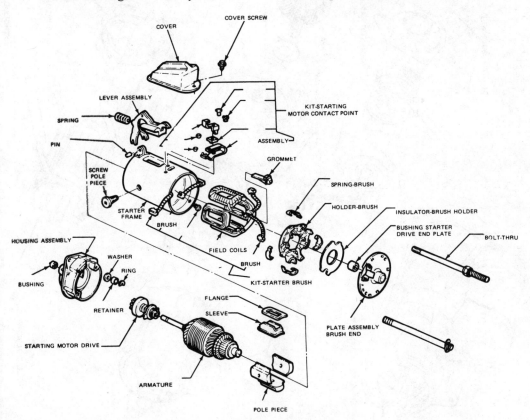

**Exploded view of a starter motor**

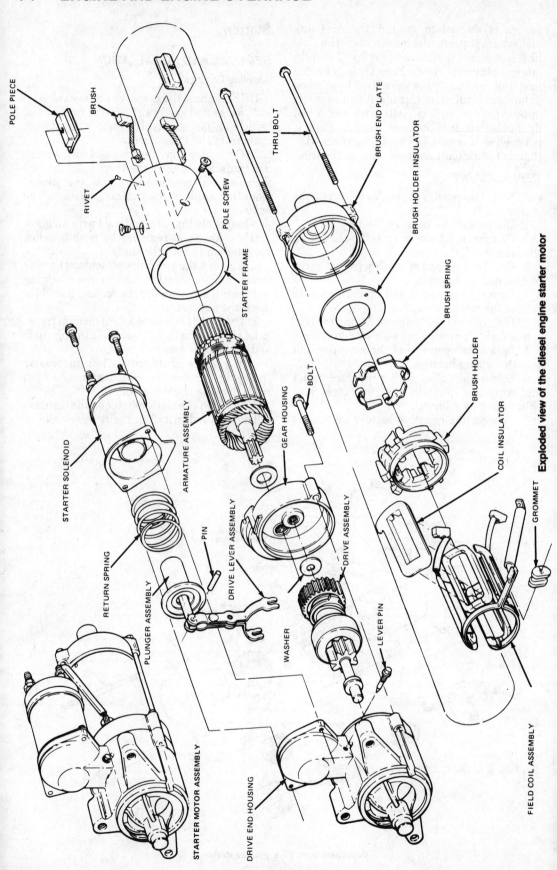

POLE PIECE

BRUSH

RIVET

POLE SCREW

STARTER FRAME

THRU BOLT

BRUSH END PLATE

BRUSH HOLDER INSULATOR

BRUSH SPRING

BRUSH HOLDER

COIL INSULATOR

BOLT

ARMATURE ASSEMBLY

GEAR HOUSING

STARTER SOLENOID

RETURN SPRING

PLUNGER ASSEMBLY

PIN

DRIVE LEVER ASSEMBLY

WASHER

DRIVE ASSEMBLY

LEVER PIN

GROMMET

STARTER MOTOR ASSEMBLY

DRIVE END HOUSING

FIELD COIL ASSEMBLY

**Exploded view of the diesel engine starter motor**

## Starter Specifications

| Years | Engine Ltr. (CID) | Current Draw Normal Load (Amps) | Lock Test | | No-Load Current Draw (Amps) | Engine Cranking Speed (rpm) | Brush Length (in.) | Brush Spring Tension (oz.) |
|---|---|---|---|---|---|---|---|---|
| | | | Volts | Torque (ft.lb.) | | | | |
| '81 | 1.3 (79) | 150–250 | 5 | 9.5 | 80 | 190–260 | 0.45 | 80 |
| | 1.6 (98) | 150–250 | 5 | 9.5 | 80 | 190–260 | 0.45 | 80 |
| '82 | 1.6 (98) | 150–250 | 5 | 9.5 | 80 | 190–260 | 0.45 | 80 |
| '83 | 1.6 (98) | 150–250 | 5 | 9.5 | 80 | 190–260 | 0.45 | 80 |
| '84 | 1.6 (98) | 150–250 | 5 | 9.5 | 80 | 190–260 | 0.45 | 80 |
| | 2.0 (122) | 375 | — | — | 190 | 250–350 | 0.485 | — |
| | 2.3 (140) | 150–250 | 5 | 9.5 | 80 | 190–260 | 0.45 | 80 |
| '85 | 1.6 (98) | 150–250 | 5 | 9.5 | 80 | 190–260 | 0.45 | 80 |
| | 2.0 (122) | 375 | — | — | 190 | 250–350 | 0.485 | — |
| | 2.3 (140) | 150–250 | 5 | 9.5 | 80 | 190–260 | 0.45 | 80 |
| '86–'87 | 1.9 (113.5) | 150–250 | 5 | 9.5 | 80 | 190–260 | 0.45 | 80 |
| | 2.0 (122) | 375 | — | — | 190 | 250–350 | 0.485 | — |
| | 2.3 (140) | 150–250 | 5 | 9.5 | 80 | 190–260 | 0.45 | 80 |

removal. Tighten the mounting bolts or studs to 30–40 ft.lb.

### OVERHAUL

#### Brush Replacement

1. Remove the top cover by taking out the retaining screw. Loosen and remove the two through bolts. Remove the starter drive end housing and the starter drive plunger lever return spring.

2. Remove the starter drive plunger lever pivot pin and lever, and remove the armature.

3. Remove the brush end plate.

4. Remove the ground brush retaining screws from the frame and remove the brushes.

5. Cut the insulated brush leads from the field coils, as close to the field connection point as possible.

6. Clean and inspect the starter motor.

7. Replace the brash end plate if the insulator between the field brush holder and the end plate is cracked or broken.

8. Position the new insulated field brushes lead on the field coil connections. Position and crimp the clip provided with the brushes to hold the brush lead to the connection. Solder the lead, clip, and connection together using rosin core solder. Use a 300W soldering iron.

9. Install the ground brush leads to the frame with the retaining screws.

10. Clean the commutator with special commutator paper.

11. Position the brush end plate to the starter frame, with the end plate boss in the frame slot.

12. Install the armature in the starter frame.

13. Install the starter drive gear plunger lever to the frame and starter drive assembly, and install the pivot pin.

14. Partially fill the drive end housing bearing bore with grease (approximately ¼ full). Position the return spring on the plunger lever, and the drive end housing to the starter frame. Install the through-bolts and tighten to specified torque (55 to 75 in.lb.). Be sure that the stop ring retainer is seated properly in the drive end housing.

15. Install the commutator brushes in the brush holders. Center the brush springs on the brushes.

16. Position the plunger lever cover and brush cover band, with its gasket, on the starter. Tighten the band retaining screw.

17. Connect the starter to a battery to check its operation.

### STARTER DRIVE REPLACEMENT

1. Remove the starter from the engine.

2. Remove the starter drive plunger lever cover.

3. Loosen the through-bolts just enough to allow removal of the drive end housing and the starter drive plunger lever return spring.

4. Remove the pivot pin which attaches the starter drive plunger lever to the starter frame and remove the lever.

5. Remove the stop ring retainer and stop ring from the armature shaft.

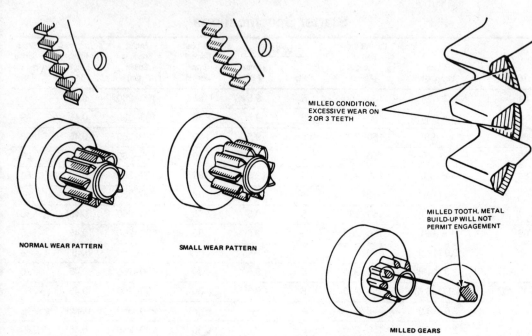

MILLED CONDITION. EXCESSIVE WEAR ON 2 OR 3 TEETH

MILLED TOOTH. METAL BUILD-UP WILL NOT PERMIT ENGAGEMENT

NORMAL WEAR PATTERN

SMALL WEAR PATTERN

MILLED GEARS

**Starter drive gear wear patterns**

6. Remove the starter drive from the armature shaft.

7. Inspect the teeth on the starter drive. If they are excessively worn, inspect the teeth on the ring gear of the flywheel. If the teeth on the flywheel are excessively worn, the flywheel ring gear should be replaced.

8. Apply a thin coat of white grease to the armature shaft, in the area in which the starter drive operates.

9. Install the starter drive on the armature shaft and install a new stopring.

10. Position the starter drive plunger lever on the starter frame and install the pivot pin. Make sure the plunger lever is properly engaged with the starter drive.

11. Install a new stop ring retainer on the armature shaft.

12. Fill the drive end housing bearing fore ¼ full with grease.

13. Position the starter drive plunger lever return spring and the drive end housing to the starter frame.

14. Tighten the starter through-bolts to 55–75 in.lb.

15. Install the starter drive plunger lever cover and the brush cover band on the starter.

16. Install the starter.

## Battery

### REMOVAL AND INSTALLATION

NOTE: *The diesel equipped models have the battery located in the luggage compartment.*

1. Loosen the battery cable bolts and spread the ends of the battery cable terminals.

2. Disconnect the negative battery cable first.

3. Disconnect the positive battery cable.

4. Remove the battery holddown.

5. Wearing heavy gloves, remove the battery from under the hood. Be careful not to tip

## Battery Specifications
## Battery Discharge Rate Table

| Battery Capacity (Ampere—Hours) | Discharge Rate (Amperes) |
|---|---|
| 36 Maintenance Free | 155 |
| 45 Maintenance Free | 190 |
| 48 Maintenance Free | 205 |

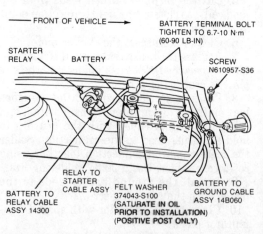

FRONT OF VEHICLE →

BATTERY TERMINAL BOLT TIGHTEN TO 6.7-10 N·m (60-90 LB-IN)

STARTER RELAY

BATTERY

SCREW N610957-S36

RELAY TO STARTER CABLE ASSY

BATTERY TO RELAY CABLE ASSY 14300

FELT WASHER 374043-S100 (SATURATE IN OIL PRIOR TO INSTALLATION) (POSITIVE POST ONLY)

BATTERY TO GROUND CABLE ASSY 14B060

**Battery mounting location—1.6L and 1.9L engines**

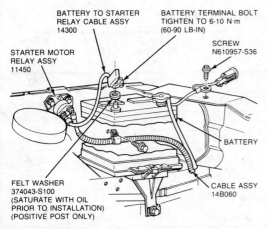

BATTERY TO STARTER
RELAY CABLE ASSY
14300

BATTERY TERMINAL BOLT
TIGHTEN TO 6-10 N·m
(60-90 LB-IN)

SCREW
N610957-S36

STARTER MOTOR
RELAY ASSY
11450

BATTERY

FELT WASHER
374043-S100
(SATURATE WITH OIL
PRIOR TO INSTALLATION)
(POSITIVE POST ONLY)

CABLE ASSY
14B060

**Battery mounting location—2.3L HSC engine**

the battery and spill acid on yourself or the car during removal.

6. To install, wearing heavy gloves, place the battery in its holder under the hood. Use care not to spill the acid.

7. Install the battery holddown.

8. Install the positive battery cable first.

9. Install the negative battery cable.

10. Apply a light coating of grease to the cable ends.

## ENGINE MECHANICAL

### Engine Overhaul

Most engine overhaul procedures are fairly standard. In addition to specific parts replacement procedures and complete specifications for each individual engine, this chapter is also

a guide to acceptable rebuilding procedures. Examples of standard rebuilding practice are shown and should be used along with specific details concerning your particular engine.

Competent and accurate machine shop services will insure maximum performance, reliability and engine life. In most instances, it is more profitable for the do-it-yourself mechanic to remove, clean and inspect the component, buy the necessary parts and deliver these to a shop for actual machine work.

On the other hand, much of the rebuilding work (crankshaft, block, bearings, piston rods, and other components) is well within the scope of the do-it-yourself mechanic.

### TOOLS

The tools required for an engine overhaul or parts replacement will depend on the depth of your involvement. With few exceptions, they will be the tools found in any mechanic's tool kit (see Chapter 1). More in-depth work will require some or all of the following:

• a dial indicator (reading in thousandths) mounted on a universal base
• micrometers and telescope gauges
• jaw and screw-type pullers
• scraper
• valve spring compressor
• ring groove cleaner
• piston ring expander and compressor
• ridge reamer
• cylinder hone or glaze breaker
• Plastigage®
• engine stand

The use of most of these tools is illustrated in

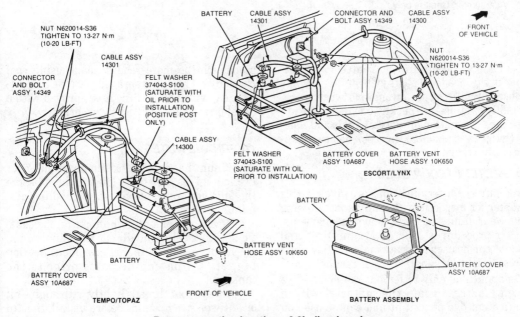

NUT N620014-S36
TIGHTEN TO 13-27 N·m
(10-20 LB-FT)

CABLE ASSY
14301

CONNECTOR
AND BOLT
ASSY 14349

FELT WASHER
374043-S100
(SATURATE WITH
OIL PRIOR TO
INSTALLATION)
(POSITIVE POST
ONLY)

CABLE ASSY
14300

BATTERY

CABLE ASSY
14301

CONNECTOR AND
BOLT ASSY 14349

CABLE ASSY
14300

FRONT
OF VEHICLE

NUT
N620014-S36
TIGHTEN TO 13-27 N·m
(10-20 LB-FT)

FELT WASHER
374043-S100
(SATURATE WITH OIL
PRIOR TO INSTALLATION)

BATTERY COVER
ASSY 10A687

BATTERY VENT
HOSE ASSY 10K650

**ESCORT/LYNX**

BATTERY

BATTERY VENT
HOSE ASSY 10K650

BATTERY

BATTERY COVER
ASSY 10A687

BATTERY COVER
ASSY 10A687

**TEMPO/TOPAZ**

FRONT OF VEHICLE

**BATTERY ASSEMBLY**

**Battery mounting location—2.0L diesel engine**

## General Engine Specifications

| Years | Engine Ltr. (CID) | Fuel System Type | SAE net Horsepower @ rpm | SAE net Torque ft.lb. @ rpm | Bore x Stroke (in.) | Comp. Ratio | Oil Press. (psi.) @ 2000 rpm |
|-------|-------------------|------------------|--------------------------|------------------------------|---------------------|-------------|------------------------------|
| '81 | 1.3 (79) | 2V | NA | NA | 3.15 x 2.40 | NA | 40 |
|  | 1.6 (98) | 2V | 65 @ 5200 | 85 @ 3000 | 3.15 x 3.13 | 8.8:1 | 45–50 |
| '82 | 1.6 (98) | 2V | 70 @ 4600 | 89 @ 3000 | 3.15 x 3.13 | 8.8:1 | 35–65 |
| '83 | 1.6 (98) | 2V | 70 @ 4600 | 89 @ 3000 | 3.15 x 3.13 | 8.8:1 | 35–65 |
| '84 | 1.6 (98) | 2V | 70 @ 4600 | 88 @ 2600 | 3.15 x 3.13 | 9.0:1 | 35–65 |
|  | 1.6 (98) ④ | 2V | 80 @ 5400 | 88 @ 3000 | 3.15 x 3.13 | 9.0:1 | 35–65 |
|  | 1.6 (98) ⑤ | EFI | 120 @ 5200 | 120 @ 3400 | 3.15 x 3.13 | 8.0:1 | 35–65 |
|  | 2.0 (122) | Diesel | 52 @ 4000 | 82 @ 2400 | 3.39 x 3.39 | 22.7:1 | 55–60 |
|  | 2.3 (140) | 1V | 84 @ 4600 | 118 @ 2600 | 3.70 x 3.30 | 9.0:1 | 55–70 |
| '85 | 1.6 (98) | 2V | 70 @ 4600 | 88 @ 2600 | 3.15 x 3.13 | 9.0:1 | 35–65 |
|  | 1.6 (98) ④ | 2V | 80 @ 5400 | 88 @ 3000 | 3.15 x 3.13 | 9.0:1 | 35–65 |
|  | 1.6 (98) | EFI | 84 @ 5200 | 90 @ 2800 | 3.15 x 3.13 | 9.0:1 | 35–65 |
|  | 1.6 (98) ⑤ | EFI | 120 @ 5200 | 120 @ 3400 | 3.15 x 3.13 | 8.0:1 | 35–65 |
|  | 2.0 (122) | Diesel | 52 @ 4000 | 82 @ 2400 | 3.39 x 3.39 | 22.7:1 | 55–60 |
|  | 2.3 (140) | CFI① | 86 @ 4000 | 124 @ 2800 | 3.70 x 3.30 | 9.0:1 | 55–70 |
|  | 2.3 (140) ② | CFI | 100 @ 4600 | 125 @ 3200 | 3.70 x 3.30 | 9.0:1 | 55–70 |
| '86–'87 | 1.9 (113.5) | 2V | 86 @ 4800 | 100 @ 3000 | 3.23 x 3.46 | 9.0:1 | 35–65 |
|  | 1.9 (113.5) ③ | EFI | 108 @ 5200 | 114 @ 4000 | 3.23 x 3.46 | 9.0:1 | 35–65 |
|  | 2.0 (122) | Diesel | 52 @ 4000 | 82 @ 2400 | 3.39 x 3.39 | 22.7:1 | 55–60 |
|  | 2.3 (140) | CFI① | 86 @ 4000 | 124 @ 2800 | 3.70 x 3.30 | 9.0:1 | 55–70 |
|  | 2.3 (140) ② | CFI | 100 @ 4600 | 125 @ 3200 | 3.70 x 3.30 | 9.0:1 | 55–70 |

NA: Not Available
EFI—Electronic Fuel Injection
CFI—Central Fuel Injection
① 1V carburetor, Canada only

② Sport option
③ Escort GT, Lynx XR3, EXP Sport Coupe
④ HO—High Output
⑤ Turbo Charged

this chapter. Many can be rented for a one-time use from a local parts jobber or tool supply house specializing in automotive work. Occasionally, the use of special tools is called for. See the information on Special Tools and Safety Notice in the front of this book before substituting another tool.

### INSPECTION TECHNIQUES

Procedures and specifications are given in this chapter for inspecting, cleaning and assessing the wear limits of most major components. Other procedures such as Magnaflux᙮ and Zyglo᙮ can be used to locate material flaws and stress cracks. Magnaflux᙮ is a magnetic process applicable only to ferrous materials. The Zyglo® process coats the material with a flourescent dye penetrant and can be used on any material Check for suspected surface

cracks can be more readily made using spot check dye. The dye is sprayed onto the suspected area, wiped off and the area sprayed with a developer. Cracks will show up brightly.

### OVERHAUL NOTES

Aluminum has become extremely popular for use in engines, due to its low weight. Observe the following precautions when handling aluminum parts:

• Never hot tank aluminum parts; the caustic hot-tank solution will eat the aluminum.

• Remove all aluminum parts (identification tag, etc.) from engine parts prior to the tanking.

• Always coat threads lightly with engine oil or anti-seize compounds before installation, to prevent seizure.

## Valve Specifications

| Year | Engine Ltr. (CID) | Seat Angle (deg) | Face Angle (deg) | Spring Test Pressure (lbs. @ in.) | Spring Installed Height (in.) | Stem to Guide Clearance (in.) | | Stem Diameter (in.) | |
|---|---|---|---|---|---|---|---|---|---|
| | | | | | | Intake | Exhaust | Intake | Exhaust |
| '81 | 1.3 (79) | 45 | 45.5 | 180 @ 1.09 | 1.46 | .0008–.0027 | .0015–.0032 | .3160 | .3150 |
| | 1.6 (98) | 45 | 45.5 | 180 @ 1.09 | 1.46 | .0008–.0027 | .0015–.0032 | .3160 | .3150 |
| '82 | 1.6 (98) | 45 | 45.5 | 180 @ 1.09 | 1.46 | .0010 | .0021 | .3200 | .3100 |
| '83 | 1.6 (98) | 45 | 45.5 | 200 @ 1.09 ① | 1.48 ② | .0008–.0027 | .0018–.0037 | .3160 | .3150 |
| '84 | 1.6 (98) | 45 | 45.5 | 200 @ 1.09 ① | 1.48 ② | .0008–.0027 | .0018–.0037 | .3160 | .3150 |
| | 2.0 (122) | 45 | 45 | NA | 1.776 | .0016–.0029 | .0018–.0031 | .3138 | .3138 |
| | 2.3 (140) | 45 | 45.5 | 182 @ 1.10 | 1.49 | .0018 | .0023 | .3415 | .3411 |
| '85 | 1.6 (98) | 45 | 45.5 | 200 @ 1.09 ① | 1.48 ② | .0008–.0027 | .0018–.0037 | .3160 | .3150 |
| | 2.0 (122) | 45 | 45 | NA | 1.776 | .0016–.0029 | .0018–.0031 | .3138 | .3138 |
| | 2.3 (140) | 45 | 45.5 | 182 @ 1.10 | 1.49 | .0018 | .0023 | .3415 | .3411 |
| '86–'87 | 1.9 (113.5) | 45 | 45.5 | 200 @ 1.09 | 1.46 | .0008–.0027 | .0018–.0037 | .3167–.3159 | .3156–.3149 |
| | 2.0 (122) | 45 | 45 | NA | 1.776 | .0016–.0029 | .0018–.0031 | .3138–.3144 | .3138–.3142 |
| | 2.3 (140) | 45 | 45.5 | 182 @ 1.10 | 1.49 | .0018 | .0023 | .3415 | .3411 |

NA: Not Available    ① H.O. and E.F.I. Engines: 206 @ 1.09    ② H.O. and E.F.I. Engines: 1.450–1.480

• Never overtorque bolts or spark plugs, especially in aluminum threads.

When assembling the engine, any parts that will be in frictional contact must be prelubed to provide lubrication at initial start-up. Any product specifically formulated for this purpose can be used, but engine oil is not recommended as a prelube.

When semi-permanent (locked, but removable) installation of bolts or nuts is desired, threads should be cleaned and coated with Loctite® or other similar, commercial non-hardening sealant.

### REPAIRING DAMAGED THREADS

Several methods of repairing damaged threads are available. Heli-Coil® (shown here), Keenserts® and Microdot® are among the most widely used. All involve basically the same principle (drilling out stripped threads, tapping the hole and installing a prewound insert), making welding, plugging and oversize fasteners unnecessary.

Two types of thread repair inserts are usually supplied: a standard type for most Inch Coarse, Inch Fine, Metric Course and Metric Fine thread sizes and a spark lug type to fit most spark plug port sizes. Consult the individual manufacturer's catalog to determine exact applications. Typical thread repair kits will contain a selection of prewound threaded inserts, a tap (corresponding to the outside diameter threads of the insert) and an installa-

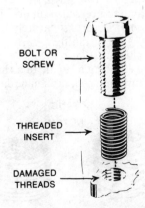

BOLT OR SCREW

THREADED INSERT

DAMAGED THREADS

**Damaged bolt holes can be repaired with thread repair inserts**

## Camshaft Specifications
All Specifications in inches

| Years | Engine Ltr. (CID) | Journal Diameter | | | | | Bearing Clearance | Valve Lift | | End Play |
|---|---|---|---|---|---|---|---|---|---|---|
| | | 1 | 2 | 3 | 4 | 5 | | Int. | Exh. | |
| '81 | 1.3 (79) | 1.761–1.762 | 1.771–1.772 | 1.781–1.782 | 1.791–1.792 | 1.801–1.802 | .0008–.0028 | .377 ① | .377 ① | .0018–.0060 |
| | 1.6 (98) | 1.761–1.762 | 1.771–1.772 | 1.781–1.782 | 1.791–1.792 | 1.801–1.802 | .0008–.0028 | .377 ① | .377 ① | .0018–.0060 |
| '82 | 1.6 (98) | 1.761–1.762 | 1.771–1.772 | 1.781–1.782 | 1.791–1.792 | 1.801–1.802 | .0008–.0028 | .377 ① | .377 ① | .0018–.0060 |
| '83 | 1.6 (98) | 1.761–1.762 | 1.771–1.772 | 1.781–1.782 | 1.791–1.792 | 1.801–1.802 | .0008–.0028 | .377 ① | .377 ① | .0018–.0060 |
| '84 | 1.6 (98) | 1.761–1.762 | 1.771–1.772 | 1.781–1.782 | 1.791–1.792 | 1.801–1.802 | .0008–.0028 | .377 ① | .377 ① | .0018–.0060 |
| | 2.0 (122) | 1.2582–1.2589 | 1.2582–1.2589 | 1.2582–1.2589 | 1.2582–1.2589 | 1.2582–1.2589 | .0010–.0026 | NA | NA | .0059–.0080 |
| | 2.3 (140) | NA | NA | NA | NA | NA | .001–.003 | .392 ② | .377 ② | .009 |
| '85 | 1.6 (98) | 1.761–1.762 | 1.771–1.772 | 1.781–1.782 | 1.791–1.792 | 1.801–1.802 | .0008–.0028 | .377 ① | .377 ① | .0018–.0060 |
| | 2.0 (122) | 1.2582–1.2589 | 1.2582–1.2589 | 1.2582–1.2589 | 1.2582–1.2589 | 1.2582–1.2589 | .0010–.0026 | NA | NA | .0059–.0080 |
| | 2.3 (140) | NA | NA | NA | NA | NA | .001–.003 | .392 ② | .377 ② | .009 |
| '86–'87 | 1.9 (113.5) | 1.8007–1.8017 | 1.8007–1.8017 | 1.8007–1.8017 | 1.8007–1.8017 | 1.8007–1.8017 | .0013–.0033 | .468 ① | .468 ① | .0018–.0060 |
| | 2.0 (122) | 1.2582–1.2589 | 1.2582–1.2589 | 1.2582–1.2589 | 1.2582–1.2589 | 1.2582–1.2589 | .0010–.0026 | NA | NA | .0059–.0080 |
| | 2.3 (140) | NA | NA | NA | NA | NA | .001–.003 | .392 ② | .377 ② | .009 |

NA—Not Available
① HO and EFI: .396 in.
② HO: .413 in.

tion tool. Spark plug inserts usually differ because they require a tap equipped with pilot threads and a combined reamer/tap section. Most manufacturers also supply blister packed thread repair inserts separately in addition to a master kit containing a variety of taps and inserts plus installation tools.

Before effecting a repair to a threaded hole, remove any snapped, broken or damaged bolts or studs. Penetrating oil can be used to free frozen threads. The offending item can be removed with locking pliers or with a screw or stud extractor. After the hole is clear, the thread can be repaired.

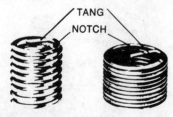

Standard thread repair insert (left) and spark plug thread insert (right)

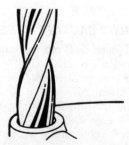

Drill out the damaged threads with specified drill. Drill completely through the hole or to the bottom of a blind hole

## Crankshaft and Connecting Rod Specifications
All Specifications in inches

| | | Crankshaft | | | | Connecting Rod | | |
|---|---|---|---|---|---|---|---|---|
| Years | Engine Ltr. (CID) | Main Bearing Journal Dia. | Main Bearing Oil Clearance | Shaft End Play | Thrust on No. | Journal Dia. | Oil Clearance | Side Clearance |
| '81 | 1.3 (79) | 2.2826–2.2834 | .0008–.0015 | .004–.008 | 3 | 1.885–1.886 | .0002–.0003 | .004–.011 |
| | 1.6 (98) | 2.2826–2.2834 | .0008–.0015 | .004–.008 | 3 | 1.885–1.886 | .0002–.0003 | .004–.011 |
| '82 | 1.6 (98) | 2.2826–2.2834 | .0008–.0015 | .004–.008 | 3 | 1.885–1.886 | .0002–.0003 | .004–.011 |
| '83 | 1.6 (98) | 2.2826–2.2834 | .0008–.0015 | .004–.008 | 3 | 1.885–1.886 | .0002–.0003 | .004–.011 |
| '84 | 1.6 (98) | 2.2826–2.2834 | .0008–.0015 | .004–.008 | 3 | 1.885–1.886 | .0002–.0003 | .004–.011 |
| | 2.0 (122) | 2.3598–2.3605 | .0012–.0020 | .0016–.0011 | 3 | 2.0055–2.0061 | .0010–.0022 | .0043–.0103 |
| | 2.3 (140) | 2.2489–2.2490 | .0008–.0015 | .004–.008 | 3 | 2.1232–2.1240 | .0008–.0015 | .0035–.0105 |
| '85 | 1.6 (98) | 2.2826–2.2834 | .0008–.0015 | .004–.008 | 3 | 1.885–1.886 | .0002–.0003 | .004–.011 |
| | 2.0 (122) | 2.3598–2.3605 | .0012–.0020 | .0016–.0111 | 3 | 2.0055–2.0061 | .0010–.0022 | .0043–.0103 |
| | 2.3 (140) | 2.2489–2.2490 | .0008–.0015 | .004–.008 | 3 | 2.1232–2.1240 | .0008–.0015 | .0035–.0105 |
| '86–'87 | 1.9 (113.5) | 2.2827–2.2835 | .0008–.0015 | .004–.008 | 3 | 1.8854–1.8862 | .0008–.0015 | .004–.011 |
| | 2.0 (122) | 2.3598–2.3605 | .0012–.0020 | .0016–.0111 | 3 | 2.0055–2.0061 | .0010–.0022 | .0043–.0103 |
| | 2.3 (140) | 2.2489–2.2490 | .0008–.0015 | .004–.008 | 3 | 2.1232–2.1240 | .0008–.0015 | .0035–.0105 |

## CHECKING ENGINE COMPRESSION

### Gasoline Engines

A noticeable lack of engine power, excessive oil consumption and/or poor fuel mileage measured over an extended period are all indica-

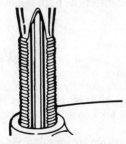

With the tap supplied, tap the hole to receive the thread insert. Keep the tap well oiled and back it out frequently to avoid clogging the threads

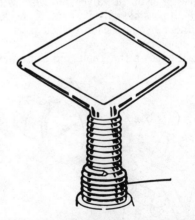

Screw the threaded insert onto the installation tool until the tang engages the slot. Screw the insert into the tapped hole until it is ¼–½ turn below the top surface. After installation break off the tang with a hammer and punch

## Piston and Ring Specifications

All Specifications in inches

| Years | Engine Ltr. (CID) | Ring Gap | | | Ring Side Clearance | | | Piston Clearance |
| | | #1 Compr. | #2 Compr. | Oil Control | #1 Compr. | #2 Compr. | Oil Control | |
|---|---|---|---|---|---|---|---|---|
| '81 | 1.3 (79) | .012–.020 | .012–.020 | .016–.055 | .001–.003 | .002–.003 | Snug | .0008–.0016 |
| | 1.6 (98) | .012–.020 | .012–.020 | .016–.055 | .001–.003 | .002–.003 | Snug | .0008–.0016 |
| '82 | 1.6 (98) | .012–.020 | .012–.020 | .016–.055 | .001–.003 | .002–.003 | Snug | .0012–.0020 |
| '83 | 1.6 (98) | .012–.020 | .012–.020 | .016–.055 | .001–.003 | .002–.003 | Snug | .0018–.0026 |
| '84 | 1.6 (98) | .012–.020 | .012–.020 | .016–.055 | .001–.003 | .002–.003 | Snug | .0018–.0026 |
| | 2.0 (122) | .0079–.0157 | .0079–.0157 | .0079–.0157 | .0020–.0035 | .0016–.0031 | Snug | .0013–.0020 |
| | 2.3 (140) | .008–.016 | .008–.016 | .015–.055 | .002–.004 | .002–.004 | Snug | .0013–.0021 |
| '85 | 1.6 (98) | .012–.020 | .012–.020 | .016–.055 | .001–.003 | .002–.003 | Snug | .0018–.0026 |
| | 2.0 (122) | .0079–.0157 | .0079–.0157 | .0079–.0157 | .0020–.0035 | .0016–.0031 | Snug | .0013–.0020 |
| | 2.3 (140) | .008–.016 | .008–.016 | .015–.055 | .002–.004 | .002–.004 | Snug | .0013–.0021 |
| '86–'87 | 1.9 (113.5) | .010–.020 | .010–.020 | .016–.055 | .0015–.0032 | .0015–.0035 | Snug | .0016–.0024 |
| | 2.0 (122) | .0079–.0157 | .0079–.0157 | .0079–.0157 | .0020–.0035 | .0016–.0031 | Snug | .0013–.0020 |
| | 2.3 (140) | .008–.016 | .008–.016 | .015–.055 | .002–.004 | .002–.004 | Snug | .0012–.0022 |

tors of internal engine war. Worn piston rings, scored or worn cylinder bores, blown head gaskets, sticking or burnt valves and worn valve seats are all possible culprits here. A check of each cylinder's compression will help you locate the problems.

As mentioned in the Tools and Equipment section of Chapter 1, a screw-in type compression gauge is more accurate that the type you simply hold against the spark plug hole, although it takes slightly longer to use. It's worth it to obtain a more accurate reading. Follow the procedures below.

1. Warm up the engine to normal operating temperature.

2. Remove all spark plugs.

3. Disconnect the high tension lead from the ignition coil.

4. Disconnect all fuel injector electrical connections.

5. Screw the compression gauge into the No. 1 spark plug hole until the fitting is snug.

NOTE: *Be careful not to crossthread the plug hole. On aluminum cylinder heads use extra care, as the threads in these heads are easily ruined.*

6. Have an assistant depress the accelerator pedal fully. Then, while you read the compression gauge, ask the assistant to crank the en-

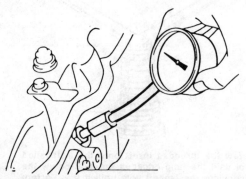

**The screw-in type compression gauge is more accurate**

## Torque Specifications
### Piston Engines

| Years | Engine Ltr. (CID) | Cyl. Head | Conn. Rod | Main Bearing | Crankshaft Damper | Flywheel | Manifold | |
|---|---|---|---|---|---|---|---|---|
| | | | | | | | Intake | Exhaust |
| '81 | 1.3 (79) | ① | 19–25 | 67–80 | 74–90 | 59–69 | 12–15 ② | 15–20 |
| | 1.6 (98) | ① | 19–25 | 67–80 | 74–90 | 59–69 | 12–15 ② | 15–20 |
| '82 | 1.6 (98) | ① | 19–25 | 67–80 | 74–90 | 59–69 | 12–15 ② | 15–20 |
| '83 | 1.6 (98) | ① | 19–25 | 67–80 | 74–90 | 59–69 | 3.7–7.4 ② | 15–20 |
| '84 | 1.6 (98) | ① | 19–25 | 67–80 | 74–90 | 59–69 | 3.7–7.4 ② | 15–20 |
| | 2.0 (122) | ① | 48–51 | 61–65 | 115–123 | 130–137 | 12–16 | 16–19 |
| | 2.3 (140) | ③ | 21–26 | 51–66 | 140–170 | 54–64 | 15–23 | ④ |
| '85 | 1.6 (98) | ① | 19–25 | 67–80 | 74–90 | 59–69 | 1.5–7.4 ② | 15–20 |
| | 2.0 (122) | ① | 48–51 | 61–65 | 115–123 | 130–137 | 12–16 | 16–19 |
| | 2.3 (140) | ③ | 21–26 | 51–66 | 140–170 | 54–64 | 15–23 | ④ |
| '86–'87 | 1.9 (113.5) | ① | 19–25 | 67–80 | 74–90 | 59–69 | 1.5–7.4 ② | 15–20 |
| | 2.0 (122) | ① | 48–51 | 61–65 | 115–123 | 130–137 | 12–16 | 16–19 |
| | 2.3 (140) | ③ | 21–26 | 51–66 | 140–170 | 54–64 | 15–23 | ④ |

① See head removal procedure for instructions
② Manifold stud nuts 12–15 ft. lbs.
③ Tighten in two stages: 52–59 ft. lbs., then 70–76 ft. lbs.
④ Tighten in two stages: 5–7 ft. lbs., then 20–30 ft. lbs.

gine two or three times in short bursts using the ignition switch.

7. Read the compression gauge at the end of each series of cranks, and record the highest of these readings. Repeat this procedure for each of the engine's cylinders. Maximum compression should be 175–185 psi. A cylinder's compression pressure is usually acceptable if it is not less than 80% of maximum. The difference between each cylinder should be no more than 12–14 psi.

8. If a cylinder is unusually low, pour a tablespoon of clean engine oil into the cylinder through the spark plug hole and repeat the compression test. If the compression comes up after adding the oil, it appears that the cylinder's piston rings or bore are damaged or worn. If the pressure remains low, the valves may not be seating properly (a valve job is needed), or the head gasket may be blown near that cylinder. If compression in any two adjacent cylinders is low, and if the addition of oil doesn't help the compression, there is leakage past the head gasket. Oil and coolant water in the combustion chamber can result from this problem. There may be evidence of water droplets on the engine dipstick when a head gasket has blown.

### Diesel Engines

Checking cylinder compression on diesel engines is basically the same procedure as on gasoline engines except for the following:

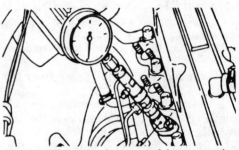

**Diesel engines require a special compression gauge adaptor**

1. A special compression gauge adaptor suitable for diesel engines (because these engines have much greater compression pressures) must be used.

2. Remove the injector tubes and remove the injectors from each cylinder.

NOTE: *Don't forget to remove the washer underneath each injector. Otherwise, it may get lost when the engine is cranked.*

3. When fitting the compression gauge adaptor to the cylinder head, make sure the bleeder of the gauge (if equipped) is closed.

4. When reinstalling the injector assemblies, install new washers underneath each injector.

## Engine

### REMOVAL AND INSTALLATION

NOTE: *A special engine support bar is necessary. The bar is used to support the engine/transaxle while disconnecting the various engine mounts Ford Part No. T81P6000A. A suitable support can be made using angle iron, a heavy J-hook and some strong chain.*

### 1.6L, 1.9L Engine — Engine w/Transaxle

NOTE: *The following procedure is for engine and transaxle removal and installation as an assembly. Procedure for removing the engine only is in following section.*

1. Mark the location of the hinges and remove the hood.

2. Remove the air cleaner, hot air tube and alternator fresh air intake tube.

3. Disconnect the battery cables, remove the battery and tray.

4. Drain the radiator, engine oil and transaxle fluid.

5. Remove the coil the mounting bracket and the coil wire harness.

6. If the vehicle is equipped with air conditioning, remove the compressor from the engine with the refrigerant hoses still attached. Position compressor to the side.

CAUTION: *Never loosen air conditioning refrigerant lines, as the escaping refrigerant is a deadly poison and can freeze exposed skin instantly.*

7. Disconnect the upper and lower radiator hose.

8. Disconnect the heater hoses from the engine.

9. If equipped with an automatic transaxle disconnect and plug the cooler lines at the rubber coupler.

10. Disconnect the electric fan.

11. Remove the fan motor, shroud assembly and the radiator.

12. If equipped with power steering, remove the filler tube.

13. Disconnect the following electrical connections:

   a. Main wiring harness
   b. Neutral safety switch (automatic only)
   c. Choke cap wire
   d. Starter cable
   e. Alternator wiring

14. Disconnect the fuel supply and return lines. Relieve fuel pressure on injected models before disconnecting fuel lines.

15. Disconnect the (3) altitude compensator lines if so equipped. Mark each line as you remove it. for easy installation.

16. Disconnect the vacuum lines from the "tree" on the firewall.

17. Disconnect the power brake booster vacuum line.

18. Disconnect the cruise control is so equipped.

19. Disconnect all carburetor linkage.

20. Disconnect all engine vacuum lines. Mark each line as you remove it, for easy installation.

21. Disconnect the clutch cable if so equipped.

22. Remove the thermactor pump bracket bolt.

23. Install engine support T81P-6000-A or equivalent. Using a short piece of chain, attach it to the engine using the 10 mm bolt holes at the transaxle, the exhaust manifold side of the head, and the thermactor bracket hole. Tighten the J-bolt. Place a piece of tape around the J-bolt threads where the bolt passes through the bottom of the support bar. This will act as a reference later.

24. Jack up the vehicle and support it with jackstands.

25. Remove the splash shields.

26. If equipped with a manual transaxle, remove the roll restrictor at the engine and body.

27. Remove the stabilizer bar.

28. Remove the lower control arm through-bolts at the body brackets.

29. Disconnect the left tie rod at the steering knuckle.

30. Disconnect the secondary air tube (catalyst) at the check valve.

31. Disconnect the exhaust system at the exhaust manifold and tail pipe.

32. Remove the right halfshaft from the transaxle. Some fluid will leak out when the shaft is removed.

33. Remove the left side halfshaft.

34. Install shipping plugs T81P-1177-B or equivalent in the differential seals.

35. Disconnect the speedometer cable.

36. If equipped with an automatic transaxle, disconnect the shift selector cable. On manual transaxles, disconnect the shift control rod.

   NOTE: *Mark the position of the shift control before disconnecting it.*

37. If equipped with power steering, disconnect the pump return line at the pump, and the pressure line at the intermediate fitting.

38. Remove the left front motor mount attaching bracket and remove the mount with its through-bolt. Remove the left rear motor mount stud nut. Carefully reach into the engine compartment and loosen the engine support bar J-bolt until the left rear motor mount stud clears the mounting bracket. Remove the left rear mount to transaxle attaching bracket.

39. Lower the vehicle, then tighten the support bar J-bolt until the piece of tape installed earlier contacts the bottom of the support bar. Attach a lifting sling to the engine, disconnect the right engine mount and lift the engine from the vehicle.

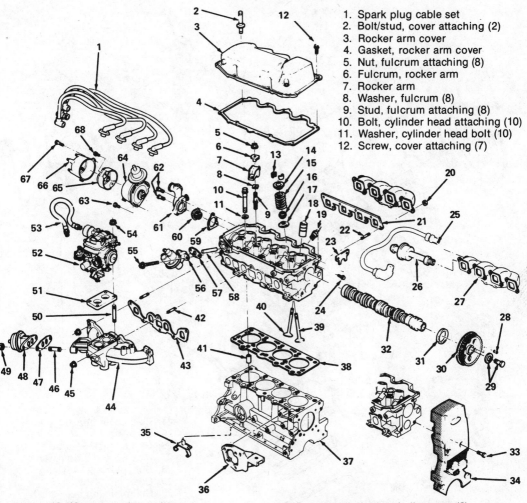

1. Spark plug cable set
2. Bolt/stud, cover attaching (2)
3. Rocker arm cover
4. Gasket, rocker arm cover
5. Nut, fulcrum attaching (8)
6. Fulcrum, rocker arm
7. Rocker arm
8. Washer, fulcrum (8)
9. Stud, fulcrum attaching (8)
10. Bolt, cylinder head attaching (10)
11. Washer, cylinder head bolt (10)
12. Screw, cover attaching (7)

13. Keepers, valve springs
14. Retainer, valve spring
15. Valve spring
16. Seal, valve stem
17. Washer, valve spring
18. Valve lifter
19. Spark plug
20. Nut, manifold attaching (8)
21. Gasket, exhaust manifold
22. Stud, manifold attaching (8)
23. Plate, camshaft thrust
24. Bolt, thrust plate attaching (2)
25. EGR tube
26. Check valve, air injection
27. Exhaust manifold
28. Shaft key, cam sprocket
29. Bolt/washer sprocket attaching (1)
30. Camshaft sprocket
31. Seal, camshaft
32. Camshaft
33. Bolts (2) & nuts (2), cover attaching (2)
34. Timing belt cover
35. Crankcase ventilation baffle
36. Engine mount
37. Cylinder block
38. Gasket, cylinder head
39. Exhaust valve
40. Intake valve

41. Dowel, cylinder head alignment (2)
42. Stud, manifold attaching (6)
43. Gasket, intake manifold
44. Intake manifold
45. Nut, manifold attaching (6)
46. Stud, valve attaching (2)
47. Gasket, EGR valve
48. EGR valve
49. Nut, valve attaching (2)
50. Stud, carburetor attaching (4)
51. Gasket, carburetor mounting
52. Carburetor
53. Fuel line
54. Nut, carburetor attaching (4)
55. Bolt, pump attaching (2)
56. Fuel pump
57. Gasket, fuel pump
58. Push rod, fuel pump
59. Gasket, housing
60. Thermostat
61. Thermostat housing
62. Bolt, housing attaching (2)
63. Bolt, distributor attaching (3)
64. Distributor
65. Rotor
66. Distributor cap
67. Screwn cap attaching (2).
68. Screw, rotor attaching (2)

**Exploded view of upper part of the 1.6L, 1.9L engines**

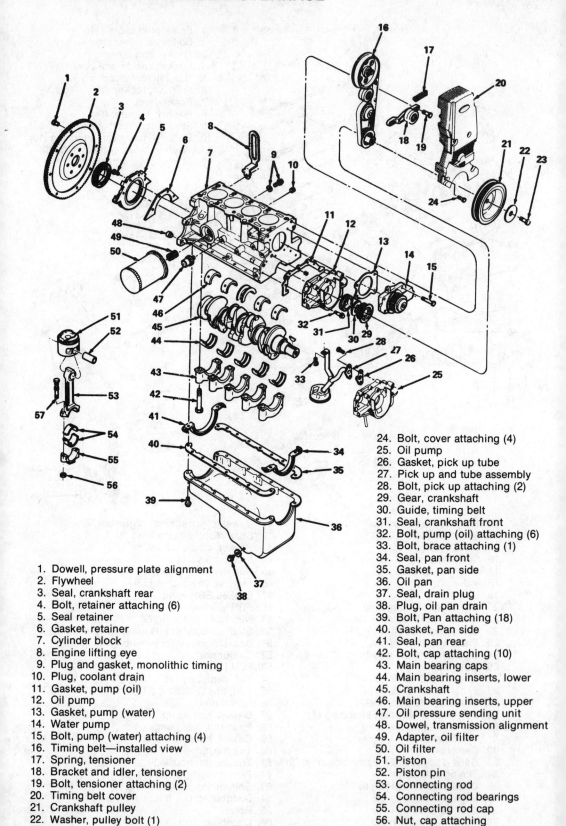

1. Dowell, pressure plate alignment
2. Flywheel
3. Seal, crankshaft rear
4. Bolt, retainer attaching (6)
5. Seal retainer
6. Gasket, retainer
7. Cylinder block
8. Engine lifting eye
9. Plug and gasket, monolithic timing
10. Plug, coolant drain
11. Gasket, pump (oil)
12. Oil pump
13. Gasket, pump (water)
14. Water pump
15. Bolt, pump (water) attaching (4)
16. Timing belt—installed view
17. Spring, tensioner
18. Bracket and idler, tensioner
19. Bolt, tensioner attaching (2)
20. Timing belt cover
21. Crankshaft pulley
22. Washer, pulley bolt (1)
23. Bolt, Pulley attaching (1)

24. Bolt, cover attaching (4)
25. Oil pump
26. Gasket, pick up tube
27. Pick up and tube assembly
28. Bolt, pick up attaching (2)
29. Gear, crankshaft
30. Guide, timing belt
31. Seal, crankshaft front
32. Bolt, pump (oil) attaching (6)
33. Bolt, brace attaching (1)
34. Seal, pan front
35. Gasket, pan side
36. Oil pan
37. Seal, drain plug
38. Plug, oil pan drain
39. Bolt, Pan attaching (18)
40. Gasket, Pan side
41. Seal, pan rear
42. Bolt, cap attaching (10)
43. Main bearing caps
44. Main bearing inserts, lower
45. Crankshaft
46. Main bearing inserts, upper
47. Oil pressure sending unit
48. Dowel, transmission alignment
49. Adapter, oil filter
50. Oil filter
51. Piston
52. Piston pin
53. Connecting rod
54. Connecting rod bearings
55. Connecting rod cap
56. Nut, cap attaching
57. Bolt, cap attaching

**Exploded view of lower part of the 1.6L, 1.9L engines**

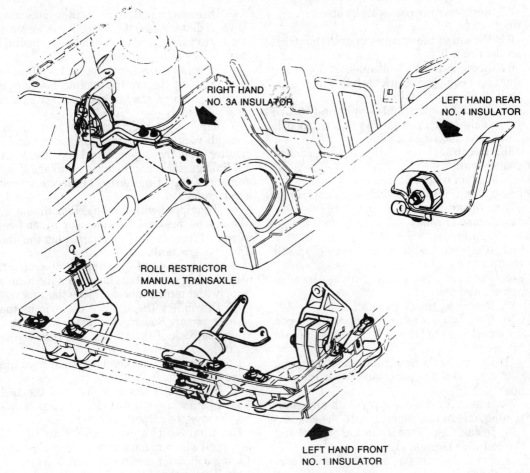

RIGHT HAND
NO. 3A INSULATOR

LEFT HAND REAR
NO. 4 INSULATOR

ROLL RESTRICTOR
MANUAL TRANSAXLE
ONLY

LEFT HAND FRONT
NO. 1 INSULATOR

**Typical 1.6L, 1.9L engine and transaxle mounting**

## To Install:

40. Attach a lowering sling to the engine, Reconnect the right engine mount and lower the engine into the vehicle.

41. Install the left front motor mount attaching bracket and install the mount with its through-bolt. Install the left rear motor mount stud nut. Reach into the engine compartment and tighten the engine support bar J-bolt until the left rear motor mount stud clears the mounting bracket. Install the left rear mount to transaxle attaching bracket.

42. If equipped with power steering, reconnect the pump return line at the pump, and the pressure line at the intermediate fitting.

43. If equipped with an automatic transaxle, reconnect the shift selector cable. On manual transaxles, reconnect the shift control rod.

44. Reconnect the speedometer cable.

45. Remove the shipping plugs T81P-1177-B or equivalent in the differential seals.

46. Install the left side halfshaft.

47. Install the right halfshaft to the transaxle.

48. Reconnect the exhaust system at the exhaust manifold and tail pipe.

49. Reconnect the secondary air tube (catalyst) at the check valve.

50. Reconnect the left tie rod at the steering knuckle.

51. Install the lower control arm through-bolts at the body brackets.

52. Install the stabilizer bar.

53. If equipped with a manual transaxle, install the roll restrictor at the engine and body.

54. Install the splash shields.

55. Jack up the vehicle and support it with jackstands.

56. Remove the engine support T81P-6000-A or equivalent.

57. Install the thermactor pump bracket bolt.

58. Reconnect the clutch cable if so equipped.

59. Reconnect all engine vacuum lines. Mark each line as you Install it, for easy installation.

60. Reconnect all carburetor linkage.

61. Reconnect the cruise control is so equipped.

62. Reconnect the power brake booster vacuum line.

63. Reconnect the vacuum lines to the "tree" on the firewall.

64. Reconnect the (3) altitude compensator lines if so equipped. Mark each line as you Install it. for easy installation.

65. Reconnect the fuel supply and return lines. Relieve fuel pressure on injected models before reconnecting fuel lines.

66. Reconnect the following electrical connections:
   a. Main wiring harness
   b. Neutral safety switch (automatic only)
   c. Choke cap wire
   d. Starter cable
   e. Alternator wiring

67. If equipped with power steering, install the filler tube.

68. Install the fan motor, shroud assembly and the radiator.

69. Reconnect the electric fan.

70. If equipped with an automatic transaxle reconnect and plug the cooler lines at the rubber coupler.

71. Reconnect the heater hoses to the engine.

72. Reconnect the upper and lower radiator hose.

73. If the vehicle is equipped with air conditioning, install the compressor to the engine.

74. Install the coil the mounting bracket and the coil wire harness.

75. Refill the radiator, engine oil and transaxle fluid.

76. Reconnect the battery cables, install the battery and tray.

77. Install the air cleaner, hot air tube and alternator fresh air intake tube.

78. Install the hood.

## 1.6L, 1.9L Engine — Engine Alone

NOTE: *The following procedure is for engine only removal and installation.*

1. Mark the position of the hinges on the hood underside and remove the hood.

2. Remove the air cleaner assembly. Remove the air feed duct and the heat tube. Remove the air duct to the alternator.

3. Disconnect the battery cables from the battery. Remove the battery. If equipped with air conditioning, remove compressor with line still connected and position out of the way.

CAUTION: *Never loosen refrigerant lines, as the escaping refrigerant is a deadly poison and can freeze exposed skin instantly.*

4. Drain the cooling system. Remove the drive belts from the alternator and thermactor pump. Disconnect the thermactor air supply hose. Disconnect the wiring harness at the alternator. Remove alternator and thermactor.

5. Disconnect and remove the upper and lower radiator hoses. If equipped with an automatic transaxle, disconnect and plug the fluid cooler lines at the radiator.

6. Disconnect the heater hoses from the engine. Unplug the electric cooling fan wiring harness. Remove the fan and radiator shroud as an assembly.

7. Remove the radiator. Label and disconnect all vacuum lines, including power brake booster, from the engine. Label and disconnect all linkage, including kickdown linkage if automatic, and wiring harness connectors from the engine.

8. If equipped with fuel injection, discharge the system pressure. Remove supply and return fuel lines to the fuel pump. Plug the line from the gas tank.

9. Raise and safely support the car on jackstands. Remove the clamp from the heater supply and return tubes. remove the tubes.

10. Disconnect the battery cable from the starter motor. Remove the brace or bracket from the back of the starter and remove the starter.

11. Disconnect the exhaust system from the exhaust manifold. Drain the engine oil.

12. Remove the brace in front of the bell housing (flywheel or converter) inspection cover. Remove the inspection cover.

13. Remove the crankshaft pulley. If equipped with a manual transaxle, remove the timing belt cover lower attaching bolts.

14. If equipped with an automatic transaxle, remove the torque converter to flywheel mounting nuts.

15. Remove the lower engine to transaxle attaching bolts.

16. Loosen the hose clamps on the bypass hose and remove the hose from the intake manifold.

17. Remove the bolt and nut attaching the right front mount insulator to the engine bracket.

18. Lower the car from the jackstands.

19. Attach an engine lifting sling to the engine. Connect a chain hoist to the lifting sling and remove all slack. Remove the through bolt from the right front engine mount and remove the insulator.

20. If the car is equipped with a manual transaxle, remove the timing belt cover upper mounting bolts and remove the cover.

21. Remove the right front insulator attaching bracket from the engine.

22. Position a floor jack under the transaxle. Raise the jack just enough to take the weight of the transaxle.

23. Remove the upper bolts connecting the engine and transaxle.

24. Slowly raise the engine and separate from the transaxle. Be sure the torque converter stays on the transxaxle. Remove the engine from the car. On models equipped with manual transaxles, the engine must be separated from the input shaft of the transaxle before raising.

**To install:**

25. Slowly lower the engine and connect it to the transaxle.

26. Install the upper bolts connecting the engine and transaxle.

27. Lower the jack under the transaxle.

28. Install the right front insulator attaching bracket to the engine.

29. If the car is equipped with a manual transaxle, install the timing belt cover upper mounting bolts and install the cover.

30. Remove the engine sling from the engine. Install the through bolt to the right front engine mount and install the insulator.

31. Raise the car and support on jackstands.

32. Install the bolt and nut attaching the right front mount insulator to the engine bracket.

33. Install the bypass hose to the intake manifold and tighten the clamps.

34. Install the lower engine to transaxle attaching bolts.

35. If equipped with an automatic transaxle, install the torque converter to the flywheel.

36. Install the crankshaft pulley. If equipped with a manual transaxle, install the timing belt cover lower attaching bolts.

37. Install the brace in front of the bell housing (flywheel or converter) inspection cover. Install the inspection cover.

38. Reconnect the exhaust system to the exhaust manifold. Refill the engine oil.

39. Reconnect the battery cable to the starter motor. Install the brace or bracket to the back of the starter and install the starter.

40. Lower the car from the jackstands. Install the clamp to the heater supply and return tubes.

41. If equipped with fuel injection, install the supply and return fuel lines to the fuel pump.

42. Install the radiator. Reconnect all vacuum lines, including power brake booster, to the engine. Reconnect all linkage, including kickdown linkage if automatic, and wiring harness connectors to the engine.

43. Reconnect the heater hoses to the engine. Unplug the electric cooling fan wiring harness. Install the fan and radiator shroud as an assembly.

44. Reconnect the upper and lower radiator hoses. If equipped with an automatic transaxle, reconnect the fluid cooler lines at the radiator.

45. Refill the cooling system. Install alterna-tor and thermactor. Install the drive belts to the alternator and thermactor pump. Reconnect the thermactor air supply hose. Reconnect the wiring harness at the alternator.

46. Install the battery. Reconnect the battery cables to the battery. If equipped with air conditioning, install the compressor.

47. Install the air cleaner assembly. Install the air feed duct and the heat tube. Install the air duct to the alternator.

48. Install the hood.

### 2.0 Diesel Engine

NOTE: *Suitable jackstands or hoisting equipment are necessary to remove the engine and transaxle assembly. The assembly is removed from underneath the vehicle.*

CAUTION: *The air conditioning system contains refrigerant (R-12) under high pressure. Use extreme care when discharging the system. If the tools and know-how are not on hand, have the system discharged prior to the start of engine removal.*

These procedures cover the removal and installation of the 2.0L Diesel engine and transaxle as an assembly.

1. Mark the position of the hood hinges and remove the hood.

2. Remove the negative ground cable from the battery that is located in luggage compartment.

3. Remove the air cleaner assembly.

4. Position a drain pan under the lower radiator hose. Remove the hose and drain the engine coolant.

5. Remove the upper radiator hose from the engine.

6. Disconnect the cooling fan at the electrical connector.

7. Remove the radiator shroud and cooling fan as an assembly. Remove the radiator.

8. Remove the starter cable from the starter.

9. Discharge air conditioning system (see opening CAUTION) if so equipped. Remove the pressure and suction lines from the air conditioning compressor.

10. Identify and disconnect all vacuum lines as necessary.

11. Disconnect the engine harness connectors (two) at the dash panel. Disconnect the glow plug relay connectors at the dash panel.

NOTE: *Connectors are located under the plastic shield on the dash panel. Remove and save plastic retainer pins. Disconnect the alternator wiring connector on RH fender apron.*

12. Disconnect the clutch cable from the shift lever on transaxle.

13. Disconnect the injection pump throttle linkage.

14. Disconnect the fuel supply and return hoses on the engine.

15. Disconnect the power steering pressure and return lines at the power steering pump, if so equipped. Remove the power steering lines bracket at the cylinder head.

16. Install Engine Support Tool D79P-8000-A or equivalent to existing engine lifting eye.

17. Raise vehicle and safely support on jackstands.

18. Remove the bolt attaching the exhaust pipe bracket to the oil pan.

19. Remove the two exhaust pipes to exhaust manifold attaching nuts.

20. Pull the exhaust system out of rubber insulating grommets and set aside.

21. Remove the speedometer cable from the transaxle.

22. position an drain pan under the heater hoses. Remove one heater hose form the water pump inlet tube. Remove the other heater hose from the oil cooler.

23. Remove the bolts attaching the control arms to the body. Remove the stabilizer bar bracket retaining bolts and remove the brackets.

24. Halfshaft assemblies must be removed from the transaxle at this time.

25. On MT models, remove the shift stabilizer bar-to-transaxle attaching bolts. Remove the shift mechanism to shift shaft attaching nut and bolt at the transaxle.

26. Remove the LH rear insulator mount bracket from body bracket by removing the two nuts.

27. Remove the LH front insulator to transaxle mounting bolts.

28. Lower vehicle (see CAUTION below). Install lifting equipment to the two existing lifting eyes on engine.

   CAUTION: *Do not allow front wheels to touch floor.*

29. Remove Engine Support Tool D79L-8000-A or equivalent.

30. Remove RH insulator intermediate bracket to engine bracket bolts, intermediate bracket to insulator attaching nuts and the nut on the bottom of the double ended stud attaching the intermediate bracket to engine bracket. Remove the bracket.

31. Carefully lower the engine and the transaxle assembly to the floor.

32. Raise the vehicle and safely support.

33. Position the engine and transaxle assembly directly below the engine compartment.

34. Slowly lower the vehicle over the engine and transaxle assembly.

CAUTION: *Do not allow the front wheels to touch the floor.*

35. Install the lifting equipment to both existing engine lifting eyes on engine.

36. Raise the engine and transaxle assembly up through engine compartment and position accordingly.

37. Install RH insulator intermediate attaching nuts and intermediate bracket to engine bracket bolts. Install nut on bottom of double ended stud attaching intermediate bracket to engine bracket. Tighten to 75–100 ft.lb.

38. Install Engine Support Tool D79L-8000-A or equivalent to the engine lifting eye.

39. Remove the lifting equipment.

40. Raise vehicle.

41. Position a suitable floor or transaxle jack under engine. Raise the engine and transaxle assembly into mounted position.

42. Install insulator to bracket nut and tighten to 75–100 ft.lb.

43. Tighen the LH rear insulator bracket to body bracket nuts to 75–100 ft.lb.

44. Install the lower radiator hose and install retaining bracket and bolt.

45. Install the shift stabilizer bar to transaxle attaching bolt. Tighten to 23–35 ft.lb.

46. Install the shift mechanism to input shift shaft (on transaxle) bolt and nut. Tighen to 7–10 ft.lb.

47. Install the lower radiator hose to the radiator.

48. Install the speedometer cable to the transaxle.

49. Connect the heater hoses to the water pump and oil cooler.

50. Position the exhaust system up and into insulating rubber grommets located at the rear of the vehicle.

51. Install the exhaust pipe to exhaust manifold bolts.

52. Install the exhaust pipe bracket to the oil pan bolt.

53. Place the stabilizer bar and control arm assembly into position. Install control arm to body attaching bolts. Install the stabilizer bar brackets and tighten all fasteners.

54. Halfshaft assemblies must be installed at this time.

55. Lower the vehicle.

56. Remove the Engine Support Tool D79L-6000-A or equivalent.

57. Connect the alternator wiring at RH fender apron.

58. Connect the engine harness to main harness and glow plug relays at dash panel.

   NOTE: *Reinstall plastic shield.*

59. Connect the vacuum lines.

60. Install the air conditioning discharge and suction lines to A/C compressor, if so equipped. Do not charge system at this time.

61. Connect the fuel supply and return lines to the injection pump.

62. Connect the injection pump throttle cable.

63. Install the power steering pressure and return lines. Install bracket.

64. Connect the clutch cable to shift lever on transaxle.

65. Connect the battery cable to starter.

66. Install the radiator shroud and coolant fan assembly. Tighten attaching bolts.

67. Connect the coolant fan electrical connector.

68. Install the upper radiator hose to engine.

69. Fill and bleed the cooling system.

70. Install the negative ground battery cable to battery.

71. Install the air cleaner assembly.

72. Install the hood.

73. Charge air conditioning system, if so equipped. System can be charged at a later time if outside source is used.

74. Check and refill all fluid levels, (power steering, engine, MT).

75. Start the vehicle. Check for leaks.

## 2.3L HSC Engine

NOTE: *The following procedure is for engine and transaxle removal and installation as an assembly.*

CAUTION: *The engine and transaxle assembly are removed together as a unit from underneath the car. Provision must be made to safely raise and support the car for power train removal and installation.*

*The air conditioning system (if equipped) must be discharged prior to engine removal. The refrigerant is contained under high pressure and is very dangerous when released. The system should be discharged by a knowledgeable person using the proper equipment.*

1. Mark the position of the lines on the underside of the hood and remove the hood.

2. Disconnect the battery cables from the battery, negative cable first. Remove the air cleaner assembly.

3. Remove the radiator cap and disconnect the lower radiator hose from the radiator to drain the cooling system.

4. Remove the upper and lower radiator hoses. On models equipped with an automatic transaxle, disconnect and plug the oil cooler lines from the rubber connectors at the radiator.

5. Disconnect and remove the coil from the cylinder head. Disconnect the cooling fan wiring harness. Remove the radiator shroud and electric fan as an assembly.

6. Be sure the air conditioning system is properly and safely discharged. Remove the hoses from the compressor. Label and disconnect all electrical harness connections, linkage and vacuum lines from the engine.

7. On automatic transaxle models disconnect the TV (throttle valve) linkage at the transaxle. On manual transaxle models disconnect the clutch cable from the lever at the transaxle.

8. Disconnect the fuel supply and return lines. Plug the fuel line from the gas tank. Disconnect the thermactor pump discharge hose at the pump.

9. Disconnect the power steering lines at the pump. Remove the hose support bracket from the cylinder head.

10. Install an engine support sling (Ford Tool T79L6000A, or equivalent), see the 1.6L removal and installating engine/transaxle assembly section for details.

11. Raise and safely support the car on jackstands.

12. Remove the starter cable from the starter motor terminal. Drain the engine oil and the transaxle lubricant.

13. Disconnect the hose from the catalytic converter. Remove the bolts retaining the exhaust pipe bracket to the oil pan.

14. Remove the exhaust pipe to exhaust manifold mounting nuts. Remove the pipes from the mounting bracket insulators and position out of the way.

15. Disconnect the speedometer cable from the transaxle. Remove the heater hoses from the water pump inlet and intake manifold connector.

16. Remove the water intake tube bracket from the engine block. Remove the two clamp attaching bolts from the bottom of the oil pan. Remove the water pump inlet tube.

17. Remove the bolts attaching the control arms to the body. Remove the stabilizer bar bracket retaining bolts and remove the brackets.

18. Remove the half shafts (drive axles) from the transaxle. Plug transaxle with shipping plugs or equivalent.

19. On models equipped with a manual transaxle, remove the roll restrictor nuts from the transaxle and pull the roll restrictor from mounting bracket.

20. On models equipped with a manual transaxle, remove the shift stabilizer bar to transaxle attaching bolts. Remove the shift mechanism to shift shaft attaching nut and bolt at the transaxle.

21. On models equipped with an automatic

transaxle, disconnect the shift cable clip from the transaxle lever. Remove the manual shift linkage bracket bolts from the transaxle and remove the bracket.

22. Remove the left rear No. 4 insulator mount bracket from the body by removing the retaining nuts.

23. Remove the left front No. 1 insulator to transaxle mounting bolts.

24. Lower the car and support with stands so that the front wheels are just above the ground. Do not allow the wheels to touch the ground.

25. Connect an engine sling to the lifting brackets provided. Connect a hoist to the sling and apply slight tension. Remove and support sling (Step 10).

26. Remove the right hand insulator intermediate bracket to engine bracket bolts, intermediate bracket to insulator attaching nuts and the nut on the bottom of the double ended stud which attaches the intermediate bracket and engine bracket. Remove the bracket.

27. Lower the engine and transaxle assembly to the ground.

28. Raise and support the car at a height suitable from assembly to be removed.

**To Install:**

29. Raise the engine and transaxle assembly and lower it into the vehicle.

30. Install the right hand insulator intermediate bracket to engine bracket bolts, intermediate bracket to insulator attaching nuts and the nut on the bottom of the double ended stud which attaches the intermediate bracket and engine bracket. Install the bracket.

31. Connect an engine sling to the Lowering brackets provided. Connect a hoist to the sling and apply slight tension. Install and support sling.

32. Raise the car and support with stands so that the front wheels are just above the ground. Do not allow the wheels to touch the ground.

33. Install the left front No. 1 insulator to transaxle mounting bolts.

34. Install the left rear No. 4 insulator mount bracket to the body by removing the retaining nuts.

35. On models equipped with an automatic transaxle, reconnect the shift cable clip to the transaxle lever. Install the manual shift linkage bracket bolts to the transaxle and install the bracket.

36. On models equipped with a manual transaxle, install the shift stabilizer bar to transaxle attaching bolts. Install the shift mechanism to shift shaft attaching nut and bolt at the transaxle.

37. On models equipped with a manual transaxle, install the roll restrictor nuts to the transaxle and pull the roll restrictor to mounting bracket.

38. Remove the shipping plugs and install the half shafts (drive axles) to the transaxle.

39. Install the bolts attaching the control arms to the body. Install the stabilizer bar bracket retaining bolts and install the brackets.

40. Install the water intake tube bracket to the engine block. Install the two clamp attaching bolts to the bottom of the oil pan. Install the water pump inlet tube.

41. Reconnect the speedometer cable to the transaxle. Install the heater hoses to the water pump inlet and intake manifold connector.

42. Install the exhaust pipe to exhaust manifold mounting nuts. Install the pipes to the mounting bracket insulators.

43. Reconnect the hose to the catalytic converter. Install the bolts retaining the exhaust pipe bracket to the oil pan.

44. Install the starter cable to the starter motor terminal. Refill the engine oil and the transaxle lubricant.

45. Lower the car from the jackstands.

46. Remove the engine support sling.

47. Reconnect the power steering lines at the pump. Install the hose support bracket to the cylinder head.

48. Reconnect the fuel supply and return lines. Reconnect the thermactor pump discharge hose at the pump.

49. On automatic transaxle models reconnect the TV (throttle valve) linkage at the transaxle. On manual transaxle models reconnect the clutch cable to the lever at the transaxle.

50. Install the hoses to the compressor. Reconnect all electrical harness connections, linkage and vacuum lines to the engine. Be sure the air conditioning system is properly and safely recharged.

51. Reconnect and install the coil to the cylinder head. Reconnect the cooling fan wiring harness. Install the radiator shroud and electric fan as an assembly.

52. Install the upper and lower radiator hoses. On models equipped with an automatic transaxle, reconnect and plug the oil cooler lines to the rubber connectors at the radiator.

53. Reconnect the lower radiator hose to the radiator. Refill the cooling system.

54. Reconnect the battery cables to the battery. Install the air cleaner assembly.

55. Install the hood.

## Rocker Arms

### *REMOVAL AND INSTALLATION*

#### Gasoline Engines

1. Disconnect the negative battery cable. Remove the air cleaner and air inlet duct. Disconnect and label all hoses and wires connected to or crossing the valve cover. Remove the cover.

2. On 1.6 & 1.9L engines, remove the rocker arm nuts and discard. On 2.3L HSC engines, remove the rocker bolts and fulcrums. Remove the rocker arms. Keep all parts in order; they must be returned to their original positions.

3. Before installation, coat the valve tips and the rocker arm contact areas with Lubriplate<sup>ж</sup> or the equivalent.

4. Rotate the engine until the lifter is on the base circle of the cam (valve closed).

CAUTION: *On 1.6 & 1.9L engines, turn the engine only in the direction of normal rotation. Backward rotation will cause the camshaft belt to slip or lose teeth, altering valve timing and causing serious engine damage.*

5. Install the rocker arm and new hex flange nuts or fulcrum and bolt. Be sure the lifter is on the base circle of the cam for each rocker arm as it is installed.

6. Clean the valve cover mating surfaces. Apply a bead of sealer to the cover flange and install the cover. Install all disconnected hoses and wires.

### *TAPPET CLEARANCE*

NOTE: *For 2.3L HSC engine refer to illustration provided for procedure. Tappet gap should be 0.072–0.174.*

The 1.6 & 1.9L engine is a cam in head engine with hydraulic tappets.

Valve stem to valve rocker arm clearance should be within specifications with the tappet completely collapsed. Repeated valve reconditioning operations (valve and/or valve seat refacing) will decrease the clearance to the point that if not compensated for, the tappet will cease to function and the valve will be held open.

To determine the rocker arm-to-tappet clearance, make the following check:

1. Connect an auxiliary starter switch in the starting circuit. Crank the engine with the ignition switch Off until No. 1 piston is on TDC after the compression stroke.

2. With the crankshaft in the position designated in Steps 3 and 4, position the hydraulic lifter compressor tool on the rocker arm. Slowly apply pressure to bleed down the tappet until it is completely bottomed. Hold the tappet in this position and check the available clearance between the rocker arm and the valve stem tip with a feeler gauge. The feeler gauge width must not exceed ⅜″ (9.5mm), in order to fit between the rails on the rocker arm. If the clearance is less than specifications, check the following for wear:

- Fulcrum.
- Tappet.
- Cam lobe.
- Valve tip.

3. With the No. 1 piston on TDC at the end of the compression stroke (Position No. 1), check the following valves:

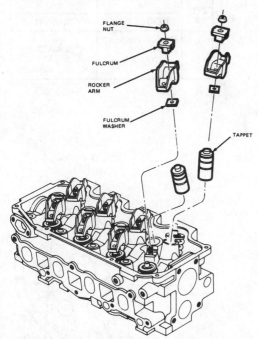

**Exploded view of the upper valve train—1.6L, 1.9L engines**

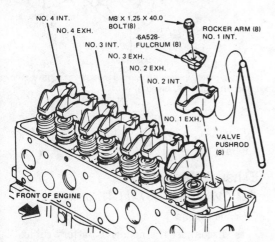

**Valve train components—2.3L HSC**

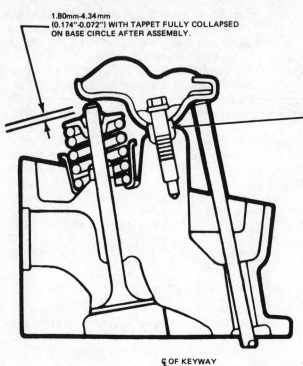

| | CAMSHAFT POSITION | |
|---|---|---|
| CYL. NO. | A | B |
| | TIGHTEN FULCRUM BOLTS AS NOTED | |
| 1 | INTAKE -EXHAUST | — |
| 2 | INTAKE | EXHAUST |
| 3 | EXHAUST | INTAKE |
| 4 | — | INTAKE - EXHAUST |

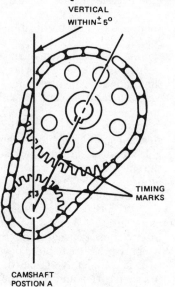

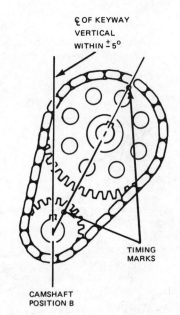

Checking the collapsed tappet gap on 2.3L HSC engine

• No. 1 Intake No. 1 Exhaust.
• No. 2 Intake.

4. Rotate the crankshaft to Position No. 2 and check the following valves:

• No. 3 Intake No. 3 Exhaust.

5. Rotate the crankshaft another 180° from Position No. 2 back to TDC and check the following valves:

• No. 4 Intake No. 4 Exhaust.
• No. 2 Exhaust.

Collapsed tappet clearance should be 1.50–4.93mm (0.59–0.194").

## Exhaust Manifold

### REMOVAL AND INSTALLATION

#### Gasoline Engine

1. Disconnect the negative battery cable.
2. Remove the air cleaner duct for access to the manifold.

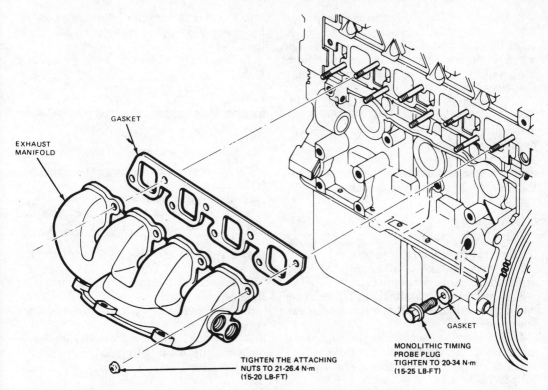

GASKET

EXHAUST
MANIFOLD

TIGHTEN THE ATTACHING
NUTS TO 21-26.4 N·m
(15-20 LB-FT)

GASKET

MONOLITHIC TIMING
PROBE PLUG
TIGHTEN TO 20-34 N·m
(15-25 LB-FT)

**Install the exhaust manifold and tighten the retaining bolts in the sequence shown—1.6L, 1.9L engines**

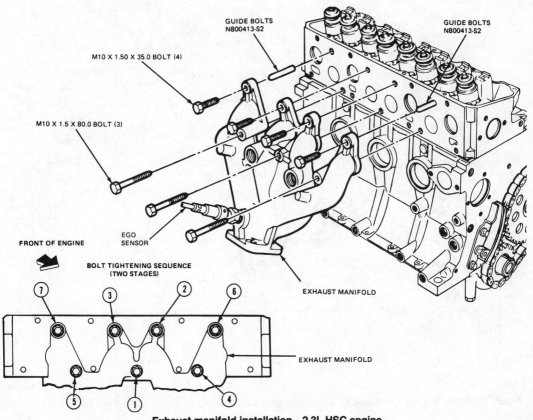

GUIDE BOLTS
N800413-S2

GUIDE BOLTS
N800413-S2

M10 X 1.50 X 35.0 BOLT (4)

M10 X 1.5 X 80.0 BOLT (3)

FRONT OF ENGINE

EGO
SENSOR

EXHAUST MANIFOLD

BOLT TIGHTENING SEQUENCE
(TWO STAGES)

EXHAUST MANIFOLD

**Exhaust manifold installation—2.3L HSC engine**

3. Disconnect the Thermactor (air pump) line from the manifold. Disconnect the EGR tube. Remove heat shield. Disconnect sensor wire if equipped. Unbolt the exhaust pipe from the manifold flange. Remove the turbocharger, if equipped.

4. Unbolt and remove the exhaust manifold.

5. Clean the manifold and cylinder head mating surfaces. Place a new gasket on the exhaust pipe-to-manifold flange.

6. Install the manifold. Tighten the bolts in a circular pattern, working from the center to the ends, in three progressive steps.

### Diesel Engine

1. Remove the nuts attaching the muffler inlet pipe to the exhaust manifold.

2. Remove the bolts attaching the heat shield to the exhaust manifold.

3. Remove the nuts attaching the exhaust manifold to cylinder head and remove the exhaust manifold.

4. Install the exhaust manifold, using new gaskets, and tighten nuts to 16–20 ft.lb.

5. Install the exhaust shield and tighten bolts to 12–16 ft.lb.

6. Connect the muffler inlet pipe to the exhaust manifold and tighten the nuts to 25–35 ft.lb.

7. Run the engine and check for exhaust leaks.

## Intake Manifold

### REMOVAL AND INSTALLATION

#### Gasoline Engine — Except Fuel Injection

1. Disconnect the negative battery terminal.

2. Remove the air cleaner housing.

3. Partially drain the cooling system and disconnect the heater hose from under the intake manifold.

4. Disconnect and label all vacuum and electrical connections.

5. Disconnect the fuel line and carburetor linkage.

6. Disconnect the EGR vacuum hose and supply tube.

7. On Escort & Lynx models, jack up the vehicle and support it with jackstands.

8. On Escort & Lynx models, remove the bottom (3) intake manifold nuts.

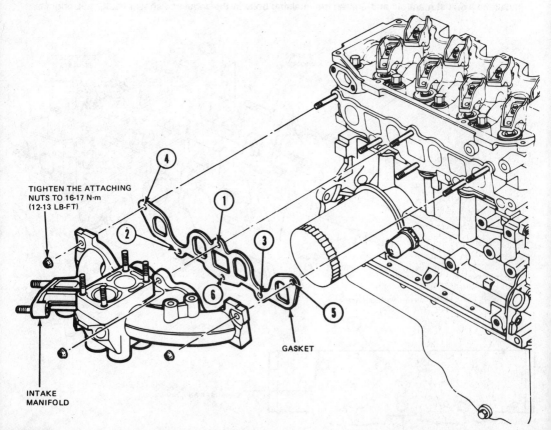

TIGHTEN THE ATTACHING NUTS TO 16-17 N·m (12-13 LB-FT)

GASKET

INTAKE MANIFOLD

Install the intake manifold and tighten the retaining bolts in the sequence shown—1.6L, 1.9L carbureted engines

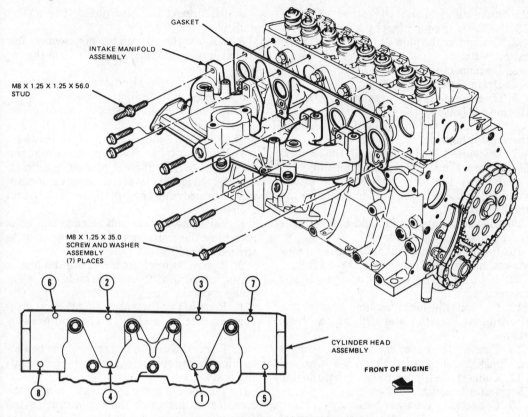

GASKET

INTAKE MANIFOLD ASSEMBLY

M8 X 1.25 X 1.25 X 56.0 STUD

M8 X 1.25 X 35.0 SCREW AND WASHER ASSEMBLY (7) PLACES

CYLINDER HEAD ASSEMBLY

FRONT OF ENGINE

**Intake manifold installation—2.3L HSC engine**

9. On Escort & Lynx models, remove the vehicle from the jackstands.

10. If equipped with automatic transmission disconnect the throttle valve linkage at the carburetor and remove the cable bracket attaching bolts.

11. If equipped with power steering (Escort/Lynx), remove the thermactor pump drive belt, the pump, the mounting bracket, and the by-pass hose.

12. Remove the fuel pump (Escort/Lynx). See the fuel pump removal procedure.

13. Remove the intake bolts, the manifold, and gasket.

NOTE: *Do not lay the intake manifold flat as the gasket surfaces may be damaged.*

**To install:**

14. Install the intake manifold, and gasket.

15. Install the fuel pump (Escort/Lynx).

16. If equipped with power steering (Escort/Lynx), install the thermactor pump drive belt, the pump, the mounting bracket, and the by-pass hose.

17. If equipped with automatic transmission reconnect the throttle valve linkage at the carburetor and install the cable bracket attaching bolts.

18. On Escort & Lynx models, jack up the vehicle and support it with jackstands.

19. On Escort & Lynx models, install the bottom (3) intake manifold nuts.

20. On Escort & Lynx models, remove the vehicle from the jackstands.

21. Reconnect the EGR vacuum hose and supply tube.

22. Reconnect the fuel line and carburetor linkage.

23. Reconnect all vacuum and electrical connections.

24. Reconnect the heater hose to under the intake manifold and refill the cooling system.

25. Install the air cleaner housing.

26. Reconnect the negative battery terminal.

**Gasoline Engine w/Fuel Injection**

NOTE: *The intake manifold is a two piece aluminum casting, with separate upper and lower pieces. Service procedures are found in Chapter 4 under the Fuel Injection section.*

**Diesel Engine**

1. Disconnect the air inlet duct from the intake manifold and install the protective cap in

the intake manifold (part or Protective Cap Set T84P-9395-A or equivalent).

2. Disconnect the glow plug resistor electrical connector.

3. Disconnect the breather hose.

4. Drain the cooling system.

5. Disconnect the upper radiator hose at the thermostat housing.

6. Disconnect the tow coolant hoses at the thermostat housing.

7. Disconnect the connectors to the temperature sensors in the thermostat housing.

8. Remove the bolts attaching the intake manifold to the cylinder head and remove the intake manifold.

9. Clean the intake manifold and cylinder head gasket mating surfaces.

10. Install the intake manifold, using a new gasket, and tighten the bolts to 12–16 ft.lb.

11. Connect the temperature sensor connectors.

12. Connect the lower coolant hose to the thermostat housing and tighten the hose clamp.

13. Connect the upper coolant tube, using a new gasket and tighten bolts to 5–7 ft.lb.

14. Connect the upper radiator hose to the thermostat housing.

15. Connect the breather hose.

16. Connect the glow plug resistor electrical connector.

17. Remove the protective cap and install the air inlet duct.

18. Fill and bleed the cooling system.

19. Run the engine and check for intake air leaks and coolant leaks.

## Turbocharger

### REMOVAL AND INSTALLATION

1. Allow engine to cool. Disconnect intake hose between turbocharger and injector unit.

2. Disconnect oil supply lines.

3. Unbolt exhaust pipe. Disconnect sensors.

4. Loosen and remove mounting bolts. Remove turbocharger.

5. Install in the reverse order.

NOTE: *When installing the turbocharger, or after an oil and filter change, disconnect the coil wire to the distributor and crank the engine with the starter motor until the oil pressure light on the dash goes out. Oil pressure must be up before starting the engine.*

## Air Conditioning Compressor

### REMOVAL AND INSTALLATION

#### ESCORT/EXP AND LYNX/LN7

*1981–83*

1. Discharge the system following the recommended service procedures in Chapter 1. Observe all safety precautions.

2. Disconnect the alternator wire at the multiple connector.

3. Remove the carburetor air cleaner and the air intake and tube assembly from the radiator support.

4. Disconnect the alternator air tube from the air inlet on the radiator support.

5. Remove the alternator from the engine.

6. Disconnect the compressor clutch wires at the field coil connector on the compressor.

7. Disconnect the discharge hose and the suction hose from the compressor manifolds. Cap the refrigerant lines and compressor manifolds to prevent the entrance of dirt and moisture.

8. Raise the vehicle and remove two bolts attaching the front legs of the compressor to the mounting bracket.

9. Remove two screws attaching the heater water return tube to the underside of the engine supports.

10. Remove two bolts attaching the compressor bracket assembly to the compressor bracket.

11. Lower the vehicle and remove one bolt attaching the top of the compressor to the mounting bracket.

12. Tilt the top of the compressor toward the radiator to disengage the top mounting tab from the compressor bracket. Then, lift the compressor from the engine compartment, rear head first.

13. If the compressor is to be replaced, remove the clutch and field coil assembly and the compressor bracket assembly from the compressor.

14. Installation is the reverse of the removal procedure.

*1984–87*

1. Disconnect the alternator wires at the multiple connector and remove the alternator from the engine.

2. Discharge the A/C system and disconnect the compressor clutch wires at the field coil connector on the compressor.

3. On the 1.6L EFI and HO engines, remove the discharge and suction hoses at the compressor manifolds.

4. On the 1.6L Turbo and 2.0L Diesel engines, remove the discharge hose from the manifold tube with a ½" lock coupling tool (#T81P-19623-G2 or equivalent). Use a ⅝" spring lock coupling tool (#T83P-19632-C or equivalent) to remove the suction hose.

5. Remove the four retaining bolts attaching the compressor to the compressor bracket and remove the compressor from the engine compartment.

6. Installation is the reverse of the removal procedure.

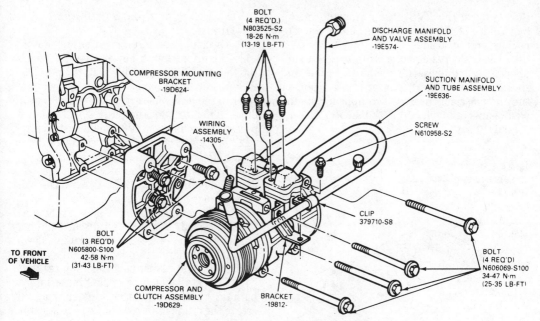

**Escort/Lynx compressor mounting—typical**

## TEMPO/TOPAZ

1. Discharge the system following the recommended service procedures in Chapter 1. Observe all safety precautions.

2. Disconnect the compressor clutch wires at the field coil connector on the compressor.

3. Disconnect the discharge hose and the suction hose from the compressor manifolds. Cap the refrigerant lines and compressor manifolds to prevent the entrance of dirt and moisture.

4. Separate the discharge refrigerant line at the spring lock coupling above the compressor with Tool T81P–19623–G or equivalent and remove the lower end of the discharge line.

5. Loosen the two idler attaching screws and release the compressor belt tension.

6. Raise the vehicle and remove the four bolts attaching the front legs of the compressor to the mounting bracket.

7. Remove two screws attaching the heater water return tube to the underside of the engine supports.

8. Move the compressor to the left and remove the compressor from the underside of the vehicle.

9. If the compressor is to be replaced, remove the clutch and field coil assembly from the compressor.

10. Installation is the reverse of the removal procedure. If the compressor is to be replaced, drain the oil from the removed compressor into a calibrated measuring container. Record the amount of oil (fluid ounces) drained from the old compressor, discard the oil. Check the system for proper operation.

## Cylinder Head

### *REMOVAL AND INSTALLATION*

#### 1.6 & 1.9L Engine

NOTE: *The engine must be overnight cold before removing the cylinder head, to reduce the possibility of warpage or distortion.*
CAUTION: *Always use new head bolts when reinstalling the cylinder head.*

1. Disconnect the negative battery cable.

2. Drain the cooling system, disconnect the heater hose under the intake manifold, and disconnect the radiator upper hose at the cylinder head.

3. Disconnect the wiring from the cooling fan switch, remove the air cleaner assembly, remove the PCV hose, and disconnect all interfering vacuum hoses after marking them for reassembly.

4. Remove the valve cover and disconnect all accessory drive belts. Remove the crankshaft pulley. Remove the timing belt cover.

5. Set the No.1 cylinder to top dead center compression stroke. See distributor removal and installation procedure for details.

6. Remove the distributor cap and spark plug wires as an assembly.

7. Loosen both belt tensioner attaching bolts using special Ford tool T81P-6254-A or the equivalent. Secure the belt tensioner as far left as possible. Remove the timing belt and discard.

NOTE: *Once the tension on the timing belt has been released, the belt cannot be used again.*

8. Disconnect the tube at the EGR valve,

then remove the PVS hose connectors using tool T81P-8564-A or equivalent. Label the connectors and set aside.

9. Disconnect the choke wire, the fuel supply and return lines, the accelerator cable and speed control cable (if equipped). Disconnect the altitude compensator, if equipped, from the dash panel and place on the heater/AC air intake.

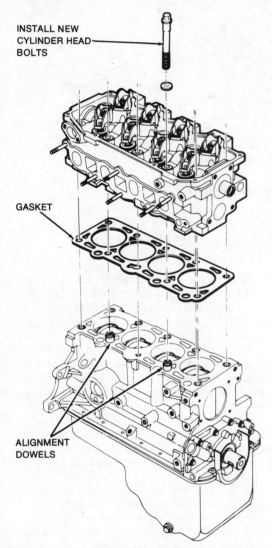

INSTALL NEW CYLINDER HEAD BOLTS

GASKET

ALIGNMENT DOWELS

**1.6L and 1.9L cylinder head installation**

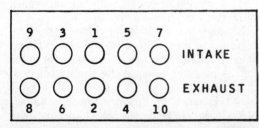

| 9 | 3 | 1 | 5 | 7 | INTAKE |
|---|---|---|---|---|---|
| 8 | 6 | 2 | 4 | 10 | EXHAUST |

**Tightening sequence for the 1.6L, 1.9L cylinder head**

NOTE: *Use caution not to damage the compensator.*

10. Disconnect and remove the alternator.

11. If equipped with power steering, remove the thermactor pump drive belt, the pump and its bracket. If equipped with a turbocharger, refer to the previous section for removal procedure. Refer to the Fuel Injection section for pressure discharge and removal instructions.

12. Raise the vehicle and disconnect the exhaust pipe from the manifold.

13. Lower the vehicle and remove the cylinder head bolts and washers. Discard the bolts, they cannot be used again.

14. Remove the cylinder head with the manifolds attached. Remove and discard the head gasket. Do not place the cylinder head with combustion chambers down or damage to the spark plugs or gasket surfaces may result.

15. To install, clean all gasket material from both the block face and the cylinder head, then rotate the crankshaft so that the No. 1 piston is 90° BTDC. In this position, the crankshaft pulley keyway is at 9 o'clock. Turn the camshaft so its keyway is at 6 o'clock. When installing the timing belt, turn the crankshaft keyway back to 12 o'clock but do not turn the camshaft from its 6 o'clock position. The crankshaft is turned 90° BTDC to prevent the valves from hitting the pistons when the cylinder head is installed.

16. Position the cylinder head gasket on the block and install the cylinder head using new bolts and washers. Tighten the bolts to 44 ft.lb. in the sequence shown, then back off 2 turns and retighten to 44 ft.lb. After tightening, turn the bolts an additional 90° in the same sequence. Complete the bolt tightening by turning an additional 90° in the same sequence.

17. Remaining installation is the reverse of removal. See Timing Belt Removal and Installation for timing belt installation procedures. Fill the cooling system only with Ford Cooling System Fluid, Prestone II or the equivalent. Using the wrong type of coolant can damage the engine.

### 2.3L HSC Engine

1. Disconnect the negative battery cable. Drain the cooling system by disconnecting the lower radiator hose.

2. Disconnect the heater hose at the fitting under the intake manifold. Disconnect the upper radiator hose at the cylinder head connector.

3. Disconnect the electric cooling fan switch at the plastic connector. Remove the air cleaner assembly. Label and disconnect any vacuum lines that will interfere with cylinder head removal.

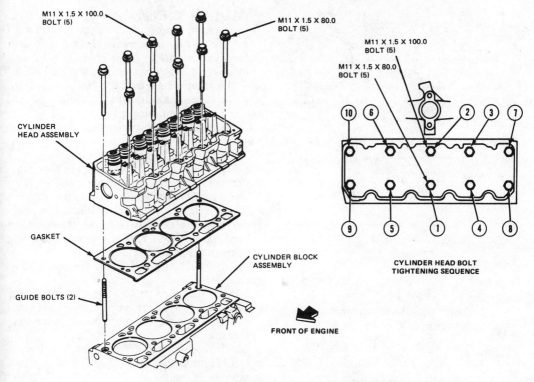

M11 X 1.5 X 100.0 BOLT (5)

M11 X 1.5 X 80.0 BOLT (5)

M11 X 1.5 X 100.0 BOLT (5)

M11 X 1.5 X 80.0 BOLT (5)

CYLINDER HEAD ASSEMBLY

GASKET

CYLINDER BLOCK ASSEMBLY

GUIDE BOLTS (2)

CYLINDER HEAD BOLT TIGHTENING SEQUENCE

FRONT OF ENGINE

**Torque sequence, cylinder head installation—2.3L HSC**

4. Disconnect all drive belts. Remove rocker arm cover. Remove the distributor cap and spark plug wires as an assembly.

5. Disconnect the EGR tube at EGR valve. Disconnect the choke wire from the choke.

6. Disconnect the fuel supply and return lines at the rubber connector. Disconnect the accelerator cable and speed control cable, if equipped. Loosen the bolts retaining the thermactor pump pulley.

7. Raise and safely support the front of the car. Disconnect the exhaust pipe from the exhaust manifold. Lower car.

8. Loosen the rocker arm bolts until the arms can pivot for pushrod removal. Remove the pushrods. Keep the pushrods in order for installation in original position.

9. Remove the cylinder head bolts. Remove the cylinder head, gasket, thermactor pump, intake and exhaust manifolds as an assembly. Do not lay the cylinder head down flat before removing the spark plugs. Take care not to damage the gasket surface.

10. Clean all gasket material from the head and block surfaces.

11. Position a new head gasket on the block surface. Do not use a sealer, unless directions with gasket specify.

12. To help with head installation alignment, purchase two head bolts and cut off the heads. Install the modified bolts at opposite corners of the block to act as guides.

13. Position the cylinder head over the guide bolts and lower onto the engine block.

14. Install head bolts, remove the guides and replace with regular bolts.

15. Tighten the heads bolts to 53–59 ft.lb. in two stages in the sequence shown.

16. The rest of the cylinder head installation is in the reverse order of removal.

### Diesel Engine

1. Disconnect the battery ground cable from the battery, which is located in the luggage compartment.

2. Drain the cooling system.

3. Remove the camshaft cover, front and rear timing bolt covers, and front and rear timing belts.

4. Raise the vehicle and safely support on jackstands.

5. Disconnect the muffler inlet pipe at the exhaust manifold. Lower the vehicle.

6. Disconnect the air inlet duct at the air cleaner and intake manifold. Install a protective cover.

7. Disconnect the electrical connectors and vacuum hoses to the temperature sensors located in the thermostat housing.

8. Disconnect the upper and lower coolant

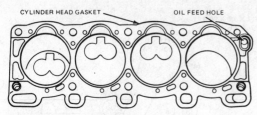

CYLINDER HEAD GASKET          OIL FEED HOLE

**Head gasket installation**

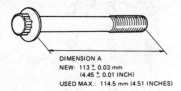

DIMENSION A
NEW: 113 ± 0.03 mm
(4.45 ± 0.01 INCH)
USED MAX.: 114.5 mm (4.51 INCHES)

**Head bolt dimension**

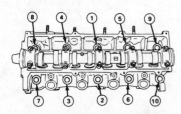

**Torque sequence, cylinder head installation**

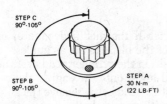

STEP C
90°-105°

STEP B
90°-105°

STEP A
30 N·m
(22 LB-FT)

**Head bolt tightening steps**

hoses, and the upper radiator hose at the thermostat housing.

9. Disconnect and remove the injection lines at the injection pump and nozzles. Cap all lines and fittings with Cap Protective Set T84P-9395-A or equivalent.

10. Disconnect the glow plug harness from the main engine harness.

11. Remove the cylinder head bolts in the sequence shown. Remove the cylinder head.

12. Remove the glow plugs. Then, remove prechamber cups from the cylinder head using a brass drift.

13. Clean the prechamber cups, prechambers in the cylinder head and the cylinder head and crankcase gasket mating surfaces.

14. Install the prechambers in the cylinder heads, making sure the locating pins are aligned with the slots provided.

15. Install the glow plugs and tighten to 11–15 ft.lb. Connect glow plug harness to the glow plugs. Tighten the nuts to 5–7 ft.lb.

CAUTION: *Carefully blow out the head bolt threads in the crankcase with compressed air. Failure to thoroughly clean the thread bores can result in incorrect cylinder head torque or possible cracking of the crankcase.*

16. Position a new cylinder head gasket on the crankcase making sure the cylinder head oil feed hold is not blocked.

17. Measure each cylinder head bolt dimension A. If the measurement is more than 114.5mm (4.51"), replace the head bolt.

CAUTION: *Rotate the camshaft in the cylinder head until the cam lobes for No. 1 cylinder are at the base circle (both valves closed). Then, rotate the crankshaft clockwise until No. 1 piston is halfway up in the cylinder bore toward TDC. This is to prevent contact between the pistons and valves.*

18. Install the cylinder head on the crankcase.

NOTE: *Before installing the cylinder head bolts, paint a white reference dot on each one, and apply a light coat of engine oil on the bolt threads.*

19. Tighten cylinder head bolts as follows:

a. Tighten bolts to 22 ft.lb. in the sequence shown.

b. Using the painted reference marks, tighten each bolt in sequence, another 90°–105°.

c. Repeat Step b turning the bolts another 90°–105°.

20. Connect the glow plug harness to main engine harness.

21. Remove the protective caps and install injection lines to the injection pump and nozzles. Tighten capnuts to 18–22 ft.lb.

22. Air bleed the system.

23. Connect the upper (with a new gasket) and lower coolant hoses, and the upper radiator hose to the thermostat housing. Tighten upper coolant hose bolts to 5–7 ft.lb.

24. Connect the electrical connectors and the vacuum hoses to the temperature sensors in the thermostat housing.

25. Remove the protective cover and install the air inlet duct to the intake manifold and air cleaner.

26. Raise vehicle and support on jackstands. Connect the muffler inlet pipe to the exhaust manifold. Tighten nuts to 25–35 ft.lb.

27. Lower the vehicle.

28. Install and adjust the front timing belt.

29. Install and adjust the rear timing belt.

30. Install the front upper timing belt cover and rear timing belt cover. Tighten the bolts to 5–7 ft.lb.

31. Check and adjust the valves as outlined. Install the valve cover and tighten the bolts to 5–7 ft.lb.

32. Fill and bleed the cooling system.

33. Check and adjust the injection pump timing.

34. Connect battery ground cable to battery. Run engine and check for oil, fuel and coolant leaks.

### OVERHAUL

1. Remove the cylinder head form the car engine (see Cylinder Head Removal and Installation). Place the head on a workbench and remove any manifolds that are still connnected. Remove all rocker arm retaining parts and the rocker arms, if still installed or the camshaft (see Camshaft Removal).

2. Turn the cylinder head over so that the mounting surface is facing up and support evenly on wooden blocks.

CAUTION: *If an aluminum cylinder head, exercise care when cleaning.*

3. Use a scraper and remove all of the gasket material stuck to the head mounting surface. Mount a wire carbon removal brush in an electric drill and clean away the carbon on the valves and head combustion chambers.

CAUTION: *When scraping or decarbonizing the cylinder head take care not to damage or nick the gasket mounting surface.*

4. Number the valve heads with a permanent felt-tip marker for cylinder location.

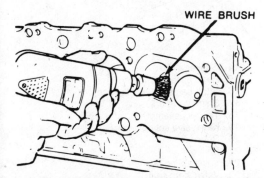

**Remove the carbon from cylinder head with a wire brush and electric drill**

### RESURFACING

If the cylinder head is warped resurfacing by a machine shop is required. Place a straightedge across the gasket surface of the head. Using feeler gauges, determine the clearance at the center and along the length between the head and straightedge. Measure clearance at the center and along the lengths of both diagonals. If warpage exceeds 0.003″ (0.076mm) in a 6″ (152mm) span, or 0.006″ (0.15mm) over the total length the cylinder head must be resurfaced.

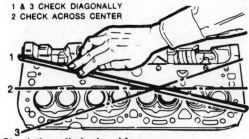

1 & 3 CHECK DIAGONALLY
2 CHECK ACROSS CENTER

**Check the cylinder head for warpage**

## Valves and Springs

### REMOVAL AND INSTALLATION

1. Block the head on its side, or install a pair of head-holding brackets made especially for valve removal.

2. Use a socket slightly larger than the valve stem and keepers, place the socket over the valve stem and gently hit the socket with a plastic hammer to break loose any varnish buildup.

3. Remove the valve keepers, retainer, spring shield and valve spring using a valve spring compressor (the locking C-clamp type is the easiest kind to use).

4. Put the parts in a separate container numbered for the cylinder being worked on. Do not mix them with other parts removed.

5. Remove and discard the valve stem oil seal, a new seal will be used at assembly time.

6. Remove the valve from the cylinder head and place, in order, through numbered holes punched in a stiff piece of cardboard or wooden valve holding stick.

NOTE: *The exhaust valve stems, on some engines, are equipped with small metal caps. Take care not to lose the caps. Make sure to reinstall them at assembly time. Replace any caps that are worn.*

7. Use an electric drill and rotary wire brush to clean the intake and exhaust valve ports, combustion chamber and valve seats. In some cases, the carbon will need to be chipped away. Use a blunt pointed drift for carbon chipping, be careful around the valve seat areas.

8. Use a wire valve guide cleaning brush and safe solvent to clean the valve guides.

9. Clean the valves with a revolving wire brush. Heavy carbon deposits may be removed with the blunt drift.

NOTE: *When using a wire brush to clean carbon on the valve ports, valves etc., be sure that the deposits are actually removed, rather than burnished.*

10. Wash and clean all valve spring, keepers, retaining caps etc., in safe solvent.

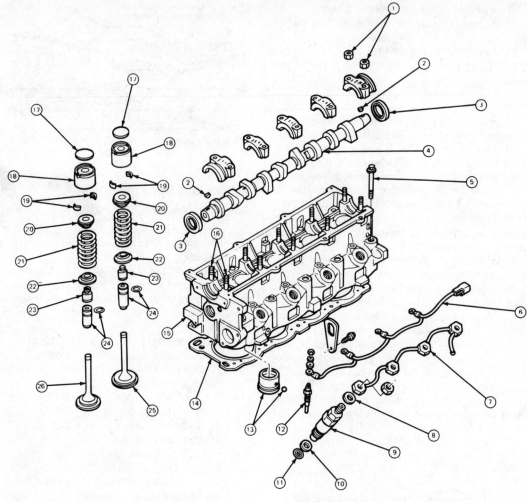

1. Nut
2. Woodruff key
3. Seal
4. Camshaft
5. Bolt
6. Glow plug harness
7. Fuel return pipe
8. Washer
9. Injector nozzle
10. Washer
11. Gasket
12. Glow plug
13. Insert assembly (combusion chamber)
14. Gasket
15. Head assembly (cylinder)
16. Stud (camshaft bearing cap)
17. Shim, valve adjusting
18. Tappet assembly
19. Key (valve spring retaining)
20. Retainer
21. Spring
22. Valve spring seat
23. Valve stem seal
24. Valve guide assembly
25. Exhaust valve
26. Intake valve

**Diesel engine, cylinder head components**

11. Clean the head with a brush and some safe solvent and wipe dry.

12. Check the head for cracks. Cracks in the cylinder head usually start around an exhaust valve seat because it is the hottest part of the combustion chamber. If a crack is suspected buy cannot be detected visually have the area checked with dye penetrant or other method by the machine shop.

13. After all cylinder head parts are reason-

ably clean check the valve stem-to-guide clearance. If a dial indicator is not on hand, a visual inspection can give you a fairly good idea if the guide, valve stem or both are worn.

14. Insert the valve into the guide until slightly away from the valve seat. Wiggle the valve sideways. A small amount of wobble is normal, excessive wobble means a worn guide or valve stem. If a dial indicator is on hand, mount the indicator so that the stem of the

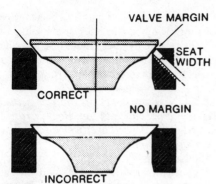

**Valve seat width and centering**

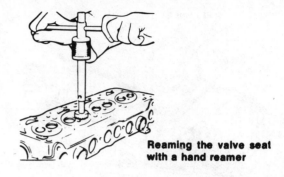

**Reaming the valve seat with a hand reamer**

valve is at 90° to the valve stem, as close to the valve guide as possible. Move the valve off the seat, and measure the valve guide-to-stem clearance by rocking the stem back and forth to actuate the dial indicator. Measure the valve stem using a micrometer and compare to specifications to determine whether stem or guide wear is causing excessive clearance.

15. The valve guide, if worn, must be repaired before the valve seats can be resurfaced. Ford supplies valves with oversize stems to fit valve guides that are reamed to oversize for repair. The machine shop will be able to handle the guide reaming for you. In some cases, if the guide is not too badly worn, knurling may be all that is required.

16. Reface, or have the valves and valve seats refaced. The valve seats should be a true 45° angle. Remove only enough material to clean up any pits or grooves. Be sure the valve seat is not too wide or narrow. Use a 60° grinding wheel to remove material from the bottom of the seat for raising and a 30° grinding wheel to remove material from the top of the seat to narrow.

17. After the valves are refaced by machine, hand lap them to the valve seat. Clean the grinding compound off and check the position of face-to-seat contact. Contact should be close to the center of the valve face. If contact is close to the top edge of the valve narrow the seat; if too close to the bottom edge, raise the seat.

18. Valves should be refaced to a true angle of 44°. Remove only enough metal to clean up the valve face or to correct runout. If the edge of the valve head, after machining, is $\frac{1}{32}''$ (0.8mm) or less replace the valve. The tip of the valve stem should also be dressed on the valve grinding machine, however, do not remove more than 0.010″ (0.25mm).

19. After all valve and valve seats have been machined, check the remaining valve train parts (springs, retainers, keepers, etc.) for wear. Check the valve springs for straightness and tension.

20. Reassemble the head in the reverse order of disassembly using new valve guide seals and lubricating the valve stems. Check the valve spring installed height, shim or replace as necessary.

### CHECKING VALVE SPRINGS

Place the valve spring on a flat surface next to a carpenters square. Measure the height of the spring, and rotate the spring against the edge of the square to measure distortion. If the spring height varies (by comparison) by more than $\frac{1}{16}''$ (1.6mm) or if the distortion exceeds $\frac{1}{16}''$ (1.6mm), replace the spring.

Have the valve springs tested for spring pressure at the installed and compressed (installed height minus valve lift) height using a valve spring tester. Springs should be within one pound, plus or minus each other. Replace spring as necessary.

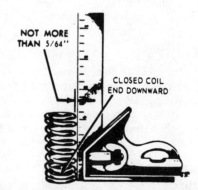

**Check the valve spring free length and squareness**

### VALVE SPRING INSTALLED HEIGHT

After installing the valve spring, measure the distance between the spring mounting pad and the lower edge of the spring retainer. Compare the measurement to specifications. If the installed height is incorrect, add shim washers between the spring mounting pad and the spring. Use only washers designed for valve springs, available at most parts houses.

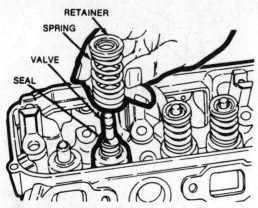

Install valve stem oil seals

## VALVE STEM OIL SEALS

Most engines are equipped with a positive valve stem seal using a Teflon® insert. Teflon® seals are available for other engines buy usually require valve guide machining, consult your automotive machine shop for advice on having positive valve stem oil seals installed.

When installing valve stem oil seals, ensure that a small amount of oil is able to pass the seal to lubricate the valve stems and guide walls; otherwise, excessive wear will occur.

## VALVE SEATS

If a valve seat is damaged or burnt and cannot be serviced by refacing, it may be possible to have the seat machined and an insert installed. Consult the automotive machine shop for their advice.

NOTE: *The aluminum heads on V6 engines are equipped with inserts.*

## VALVE GUIDES

Worn valve guides can, in most cases, be reamed to accept a valve with an oversized stem. Valve guides that are not excessively worn or distorted may, in some cases, be knurled rather than reamed. However, if the valve stem is worn reaming for an oversized valve stem is the answer since a new valve would be required.

Knurling is a process in which metal is displaced and raised, thereby reducing clearance. Knurling also produces excellent oil control. The possibility of knurling instead of reaming the valve guides should be discussed with a machinist.

## Timing Belt

### CHECKING ENGINE TIMING

#### 1.6 & 1.9L Engine

Should the camshaft drive belt jump timing by a tooth or two, the engine could still run, although very poorly. To visually check for correct timing, remove the No.1 spark plug and place your thumb over the hole. Use a wrench on the crankshaft pulley bolt to rotate the engine to TDC of the compression stroke for No. 1 cylinder.

CAUTION: *Turn the crankshaft only in the direction of normal rotation. Backward rotation will cause the belt to slip or lose teeth, altering engine timing.*

As the No. 1 piston rises on the compression stroke, your thumb will be pushed out by compression pressure. At the same time, the timing notch on the crankshaft pulley will be approaching the **0**, or **TDC**, mark on the timing degree scale molded into the camshaft belt cover. Continue to turn the crankshaft until the pulley mark and **0** mark are aligned, indicating that No. 1 cylinder is at TDC.

Remove the alternator drive belt, and the power steering pump and air conditioning compressor drive belts, if so equipped. Remove the camshaft belt cover.

The camshaft sprocket has a mark next to one of the holes. The cylinder head is similarly marked. These marks should be aligned, dot-to-dot, indicating that camshaft timing is correct.

NOTE: *As a further check, the distributor cap can be removed. The ignition rotor should be pointing toward the No. 1 spark plug tower in the cap.*

If the marks are aligned, the engine timing is correct. If not, the belt must be removed from the cam sprocket and the camshaft turned until its marks are aligned (crankshaft still at TDC).

CAUTION: *Never attempt to rotate the engine by means of the camshaft sprocket. The 2:1 ratio between the camshaft and crankshaft sprockets will place a severe strain on the belt, stretching or tearing it.*

### REMOVAL AND INSTALLATION

NOTE: *With the timing belt removed and pistons at TDC, do not rotate the camshaft for fear of bending the valves. If the camshaft must be rotated, align the crankshaft pulley 90° BTDC. When actually installing the belt, the crankshaft pulley must be at TDC.*

1. Disconnect the negative battery cable. Remove all accessory drive belts and remove the timing belt cover.

NOTE: *Align the timing mark on the camshaft sprocket with the timing mark on the cylinder head.*

2. After aligning the camshaft timing marks, reinstall the timing belt cover and confirm that the timing mark on the crankshaft

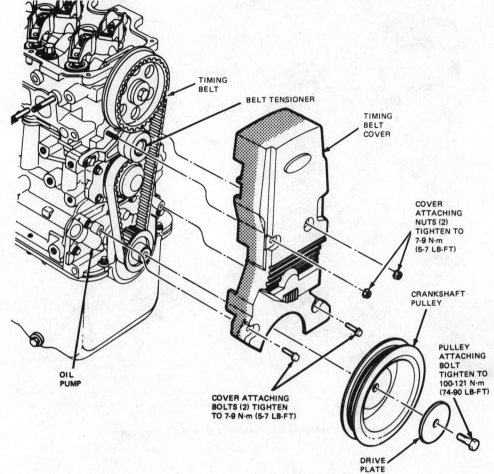

**Timing cover and parts—1.6L and 1.9L engines**

pulley aligns with the TDC mark on the front cover. Remove the timing belt cover.

3. Loosen both timing belt attaching bolts using tool T81P-6254-A or equivalent. Pry the tensioner away from the belt as far as possible and hold it in that position by tightening one of the tensioner attaching bolts.

NOTE: *Due to limited working space, special tools are required to remove the crankshaft pulley. Crankshaft wrench (Ford) tool number YA826 (to hold the pulley stationary) and crankshaft pulley wrench (Ford) T81P6312A or equivalents will make the job easier.*

4. Remove the crankshaft pulley and remove and discard the timing belt.

5. To install new belt, fit the timing belt over the gears in a counterclockwise direction starting at the crankshaft. Ensure that belt span between crankshaft and camshaft is kept tight as belt is installed over remaining gears.

6. Loosen belt tensioner attaching bolts and allow tensioner to extend against the belt.

7. Tighten one tensioner attaching bolt using special tool mentioned earlier or its equivalent.

8. Install the crankshaft pulley, drive plate and pulley attaching bolt.

9. Hold the crankshaft pulley stationary using tool YA-826 or equivalent and torque pulley bolt to 74–90 ft.lb.

10. Disconnect the distributor wire harness. Crank the engine for 30 seconds after reconnecting the negative battery cable. Disconnect cable and realign timing marks. Check that the camshaft sprocket pointer is aligned with the TDC mark, and that the crankshaft is in the TDC position.

11. Loosen belt tensioner attaching bolt (tightened in step 7) ¼ to ½ turn maximum. If the marks do not align, remove and reinstall the belt.

12. Turn the camshaft sprocket counterclockwise with Tool D81P6256A or equivalent and a torque wrench. Tighten the belt tension-

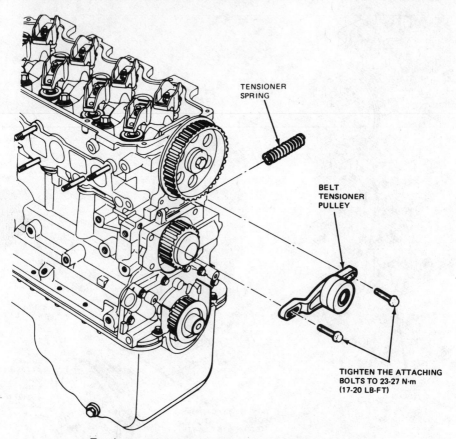

TENSIONER
SPRING

BELT
TENSIONER
PULLEY

TIGHTEN THE ATTACHING
BOLTS TO 23-27 N·m
(17-20 LB-FT)

**Tensioner and spring installation—1.6L and 1.9L engines**

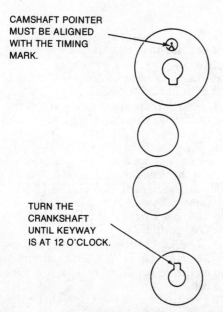

CAMSHAFT POINTER
MUST BE ALIGNED
WITH THE TIMING
MARK.

TURN THE
CRANKSHAFT
UNTIL KEYWAY
IS AT 12 O'CLOCK.

**Camshaft and crankshaft alignment—1.6L and 1.9L engines**

er mounting screw when the torque wrench reaches a reading of 27–32 ft.lb. for a new belt, or 10 lbs. if an old belt was installed.

NOTE: *Do not apply torque to the camshaft sprocket attaching bolt. Apply it to the hex on the sprocket.*

13. Install the timing belt cover and remaining parts in reverse order of removal.

## Timing Cover, Oil Seal, Timing Chain and Gears

### REMOVAL AND INSTALLATION

#### 2.3L HSC Engine

NOTE: *The engine must be removed from the car for the following procedure.*

1. The front seal can be replaced after the drive pulley has been removed. Remove the bolt and washer retaining the pulley. Use a suitable puller and remove the crankshaft pulley. Install a front seal remover tool (Ford No. T74P6700A or equivalent) and remove the

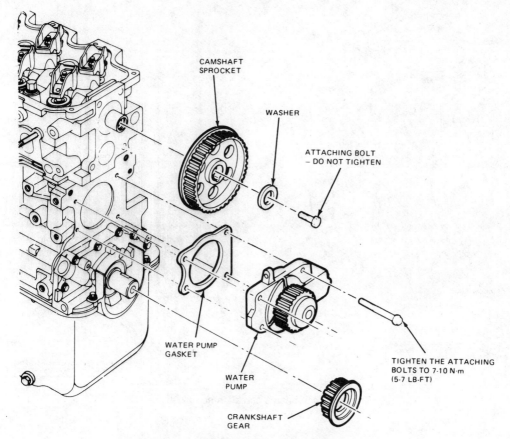

**Timing components installation—1.6L and 1.9L engines**

seal. Coat a new seal with grease and install with suitable tool (Ford No. T83T4676A or the equivalent). Drive the seal in until fully seated. Check the seal after installation to make sure the spring is in proper position around the seal. Install the crankshaft pulley, washer and bolt.

2. To remove the front cover, remove the crankshaft pulley as described above. Remove the front cover retaining bolts, pry the top of the cover away from the engine block and remove the cover.

3. Clean all gasket mounting surfaces. Check the play in the timing chain, replace chain if play is excessive. Check the timing chain tensioner blade for wear, if excessive replace the blade.

4. Turn the engine until the timing marks on the crank and cam gears align.

5. Remove the camshaft gear attaching bolt and washer. Slide the tow gears and chain forward and remove as an assembly.

6. Install in the reverse order. Make sure the timing marks on the camshaft and crank gears are in alignment. Check the timing

chain damper, located in the front cover, for wear and replace damper if necessary. Lubricate gears, chain, tensioner blade and front cover oil seal before cover installation. Apply an oil resistant sealer to both sides of the front cover gasket.

**2.0L Diesel Engine**

*IN CAR SERVICE*

NOTE: *This procedure is for Removal and Installation of the front timing belt for in-vehicle service of the water pump, camshaft, or cylinder head. The timing belt cannot be replaced with the engine installed in the vehicle.*

1. Remove the front timing belt upper cover and the flywheel timing mark cover.

2. Rotate engine clockwise until the timing marks on the flywheel and the front camshaft sprocket are aligned with their pointers.

3. Loosen tensioner pulley lockbolt and slide the timing belt off the water pump and camshaft sprockets.

4. The water pump and/or camshaft can now be serviced.

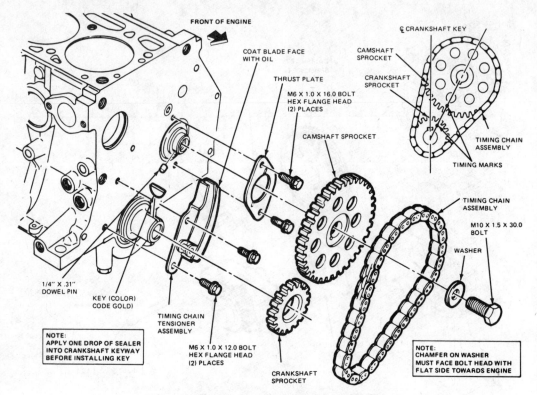

Timing gear components and alignment, 2.3L engine

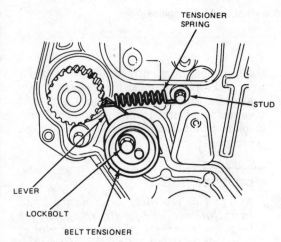

**Front timing belt tensioner—diesel engine**

*FRONT BELT ADJUSTMENTS*

1. Remove the flywheel timing mark cover.
2. Remove the front timing belt upper cover.
3. Remove the belt tension spring from the storage pocket in the front cover.
4. Install the tensioner spring in the belt tensioner lever and over the stud mounted on the front of the crankcase.
5. Loosen the tensioner pulley lockbolt.
6. Rotate the crankshaft pulley two revolutions clockwise until the flywheel TDC timing mark aligns with the pointer on the rear cover plate.
7. Check the front camshaft sprocket to see that it is aligned with its timing mark.

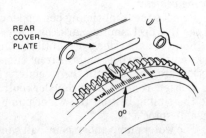

**Flywheel timing marks—diesel engine**

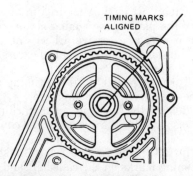

**Camshaft timing mark—diesel engine**

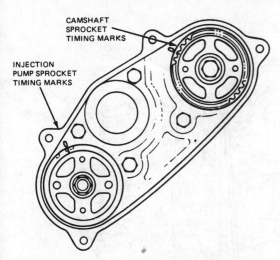

Camshaft and injector pump timing marks—diesel engine

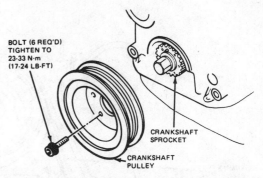

Crankshaft sprocket and pulley removal—diesel engine

8. Tighten the tensioner lockbolt to 23–34 ft.lb.

9. Check the belt tension using Rotunda Belt Tension Gauge model 21-0028 or equivalent. Belt tension should be 33–44 lbs.

10. Remove the tensioner spring and install it in the storage pocket in the front cover.

11. Install the front cover and tighten the attaching bolts to 5–7 ft.lb.

12. Install the flywheel timing mark cover.

### REAR BELT ADJUSTMENTS

1. Remove the flywheel timing mark cover.
2. Remove the rear timing belt cover.
3. Loosen the tensioner pulley locknut.
4. Rotate the crankshaft two revolutions until the flywheel TDC timing mark aligns with the pointer on the rear cover plate.
5. Check that the camshaft sprocket and injection pump sprocket are aligned with their timing marks.

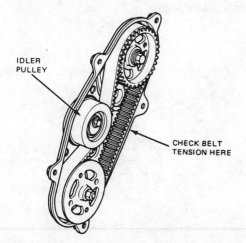

Timing belt tensioner, rear—diesel engine

6. Tighten tensioner locknut to 15–20 ft.lb.

7. Check belt tension using Rotunda Belt Tension Gauge model 21-0028 or equivalent. Belt tension should be 22–33 lbs.

8. Install the rear timing belt cover. Tighten the 6mm bolts to 5–7 ft.lb. and the 8mm bolt to 12–16 ft.lb.

9. Install the flywheel timing mark cover.

### REAR BELT REMOVAL AND INSTALLATION

1. Remove the rear timing belt cover.
2. Remove the flywheel timing mark cover from clutch housing.
3. Rotate the crankshaft until the flywheel timing mark is at TDC on No. 1 cylinder.
4. Check that the injection pump and camshaft sprocket timing marks are aligned.
5. Loosen the tensioner locknut. With a screwdriver, or equivalent tool, inserted in the slot provided, rotate the tensioner clockwise to relieve belt tension. Tighten locknut snug.
6. Remove the timing belt.
7. Install the belt.
8. Loosen the tensioner locknut and adjust timing belt as outlined in previous section.
9. Install rear timing belt cover and tighten belts to 5–7 ft.lb.

### FRONT BELT REMOVAL AND INSTALLATION

NOTE: *The engine must be removed from the vehicle to replace the front timing belt.*

1. With engine removed from the vehicle and installed on an engine stand, remove front timing belt upper cover.
2. Install a Flywheel Holding Tool T84P6375A or equivalent.
3. Remove the six bolts attaching the crankshaft pulley to the crankshaft sprocket.
4. Install a crankshaft pulley Remover T58P6316D or equivalent using Adapter T74P6700B or equivalent, and remove crankshaft pulley.
5. Remove the front timing belt lower cover.
6. Loosen the tensioning pulley and remove timing belt.

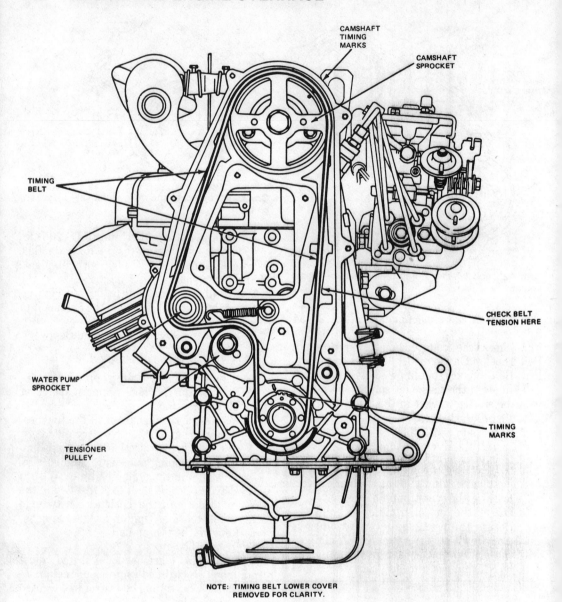

NOTE: TIMING BELT LOWER COVER
REMOVED FOR CLARITY.

**Front timing belt installation, diesel engine**

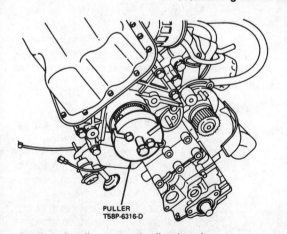

**Crankshaft pulley removal—diesel engine**

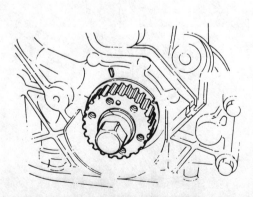

**Loosening tensioner pulley—diesel engine**

7. Align the camshaft sprocket with the timing mark.

NOTE: *Check the crankshaft sprocket to see that the timing marks are aligned.*

8. Remove the tensioner spring from the pocket in the front timing belt upper cover and install it in the slot in the tensioner lever and over the stud in the crankcase.

9. Push the tensioner lever toward the water pump as far as it will travel and tighten lockbolt snug.

10. Install timing belt.

11. Adjust the timing belt tension as outlined in previous section.

12. Install the front timing belt lower cover and tighten bolts to 5–7 ft.lb.

13. Install the crankshaft pulley and tighten bolts to 17–24 ft.lb.

14. Install the front timing belt upper cover and tighten bolts to 5–7 ft.lb.

## Camshaft

### REMOVAL AND INSTALLATION

#### 1.6 & 1.9L Engine

The camshaft can be removed with the engine in the car.

1. Remove the fuel pump and plunger. Set the engine to TDC on the compression stroke of No. 1 cylinder. Remove the negative battery cable.

2. Remove the alternator drive belt. Remove the power steering and air conditioning compressor drive belts, if equipped.

3. Remove the camshaft belt cover.

4. Remove the distributor.

5. Remove the rocker arms.

6. Remove the hydraulic valve lash adjusters. Keep the parts in order, as they must be returned to their original positions.

7. Remove and discard the timing belt.

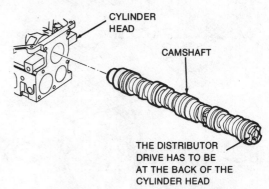
Camshaft installation—1.6L and 1.9L engines

8. Remove the camshaft sprocket and key.

9. Remove the camshaft thrust plate.

10. Remove the ignition coil and coil bracket.

11. Remove the camshaft through the back of the head towards the transaxle.

12. Before installing the camshaft, coat the bearing journals, cam lobe surfaces, seal and thrust plate groove with engine oil. Install the camshaft through the rear of the cylinder head. Rotate the camshaft during installation.

13. Install the camshaft thrust plate and tighten the two attaching bolts to 7–11 ft.lb.

14. Install the cam sprocket and key.

15. Install a new timing belt. See timing belt removal and installation procedure.

16. Install remaining parts in the reverse order of removal. When installing rocker arms, use new hex flange nuts.

#### 2.3L HSC Engine

NOTE: *The engine must be removed from the car to perform the following procedure.*

1. Remove the oil dipstick, all drive belts and pulleys and remove the cylinder head.

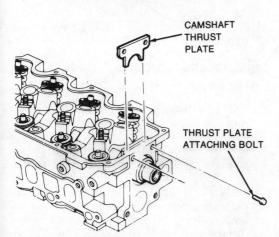
Camshaft thrust plate removal—1.6L and 1.9L engines

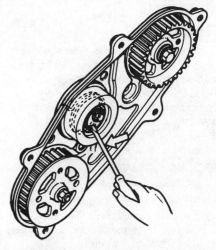
Front timing case cover installation—2.3L HSC engine

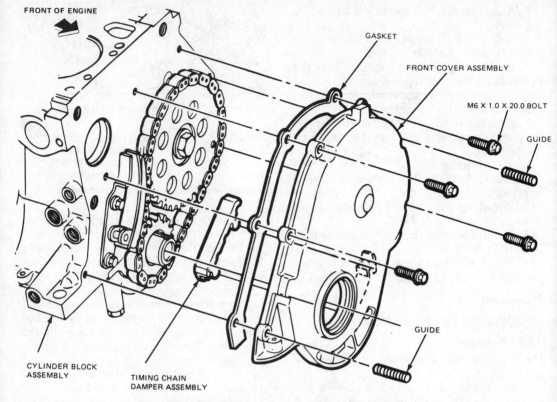

FRONT OF ENGINE

GASKET

FRONT COVER ASSEMBLY

M6 X 1.0 X 20.0 BOLT

GUIDE

GUIDE

CYLINDER BLOCK
ASSEMBLY

TIMING CHAIN
DAMPER ASSEMBLY

**2.3 HSC Engine timing cover components**

2. Use a magnet or suitable tools to remove the hydraulic lifters from the engine. Keep the lifters in order if reusable.

3. Remove the crankshaft pulley and timing case cover.

4. Check camshaft end play, if excessive replace the thrust plate.

5. Remove the fuel pump and pushrod. Remove the timing chain, sprockets and tensioner.

6. Remove the camshaft thrust plate retaining bolts and the plate.

7. Carefully remove the camshaft from the engine. Use caution to avoid damage to the bearings, journals and lobes.

8. Install in reverse order. Apply lubricant to the camshaft lobes and journals and to the bottom of the lifters. Lubricate all assemblies with oil. Remove to gear and chain replacement section for alignment procedures.

### CHECKING CAMSHAFT

Degrease the camshaft using safe solvent, clean all oil grooves. Visually inspect the cam lobes and bearing journals for excessive wear. If a lobe is questionable, check all lobes and journals with a micrometer.

Measure the lobes from nose to base and again at 90°. The lift is determined by sub-

tracting the second measurement from the first. If all exhaust lobes and all intake lobes are not identical, the camshaft must be reground or replaced. Measure the bearing journals and compare to specifications. If a journal is worn there is a good chance that the cam bearings are worn too, requiring replacement.

If the lobes and journals appear intact, place the front and rear cam journals in V-blocks and rest a dial indicator on the center journal. Rotate the camshaft to check for straightness, if deviation exceeds 0.001″ (0.025mm), replace the camshaft.

## Pistons and Connection Rods

### REMOVAL AND INSTALLATION

NOTE: *Although, in most cases, the pistons and connecting rods can be removed from the engine (after the cylinder head and oil pan are removed) while the engine is still in the car, it is far easier to remove the engine from the car. If removing pistons with the engine still installed, disconnect the radiator hoses, automatic transmission cooler lines and radiator shroud. Unbolt front mounts before jacking up the engine. Block the engine in position with wooden blocks between the mounts.*

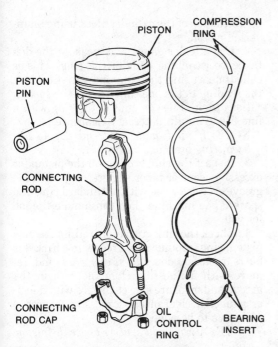

**Piston and connecting rod assembly**

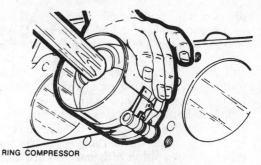

RING COMPRESSOR

**Install the piston using a ring compressor**

1. Remove the engine from the car. Remove cylinder head(s), oil pan and front cover (if necessary).

2. Because the top piston ring does not travel to the very top of the cylinder bore, a ridge is built up between the end of the travel and the top of the cylinder. Pushing the piston and connecting rod assembly past the ridge is difficult and may cause damage to the piston. If new rings are installed and the ridge has not been removed, ring breakage and piston damage can occur when the ridge is encountered at engine speed.

3. Turn the crankshaft to position the piston at the bottom of the cylinder bore. Cover the

top of the piston with a rag. Install a ridge reamer in the bore and follow the manufacturer's instructions to remove the ridge. Use caution. Avoid cutting too deeply or into the ring travel area. Remove the rag and cuttings from the top of the piston. Remove the ridge from all cylinders.

4. Check the edges of the connecting rod and bearing cap for numbers or matchmarks, if none are present mark the rod and cap numerically and in sequence from front to back of engine. The numbers or marks not only tell from which cylinder the piston came from buy also ensures that the rod caps are installed in the correct matching position.

5. Turn the crankshaft until the connecting rod is at the bottom of travel. Remove the two attaching nuts and the bearing cap. Take two

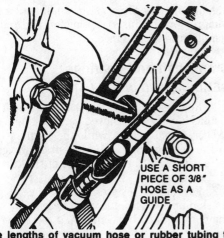

USE A SHORT PIECE OF 3/8" HOSE AS A GUIDE

**Use lengths of vacuum hose or rubber tubing to protect the crankshaft journals and cylinder walls during installation**

## PISTON RING SPACING

**Recommended piston ring spacing. Refer to the ring manufacturer's instruction sheet before installing new piston rings**

pieces of rubber tubing and cover the rod bolts to prevent crank or cylinder scoring. Use a wooden hammer handle to help push the piston and rod up and out of the cylinder. Reinstall the rod cap in proper position. Remove all pistons and connecting rods. Inspect cylinder walls and deglaze or hone as necessary.

6. Installation is the reverse order of removal. Lubricate each piston, rod bearing and cylinder wall. Install a ring compressor over the piston, position piston with mark toward front of engine and carefully install. Position connecting rod with bearing insert installed over the crank journal. Install the rod cap with bearing in proper position. Secure with rod nuts and torque to proper specifications. Install all rod and piston assemblies.

### CLEANING AND INSPECTION

1. Use a piston ring expander and remove the rings from the piston.
2. Clean the ring grooves using an appropriate cleaning tool, exercise care to avoid cutting too deeply.
3. Clean all varnish and carbon from the piston with a safe solvent. Do not use a wire brush or caustic solution on the pistons.
4. Inspect the pistons for scuffing, scoring, cracks, pitting or excessive ring groove wear. If wear is evident, the piston must be replaced.
5. Have the piston and connecting rod assembly checked by a machine shop for correct alignment, piston pin wear and piston diameter. If the piston has collapsed it will have to be replace or knurled to restore original diameter. Connecting rod bushing replacement, piston pin fitting and piston changing can be handled by the machine shop.

### CYLINDER BORE

Check the cylinder bore for wear using a telescope gauge and a micrometer, measure the cylinder bore diameter perpendicular to the piston pin at a point 2½" (63.5mm) below the top of the engine block. Measure the piston skirt perpendicular to the piston pin. The difference between the two measurements is the piston clearance. If the clearance is within specifications, finish honing or glaze breaking is all that is required. If clearance is excessive a slightly oversize piston may be required. If greatly oversize, the engine will have to be bored and 0.010" (0.25mm) or larger oversized pistons installed.

### FITTING AND POSITIONING PISTON RINGS

1. Take the new piston rings and compress them, one at a time into the cylinder that they will be used in. Press the ring about 1" (25mm)

below the top of the cylinder block using an inverted piston.
2. Use a feeler gauge and measure the distance between the ends of the ring. This is called measuring the ring end gap. Compare the reading to the one called for in the specifications table. File the ends of the ring with a fine file to obtain necessary clearance.
NOTE: *If inadequate ring end gap is utilized, ring breakage will result.*
3. Inspect the ring grooves on the piston for excessive wear or taper. If necessary have the grooves recut for use with a standard ring and spacer. The machine shop can handle the job for you.
4. Check the ring grooves by rolling the new piston ring around the groove to check for burrs or carbon deposits. If any are found, remove with a fine file. Hold the ring in the groove and measure side clearance with a feeler gauge. If clearance is excessive, spacer(s) will have to be added.
NOTE: *Always add spacers above the piston ring.*
5. Install the ring on the piston, lower oil ring first. Use a ring installing tool on the compression rings. Consult the instruction sheet that comes with the rings to be sure they are installed with the correct side up. A mark on the ring usually faces upward.
6. When installing oil rings, first, install the expanding ring in the groove. Hold the ends of the ring butted together (they must not overlap) and install the bottom rail (scraper) with the end about 1" (25mm) away from the butted end of the control ring. Install the top rail about 1" (25mm) away from the butted end of the control but on the opposite side from the lower rail.
7. Install the two compression rings.
8. Consult the illustration for ring positioning, arrange the rings as shown, install a ring compressor and insert the piston and rod assembly into the engine.

## Crankshaft and Bearings
### REMOVAL AND INSTALLATION

1. Rod bearings can be installed when the pistons have been removed for servicing (rings etc.) or, in most cases, while the engine is still in the car. Bearing replacement, however, is far easier with the engine out of the car and disassembled.
2. For in car service, remove the oil pan, spark plugs and front cover if necessary. Turn the engine until the connecting rod to be serviced is at the bottom of travel. Remove the bearing cap, place two pieces of rubber hose over the rod cap bolts and push the piston and

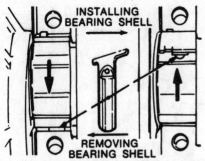

Remove or install the upper main bearing insert using a roll-out pin

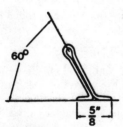

**Home made roll-out pin**

rod assembly up the cylinder bore until enough room is gained for bearing insert removal. Take care not to push the rod assembly up too far or the top ring will engage the cylinder ridge or come out of the cylinder and require head removal for installation.

3. Clean the rod journal, the connecting rod end and the bearing cap after removing the old bearing inserts. Install the new inserts in the rod and bearing cap, lubricate them with oil. Position the rod over the crankshaft journal and install the rod cap. Make sure the cap and rod numbers match, torque the rod nuts to specifications.

4. Main bearings may be replaced while the engine is still in the car by rolling them out and in.

5. Special roll out pins are available from automotive parts houses or can be fabricated from a cotter pin. The roll out pin fits in the oil hole of the main bearing journal. When the crankshaft is rotated opposite the directions of the bearing lock tab, the pin engages the end of the bearing and rolls out the insert.

6. Remove main bearing cap and roll out upper bearing insert. Remove insert from main bearing cap. Clean the inside of the bearing cap and crankshaft journal.

7. Lubricate and roll upper insert into position, make sure the lock tab is anchored and the insert is not cocked. Install the lower bearing insert into the cap, lubricate and install on the engine. Make sure the main bearing cap is installed facing in the correct direction and torque to specifications.

8. With the engine out of the car, remove the intake manifold, cylinder heads, front cover, timing gears and/or chain, oil pan , oil pump and flywheel.

9. Remove the piston and rod assemblies. Remove the main bearing caps after marking them for position and direction.

10. Remove the crankshaft, bearing inserts and rear main oil seal. Clean the engine block and cap bearing saddles. Clean the crankshaft and inspect for wear. Check the bearing journals with a micrometer for out-of-round condition and to determine wheat size rod and main bearing inserts to install.

11. Install the main bearing upper inserts and rear main oil seal half into the engine block.

12. Lubricate the bearing inserts and the crankshaft journals. Slowly and carefully lower the crankshaft into position.

13. Install the bearing inserts and rear main seal into the bearing caps, install the caps working from the middle out. Torque cap bolts to specifications in stages, rotate the crankshaft after each torque state. Note the illustration for thrust bearing alignment.

14. Remove bearing caps, one at a time and check the oil clearance with Plastigage\*. Reinstall if clearance is within specifications. Check the crankshaft endplay, if within specifications install connecting rod and piston assemblies with new rod bearing inserts. Check connecting rod bearing oil clearance and side play, if correct assemble the rest of the engine.

### BEARING OIL CLEARANCE

Remove cap from the bearing to be checked. Using a clean, dry rag, thoroughly clean all oil from crankshaft journal and bearing insert.

NOTE: *Plastigage® is soluble in oil, therefore, oil on the journal or bearing could result in erroneous readings.*

Place a pieced of Plastigage® along the full width of the bearing insert, reinstall cap, and torque to specifications.

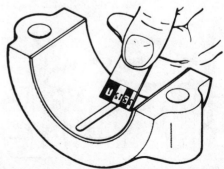

**Measure the Plastigage® to determine bearing clearance**

NOTE: *Specifications are given in the engine specifications earlier in this chapter.*

Remove bearing cap, and determine bearing clearance by comparing width of Plastigage® to the scale on Plastigage® envelope. Journal taper is determined by comparing width of the bearing insert, reinstall cap, and torque to specifications.

NOTE: *Do not rotate crankshaft with Plastigage® installed. If bearing insert and journal appear intact, and are within tolerances, no further main bearing service is required. If bearing or journal appear defective, cause of failure should be determined before replacement.*

## CRANKSHAFT ENDPLAY/CONNECTING ROD SIDE PLAY

Place a pry bar between a main bearing cap and crankshaft casting taking care not to damage any journals. Pry backward and forward, measure the distance between the thrust bearing and crankshaft with a feeler gauge. Compare reading with specifications. If too great a clearance is determined, a main bearing with a larger thrust surface or crank machining may be required. Check with an automotive machine shop for their advice.

Connecting rod clearance between the rod and crankthrow casting can be checked with a feeler gauge. Pry the rod carefully on one side as far as possible and measure the distance on the other side of the rod.

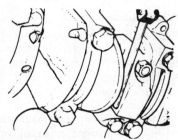

**Check the connecting rod side clearance with a feeler gauge**

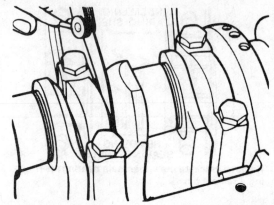

**Check the crankshaft end-play with a feeler gauge**

## CRANKSHAFT REPAIRS

If a journal is damaged on the crankshaft, repair is possible by having the crankshaft machined to a standard undersize.

In most cases, however, since the engine must be removed from the car and disassembled, some thought should be given to replacing the damaged crankshaft with a reground shaft kit. A reground crankshaft kit contains the necessary main and rod bearings for installation. The shaft has been ground and polished to undersize specifications and will usually hold up well if installed correctly.

## Oil Pan

### REMOVAL AND INSTALLATION

#### Gasoline Engines

The oil pan can be removed with the engine in the car. No suspension or chassis components need be removed. However, on Tempo/Topaz model, the transaxle case must be mounted to the engine.

1. Disconnect the negative battery terminal.

2. Jack up the vehicle and support it with stands.

3. Drain the oil. On Tempo/Topaz, drain cooling system and remove coolant tube (lower

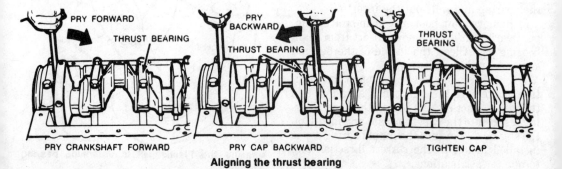

PRY CRANKSHAFT FORWARD          PRY CAP BACKWARD          TIGHTEN CAP

**Aligning the thrust bearing**

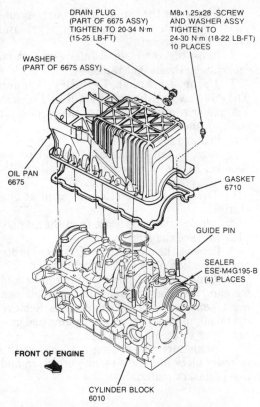

DRAIN PLUG
(PART OF 6675 ASSY)
TIGHTEN TO 20-34 N·m
(15-25 LB-FT)

M8x1.25x28 -SCREW
AND WASHER ASSY
TIGHTEN TO
24-30 N·m (18-22 LB-FT)
10 PLACES

WASHER
(PART OF 6675 ASSY)

OIL PAN
6675

GASKET
6710

GUIDE PIN

SEALER
ESE-M4G195-B
(4) PLACES

FRONT OF ENGINE

CYLINDER BLOCK
6010

**Oil pan installation—1.6L and 1.9L engines**

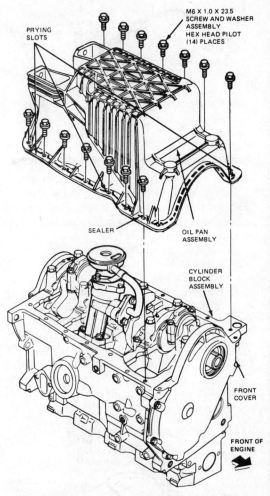

PRYING
SLOTS

M6 X 1.0 X 23.5
SCREW AND WASHER
ASSEMBLY
HEX HEAD PILOT
(14) PLACES

SEALER

OIL PAN
ASSEMBLY

CYLINDER
BLOCK
ASSEMBLY

FRONT
COVER

FRONT OF
ENGINE

**Oil pan installation—2.3L HSC engine**

hose). Disconnect exhaust pipe. Move A/C line out of the way.

4. Disconnect the starter wires.

5. Remove the knee brace and roll restrictor.

6. Remove the starter bolts and the starter.

7. Remove the knee braces at the transaxle on Escort/Lynx models.

8. Remove the oil pan bolts and the pan.

9. Remove the front and rear oil pan seal, and the pan gasket.

10. Installation is the reverse or removal.

a. When installing the pan on Escort/Lynx, apply a thin coating of sealer to the front and rear seals and also to the pan before installing the gasket. Tighten the pan bolts 6–8 ft.lb.

b. When installing the pan on Tempo/Topaz bolt transaxle case to rear face of cylinder block to align oil pan.

c. Apply a continuous $\frac{3}{16}$" (4.8mm) wide bead of Ford Silcone Gasket Sealer E3AZ-19562-A or equivalent, to the groove in the oil pan flange.

d. Apply an extra beard of sealer to the cylinder block on each side of the front cover.

e. Immediately place the oil pan against the cylinder block and install four corner bolts. Tighten bolts snug enough to allow

horizontal movement of pan. Install and tighten oil pan to transaxle bolts, then back off bolts. Install the oil pan attaching bolts and tighten to 6–9 ft.lb.

**Diesel Engine**

1. Disconnect the negative battery cable.

2. Raise and safely support the vehicle on jackstands. Drain the engine oil.

3. Remove the bolts that attach the oil pan to the engine and remove the oil pan.

4. Clean all gasket mounting surfaces.

5. Apply a $\frac{1}{8}$" (3mm) bead of Silicone Sealer on the oil pan mounting surface.

6. Install the oil pan and tighten the bolts to 5–7 ft.lb.

## Oil Pump

### REMOVAL AND INSTALLATION

#### 1.6 & 1.9L Engine

1. Disconnect the negative cable at the battery.

3.18 mm (1/8 INCH)
BEAD OF SILICONE
SEALER – D6AZ-19562-B

OIL PAN

**Applying sealant to the oil pan—2.0L diesel engine**

2. Loosen the alternator bolt on the alternator adjusting arm. Lower the alternator to remove the accessory drivebelt from the crankshaft pulley.

3. Remove the timing belt cover.

NOTE: *Set No. 1 cylinder at TDC prior to timing belt removal.*

4. Loosen both belt tensioner attaching bolts using Tool T8AP-6254-A or equivalent on the left bolt. Using a pry bar or other suitable tool pry the tensioner away from the belt. While holding the tensioner away from the belt, tighten one of the tensioner attaching bolts.

5. Disengage the timing belt from the camshaft sprocket, water pump sprocket and crankshaft sprocket.

6. Raise the vehicle and safely support on jackstands. Drain the crankcase.

7. Using a crankshaft Pulley Wrench T81P6312A and Crankshaft Bolt Wrench YA-826 or equivalent, remove the crankshaft pulley attaching bolt.

8. Remove the timing belt.

9. Remove the crankshaft drive plate assembly. Remove the crankshaft pulley. Remove the crankshaft sprocket.

10. Disconnect the starter cable at the starter.

11. Remove the knee brace from the engine.

12. Remove the starter.

13. Remove the rear section of the knee brace and inspection plate at the transmission.

14. Remove the oil pan retaining bolts and oil pan. Remove the front and rear oil pan seals. Remove the oil pan side gaskets. Remove the oil pump attaching bolts, oil pump and gasket. Remove the oil pump seal.

15. Make sure the mating surfaces on the cylinder block and the oil pump are clean and free of gasket material.

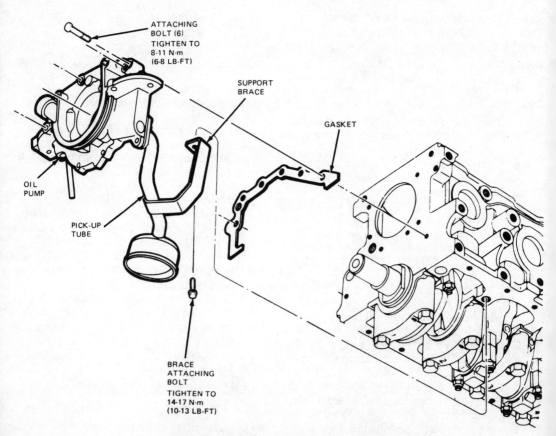

ATTACHING
BOLT (6)
TIGHTEN TO
8-11 N·m
(6-8 LB-FT)

SUPPORT
BRACE

GASKET

OIL
PUMP

PICK-UP
TUBE

BRACE
ATTACHING
BOLT
TIGHTEN TO
14-17 N·m
(10-13 LB-FT)

**Oil pump installation—1.6L and 1.9L engines**

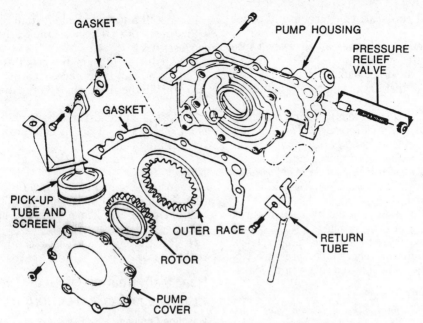

**Exploded view of the oil pump—1.6L and 1.9L engines**

16. Remove the oil pick-up tube and screen assembly from the pump for cleaning.

17. Lubricate the outside diameter of the oil pump seal with engine oil.

18. Install the oil pump seal using Seal Installer T81P-6700-A or equivalent.

19. Install the pick-up tube and screen assembly on the oil pump. Tighten attaching bolts to 6–9 ft.lb.

20. Lubricate the oil pump seal lip with light engine oil.

21. Position the oil pump gasket over the locating dowels. Install attaching bolts and tighten to 5–7 ft.lb.

22. Apply a bead of Silicone Sealer approximately 3.0mm wide at the corner of the front and rear oil pan seals, and at the seating point of the oil pump to the block retainer joint.

23. Install the front oil pan seal by pressing firmly into the slot cut into the bottom of the pump.

24. Install the rear oil seal by pressing firmly into the slot cut into rear retainer assembly.

NOTE: *Install the seal before the sealer has cured (within 10 minutes of application).*

25. Apply adhesive sealer evenly to oil pan flange and to the oil pan side of the gasket. Allow the adhesive to dry past the wet stage and then install the gaskets on the oil pan. Position the oil pan on the cylinder block.

26. Install oil pan attaching bolts. Tighten bolts in the proper sequence to 6–8 ft.lb.

27. Position the transmission inspection plate and the rear section of the knee brace on the transmission. Install the two attaching bolts and tighten to specification.

28. Install the starter.

29. Install the knee brace.

30. Connect the starter cable.

31. Install the crankshaft gear. Install crankshaft pulley. Install crankshaft drive plate assembly. Install timing belt over the crankshaft pulley.

32. Using the Crankshaft Pulley Wrench T81P-6312-A and Crankshaft Bolt Wrench YA-826 or equivalent, install the crankshaft pulley attaching bolt. Tighten bolt to specification. (Refer to Timing Belt section).

33. Lower the vehicle.

34. Install the engine front timing cover.

35. Position the accessory drive belts over the alternator and crankshaft pulleys. Tighten the drive belts to specification.

36. Connect the negative cable at the battery. Fill crankcase to the proper level with the specified oil.

37. Start the engine and check for oil leaks. Make sure the oil pressure indicator lamp has gone out. If the lamp remains On, immediately shut off the engine, determine the case and correct the condition.

## 2.3L HSC Engine

1. Remove the oil pan.

2. Remove the oil pump attaching bolts an remove the oil pump and intermediate driveshaft.

3. Prime the oil pump by filling inlet port with engine oil. Rotate the pump shaft until oil flows from outlet port.

4. If the screen and cover assembly have been removed, replace the gasket. Clean the

screen and reinstall the screen and cover assembly.

5. Position the intermediate driveshaft into the distributor socket.

6. Insert the intermediate driveshaft into the oil pump. Install the pump and shaft as an assembly.

CAUTION: *Do not attempt to force the pump into position if it will not seat. The shaft hex may be misaligned with the distributor shaft. To align, remove the oil pump and rotate the intermediate driveshaft into a new position.*

7. Tighten the two attaching bolts to specification.

8. Install the oil pan and all related parts, refer to Oil Pan Installation.

9. Fill the crankcase to the proper level. Start the engine and check for oil pressure. Operate engine at fast idle and check for oil leaks.

**Diesel Engine**

NOTE: *The engine must be removed from the car.*

1. Disconnect the battery ground cable from the battery, which is located in the luggage compartment.

2. Remove the engine from the vehicle.

3. Remove accessory drive belts.

4. Drain the engine oil.

5. Remove the oil pan.

6. Remove the crankshaft pulley, front timing belt, front timing belt tensioner, and crankshaft sprocket as outlined.

7. Remove the bolts attaching the oil pump to the crankcase and remove the pump. Remove the crankshaft front oil seal.

8. Clean the oil pump and the crankcase gasket mating surfaces.

9. Apply a ⅛″ (3mm) bead of Silicone Sealer on the oil pump-to-crankcase mating surface.

10. Install a new O-ring.

11. Install the oil pump, making sure the oil pump inner gear engages with the splines on the crankshaft. Tighten the 10mm bolts to 23–34 ft.lb. and the 8mm bolts to 12–16 ft.lb.

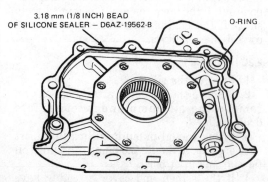

3.18 mm (1/8 INCH) BEAD OF SILICONE SEALER — D6AZ-19562-B    O-RING

**Oil pump assembly—2.0L diesel engine**

12. Install a new crankshaft front oil seal.

13. Clean the oil pan-to-crankcase mating surfaces.

14. Apply a ⅜″ (3.8mm) bead of Silicone Sealer on the oil-pan-to-crankcase mating surface.

15. Install the oil pan and tighten the bolts to 5–7 ft.lb.

16. Install and adjust as necessary the crankshaft sprocket, front timing belt tensioner and front timing belt.

17. Install and adjust the accessory drive belts.

18. Install engine in the vehicle.

19. Fill and bleed the cooling system.

20. Fill the crankcase with the specified quantity and quality of oil.

21. Run the engine and check for oil, fuel and coolant leaks.

## Rear Main Bearing Oil Seal
### REMOVAL AND INSTALLATION
**Gasoline Engines**

1. Remove the transaxle.

2. Remove the rear cover plate, and flywheel.

3. Using a suitable tool, punch two holes in the metal surface of the seal between the lip and block.

4. Screw in the threaded end of a small slide hammer and remove the seal.

5. Clean the seal mounting surfaces. Coat the crankshaft and seal with engine oil.

6. Install the oil seal using a seal installing tool.

7. Reassembly the remaining parts in the reverse order of removal.

## Completing the Rebuilding Process

Complete the rebuilding process as follows:

1. Fill the oil pump with oil, to prevent cavitating (sucking air) on initial engine start up. Install the oil pump and the pickup tube on the engine. Coat the oil pan gasket as necessary, and install the gasket and the oil pan. Mount the flywheel and the crankshaft vibration damper or pulley on the crankshaft.

NOTE: *Always use new bolts when install the flywheel. Inspect the clutch shaft pilot bushing in the crankshaft. If the bushing is excessively worn, remove it with an expanding puller and a slide hammer, and tap a new bushing into place.*

2. Position the engine, cylinder head side up. Lubricate the lifters, and install them into their bores. Install the cylinder head, and torque it as specified. Insert the pushrods (where applicable), and install the rocker shaft(s) (if so equipped) or position the rocker.

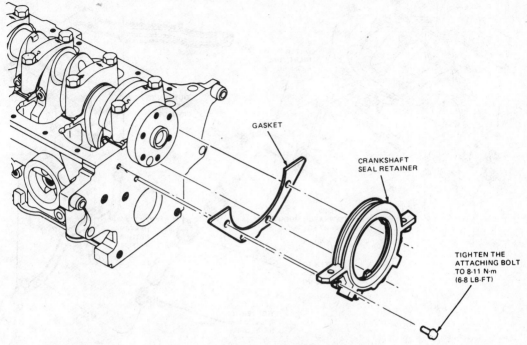

**Typical rear main bearing oil seal installation**

3. Install the intake and exhaust manifolds, the carburetor(s), the distributor and spark plugs. Mount all accessories and install the engine in the car. Fill the radiator with coolant, and the crankcase with high quality engine oil.

## Radiator

### REMOVAL AND INSTALLATION

1. Disconnect the negative battery cable. Drain the cooling system.

2. On models equipped, remove the carbure-

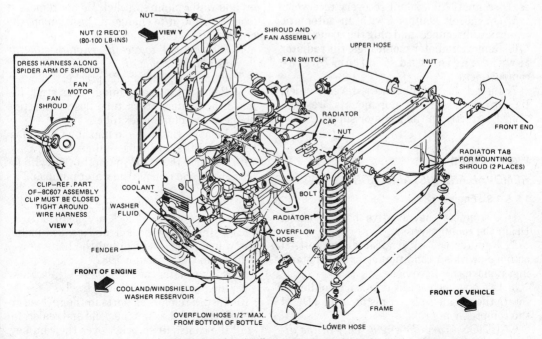

**Typical engine cooling system components**

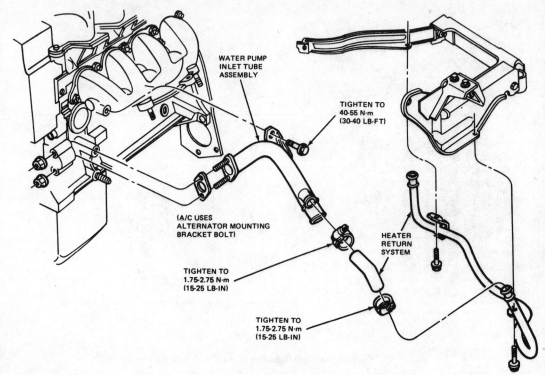

WATER PUMP
INLET TUBE
ASSEMBLY

TIGHTEN TO
40-55 N·m
(30-40 LB-FT)

(A/C USES
ALTERNATOR MOUNTING
BRACKET BOLT)

HEATER
RETURN
SYSTEM

TIGHTEN TO
1.75-2.75 N·m
(15-25 LB-IN)

TIGHTEN TO
1.75-2.75 N·m
(15-25 LB-IN)

**Typical water inlet system, car shown non air conditioned**

tor air intake tube and alternator air tube from the radiator support.

3. Remove the upper shroud mountings, disconnect the wire harness to the electric fan motor and remove the shroud and fan as an assembly.

4. Remove the upper and lower radiator hoses. Disconnect the coolant recovery reservoir.

5. On models equipped with an automatic transaxle, disconnect and plug the cooler lines.

6. Remove radiator mountings, tilt radiator toward engine and lift from engine compartment.

7. Install the radiator in the reverse order. Be sure the lower radiator mounts are positioned correctly on the radiator support.

## Water Pump

### REMOVAL AND INSTALLATION

#### 1.6 & 1.9L Engine

1. Disconnect the negative battery cable. Drain the cooling system.

2. Remove the alternator drive belt. If equipped with air conditioning or power steering, remove the drive belts.

3. Use a wrench on the crankshaft pulley to rotate the engine so No. 1 piston is on TDC of the compression stroke.

CAUTION: *Turn the engine only in the direction of normal rotation. Backward rota-*

*tion will cause the camshaft belt to slip or lose teeth.*

4. Remove the cam belt cover.

5. Loosen the bolt tensioner attaching bolts, then secure the tensioner over as far as possible.

6. Pull the bolt from the camshaft, tensioner, and water pump sprocket. Do not remove it from, or allow it to change its position on, the crankshaft sprocket.

NOTE: *Do not rotate the engine with the camshaft belt removed.*

7. Remove the camshaft sprocket.

8. Remove the rear timing cover stud. Remove the heater return tube hose connection at the water pump inlet tube.

9. Remove the water pump inlet tube fasteners and the inlet tube and gasket.

10. Remove the water pump to the cylinder block bolts and remove the water pump and its gasket.

11. To install, make sure the mating surfaces on the pump and the block are clean.

12. Using a new gasket and sealer, install the water pump and tighten the bolts to 5–7 ft.lb. on models through 1982.

1983 and later models – 30–40 ft.lb. Make sure the pump impeller turns freely.

13. Install remaining parts in the reverse order of removal. Use new gaskets and sealer. Install the camshaft sprocket over the cam key. See below the procedure. Install new timing

belt and adjust tension. See Timing Belt Removal and Installation for procedure.

### 2.3L HSC Engine

1. Disconnect the negative battery cable. Drain the cooling system.
2. Loosen the thermactor pump mounting and remove the drive belt. Disconnect and remove the hose clamp below the pump. Remove the thermactor pump bracket mounting bolts and remove the thermactor and bracket as an assembly.
3. Loosen the water pump drive belt idler pulley and remove the drive belt.
4. Disconnect the heater hose from the water pump.
5. Remove the water pump mounting bolts and the pump.
6. Clean the engine mounting surface. Apply gasket cement to both sides of the mounting gasket and position the gasket on the engine.
7. Install the pump in reverse order of removal. Torque the mounting bolts to 15–22 ft.lb.
8. Add the proper coolant mixture, start the engine and check for leaks.

### 2.0L Diesel Engine

1. Remove the front timing belt upper cover.
2. Loosen and remove the front timing belt, refer to timing belt in-vehicle services.
3. Drain the cooling system.
4. Raise the vehicle and support safely on jackstands.
5. Disconnect the lower radiator hose and heater hose from the water pump.
6. Disconnect the coolant tube from the thermostat housing and discard gasket.
7. Remove the three bolts attaching the water pump to the crankcase. Remove the water pump. Discard gasket.
8. Clean the water pump and crankshaft gasket mating surfaces.
9. Install the water pump, using a new gasket. Tighten bolts to 23–34 ft.lb.
10. Connect the coolant tube from the thermostat housing to the water pump using a new gasket. Tighten bolts to 5–7 ft.lb.
11. Connect the heater hose and lower radiator hose to the water pump.
12. Lower vehicle.
13. Fill and bleed the cooling system.
14. Install and adjust the front timing belt.
15. Run the engine and check for coolant leaks.
16. Install the front timing belt upper cover.

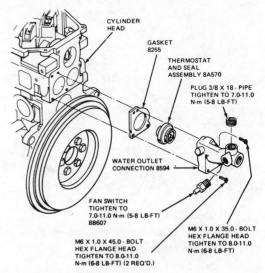

**Typical thermostat installation**

## Thermostat

### REMOVAL AND INSTALLATION

1. Disconnect the negative battery cable. Drain the radiator until the coolant level is below the thermostat.
2. Disconnect the wire connector at the thermostat housing thermoswitch.
3. Loosen the top radiator hose clamp. Remove the thermostat housing mounting bolts and lift up the housing.
4. Remove the thermostat by turning counterclockwise.
5. Clean the thermostat housing and engine gasket mounting surfaces. Install new mounting gasket and fully insert the thermostat to compress the mounting gasket. Turn the thermostat clockwise to secure in housing.
6. Position the housing onto the engine. Install the mounting bolts and torque to 6–8 ft.lb. on 1.6 & 1.9L engines and 12–18 ft.lb. on 2.3L HSC engines.
7. The rest of the installation is in the reverse order of removal.

## Electric Fan

### OPERATION

The electric cooling fan is mounted in the shroud behind the radiator.

A thermal switch mounted in the thermostat housing activates the fan when the coolant reaches a specified temperature. When the temperature is approximately 221°F (105°C) the thermal switch closes thus starting the fan.

The electric fan also operates when the air conditioner (if equipped) is turned on. When

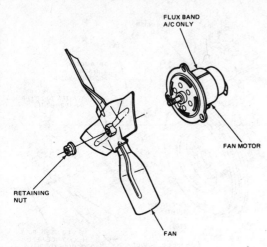

FLUX BAND
A/C ONLY

FAN MOTOR

RETAINING
NUT

FAN

**Cooling fan and electric motor**

the temperature drops to between 185–193°F (85–90°C) the thermal switch opens and the fan shuts off.

CAUTION: *Since the fan is governed by temperature the engine does not have to be* **ON** for the fan to operate. If any underhood operations must be performed on a warm engine, disconnect the wiring harness to the fan.

## EXHAUST SYSTEM

Inspect inlet pipes, outlet pipes and mufflers for cracked joints, broken welds and corrosion damage that would result in a leaking exhaust system. It is normal for a certain amount of moisture and staining to be present around the muffler seams. The presence of soot, light surface rust or moisture does not indicate a faulty muffler. Inspect the clamps, brackets and insulators for cracks and stripped or badly corroded bolt threads. When flat joints are loosened and/or disconnected to replace a shield pipe or muffler, replace the bolts and flange nuts if there is reasonable doubt that its service life is limited.

The exhaust system, including brush shields, must be free of leaks, binding, grounding and excessive vibrations. These conditions are usually caused by loose or broken flange bolts, shields, brackets or pipes. If any of these conditions exist, check the exhaust system components and alignment. Align or replace as necessary. Brush shields are positioned on the underside of the catalytic converter and should be free from bends which would bring any part of the shield in contact with the catalytic converter or muffler. The shield should also be clear of any combustible material such as dried grass or leaves.

## Muffler and Outlet Pipe Assembly
### REMOVAL AND INSTALLATION

1. Raise the vehicle and support on jackstands.
2. Remove the U-bolt assembly and the rubber insulators from the hanger brackets and remove the muffler assembly. Slide the muffler assembly toward the rear of the car to disconnect it from the converter.
3. Replace parts as needed.
4. Position the muffler assembly under the car and slide it forward onto the converter outlet pipe. Check that the slot in the muffler and the tab on the converter are fully engaged.
5. Install the rubber insulators on the hanger assemblies. Install the U-bolt and tighten
6. Check the system for leaks. Lower the vehicle.

## Catalytic Converter and/or Pipe Assembly
### REMOVAL AND INSTALLATION

1. Raise the vehicle and support on jackstands.
2. Remove the front catalytic converter flange fasteners, loosen the rear U-bolt connection and disconnect the air hoses.
3. Separate the catalytic converter inlet and outlet connections. Remove the converter.
4. Install the converter to the muffler.
5. Install the converter and muffler assembly to the inlet pipe/flex joint. Connect the air hoses and position the U-bolt.
6. Align the exhaust system into position and, starting at the front of the system, tighten all the nuts and bolts.
7. Check the system for leaks. Lower the vehicle.

## Troubleshooting Basic Charging System Problems

| Problem | Cause | Solution |
| --- | --- | --- |
| Noisy alternator | • Loose mountings | • Tighten mounting bolts |
| | • Loose drive pulley | • Tighten pulley |
| | • Worn bearings | • Replace alternator |
| | • Brush noise | • Replace alternator |
| | • Internal circuits shorted (High pitched whine) | • Replace alternator |

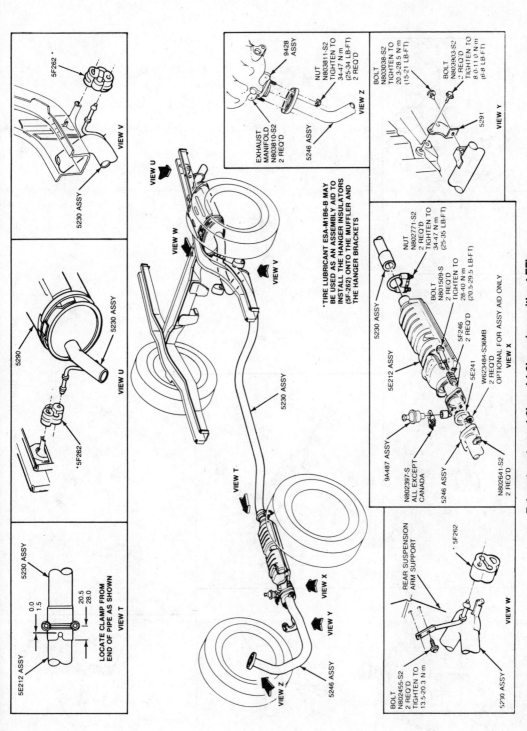

VIEW V

5F262

5230 ASSY

VIEW U

5290

5230 ASSY

5F262

VIEW U

5E212 ASSY

5230 ASSY

0.0
1.5

20.5
28.0

LOCATE CLAMP FROM
END OF PIPE AS SHOWN

VIEW T

VIEW U

VIEW W

VIEW V

5230 ASSY

5230 ASSY

VIEW T

VIEW X

VIEW Y

VIEW Z

5246 ASSY

*TIRE LUBRICANT ESA-M1B6-B MAY
BE USED AS AN ASSEMBLY AID TO
INSTALL THE HANGER INSULATORS
(5F-262) ONTO THE MUFFLER AND
THE HANGER BRACKETS

9428
ASSY

NUT
N803811-S2
TIGHTEN TO
34-47 N·m
(25-34 LB-FT)
2 REQ'D

EXHAUST
MANIFOLD
N803810-S2
2 REQ'D

5246 ASSY

VIEW Z

BOLT
N803038-S2
TIGHTEN TO
20.3-28.5 N·m
(15-21 LB-FT)

BOLT
N803903-S2
2 REQ'D
TIGHTEN TO
8.0-11.0 N·m
(6-8 LB-FT)

5291

VIEW Y

5230 ASSY

NUT
N802771-S2
2 REQ'D
TIGHTEN TO
34-47 N·m
(25-35 LB-FT)

BOLT
N801509-S
2 REQ'D
TIGHTEN TO
28-40 N·m
(20.5-29.5 LB-FT)

5E212 ASSY

5F246
2 REQ'D

5E241

W623484-S36MB
2 REQ'D
OPTIONAL FOR ASSY AID ONLY

VIEW X

9A487 ASSY

N802397-S
ALL EXCEPT
CANADA

5246 ASSY

N802641-S2
2 REQ'D

REAR SUSPENSION
ARM SUPPORT

5F262

BOLT
N802455-S2
2 REQ'D
TIGHTEN TO
13.5-20.3 N·m

5290 ASSY

VIEW W

**Exhaust system—1.6L and 1.9L engines without EFI**

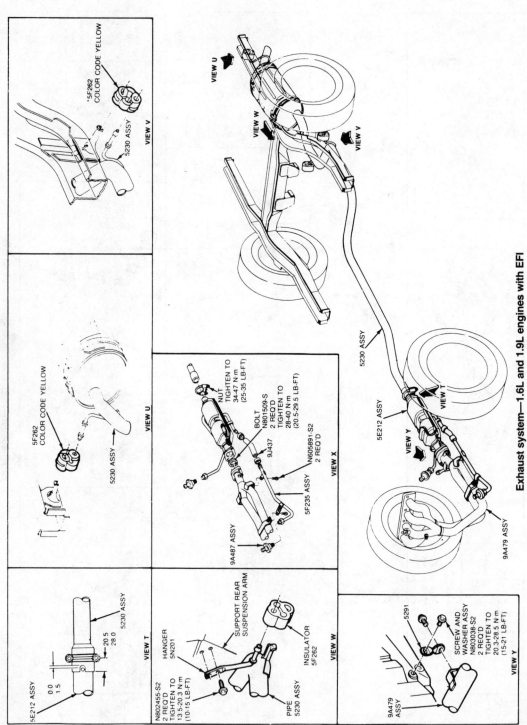

VIEW U

VIEW W

VIEW V

5230 ASSY

5E212 ASSY

VIEW T

VIEW Y

9A479 ASSY

**Exhaust system—1.6L and 1.9L engines with EFI**

**VIEW V**

5F262
COLOR CODE YELLOW

5230 ASSY

**VIEW U**

5F262
COLOR CODE YELLOW

5230 ASSY

**VIEW X**

NUT
TIGHTEN TO
34-47 N·m
(25-35 LB-FT)

BOLT
N801509-S
2 REQ'D
TIGHTEN TO
28-40 N·m
(20.5-29.5 LB-FT)

9J437

N605891-S2
2 REQ'D

5F235 ASSY

9A487 ASSY

**VIEW T**

5230 ASSY

20.5
28.0

5E212 ASSY

0.0
1.5

**VIEW W**

SUPPORT REAR
SUSPENSION ARM

HANGER
5N201

INSULATOR
5F262

PIPE
5230 ASSY

N802455-S2
2 REQ'D
TIGHTEN TO
13.5-20.3 N·m
(10-15 LB-FT)

**VIEW Y**

5291

SCREW AND
WASHER ASSY
N803038-S2
2 REQ'D
TIGHTEN TO
20.3-28.5 N·m
(15-21 LB-FT)

9A479
ASSY

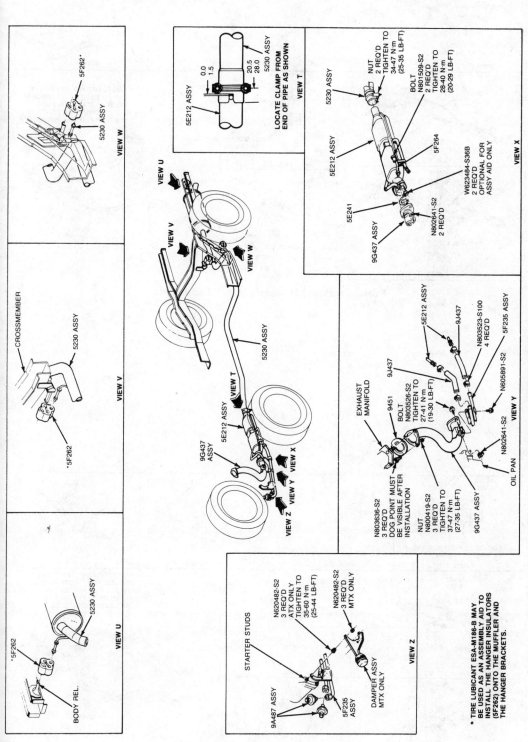

Exhaust system 2.3L HSC engine

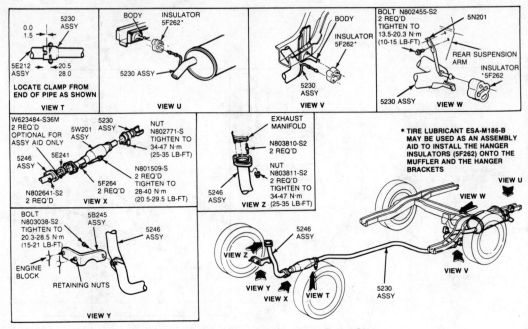

Exhaust system 2.0L diesel engine—Escort/Lynx

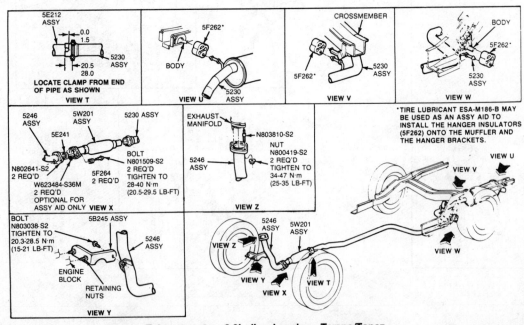

Exhaust system 2.0L diesel engine—Tempo/Topaz

## Troubleshooting Basic Charging System Problems

| Problem | Cause | Solution |
|---|---|---|
| Squeal when starting engine or accelerating | • Glazed or loose belt | • Replace or adjust belt |
| Indicator light remains on or ammeter indicates discharge (engine running) | • Broken fan belt<br>• Broken or disconnected wires<br>• Internal alternator problems<br>• Defective voltage regulator | • Install belt<br>• Repair or connect wiring<br>• Replace alternator<br>• Replace voltage regulator |
| Car light bulbs continually burn out— battery needs water continually | • Alternator/regulator overcharging | • Replace voltage regulator/alternator |
| Car lights flare on acceleration | • Battery low<br>• Internal alternator/regulator problems | • Charge or replace battery<br>• Replace alternator/regulator |
| Low voltage output (alternator light flickers continually or ammeter needle wanders) | • Loose or worn belt<br>• Dirty or corroded connections<br>• Internal alternator/regulator problems | • Replace or adjust belt<br>• Clean or replace connections<br>• Replace alternator or regulator |

## Troubleshooting Basic Starting System Problems

| Problem | Cause | Solution |
|---|---|---|
| Starter motor rotates engine slowly | • Battery charge low or battery defective<br>• Defective circuit between battery and starter motor<br>• Low load current<br><br>• High load current | • Charge or replace battery<br>• Clean and tighten, or replace cables<br>• Bench-test starter motor. Inspect for worn brushes and weak brush springs.<br>• Bench-test starter motor. Check engine for friction, drag or coolant in cylinders. Check ring gear-to-pinion gear clearance. |
| Starter motor will not rotate engine | • Battery charge low or battery defective<br>• Faulty solenoid<br><br>• Damage drive pinion gear or ring gear<br>• Starter motor engagement weak<br>• Starter motor rotates slowly with high load current<br><br><br>• Engine seized | • Charge or replace battery<br>• Check solenoid ground. Repair or replace as necessary.<br>• Replace damaged gear(s)<br><br>• Bench-test starter motor<br>• Inspect drive yoke pull-down and point gap, check for worn end bushings, check ring gear clearance<br>• Repair engine |
| Starter motor drive will not engage (solenoid known to be good) | • Defective contact point assembly<br>• Inadequate contact point assembly ground<br>• Defective hold-in coil | • Repair or replace contact point assembly<br>• Repair connection at ground screw<br>• Replace field winding assembly |
| Starter motor drive will not disengage | • Starter motor loose on flywheel housing<br>• Worn drive end busing<br>• Damaged ring gear teeth<br>• Drive yoke return spring broken or missing | • Tighten mounting bolts<br>• Replace bushing<br>• Replace ring gear or driveplate<br>• Replace spring |
| Starter motor drive disengages prematurely | • Weak drive assembly thrust spring<br>• Hold-in coil defective | • Replace drive mechanism<br>• Replace field winding assembly |
| Low load current | • Worn brushes<br>• Weak brush springs | • Replace brushes<br>• Replace springs |

## Troubleshooting Engine Mechanical Problems

| Problem | Cause | Solution |
| --- | --- | --- |
| External oil leaks | • Fuel pump gasket broken or improperly seated | • Replace gasket |
| | • Cylinder head cover RTV sealant broken or improperly seated | • Replace sealant; inspect cylinder head cover sealant flange and cylinder head sealant surface for distortion and cracks |
| | • Oil filler cap leaking or missing | • Replace cap |
| | • Oil filter gasket broken or improperly seated | • Replace oil filter |
| | • Oil pan side gasket broken, improperly seated or opening in RTV sealant | • Replace gasket or repair opening in sealant; inspect oil pan gasket flange for distortion |
| | • Oil pan front oil seal broken or improperly seated | • Replace seal; inspect timing case cover and oil pan seal flange for distortion |
| | • Oil pan rear oil seal broken or improperly seated | • Replace seal; inspect oil pan rear oil seal flange; inspect rear main bearing cap for cracks, plugged oil return channels, or distortion in seal groove |
| | • Timing case cover oil seal broken or improperly seated | • Replace seal |
| | • Excess oil pressure because of restricted PCV valve | • Replace PCV valve |
| | • Oil pan drain plug loose or has stripped threads | • Repair as necessary and tighten |
| | • Rear oil gallery plug loose | • Use appropriate sealant on gallery plug and tighten |
| | • Rear camshaft plug loose or improperly seated | • Seat camshaft plug or replace and seal, as necessary |
| | • Distributor base gasket damaged | • Replace gasket |
| Excessive oil consumption | • Oil level too high | • Drain oil to specified level |
| | • Oil with wrong viscosity being used | • Replace with specified oil |
| | • PCV valve stuck closed | • Replace PCV valve |
| | • Valve stem oil deflectors (or seals) are damaged, missing, or incorrect type | • Replace valve stem oil deflectors |
| | • Valve stems or valve guides worn | • Measure stem-to-guide clearance and repair as necessary |
| | • Poorly fitted or missing valve cover baffles | • Replace valve cover |
| | • Piston rings broken or missing | • Replace broken or missing rings |
| | • Scuffed piston | • Replace piston |
| | • Incorrect piston ring gap | • Measure ring gap, repair as necessary |
| | • Piston rings sticking or excessively loose in grooves | • Measure ring side clearance, repair as necessary |
| | • Compression rings installed upside down | • Repair as necessary |
| | • Cylinder walls worn, scored, or glazed | • Repair as necessary |
| | • Piston ring gaps not properly staggered | • Repair as necessary |
| | • Excessive main or connecting rod bearing clearance | • Measure bearing clearance, repair as necessary |
| No oil pressure | • Low oil level | • Add oil to correct level |
| | • Oil pressure gauge, warning lamp or sending unit inaccurate | • Replace oil pressure gauge or warning lamp |
| | • Oil pump malfunction | • Replace oil pump |
| | • Oil pressure relief valve sticking | • Remove and inspect oil pressure relief valve assembly |
| | • Oil passages on pressure side of pump obstructed | • Inspect oil passages for obstruction |

## Troubleshooting Engine Mechanical Problems (cont.)

| Problem | Cause | Solution |
|---|---|---|
| No oil pressure (cont.) | • Oil pickup screen or tube obstructed | • Inspect oil pickup for obstruction |
| | • Loose oil inlet tube | • Tighten or seal inlet tube |
| Low oil pressure | • Low oil level | • Add oil to correct level |
| | • Inaccurate gauge, warning lamp or sending unit | • Replace oil pressure gauge or warning lamp |
| | • Oil excessively thin because of dilution, poor quality, or improper grade | • Drain and refill crankcase with recommended oil |
| | • Excessive oil temperature | • Correct cause of overheating engine |
| | • Oil pressure relief spring weak or sticking | • Remove and inspect oil pressure relief valve assembly |
| | • Oil inlet tube and screen assembly has restriction or air leak | • Remove and inspect oil inlet tube and screen assembly. (Fill inlet tube with lacquer thinner to locate leaks.) |
| | • Excessive oil pump clearance | • Measure clearances |
| | • Excessive main, rod, or camshaft bearing clearance | • Measure bearing clearances, repair as necessary |
| High oil pressure | • Improper oil viscosity | • Drain and refill crankcase with correct viscosity oil |
| | • Oil pressure gauge or sending unit inaccurate | • Replace oil pressure gauge |
| | • Oil pressure relief valve sticking closed | • Remove and inspect oil pressure relief valve assembly |
| Main bearing noise | • Insufficient oil supply | • Inspect for low oil level and low oil pressure |
| | • Main bearing clearance excessive | • Measure main bearing clearance, repair as necessary |
| | • Bearing insert missing | • Replace missing insert |
| | • Crankshaft end play excessive | • Measure end play, repair as necessary |
| | • Improperly tightened main bearing cap bolts | • Tighten bolts with specified torque |
| | • Loose flywheel or drive plate | • Tighten flywheel or drive plate attaching bolts |
| | • Loose or damaged vibration damper | • Repair as necessary |
| Connecting rod bearing noise | • Insufficient oil supply | • Inspect for low oil level and low oil pressure |
| | • Carbon build-up on piston | • Remove carbon from piston crown |
| | • Bearing clearance excessive or bearing missing | • Measure clearance, repair as necessary |
| | • Crankshaft connecting rod journal out-of-round | • Measure journal dimensions, repair or replace as necessary |
| | • Misaligned connecting rod or cap | • Repair as necessary |
| | • Connecting rod bolts tightened improperly | • Tighten bolts with specified torque |
| Piston noise | • Piston-to-cylinder wall clearance excessive (scuffed piston) | • Measure clearance and examine piston |
| | • Cylinder walls excessively tapered or out-of-round | • Measure cylinder wall dimensions, rebore cylinder |
| | • Piston ring broken | • Replace all rings on piston |
| | • Loose or seized piston pin | • Measure piston-to-pin clearance, repair as necessary |
| | • Connecting rods misaligned | • Measure rod alignment, straighten or replace |
| | • Piston ring side clearance excessively loose or tight | • Measure ring side clearance, repair as necessary |
| | • Carbon build-up on piston is excessive | • Remove carbon from piston |

## Troubleshooting Engine Mechanical Problems (cont.)

| Problem | Cause | Solution |
|---|---|---|
| Valve actuating component noise | • Insufficient oil supply | • Check for:<br>(a) Low oil level<br>(b) Low oil pressure<br>(c) Plugged push rods<br>(d) Wrong hydraulic tappets<br>(e) Restricted oil gallery<br>(f) Excessive tappet to bore clearance |
| | • Push rods worn or bent | • Replace worn or bent push rods |
| | • Rocker arms or pivots worn | • Replace worn rocker arms or pivots |
| | • Foreign objects or chips in hydraulic tappets | • Clean tappets |
| | • Excessive tappet leak-down | • Replace valve tappet |
| | • Tappet face worn | • Replace tappet; inspect corresponding cam lobe for wear |
| | • Broken or cocked valve springs | • Properly seat cocked springs; replace broken springs |
| | • Stem-to-guide clearance excessive | • Measure stem-to-guide clearance, repair as required |
| | • Valve bent | • Replace valve |
| | • Loose rocker arms | • Tighten bolts with specified torque |
| | • Valve seat runout excessive | • Regrind valve seat/valves |
| | • Missing valve lock | • Install valve lock |
| | • Push rod rubbing or contacting cylinder head | • Remove cylinder head and remove obstruction in head |
| | • Excessive engine oil (four-cylinder engine) | • Correct oil level |

## Troubleshooting the Cooling System

| Problem | Cause | Solution |
|---|---|---|
| High temperature gauge indication— overheating | • Coolant level low | • Replenish coolant |
| | • Fan belt loose | • Adjust fan belt tension |
| | • Radiator hose(s) collapsed | • Replace hose(s) |
| | • Radiator airflow blocked | • Remove restriction (bug screen, fog lamps, etc.) |
| | • Faulty radiator cap | • Replace radiator cap |
| | • Ignition timing incorrect | • Adjust ignition timing |
| | • Idle speed low | • Adjust idle speed |
| | • Air trapped in cooling system | • Purge air |
| | • Heavy traffic driving | • Operate at fast idle in neutral intermittently to cool engine |
| | • Incorrect cooling system component(s) installed | • Install proper component(s) |
| | • Faulty thermostat | • Replace thermostat |
| | • Water pump shaft broken or impeller loose | • Replace water pump |
| | • Radiator tubes clogged | • Flush radiator |
| | • Cooling system clogged | • Flush system |
| | • Casting flash in cooling passages | • Repair or replace as necessary. Flash may be visible by removing cooling system components or removing core plugs. |
| | • Brakes dragging | • Repair brakes |
| | • Excessive engine friction | • Repair engine |
| | • Antifreeze concentration over 68% | • Lower antifreeze concentration percentage |
| | • Missing air seals | • Replace air seals |
| | • Faulty gauge or sending unit | • Repair or replace faulty component |
| | • Loss of coolant flow caused by leakage or foaming | • Repair or replace leaking component, replace coolant |
| | • Viscous fan drive failed | • Replace unit |

## Troubleshooting the Cooling System (cont.)

| Problem | Cause | Solution |
|---|---|---|
| Low temperature indication—undercooling | • Thermostat stuck open<br>• Faulty gauge or sending unit | • Replace thermostat<br>• Repair or replace faulty component |
| Coolant loss—boilover | • Overfilled cooling system | • Reduce coolant level to proper specification |
| | • Quick shutdown after hard (hot) run | • Allow engine to run at fast idle prior to shutdown |
| | • Air in system resulting in occasional "burping" of coolant | • Purge system |
| | • Insufficient antifreeze allowing coolant boiling point to be too low | • Add antifreeze to raise boiling point |
| | • Antifreeze deteriorated because of age or contamination | • Replace coolant |
| | • Leaks due to loose hose clamps, loose nuts, bolts, drain plugs, faulty hoses, or defective radiator | • Pressure test system to locate source of leak(s) then repair as necessary |
| | • Faulty head gasket | • Replace head gasket |
| | • Cracked head, manifold, or block | • Replace as necessary |
| | • Faulty radiator cap | • Replace cap |
| Coolant entry into crankcase or cylinder(s) | • Faulty head gasket<br>• Crack in head, manifold or block | • Replace head gasket<br>• Replace as necessary |
| Coolant recovery system inoperative | • Coolant level low<br>• Leak in system | • Replenish coolant to FULL mark<br>• Pressure test to isolate leak and repair as necessary |
| | • Pressure cap not tight or seal missing, or leaking | • Repair as necessary |
| | • Pressure cap defective<br>• Overflow tube clogged or leaking<br>• Recovery bottle vent restricted | • Replace cap<br>• Repair as necessary<br>• Remove restriction |
| Noise | • Fan contacting shroud | • Reposition shroud and inspect engine mounts |
| | • Loose water pump impeller<br>• Glazed fan belt<br>• Loose fan belt<br>• Rough surface on drive pulley<br>• Water pump bearing worn | • Replace pump<br>• Apply silicone or replace belt<br>• Adjust fan belt tension<br>• Replace pulley<br>• Remove belt to isolate. Replace pump. |
| | • Belt alignment | • Check pulley alignment. Repair as necessary. |
| No coolant flow through heater core | • Restricted return inlet in water pump | • Remove restriction |
| | • Heater hose collapsed or restricted<br>• Restricted heater core<br>• Restricted outlet in thermostat housing | • Remove restriction or replace hose<br>• Remove restriction or replace core<br>• Remove flash or restriction |
| | • Intake manifold bypass hole in cylinder head restricted | • Remove restriction |
| | • Faulty heater control valve<br>• Intake manifold coolant passage restricted | • Replace valve<br>• Remove restriction or replace intake manifold |

**NOTE:** *Immediately after shutdown, the engine enters a condition known as heat soak. This is caused by the cooling system being inoperative while engine temperature is still high. If coolant temperature rises above boiling point, expansion and pressure may push some coolant out of the radiator overflow tube. If this does not occur frequently it is considered normal.*

## Troubleshooting the Serpentine Drive Belt

| Problem | Cause | Solution |
|---|---|---|
| Tension sheeting fabric failure (woven fabric on outside circumference of belt has cracked or separated from body of belt) | • Grooved or backside idler pulley diameters are less than minimum recommended<br>• Tension sheeting contacting (rubbing) stationary object<br>• Excessive heat causing woven fabric to age<br>• Tension sheeting splice has fractured | • Replace pulley(s) not conforming to specification<br>• Correct rubbing condition<br>• Replace belt<br>• Replace belt |
| Noise (objectional squeal, squeak, or rumble is heard or felt while drive belt is in operation) | • Belt slippage<br>• Bearing noise<br>• Belt misalignment<br>• Belt-to-pulley mismatch<br>• Driven component inducing vibration<br>• System resonant frequency inducing vibration | • Adjust belt<br>• Locate and repair<br>• Align belt/pulley(s)<br>• Install correct belt<br>• Locate defective driven component and repair<br>• Vary belt tension within specifications. Replace belt. |
| Rib chunking (one or more ribs has separated from belt body) | • Foreign objects imbedded in pulley grooves<br>• Installation damage<br>• Drive loads in excess of design specifications<br>• Insufficient internal belt adhesion | • Remove foreign objects from pulley grooves<br>• Replace belt<br>• Adjust belt tension<br>• Replace belt |
| Rib or belt wear (belt ribs contact bottom of pulley grooves) | • Pulley(s) misaligned<br>• Mismatch of belt and pulley groove widths<br>• Abrasive environment<br>• Rusted pulley(s)<br>• Sharp or jagged pulley groove tips<br>• Rubber deteriorated | • Align pulley(s)<br>• Replace belt<br>• Replace belt<br>• Clean rust from pulley(s)<br>• Replace pulley<br>• Replace belt |
| Longitudinal belt cracking (cracks between two ribs) | • Belt has mistracked from pulley groove<br>• Pulley groove tip has worn away rubber-to-tensile member | • Replace belt<br>• Replace belt |
| Belt slips | • Belt slipping because of insufficient tension<br>• Belt or pulley subjected to substance (belt dressing, oil, ethylene glycol) that has reduced friction<br>• Driven component bearing failure<br>• Belt glazed and hardened from heat and excessive slippage | • Adjust tension<br>• Replace belt and clean pulleys<br>• Replace faulty component bearing<br>• Replace belt |
| "Groove jumping" (belt does not maintain correct position on pulley, or turns over and/or runs off pulleys) | • Insufficient belt tension<br>• Pulley(s) not within design tolerance<br>• Foreign object(s) in grooves<br>• Excessive belt speed<br>• Pulley misalignment<br>• Belt-to-pulley profile mismatched<br>• Belt cordline is distorted | • Adjust belt tension<br>• Replace pulley(s)<br>• Remove foreign objects from grooves<br>• Avoid excessive engine acceleration<br>• Align pulley(s)<br>• Install correct belt<br>• Replace belt |
| Belt broken (Note: identify and correct problem before replacement belt is installed) | • Excessive tension<br>• Tensile members damaged during belt installation<br>• Belt turnover<br>• Severe pulley misalignment<br>• Bracket, pulley, or bearing failure | • Replace belt and adjust tension to specification<br>• Replace belt<br>• Replace belt<br>• Align pulley(s)<br>• Replace defective component and belt |

## Troubleshooting the Serpentine Drive Belt (cont.)

| Problem | Cause | Solution |
|---|---|---|
| Cord edge failure (tensile member exposed at edges of belt or separated from belt body) | • Excessive tension<br>• Drive pulley misalignment<br>• Belt contacting stationary object<br>• Pulley irregularities<br>• Improper pulley construction<br>• Insufficient adhesion between tensile member and rubber matrix | • Adjust belt tension<br>• Align pulley<br>• Correct as necessary<br>• Replace pulley<br>• Replace pulley<br>• Replace belt and adjust tension to specifications |
| Sporadic rib cracking (multiple cracks in belt ribs at random intervals) | • Ribbed pulley(s) diameter less than minimum specification<br>• Backside bend flat pulley(s) diameter less than minimum<br>• Excessive heat condition causing rubber to harden<br>• Excessive belt thickness<br>• Belt overcured<br>• Excessive tension | • Replace pulley(s)<br><br>• Replace pulley(s)<br><br>• Correct heat condition as necessary<br>• Replace belt<br>• Replace belt<br>• Adjust belt tension |

# Emission Controls and Fuel System

## EMISSION CONTROLS

There are three basic sources of automotive pollution in the modern internal combustion engine. They are the crankcase with its accompanying blow-by vapors, the fuel system with its evaporation of unburned gasoline and the combustion chambers with their resulting exhaust emissions. Pollution arising from the incomplete combustion of fuel generally falls into three categories: hydrocarbons (HC), carbon monoxide (CO) and oxides of nitrogen (NOx).

Engines are equipped with an air pump system, positive crankcase ventilation, exhaust gas recirculation, electronic ignition, catalytic converter, thermostatically controlled air cleaner, and an evaporative emissions system. Electronic engine controls are used on various engines, depending on model and year.

The belt driven air pump injects clean air either into the exhaust manifold, or downstream into the catalytic converter, depending on engine conditions. The oxygen contained in the injected air supports continued combustion of the hot carbon monoxide (CO) and hydrocarbon (HC) gases, reducing their release into the atmosphere.

No external PCV valve is necessary on the Escort and Lynx PCV system. Instead, an internal baffle and an orifice control flow of crankcase gases.

The back pressure modulated EGR valve is mounted next to the carburetor on the intake manifold. Vacuum applied to the EGR diaphragm raises the pintle valve from its seat, allowing hot exhaust gases to be drawn into the intake manifold with the intake charge. The exhaust gases reduce peak combustion temperature; lower temperatures reduce the formation of oxides of nitrogen (NOx).

The dual brick catalytic converter is mounted in the exhaust system, ahead of the muffler.

Catalytic converters use noble metals (platinum and palladium) and great heat — 1,200°F (650°C) to catalytically oxidize HC and CO gases into $H_2O$ and $CO_2$. The Thermactor system is used as a fresh air (and therefore, oxygen) supply.

The thermostatically controlled air cleaner housing is able to draw fresh air from two sources: cool air from outside the car (behind the grille), or warm air obtained from a heat stove encircling the exhaust manifold. A warm air supply is desirable during cold engine operation. Because it promotes better atomization of the air/fuel mixture, while cool air promotes better combustion in a hot engine.

Instead of venting gasoline vapors from the carburetor float bowl into the atmosphere, an evaporative emission system captures the vapors and stores them in a charcoal filled canister, located ahead of the left front wheel arch. When the engine is running, a purge control solenoid allows fresh air to be drawn through the canister. The fresh air and vapors are then routed to the carburetor, to be mixed with the intake charge.

### Thermactor Air Pump System
#### OPERATION

A typical air injection system consists of an air supply pump and centrifugal filter, an air bypass valve, check valve, air manifold and air hoses.

Simply, the air pump injects air into the engine which reduces the hydrocarbon and carbon monoxide content of exhaust gases by continuing the combustion of the unburned gases after they leave the combustion chamber. Fresh air mixed with the hot exhaust gases promotes further oxidation of both the hydrocarbons and carbon monoxide, thereby reducing their concentration and converting some of them into harmless carbon dioxide and water.

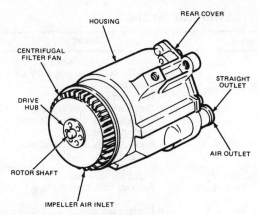

**Thermactor (Air) Pump**

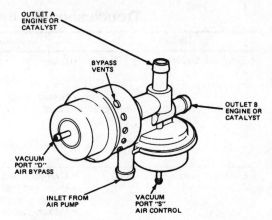

**Typical combination valve bypass and air control valve**

Air for the system is cleaned by means of a centrifugal filter fan mounted on the air pump driveshaft.

To prevent excessive pressure, the air pump is equipped with a pressure relief valve.

The air pump has sealed bearings which are lubricated for the lift of the unit, and preset rotor vane ad bearing clearances, which do not require any periodic adjustments.

The air supply from the pump is controlled by the air by-pass valve, sometimes a dump valve. During deceleration, the air by-pass valve opens, momentarily diverting the air supply into the atmosphere, thus preventing backfires within the exhaust system.

A check valve is incorporated in the air inlet side of the air manifold. It purpose is to prevent the exhaust gases from backing up into the system. The valve is especially important in the event of drive belt failure and during deceleration, when the air by-pass valve is dumping the air supply. The air manifold channel the air from the pump into the exhaust thus completing the cycle of the Thermactor system.

## COMBINATION AIR BYPASS – AIR CONTROL VALVE

### Functional Test

1. Disconnect the two hoses that go to the engine or converter (outlet **A** and outlet **B**, see the illustration).

2. Disconnect and plug the vacuum line at port **D**.

3. With the engine operating at 1,500 rpm, air flow should be coming out of the bypass vents.

4. Reconnect the vacuum line to port **D**. Disconnect and plug the vacuum line to port **S**. Make sure vacuum is present at vacuum port **D**.

5. Operate the engine at 1,500 rpm, air flow

should be detected at outlet B. No air flow should be at outlet **A**.

6. Use a hand vacuum pump and apply 8–10 in.Hg to port S. With the engine operating at 1,500 rpm, air flow should be noted coming out of outlet **A**.

7. Replace the combination valve if any of the tests indicate a problem.

## CHECK VALVE

The check valve is a one way valve. Pressure at the inlet allows air to flow past a viton disc. Vacuum at the outlet causes the reed to open, effecting one-way air flow in reed type valves. Air is prevented from passing through the valve if pressure at the outlet side of the valve is positive.

### Functional Test

1. Disconnect the air supply at the pump side of the valve.

2. Blow through the check valve, toward the manifold, then attempt to suck back through the valve. Air should pass in the direction of

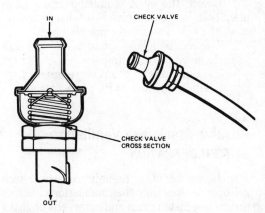

**Typical air check valve**

## Troubleshooting the Thermactor System

| Condition | Possible Source | Resolution |
|---|---|---|
| • Excessive Belt Noise | • Loose belt | • Tighten to specification CAUTION: *Do not use a pry bar to move the air pump.* |
| | • Seized pump | • Replace pump. |
| | • Loose pulley | • Replace pulley and/or pump if damaged. Tighten bolts to specification 130–180 in. lbs. |
| | • Loose or broken mounting brackets or bolts | • Replace parts as required and tighten bolts to specification. |
| • Excessive Mechanical Clicking | • Over-tightened mounting bolt | • Tighten to 25 ft. lbs. |
| | • Excessive flash on the air pump adjusting arm boss. | • Remove flash from the boss. |
| | • Distorted adjusting arm. | • Replace adjusting arm. |
| • Excessive Thermactor System Noise (Putt-Putt, Whirling or Hissing) | • Leak in hose | • Locate source of leak using soap solution, and replace hoses as necessary. |
| | • Loose, pinched or kinked hose | • Reassemble, straighten, or replace hose and clamps as required. |
| | • Hose touching other engine parts | • Adjust hose to prevent contact with other engine parts. |
| | • Bypass valve inoperative | • Test the valve. |
| | • Check valve inoperative | • Test the valve. |
| | • Pump mounting fasteners loose | • Tighten fasteners to specification. |
| | • Restricted or bent pump outlet fitting | • Inspect fitting, and remove any flash blocking the air passage way. Replace bent fittings. |
| | • Air dumping through bypass valve (at idle only) | • On many vehicles, the thermactor system has been designed to dump air at idle to prevent overheating the catalyst. This condition is normal. Determine that the noise persists at higher speeds before proceeding further. |
| • Excessive Pump Noise (Chirps, Squeaks and Ticks) | • Insufficient break-in or worn or damaged pump | • Check the thermactor system for wear or damage and make any necessary corrections. |

the exhaust manifold only. Replace the valve if air flows both ways.

### AIR PUMP

#### Removal and Installation

1. Loosen the pivot mounting and adjustment bolt. Relax the drive belt tension and remove the belt. Disconnect the air hoses.

2. Remove the adjuster and pivot nuts and bolts. Remove the air pump.

3. Installation is in the reverse order of removal. Adjust the belt to its proper tension.

## Positive Crankcase Ventilation

### SYSTEM OPERATION

A small amount of the fuel/air mixture in each cylinder escapes from the combustion chamber around the piston rings and enters the engine's crankcase, above the oil level. Since this material has been cooled by the lubricating oil and metal parts well below burning temperature, it is only partially burned and constitutes a large source of pollution. The PCV system allows outside air to be drawn in to the crankcase and to sweep this material back into the intake passages of the engine to be reburned before it either dirties the oil or escaped to the outside air. An internal baffle and an orifice control the flow of crankcase gases.

## Exhaust Emission Control

All engines are equipped with a single muffler, a single catalytic converter and connecting pipes. The converter is of the dual brick type which uses both a three way catalyst and a conventional oxidation catalyst.

### CONVERTER

#### Removal and Installation

1. Jack up the car and safely support it on jackstands.

2. Remove the front and rear converter mounting bolts. Separate the flange connections and remove the converter.

3. To install, align the flanges, install new gaskets and install the attaching bolts.

4. Align the exhaust system so that it won't rattle, and tighten the mounting bolts.

5. Remove the car from the jackstands.

## Thermostatically Controlled Air Cleaner

The air cleaner assembly intake duct is attached to a cold air intake as well as a heat shroud that surrounds the exhaust manifold. Air flow from these two sources is controlled by a door in the intake duct operated by a vacuum motor. The vacuum motor is controlled by a thermal sensor and a vacuum control system.

The thermal sensor is attached to the air valve actuating lever, along with the vacuum motor lever, both of which control the position of the air valve to supply either heated air from the exhaust manifold or cooler air from the engine compartment.

During the warm-up period, when the under-the-hood temperatures are low, the thermal sensor doesn't exert enough tension on the air valve actuating lever to close (heat off) the air valve. Thus, the carburetor receives heated air from around the exhaust manifold.

As the temperature of the air entering the air cleaner approaches approximately 110°F (43°C), the thermal sensor begins to push on the air valve actuating lever and overcome the spring tension which holds the air valve in the open (heat on) position. The air valve begins to move to the closed (heat off position, allowing only under-the-hood air to enter the air cleaner.

The air valve in the air cleaner will also open, regardless of the air temperature, during heavy acceleration to obtain maximum airflow through the air cleaner. The extreme decrease in intake manifold vacuum during heavy acceleration permits the vacuum motor to override the thermostatic control. This opens the system to both heated air and air from the engine compartment.

### HEATED AIR INTAKE TEST

1. With the engine completely cold, look inside the cold air duct and make sure that the valve plate is fully in the up position (closing the cold air duct).

2. Start the engine and bring it to operating temperature.

3. Stop the engine and look inside the cold air duct again. The valve plate should be down, allowing an opening from the cold air duct into the air cleaner.

4. If the unit appears to be malfunctioning, remove it and examine it to make sure that the springs are not broken or disconnected, and replace the thermostat if all other parts appear intact and properly connected.

## Evaporative Emission Controls

Changes in atmospheric temperature cause fuel tanks to breathe, that is, the air within the tank expands and contracts with outside temperature changes. As the temperature rises, air escapes through the tank vent tube or the vent in the tank cap. The air which escapes contains gasoline vapors. In a similar manner, the gasoline which fills the carburetor float bowl expands when the engine is stopped. Engine heat causes this expansion. The vapors escape through the carburetor and air cleaner.

The Evaporative Emission Control System provides a sealed fuel system with the capability to store and condense fuel vapors. The system has three parts: a fill control vent system; a vapor vent and storage system; and a pressure and vacuum relief system (special fill cap).

The fill control vent system is a modification to the fuel tank. It uses an air space within the tank which is 10–12% of the tank's volume. The air space is sufficient to provide for the thermal expansion of the fuel. The space also serves as part of the in-tank vapor vent system.

The in-tank vent system consists of the air space previously described and a vapor separator assembly. The separator assembly is mounted on the top of the fuel tank and is secured by a cam lockring, similar to the one which secures the fuel sending unit. Foam material fills the vapor separator assembly. The foam material separates raw fuel and vapors, thus retarding the entrance of fuel into the vapor line.

The sealed filler cap has a pressure vacuum relief valve. Under normal operating conditions, the filler cap operates as a check valve, allowing air to enter the tank to replace the fuel consumed. At the same time, it prevents vapors from escaping through the cap. In case of excessive pressure within the tank, the filler cap valve opens to relieve the pressure.

Because the filler cap is sealed, fuel vapors have but one place through which they may escape — the vapor separator assembly at the top of the fuel tank. The vapors pass through the foam material and continue through a single vapor line which leads to a canister in the engine compartment. The canister is filled with activated charcoal.

Another vapor line runs from the top of the carburetor float chamber to the charcoal canister.

As the fuel vapors (hydrocarbons) enter the charcoal canister, they are absorbed by the charcoal. The air is dispelled through the open bottom of the charcoal canister, leaving the hydrocarbons trapped within the charcoal. When the engine is started, vacuum causes fresh air to be drawn into the canister from its open bottom. The fresh air passes through the charcoal picking up the hydrocarbons which are trapped there and feeding them into the carburetor for burning with the fuel mixture.

## Exhaust Gas Recirculation (EGR)

The Exhaust Gas Recirculation System is designed to introduce small amounts of exhaust gas into the combustion cycle. Re-introducing the exhaust gas helps reduce the generation of nitrous oxides (NOx). The amount of exhaust gases re-introduced and the timing of the cycle varies as to engine speed, altitude, engine vacuum and exhaust system.

### EGR MAINTENANCE REMINDER SYSTEM

Some models are equipped with an EGR Maintenance Reminder System that consists of a mileage sensor module, an instrument panel warning light and associated wiring harness. The system provides a visual warning to indicate EGR service at 30,000 miles. The sensor is

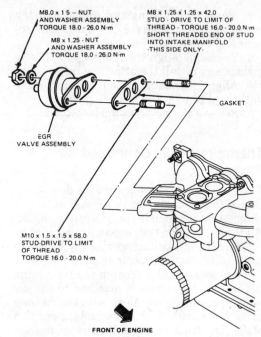

Typical EGR valve installation

an blue plastic box mounted on the dash panel in the passenger's compartment forward of the glove box. After performing the required service, the warning light is reset by installing a new sensor module.

## FUEL SYSTEM

## Mechanical Fuel Pump

The mechanical fuel pump provides fuel for the engine from the gas tank. The lever arm is actuated by a pushrod driven by an eccentric on the camshaft. The pump lever arm actuates the internal diaphragm and provides fuel on demand of the carburetor when the engine is running.

### REMOVAL AND INSTALLATION

1. Loosen the fuel outlet line using two flare wrenches. Loosen the fuel pump mounting bolts two turns.

2. Turn the engine until the fuel pump moves with just a little resistance on the mounting. The cam eccentric and pump lever are now in the low position.

3. Remove the rubber hose and clamp from the inlet side of the fuel pump.

4. Remove the outlet fuel line from the pump. Remove the mounting bolts and the fuel pump.

5. Installation is in the reverse order of removal. Mounting bolt torque is 14–21 ft.lb.

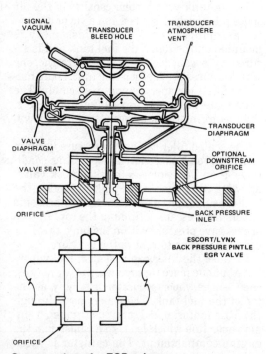

Cutaway view of a EGR valve

## Troubleshooting the EGR System

| Conditon | Possible Source | Resolution |
|---|---|---|
| • Rough Idle and/or Stalling | • EGR valve receiving vacuum at idle, vacuum hoses misrouted | • Check EGR valve vacuum hose routing. Correct as required. Check vacuum supply at idle with engine at operating temperature. |
| | • EGR valve not closing fully or stuck open | • Remove EGR valve to inspect for proper closing and seating of valve components. Clean or replace valve as required. |
| | • EGR valve gasket blown, or valve attachment loose. | • Check EGR valve attaching bolts for tightness. Inspect gasket. Tighten valve or replace gasket as required. |
| | • EGR valve air bleeds plugged | • Check to see if valve holds vacuum with engine off. If so, replace valve. |
| • Rough running, surge, hesitation and general poor performance at part throttle when engine is cold | • EGR valve receiving vacuum. Vacuum hoses misrouted. | • Check EGR valve vacuum hose routing. Correct as required. |
| | • EGR valve not closing fully or stuck open | • Remove EGR valve to inspect for proper closing and seating of valve components. Clean or replace valve as required. |
| | • EGR valve gasket blown, or valve attachment loose. | • Check EGR valve attaching bolts for tightness. Inspect gasket. Tighten valve or replace gasket as required. |
| | • EGR valve air bleeds plugged (back pressure-type valve only) | • Check to see if valve holds vacuum with engine off. If so, replace valve. |
| • Rough running, surge, hesitation, and general poor performance at part-throttle when engine is hot or cold. | Excessive EGR due to: • EGR valve stuck wide open | • Remove EGR valve to inspect for proper freedom of movement of valve components. Clean or replace as required. |
| • Engine stalls on deceleration | • EGR valve sticking open or not closing fully | • Remove EGR valve to inspect for proper closing and seating of valve components. Clean or replace as required. |
| • Part-throttle engine detonation | Insufficient EGR due to: • EGR valve stuck closed | • Check EGR valve for freedom of operation by pressing and releasing valve diaphragm to stroke the valve mechanism. Clean or replace valve if not operating smoothly. |
| | • Leaky valve diaphragm not actuating valve | • Check valve by applying vacuum. (Back pressure-type valves only—block tailpipe with drive socket of outside diameter approximately $\frac{1}{16}''$ less than inside diameter of tailpipe. DO NOT BLOCK FULLY. Idle engine while applying vacuum to valve. DO NOT RUN ENGINE FASTER THAN IDLE OR FOR PROLONGED PERIODS OF TIME. BE SURE TO REMOVE SOCKET FROM TAILPIPE AT END OF THIS TEST. IF THESE PRECAUTIONS ARE NOT OBSERVED, ENGINE AND/OR EXHAUST SYSTEM DAMAGE COULD OCCUR.) If valve leaks vacuum, replace it. |
| | • Vacuum restricted to EGR valve | • Check vacuum hoses, fittings, routing, and supply for blockage. |

## Troubleshooting the EGR System (cont.)

| Conditon | Possible Source | Resolution |
|---|---|---|
| • Part-throttle engine detonation (cont'd). | • EGR disconnected | • Check connections and reconnect as required. |
| | • Load control valve venting | • Check for proper functioning. Vacuum should be present at load control valve vacuum port to EGR valve. Replace if damaged. |
| | • EGR passages blocked. | • Check EGR passages for restrictions and blockage. |
| | • Insufficient exhaust back pressure (back pressure EGR valve only) | • Check for exhaust leaks ahead of muffler/catalyst or for blown-out muffler/catalyst. Also check for blockage to EGR valve. Service or replace all damaged components. |
| | • Vacuum hose leaking (cracked, split, broken, loose connections) | • Check all vacuum hoses for breaks and all connections for proper fit. Service or replace as required. |
| (NOTE: *Detonation can also be due to carburetor or ignition malfunction.*) | | |
| • Abnormally low power at wide open throttle. | • Load control valve not venting | • Check for proper functioning. Vacuum should not be present at vacuum port to EGR valve at wide-open throttle or heavy load. If vacuum is present, replace damaged valve. |
| • Engine starts but stalls immediately thereafter when cold | • EGR valve receiving vacuum, vacuum hoses misrouted | • Check EGR valve hose routing. Correct as required. |
| | • EGR valve not closing fully | • Remove EGR valve to inspect for proper closing and seating of valve components. Clean or replace as required. |
| (NOTE: *Stalling can also be due to carburetor malfunction.*) | | |
| • Engine hard to start, or no start condition | • EGR valve receiving vacuum. Vacuum hoses misrouted | • Check EGR valve hose routing. Correct as required. |
| | • EGR valve stuck open | • Remove EGR valve to inspect for proper closing and seating of valve components. Clean or replace as required. |
| • Poor Fuel Economy | EGR related if: • Caused by detonation or other symptom of restricted or no EGR flow | • See Resolution for part-throttle engine detonation condition. |

Use a new mounting gasket, be sure the cam eccentric is in the lower position before installing the fuel pump.

NOTE: *The fuel pump pushrod may come out when the fuel pump is removed. Be sure to install the pushrod before installing the fuel pump.*

6. After installing the pump, start the engine and check for fuel leaks.

### *FUEL PUMP CAPACITY CHECK*

The fuel pump can fail in two ways: it can fail to provide a sufficient volume of gasoline un-

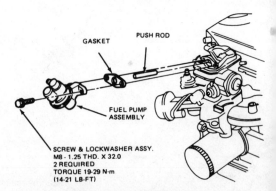

**Typical fuel pump pushrod installation**

der the proper pressure to the carburetor, or it can develop an internal or external leak. An external leak will be evident; not so with an internal leak. A quick check for an internal leak is to remove the oil dipstick and examine the oil on it. A fuel pump with an internal leak will leak fuel into the oil pan. If the oil on the dipstick is very thin and smells of gas, a defective fuel pump could be the cause.

To check the volume of gasoline from the fuel pump, disconnect the fuel pump line at the fuel filter. Connect a suitable rubber hose and clamp it to the fuel line. Insert it into a quart container. Start the engine. The fuel pump should provide one pint of gasoline in thirty seconds.

## Electric Fuel Pump

1.6 & 1.9L fuel injected models are equipped with an externally mounted electric fuel pump. The pump is located at the right rear, under the car, near the fuel tank. The pump is controlled by the EEC system, via a pump relay, which provides power to the pump under various operating conditions.

### REMOVAL AND INSTALLATION

NOTE: *Fuel pressure must be relieved before servicing the fuel system. A valve is provided on the fuel rail assembly for this purpose. Remove the air cleaner and attach a special pressure gauge tool (Rotunda T80L9974A or equivalent) to the valve and relieve the pressure.*

1. Raise and support the rear of the car on jackstands.

2. Remove the pump mounting assembly by loosening the upper mounting bolt until the pump can be lowered. Remove the parking brake cable from mounting clip to provide necessary working room.

3. Disconnect the electrical connector and disconnect the fuel pump outlet fitting.

4. Disconnect the fuel pump inlet line from the pump.

CAUTION: *Either drain the tank or raise the end of the line above the tank level to prevent draining.*

5. Install the fuel pump in the reverse order of removal.

6. Install the pressure gauge on the fuel rail. Turn the ignition ON for 2 seconds. Turn the switch OFF. Repeat procedure several times, until the pressure gauge shows 35 psi. Remove the gauge. Start the engine and check for leaks.

### INERTIA SWITCH

A safety inertia switch is installed to shut off the electric fuel pump in case of collision. The switch is located on the left hand side of the car, behind the rearmost seat side trim panel, or inside the rear quarter shock tower access door. If the pump shuts off, or if the vehicle has been hit and will not start, check for leaks fist then reset the switch. The switch is reset by pushing down on the button provided.

## Push Connect Fittings

Push connect fittings are designed with two different retaining clips. The fittings used with $^5/_{16}$" (8mm) diameter tubing use a hairpin clip. The fittings used with ¼" (6mm) and ½" (12.7mm) diameter tubing use a "duck bill" clip. Each type of fitting requires different procedures for service.

Push connect fitting disassembly must be accomplished prior to fuel component removal (filter, pump, etc.) except for the fuel tank where removal is necessary for access to the push connects.

### REMOVAL AND INSTALLATION

#### $^5/_{16}$" Fittings (Hairpin Clip)

1. Inspect internal portion of fitting for dirt accumulation. If more than a light coating of dust is present, clean the fitting before disassembly.

2. Remove hairpin type clip from fitting. This is done (using hands only) by spreading the two clip legs about ⅛" (3mm) each to disengage the body and pushing the legs into the fitting. Complete removal is accomplished by lightly pulling from the triangular end of the clip and working it clear of the tube and fitting.

NOTE: *Do not use any tools.*

3. Grasp the fitting and hose assembly and pull in an axial direction to remove the fitting from the steel tube. Adhesion between sealing surfaces may occur. A slight twist of the fitting may be required to break this adhesion and permit effortless removal.

4. When fitting is removed from the tube end, inspect clip t ensure it has not been damaged. If damaged, replace the clip. If undamaged, immediately reinstall clip, insert clip into any two adjacent openings with the trian-

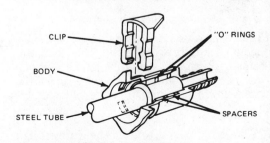

CLIP    "O" RINGS

BODY

STEEL TUBE    SPACERS

**Push connect fittings with hairpin clip**

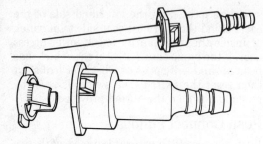

**Push connect fittings with duck bill clip**

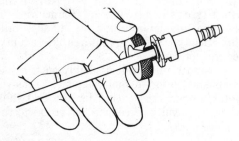

**Removing push connect with tool**

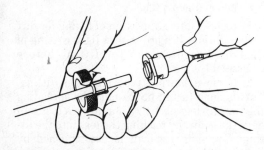

**Pulling off push connect fitting**

gular portion pointing away from the fitting opening. Install clip to fully engage the body (legs of hairpin clip locked on outside of body). Piloting with an index finger is necessary.

5. Before installing fitting on the tube, wipe tube end with a clean cloth. Inspect the inside of the fitting to ensure it is free of dirt and/or obstructions.

6. To reinstall the fitting onto the tube, align the fitting and tube axially and push the fitting onto the tube end. When the fitting is engaged, a definite click will be heard. Pull on fitting to ensure it is fully engaged.

### ½" and ¼" Fittings (Duck Bill Clip)

The fitting consists of a body, spacers, O-rings and a duck bill retaining clip. The clip maintains the fitting to steel tube juncture. When disassembly is required for service, one of the two following methods are to be followed:

#### ¼" FITTINGS

To disengage the tube from the fitting, align the slot on push connect disassembly Tool

T82L-9500-AH or equivalent with either tab on the clip (90° from slots on side of fitting) and insert the tool. This disengages the duck bill from the tube. Holding the tool and the tube with one hand, pull fitting away from the tube.

NOTE: *Only moderate effort is required if the tube has been properly disengaged. Use hands only. After disassembly, inspect and clean the tube sealing surface. Also inspect the inside of the fitting for damage to the retaining clip. If the retaining clip appears to be damaged, replace it.*

Some fuel tubes have a secondary bead which aligns with the outer surface of the clip. These beads can make tool insertion difficult. If there is extreme difficulty, use the disassembly method following.

#### ½" FITTING AND ALTERNATE METHOD FOR ¼" FITTING

This method of disassembly disengages the retaining clip from the fitting body.

Use a pair of narrow pliers, (6" [153mm] locking pliers are ideal). The pliers must have a jaw width of 0.2" (5mm) or less.

Align the jaws of the pliers with the openings in the side of the fitting case and compress the portion of the retaining clip that engages the fitting case. This disengages the retaining clip from the case (often one side of the clip will disengage before the other. It is necessary to disengage the clip from both openings). Pull the fitting off the tube.

NOTE: *Only moderate effort is required if the retaining clip has been properly disengaged. Use hands only.*

The retaining clip will remain on the tube. Disengage the clip from the tube bead and remove. Replace the retaining clip if it appears to be damaged.

NOTE: *Slight ovality of the ring of the clip will usually occur. If there are no visible cracks and the ring will pinch back to its circular configuration, it is not damaged. If there is any doubt, replace the clip.*

Install the clip into the body by inserting one of the retaining clip serrated edges on the duck bill portion into one of the window openings. Push on the other side until the clip snaps into place. Slide fuel line back into the clip.

## Carburetor

Your car uses, depending on year and model, a staged two barrel unit (the second barrel is opened under heavy throttle situations), or a single barrel carburetor. Carburetors may be of the feed back or non-feedback type.

The staged carburetor usually has five basic metering system. They are: the choke system, idle system, main metering system, acceleration system and the power enrichment system.

The choke system is used for cold starting. It incorporates a bimetal spring and an electric heater for faster cold weather starts and improved driveability during warm-up.

The idle system is a separate and adjustable system for the correct air/fuel mixture at both idle and low speed operation.

The main metering system provides the necessary air/fuel mixture for normal driving speeds. A main metering system is provided for both primary and secondary stages of operation.

The accelerating system is operated from the primary stage throttle linkage. The system provides fuel to the primary stage during acceleration. Fuel is provided by a diaphragm pump located on the carburetor.

The power enrichment system consists of a vacuum operated power valve and airflow regulated pullover system for the secondary carburetor barrel. The system is used in conjunction with the main metering system to provide acceptable performance during mid and heavy acceleration.

## REMOVAL AND INSTALLATION

1. Remove the air cleaner assembly. Disconnect the throttle control cable and speed control (if equipped). Disconnect the fuel line at the filter.

2. Label and disconnect all vacuum hoses, wires and linkage attached to the carburetor. If your car is equipped with an automatic transaxle, disconnect the TV linkage.

3. Remove the four mounting bolts that attach the carburetor to the intake manifold, remove the carburetor.

4. Installation is in the reverse order of removal. If you car is equipped with an automatic transaxle, a TV linkage adjustment may be required.

## OVERHAUL NOTES

NOTE: *All major and minor repair kits contain detailed instructions and illustrations. Refer to them for complete rebuilding instructions.*

*To prevent damage to the throttle plates, make a stand using four bolts, eight flat washers and eight nuts. Place a washer and nut on the bolt, install through the carburetor base and secure with a nut.*

Generally, when a carburetor requires major service, rebuilt one is purchased on an exchange basis, or a kit may be bought for overhauling the carburetor.

The kit contains the necessary parts (see below) and some form of instructions for carburetor rebuilding. The instructions may vary between a simple exploded view and detailed step-by-step rebuilding instructions. Unless you are familiar with carburetor overhaul, the latter should be used.

There are some general overhaul procedures which should always be observed:

Efficient carburetion depends greatly on careful cleaning and inspection during overhaul since dirt, gum, water, or varnish in or on the carburetor parts are often responsible for poor performance.

Overhaul you carburetor in a clean, dust free area. Carefully disassembly the carburetor, referring often to the exploded views. Keep all similar and lookalike parts segregated during disassembly and cleaning to avoid accidental interchange during assembly. Make a note of all jet sizes.

When the carburetor is disassembled, wash all parts (except diaphragms, electric choke units. pump plunger, and any other plastic, leather, fiber, or rubber parts) in clean carburetor solvent. Do not leave parts in the solvent any longer than is necessary to sufficiently loosen the deposits. Excessive cleaning may remove the special finish from the float bowl and choke valve bodies, leaving these parts unfit for service. Rinse all parts in clean solvent and blow them dry with compressed air or allow them to air dry. Wipe clean all cork, plastic, leather, and fiber parts with a clean, lint free cloth.

Blow out all passages and jets with compressed air and be sure that there are no restrictions or blockages. Never use wire or similar tools to clean jets, fuel passages, or air bleeds. Clean all jets and valves separately to avoid accidental interchange.

Check all parts for wear or damage. If wear or damage is found, replace the defective parts. Especially check the following:

1. Check the float needle and seat for wear. If wear is found, replace the complete assembly.

2. Check the float hinge pin for wear and the float(s) for dents or distortion. Replace the float if fuel has leaked into it.

3. Check the throttle and choke shaft bores for wear or an out-of-round condition. Damage or wear to the throttle arm, shaft, shaft bore will often require replacement of the throttle body. These parts require a close tolerance; wear may allow air leakage, which could affect starting and idling.

NOTE: *Throttle shafts and bushings are usually not included in overhaul kits. They can be purchased separately.*

4. Inspect the idle mixture adjusting needles for burrs or grooves. Any such condition requires replacement of the needle, since you

will not be able to obtain a satisfactory idle.

5. Test the accelerator pump check valves. They should pass air one way but not the other. Test for proper seating by blowing and sucking on the valve. Replace the valve if necessary. If the valve is satisfactory, wash the valve again to remove breath moisture.

6. Check the bowl cover for warped surfaces with a straightedge.

7. Closely inspect the valves and seats for wear and damage, replacing as necessary.

8. After the carburetor is assembled, check the choke valve for freedom of operation.

Carburetor overhaul kits are recommended for each overhaul. These kits contain all gaskets and new parts to replace those that deteriorate most rapidly. Failure to replace all parts supplied with the kit (especially gaskets) can result in poor performance later.

Some carburetor manufacturers supply overhaul kits of three basic types: minor repair, major repair, and gasket kits. Basically, they contain the following:

**Minor Repair Kits:**
- All gaskets
- Float needle valve
- Volume control screw
- All diaphragms
- Spring for the pump diaphragm

**Major Repair Kits:**
- All jets and gaskets
- All diaphragms
- Float needle valve
- Volume control screw
- Pump ball valve
- Main jet carrier
- Float
- Other necessary items
- Some cover holddown screws and washers

**Gasket Kits:**
- All gaskets

After cleaning and checking all components, reassemble the carburetor, using new parts and referring to the exploded view. When reassembling, make sure that all screw and jets are tight in their seats, buy do not overtighten, as the tips will be distorted. Tighten all screws gradually, in rotation. Do not tighten needle valves into their seat; uneven jetting will result. Always use new gaskets. Be sure to adjust the float level when reassembling.

## Motorcraft 740/5740 Carburetor

### ADJUSTMENTS

#### Fast Idle Cam

1. Set the fast idle screw on the kickdown step of the cam against the shoulder of the top step.

2. Manually close the primary choke plate, and measure the distance between the downstream side of the choke plate and the air horn wall.

3. Adjust the right fork of the choke bimetal shaft, which engages the fast idle cam, by bending the fork up and down to obtain the required clearance.

#### Fast Idle

1. Place the transmission in neutral or park.

2. Bring the engine to normal operating temperature.

3. Disconnect and plug the vacuum hose at the EGR and purge valves.

4. Identify the vacuum source to the air bypass section of the air supply control valve. If a vacuum hose is connected to the carburetor, disconnect the hose and plug the hose at the air supply control valve.

5. Place the fast idle adjustment on the second step of the fast idle cam. Run the engine until the cooling fan comes on.

6. While the cooling fan is on, check the fast idle rpm. If adjustment is necessary, loosen the locknut and adjust to specification on underhood decal.

7. Remove all plugs and reconnect hoses to their original position.

#### Dashpot

With the throttle set at the curb idle position, fully depress the dashpot stem and measure the distance between the stem and the throttle lever. Adjust by loosening the locknut and turning the dashpot.

#### Choke Plate Pulldown

NOTE: *The following procedure requires the removal of the carburetor and also the choke cap which is retained by two rivets.*

1. Remove the carburetor from the engine.

2. Remove the choke cap as follows:

   a. Check the rivets to determine if mandrel is well below the rivet head. If mandrel is within the rivet head thickness, drive it down or out with a $\frac{1}{16}''$ (1.6mm) diameter tip punch.

   b. With a $\frac{1}{8}''$ (3mm) diameter drill, drill into the rivet head until the rivet head comes loose from the rivet body. Use light pressure on the drill bit or the rivet will just spin in the hole.

   c. After drilling off the rivet head, drive the remaining rivet out of the hole with a $\frac{1}{8}''$ (3mm) diameter punch.

   d. Repeat steps (a thru c) to remove the remaining rivet.

3. Set the fast idle adjusting screw on the high step of the fast idle cam by temporarily

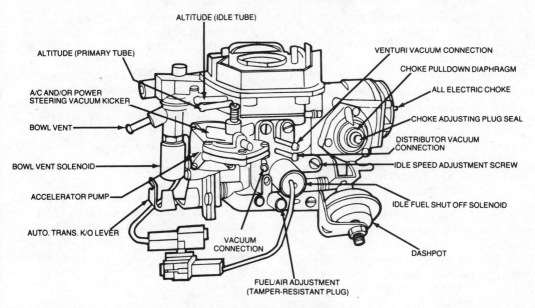

**Motorcraft 740/5740 carburetor**

opening the throttle lever and rotating the choke bimetal shaft lever counterclockwise until the choke plates are in the fully closed position.

4. With an external vacuum source, set to 17 in.Hg. Vacuum should be applied to the vacuum channel adjacent to the primary bore on the base of the carburetor.

NOTE: *The modulator spring should not be depressed.*

5. Measure the clearance between the downstream side of the choke plate and the air horn wall.

6. If an adjustment is necessary, turn the vacuum diaphragm adjusting screw in or out as required.

### Float Level

1. Hold the air horn upside down, at about a 45° angle with the air horn gasket in position.

2. Use the gauge (supplied with the rebuilding kit) and measure the clearance between the float toe and air horn casting.

3. Adjust, if necessary, by removing the float and bending the adjusting tang. Use care when handling the float.

### Float Drop

Hold the air horn in its normal installed position. Measure the clearance from the gasket to the bottom of the float. Adjust, if necessary, by removing the float and bending the float drop adjusting tab.

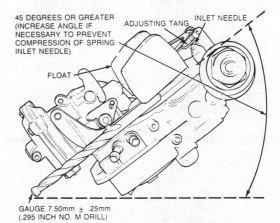

GAUGE 7.50mm ± .25mm
(.295 INCH NO. M DRILL)

**Float level adjustment—Motorcraft 740/5740 carburetor**

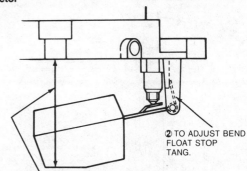

② TO ADJUST BEND FLOAT STOP TANG.

① AIR HORN HELD IN NORMAL POSITION. FLOAT HANGING IN FULL DOWN POSITION. MEASURE FROM AIR HORN TO FLOAT, AS SHOWN.

43.5mm ± 8mm
(1.71 ± 0.31 INCH) SETTING

**Float drop adjustment—Motorcraft 740/5740 carburetor**

## Holley 1949/6149 (Feedback) Carburetor

### ADJUSTMENTS

#### Float Level

1. Remove the carburetor air horn.

2. With the air horn assembly removed, place a finger over float hinge pin retainer, and invert the main body. Catch the accelerator pump check ball and weight.

3. Using a straight edge, check the position of the floats. The correct dry float setting is that both pontoons at the extreme outboard edge be flush with the surface of the main body casting (without gasket). If adjustment is required, bend the float tabs to raise or lower the float level.

4. Once adjustment is correct, turn main body right side up, and check the float alignment. The float should move freely throughout its range without contacting the fuel bowl walls. If the float pontoons are misaligned, straighten by bending the float arms. Recheck the float level adjustment.

5. During assembly, insert the check ball first and then the weight.

#### Feedback Controlled Main System — Diaphragm Adjustment (6149 Only)

1. Remove the main system feedback diaphragm adjustment screw lead sealing disc from the air horn screw boss, by drilling a 2.38mm diameter hole through the disc. Then, insert a small punch to pry the disc out.

2. Turn the main system feedback adjustment screw as required to position the top of the screw 4.57mm ± 0.25mm below the top of the air horn adjustment screw boss.

NOTE: *For carburetors stamped with as* **S** *on the top of the air horn adjustment screw boss, adjust screw position to 6.35mm ± 0.25mm.*

3. Install a new lead sealing disc and stake with a ¼″ (6mm) flat ended punch.

4. Apply an external vacuum source (hand vacuum pump — 10 in.Hg max.) and check for leaks. The diaphragm should hold vacuum.

#### Auxiliary Main Jet/Pullover Valve — Timing Adjustment

The length of the auxiliary main jet/pullover valve adjustment screw which protrudes through the back side (side opposite the adjustment screw head) of the throttle pick-up lever must be 8.76mm ± 0.25mm. To adjust turn screw in or out as required.

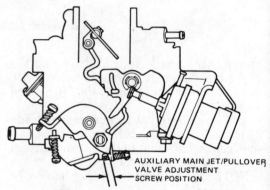

**Timing adjustment—6149 carb**

#### Mechanical Fuel Bowl Vent Adjustment Lever Clearance

##### OFF VEHICLE ADJUSTMENT

NOTE: *There are two methods for adjusting lever clearance.*

1. Secure the choke plate in the wide open position.

2. Set the throttle at the TSP Off position.

3. Turn the TSP Off idle adjustment screw

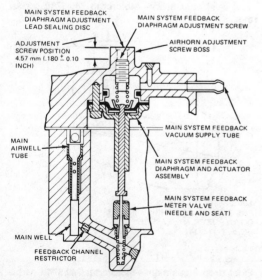

**Diaphragm adjustment—6149 carb**

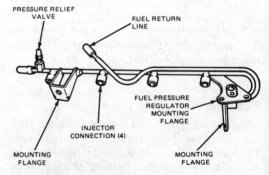

**Vent adjustment—6149 carb**

counterclockwise until the throttle plate is closed in the throttle bore.

4. Fuel bowl vent clearance, Dimension **A**, should be 3.05mm ± 0.25mm.

5. If out of specification, bend the bowl vent actuator lever at the adjustment point to obtain the required clearance.

CAUTION: *Do not bend fuel bowl vent arm and/or adjacent portion of the actuator lever.*

NOTE: *TSP Off rpm must be set after carburetor installation.*

### ON VEHICLE ADJUSTMENT

NOTE: *This adjustment must be performed after curb idle speed has been set to specification.*

1. Secure the choke plate in the wide open position.

2. Turn ignition key to the ON position to activate the TSP (engine not running). Open throttle so that the TSP plunger extends.

3. Verify that the throttle is in the idle set position (contacting the TSP plunger). Measure the clearance of the fuel bowl vent arm to the bowl vent actuating lever.

4. Fuel bowl vent clearance, Dimension **A**, should be 0.76mm.

NOTE: *There is a difference in the on-vehicle and off-vehicle specification.*

5. If out of specification, bend the bowl vent actuator lever at the adjustment point to obtain the required clearance.

CAUTION: *Do not bend fuel bowl vent arm and/or adjacent portion of the actuating lever.*

### Accelerator Pump Stroke Adjustment

1. Check the length of the accelerator pump operating link from its inside edge at the accelerator pump operating rod to its inside edge at the throttle lever hole. The dimension should be 54.61 ± 0.25mm.

2. Adjust to proper length by bending loop in operating link.

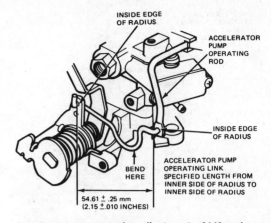

Accelerator pump stroke adjustment—6149 carb

### WOT A/C Cut–Off Switch Adjustment (1949 Only)

The WOT A/C cutoff switch is a normally closed switch (allowing current to flow at any throttle position other than wide open throttle).

1. Disconnect the wiring harness at the switch connector.

2. Connect a 12 volt DC power supply and test lamp. With the throttle at curb idle, TSP Off idle or fast idle position, the test light must be On. If the test lamp does not light, replace the switch assembly.

3. Rotate the throttle to the wide open position. The test lamp must go Off, indicating an open circuit.

4. If the lamp remains On, insert a 4.19mm drill or gauge between the throttle lever WOT stop and the WOT stop boss on the carburetor main body casting. Hold the throttle open as far as possible against the gauge. Loosen the two switch mounting screws sufficiently to allow the switch to pivot. Rotate the switch assembly so the test lamp just goes out with the throttle held in the above referenced position. If the lamp does not go Off within the allowable adjustment rotation, replace the switch. If the light goes out, tighten the two switch

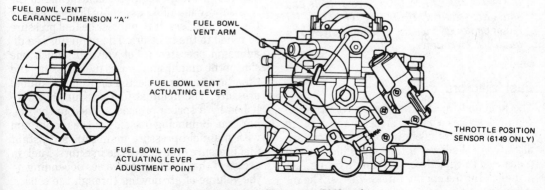

Lever clearance adjustment—6149 carb

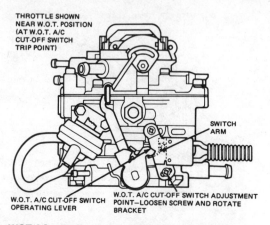

THROTTLE SHOWN
NEAR W.O.T. POSITION
(AT W.O.T. A/C
CUT-OFF SWITCH
TRIP POINT)

SWITCH
ARM

W.O.T. A/C CUT-OFF SWITCH
OPERATING LEVER

W.O.T. A/C CUT-OFF SWITCH ADJUSTMENT
POINT—LOOSEN SCREW AND ROTATE
BRACKET

**WOT/AC cut-off switch adjustment—6149 carb**

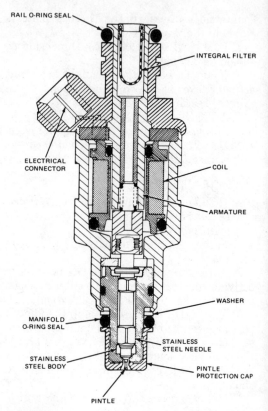

RAIL O-RING SEAL

INTEGRAL FILTER

ELECTRICAL
CONNECTOR

COIL

ARMATURE

MANIFOLD
O-RING SEAL

WASHER

STAINLESS
STEEL NEEDLE

STAINLESS
STEEL BODY

PINTLE
PROTECTION CAP

PINTLE

**Fuel injector**

bracket-to-carburetor screws to 45 in.lb. and remove drill or gauge and repeat Step 3.

## ELECTRONIC FUEL INJECTION

NOTE: *This book contains simple testing and service procedures for for your car's fuel injection system. More comprehensive testing and diagnosis procedures, which cannot be included here, may be found in CHILTON'S GUIDE TO FUEL INJECTION AND FEEDBACK CARBURETORS, book part number 7488, available at your local retailer.*

The Electronic Fuel Injection System (EFI) is a multi-point, pulse time, mass air flow fuel injection system. Fuel is metered into the air intake stream in accordance with engine demand through four injectors mounted on a tuned intake manifold. An onboard (EEC) computer receives input from various sensors to compute the required fuel flow rate necessary to maintain the necessary air/fuel ratio throughout the entire engine operational range.

The EFI system can be separated into four categories: Fuel Delivery, Air Induction, Sensors, and the Electronic Control Circuit.

NOTE: *A brief testing section is included at the end of the EFI section: Special tools and skills are required. If the tools or knowledge is not on hand, have the system serviced by a qualified mechanic.*

### Fuel Injectors

The four fuel injector nozzles are electro-mechanical devices which both meter and atomize fuel delivered to the engine. The injectors are mounted in the lower intake manifold and are positioned so that their tips are directing fuel just ahead of the engine intake valves. The injector bodies consist of a solenoid actuated pin-

tle and needle valve assembly. An electrical control signal from the Electronic Engine Control unit activates the injector solenoid causing the pintle to move inward off the seat, allowing fuel to flow. Since the injector flow orifice if fixed and the fuel pressure drop across the injector tip is constant, fuel flow to the engine is regulated by how long the solenoid is energized. Atomization is obtained by contouring the pintle at the point where the fuel separates.

### Fuel Pressure Regulator

The fuel pressure regulator is attached to the fuel supply manifold assembly downstream of the fuel injectors. It regulates the fuel pressure supplied to the injectors. The regulator is a diaphragm operated relief valve in which one side of the diaphragm senses fuel pressure and the other side is subjected to intake manifold pressure. The nominal fuel pressure is established by a spring preload applied to the diaphragm. Balancing one side of the diaphragm with manifold pressure maintains a constant fuel pressure drop across the injectors. Fuel, in excess of that used by the varies depending on the volume of air flowing through the sensor. The temperature sensor in the air vane meter

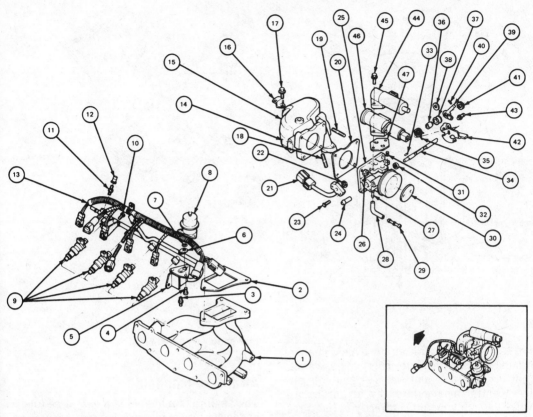

1. Manifold—intake lower
2. Gasket—intake manifold upper
3. Connector—¼ flareless x ⅛ external pipe
4. Screw—M5 x .8 x 10 socket head
5. Manifold assembly—fuel injection fuel supply
6. Gasket—fuel pressure regulator
7. Seal—⁵⁄₁₆ x .070 "O" ring
8. Regulator assembly—fuel pressure
9. Injector assembly—fuel
10. Bolt—M8 x 1.25 x 20 hex flange head
11. Valve assembly—fuel pressure relief
12. Cap—fuel pressure relief
13. Wiring harness—fuel charging
14. Decal—carburetor identification
15. Manifold—intake upper
16. Retainer—wiring harness
17. Bolt—M8 x 1.25 x 30 hex flange head
18. Stud—M6 x 1.0 x 1.0 x 40
19. Stud—M8 x 1.25 x 1.25 x 47.5
20. Gasket—air intake charge to intake manifold
21. Potentiometer—throttle position
22. Bushing—carburetor throttle shaft
23. Screw and washer assembly M4 x 22
24. Tube—emission inlet

25. Body—air intake charge throttle
26. Nut—M8 x 1.25
27. Tube
28. Hose—vacuum
29. Connector
30. Plate—air intake charge throttle
31. Screw—M4 x .7 x 8
32. Seal—throttle control shaft
33. Pin—spring coiled ¹⁄₁₆ x .42
34. Shaft
35. Spring—throttle return
36. Bushing—accelerator pump overtravel spring
37. Bearing—throttle control linkage
38. Spacer—throttle control torsion spring (MTX only)
39. Lever—carburetor transmission linkage
40. Screw—M5 x .8 x 16.25 slot head
41. Spacer—carburetor throttle shaft
42. Lever—carburetor throttle
43. Ball—carburetor throttle lever
44. Valve assembly—throttle air bypass (alt)
45. Bolt—M6 x 1.0 x 20 hex flange head
46. Valve assembly—throttle air bypass
47. Gasket—air bypass valve

**EFI components**

measures the incoming air temperature. These two inputs, air volume and temperature, are used by the Electronic Control Assembly to compute the mass air flow. This value is then used to compute the fuel flow necessary for the optimum air/fuel ration which is fed to the injectors.

## Air Throttle Body Assembly

The throttle body assembly controls air flow to the engine through a sing butterfly type valve. The throttle position is controlled by conventional cable/cam throttle linkage. The body is a single piece die casting made of aluminum. It

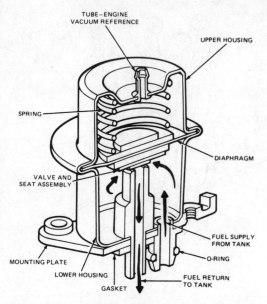

**Fuel pressure regulator—EFI**

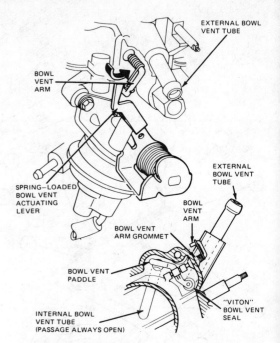

**Fuel supply manifold-EFI**

has a single bore with an air bypass channel around the throttle plate. This bypass channel controls both cold and warm engine idle airflow control as regulated by an air bypass valve assembly mounted directly to the throttle body.

The valve assembly is an electro-mechanical device controlled by the EEC computer. It incorporates a linear actuator which positions a variable area metering valve.

Other features of the air throttle body assembly include:

1. An adjustment screw to set the throttle plate a a minimum idle airflow position.

2. A preset stop to locate the WOT position.

3. A throttle body mounted throttle position sensor.

4. A PCV fresh air source located upstream of the throttle plate.

5. Individual ported vacuum taps (as required) for PCV and EVAP control signals.

## Fuel Supply Manifold Assembly

The fuel supply manifold assembly is the component that delivers high pressure fuel from the vehicle fuel supply line to the four fuel injectors. The assembly consists of a single preformed tube or stamping with four injector connectors, a mounting flange for the fuel pressure regulator, a pressure relief valve for diagnostic testing or field service fuel system pressure bleed down and mounting attachments which locate the fuel manifold assembly and provide fuel injector retention.

## Air Intake Manifold

The air intake manifold is a two piece (upper and lower intake manifold) aluminum casting. Runner lengths are tuned to optimize engine torque and power output. The manifold provides mounting flanges for the air throttle body assembly, fuel supply manifold and accelerator control bracket and the EGR valve and supply tube. Vacuum taps are provided to support various engine accessories. Pockets for the fuel injectors are machined to prevent both air and fuel leakage. The pockets, in which the injectors are mounted, are placed to direct the injector fuel spray immediately in front of each engine intake valve.

## Fuel Charging Assembly

NOTE: *If sub-assemblies are to be serviced and/or removed, with the fuel charging assembly mounted to the engine, the following steps must be taken:*

1. Open hood and install protective covers.

2. Make sure that ignition key is in Off position.

3. Drain coolant from radiator.

4. Disconnect the negative battery lead and secure it out of the way.

5. Remove fuel cap to relieve fuel tank pressure.

6. Release pressure from the fuel system at the fuel pressure relief valve on the fuel injection manifold assembly. Use tool T80L-9974-A or equivalent. To gain access to the fuel pres-

sure relief valve, the valve cap must first be removed.

7. Disconnect the push connect fuel supply line. Using a small bladed screwdriver inserted under the hairpin clip tab, pop the clip free from the push connect tube fitting and disconnect the tube. Save the hairpin clip for use in reassembly.

8. Identify and disconnect the fuel return lines and vacuum connections.

NOTE: *Care must be taken to avoid combustion from fuel spillage.*

9. Disconnect the injector wiring harness by disconnecting the ECT sensor in the heater supply tube under lower intake manifold and the electronic engine control harness.

10. Disconnect air bypass connector from EEC harness.

NOTE: *Not all assemblies may be serviceable while on the engine. In some cases, removal of the fuel charging assembly may facilitate service of the various sub-assemblies. To remove the entire fuel charging assembly, the following procedure should be followed:*

## REMOVAL AND INSTALLATION

1. Remove the engine air cleaner outlet tube between the vane air meter and air throttle body by loosening two clamps.

2. Disconnect and remove the accelerator and speed control cables (if so eqiupped) from the accelerator mounting bracket and throttle lever.

3. Disconnect the top manifold vacuum fitting connections by disconnecting:

   a. Rear vacuum line to the dash panel vacuum tree.

   b. Front vacuum line to the air cleaner and fuel pressure regulator.

4. Disconnect the PCV system by disconnecting the hoses from:

   a. Two large forward facing connectors on the throttle body and intake manifold.

   b. Throttle body port hose at the straight plastic connector.

   c. Canister purge line at the straight plastic connector.

   d. PCV hose at rocker cover.

   e. Unbolt PCV separator support bracket from cylinder head and remove PCV system.

5. Disconnect the EGR vacuum line at the EGR valve.

6. Disconnect the EGR tube from the upper intake manifold by removing the two flange nuts.

7. Withdraw the dipstick and remove the dipstick tube by removing the tube bracket mounting nut and working the tube out of the block hole.

8. Remove the fuel return line.

9. Remove six manifold mounting nuts.

10. Remove the manifold with wiring harness and gasket.

11. Clean and inspect the mounting faces of the fuel charging manifold assembly and the cylinder head. Both surfaces must be clean and flat.

12. Clean and oil manifold stud threads.

13. Install a new gasket.

14. Install manifold assembly to head and secure with top middle nut (tighten nut finger tight only at this time).

15. Install fuel return line to the fitting in the fuel supply manifold. Install two manifold mounting nuts, fingertight.

16. Install dipstick in block and secure with bracket nut fingertight.

17. Install remaining three manifold mounting nuts and tighten all six nuts to 12–15 ft.lb. observing specified tightening sequence.

18. Install EGR tube with two oil coated flange nuts tightened to 6–8.5 ft.lb.

19. Reinstall PCV system.

   a. Mount separator bracket to head.

   b. Install hose on rocker cover, tighten clamps.

   c. Connect vacuum line to canister purge.

   d. Connect vacuum line to throttle body port.

   e. Connect large PCV vacuum line to throttle body.

   f. Connect large PCV vacuum line to upper manifold.

20. Connect manifold vacuum connections:

   a. Rear connection to vacuum tree.

   b. Front connection to fuel pressure regulator and air cleaner.

21. Connect accelerator and speed control cables (if so equipped).

22. Install air supply tube and tighten clamps to 25 in.lb.

23. Connect the wiring harness at:

   a. ECT sensor in heater supply tube.

   b. Electronic Engine Control harness.

24. Connect the fuel supply hose from the fuel filter to the fuel rail.

25. Connect the fuel return line.

26. Connect negative battery cable.

27. Install engine coolant using prescribed fill procedure.

28. Start engine and allow to run at idle until engine temperature is stabilized. Check for coolant leaks.

29. If necessary, reset idle speed.

## REMOVAL AND INSTALLATION OF SUB-ASSEMBLIES

NOTE: *To prevent damage to fuel chargine assembly, the unit should be placed on a work bench during disassembly and assem-*

bly procedures. *The following is a step by step sequence of operations for servicing the assemblies of the fuel charging manifold. Some components may be serviced without a complete disassembly of the fuel charging manifold. To replace individual components, follow only the applicable steps.*

These procedures are based on the fuel charging manifold having been removed from the vehicle.

### Upper Intake Manifold

1. Disconnect the engine air cleaner outlet tube from the air intake throttle body.
2. Unplug the throttle position sensor from the wiring harness.
3. Unplug the air bypass valve connector.
4. Remove three upper manifold retaining bolts.
5. Remove upper manifold assembly and set it aside.
6. Remove and discard the gasket from the lower manifold assembly.
NOTE: *If scraping is necessary, be careful not to damage the gasket surfaces of the upper and lower manifold assemblies, or allow material to drop into lower manifold.*
7. Ensure that the gasket surfaces of the upper and lower intake manifolds are clean.
8. Place a new service gasket on the lower manifold assembly and mount the upper intake manifold to the lower, securing it with three retaining bolts. Tighten bolts to 15–22 ft.lb.
9. Ensure the wiring harness is properly installed.
10. Connect electrical connectors t air bypass valve and throttle position sensor and the vacuum hose to the fuel pressure regulator.
11. Connect the engine air cleaner outlet tube to the throttle body intake securing it with a hose clamp. Tighten to 15–25 in.lb.

### Air Intake Throttle Body

1. Remove four throttle body nuts. Ensure that the throttle position sensor connector and air bypass valve connector have been disconnected from the harness. Disconnect air cleaner outlet tube.
2. Identify and disconnect vacuum hoses.
3. Remove throttle bracket.
4. Carefully separate the throttle body from the upper intake manifold.
5. Remove and discard the gasket between the throttle body and the upper intake manifold.
NOTE: *If scraping is necessary, be careful not to damage the gasket surfaces of the throttle body and upper manifold assemblies, or allow material to drop into manifold.*

6. Ensure that both throttle body and upper intake manifold gasket surfaces are clean.
7. Install the upper/throttle body gasket on the four studs of the upper intake manifold.
8. Secure the throttle bracket and secure with two nuts. Tighten to 12–15 ft.lb.
9. Install throttle bracket and secure with two nuts. Tighten to 12–15 ft.lb.
10. Connect the air bypass valve and throttle position sensor electrical connectors and appropriate vacuum lines.
11. If the fuel charging assembly is still mounted to the engine, connect the engine air cleaner outlet tube to the throttle body intake securing it with a hose clamp. Tighten the clamp to 15–25 in.lb.

### Air Bypass Valve Assembly

1. Disconnect the air bypass valve assembly connector from the wiring harness.
2. Remove the two air bypass valve retaining screws.
3. Remove the air bypass valve and gasket.
NOTE: *If scraping is necessary, be careful not to damage the air bypass valve or throttle body gasket surfaces, or drop material into throttle body.*
4. Ensure that both the throttle body and air bypass valve gasket surfaces are clean.
5. Install gasket on throttle body surface and mount the air bypass valve assembly securing it with two retaining screws. Tighten to 71–102 in.lb.
6. Connect the electircal connector for the air bypass valve.

### Throttle Position Sensor

1. Disconnect the throttle position sensor from the wiring harness.
2. Remove two throttle position sensor retaining screws.
3. Remove the throttle position sensor.
4. Install the throttle position sensor. Make sure that the rotary tangs on the sensor are in the proper alignment and the wires are pointing down.
5. Secure the sensor to the throttle body assembly with two retaining screws. Tighten to 11–16 in.lb.
NOTE: *This throttle position sensor is not adjustable.*
6. Connect the electrical connector to the harness.

### Pressure Relief Valve

1. If the fuel charging assembly is mounted to the engine, remove fuel tank cap then release pressure from the system at the pressure relief valve on the fuel injection manifold us-

ing Tool T80L-9974-A or equivalent. Note the cap on the relief valve must be removed.

2. Using an open end wrench or suitable deep well socket, remove pressure relief valve for fuel injection manifold.

3. Install pressure relief valve and cap. Tighten valve to 48–84 in.lb. and the cap to 4–6 in.lb.

### Fuel Injector Manifold Assembly

1. Remove fuel tank cap and release pressure from the fuel system at the fuel pressure relief valve using Tool T80L-9974-A or equivalent.

2. Disconnect the fuel supply and fuel return lines.

3. Disconnect the wiring harness from the injectors.

4. Disconnect vacuum line from fuel pressure regulator valve.

5. Remove two fuel injector manifolds retaining bolts.

6. Carefully disengage manifold from the fuel injectors and remove manifold.

7. Make sure the injector caps are clean and free of contamination.

8. Place fuel injector manifold over the four injectors making sure the injectors are well seated in the fuel manifold assembly.

9. Secure the fuel manifold assembly to the charging assembly using two retaining bolts.

10. Connect fuel supply and fuel return lines.

11. Connect fuel injector wiring harness.

12. Connect vacuum line to fuel pressure regulator.

### Fuel Pressure Regulator

1. Be sure that the assembly is depressurized by removing fuel tank cap and releasing pressure from the fuel system at the pressure relief valve on the fuel injection manifold using Tool T80L-9974-A or equivalent.

2. Remove the vacuum line at the pressure regulator.

3. Remove three Allen retaining screws from regulator housing.

4. Remove pressure regulator assembly, gasket and O-ring. Discard gasket and inspect O-ring for signs of cracks or deterioration.

NOTE: *If scraping is necessary, be careful not to damage the fuel pressure regulator or fuel supply line gasket surfaces.*

5. Lubricate fuel pressure regulator O-ring with light oil ESF-M6C2-A or equivalent.

6. Make sure gasket surfaces of fuel pressure regulator and fuel injection manifold are clean.

7. Install O-ring and new gasket on regulator.

8. Install the fuel pressure regulator on the injector manifold. Tighten the three retaining screws to 27–40 in.lb.

### Fuel Injector

1. Remove fuel tank cap and release pressure from the fuel system at the fuel pressure relief valve using Tool T80L-9974-A or equivalent.

2. Disconnect fuel supply and return lines.

3. Remove vacuum line from fuel pressure regulator.

4. Disconnect the fuel injector wiring harness.

5. Remove fuel injector manifold assembly.

6. Carefully remove connectors from individual injector(s) as required.

7. Grasping the injector's body, pull up while gently rocking the injector from side-to-side.

8. Inspect the injector O-rings (two per injector) for signs of deterioration. Replace as requried.

9. Inspect the injector plastic cover (covering the injector pintle) and washer for signs of deterioration. Replace as required. If hat is missing, look for it in intake manifold.

10. Lubricate new O-rings and install two on each injector (use a light grade oil ESF-M6C2-A or equivalent).

11. Install the injector(s). Use a light, twisting, pushing motion to install the injector(s).

12. Carefully seat the fuel injector manifold assembly on the four injectors and secure the manifold with two attaching bolts. Tighten to 15–22 ft.lb.

13. Connect the vacuum line to the fuel pressure regulator.

14. Connect fuel injector wiring harness.

15. Connect fuel supply and fuel return lines. Tighten fuel return line to 15–18 ft.lb.

16. Check entire assembly for proper alignment and seating.

### Fuel Injector Wiring Harness

NOTE: *Be sure the ignition if Off and the fuel system is depressurized.*

1. Disconnect the electrical connectors from the four fuel injectors.

2. Disconnect the connectors from the main wiring harness and the throttle position sensor.

3. Remove wiring assembly.

4. Position wiring harness alongside the fuel injectors.

5. Snap the electrical connectors into position on the four injectors.

6. Connect the throttle position sensor, ECT sensor and main harness connectors.

7. Verify that all electrical connectors are firmly seated.

### Vane Air Meter

1. Loosen the hose clamp which secures engine air cleaner outlet hose to the vane air meter assembly and position outlet hose out of the way.

2. Remove air intake and air outlet tube from the air cleaner.

3. Disengage four spring clamps and remove air cleaner front cover and air cleaner filter panel.

4. Remove four screws and washers from the flange of the air cleaner where it is attached to the vane air meter assembly. Pull the air cleaner base away from the vane air meter and remove the air cleaner gasket. If the gasket shoes signs of deterioration, replace it.

NOTE: *If scraping is necessary, be careful not to damage the air cleaner outlet and vane air meter gasket surfaces.*

5. Remove the electrical connector from the vane air meter assembly.

6. Remove the two screw and washer assemblies which secure the vane air meter assembly to the vane air meter bracket and remove the vane air meter assembly.

7. Clean mounting surfaces of air cleaner outlet flange and the vane air meter housing.

8. Place four retaining screws through the four holes in the air cleaner outlet flange and place a new gasket over the screws.

9. Mount the vane air meter assembly to the vane air meter bracket using two screw and washer assemblies. Note that these screws are not the physical size and care must be taken to ensure that the proper screw is in the proper hole. Tighten screws to 6–9 ft.lb.

10. Secure the air cleaner outlet to the vane air meter with the four screws mentioned in Step 2. Tighten to 6–9 ft.lb. Make sure the gasket is properly sealed and aligned.

11. Secure the engine air cleaner outlet tube to the vane air meter assembly with the hose clamp. Tighten to 15–25 in.lb.

12. Install the engine air cleaner cover and snap spring clips into position.

13. Secure the air intake duct to air cleaner.

14. Connect all hoses to air cleaner.

# EFI – EEC IV FUEL SYSTEM

## Components and Operation

The fuel subsystem included a high pressure electric fuel pump, fuel charging manifold, pressure regulator, fuel filter and both solid and flexible fuel lines. The fuel charging manifold includes four electronically controlled fuel injectors, each mounted directly above an intake port in the lower intake manifold. All injectors are energized simultaneously and spray once every crankshaft revolution, delivering a predetermined quantity of fuel into the intake airstream.

The fuel pressure regulator maintains a constant pressure drop across the injector nozzles. The regulator is referenced to intake manifold vacuum and is connected parallel to the fuel injectors and positioned on the far end of the fuel rail. Any excess fuel supplied by the pump passes through the regulator and is returned to the fuel tank via a return line.

NOTE: *The pressure regulator reduces fuel pressure to 39–40 psi under normal operating conditions. At idle or high manifold vacuum condition, fuel pressure is reduced to about 30 psi.*

The fuel pressure regulator is a diaphragm operated relief valve in which one side of the diaphragm senses fuel pressure and the other side senses manifold vacuum. Normal fuel pressure is established by a spring preload applied to the diaphgram. Control of the fuel system is maintained through the EEC power relay and the EEC-IV control unit, although electrical power is routed through the fuel pump relay and an inertia switch. The fuel pump relay is normally located on a bracket somewhere above the Electronic Control Assembly (ECA) and the Inertia Switch is located in the left rear kick panel. The fuel pump is usually mounted on a bracket at the fuel tank.

The inertia switch opens the power circuit to the fuel pump in the event of a collision. Once tripped, the switch must be reset manually by pushing the reset button on the assembly. Check that the inertia switch is reset before diagnosing power supply problems.

## On-Car Service – EEC-IV

The EFI-EEC IV system has a self-diagnostic capability to aid the technician in locating faults and troubleshooting components. Before removing any fuel lines or fuel system components, first relieve the fuel system pressure by using the same Schraeder adapter and fitting that is used to check fuel pressure at the fuel rail.

CAUTION: *Exercise care to avoid the chance of fire whenever removing or installing fuel system components.*

As in any service procedure, a routine inspection of the system for loose connections, broken wires or obvious damage is the best way to start. Perform the system Quick Test outlined below before going any further. Check all vacuum connections and secondary ignition wiring before assuming that the problem lies with the EEC-IV system. A self-diagnosis capability is built in to the EEC-IV system to aid in troubleshooting. The primary tool necessary to read the trouble codes stored in the system is an analog voltmeter or special Self Test Automatic Readout (STAR) tester (Motorcraft No. 007-0M004, or equivalent). While the self-test is not conclusive by itself, when activated it checks the EEC-IV system by testing its memory integrity and processing capability. The self-test also verifies that all sensors and actuators are connected and working properly.

When a service code is displayed on an analog voltmeter, each code number is represented by pulses or sweeps of the meter needle. A code 3, for example, will be read as three needle pulses followed by a 6 second delay. If a two digit code is stored, there will be a two second delay between the pulses for each digit of the number. Code 23, for example, will be displayed as two needle pulses, a two second pause, then three more pulses followed by a four second pause. All testing is complete when the codes have been repeated once. The pulse format is ½ second on-time for each digit, 2 seconds off-time between digits, 4 seconds off-time between codes and 6 seconds off-time before and after the ½ second separator pulse.

NOTE: *If using the STAR tester, or equivalent, consult the manufacturers instructions included with the unit for correct hookup and trouble code interpretation.*

In addition to the service codes, two other types of coded information are outputted during the self-test: engine identification and fast codes. Engine ID codes are one digit numbers equal to ½ the number of engine cylinders (e.g. 4 cylinder is code 2, 8 cylinder is code 4, etc.) Fast codes are simply the service codes transmitted at 100 times the normal rate in a short burst of information. Some meters may detect these codes and register a slight meter deflection just before the trouble codes are flashed. Both the ID and fast codes serve no purpose in the field and this meter deflection should be ignored.

## ACTIVATING SELF–TEST MODE ON EEC-IV

Turn the ignition key OFF. On the 1.6 & 1.9L engine, connect a jumper wire from pin 5 self-test input to pin 2 (signal return) on the self-test connector. Set the analog voltmeter on a DC voltage range to read from 0–15 volts, then connect the voltmeter from the battery positive (+) terminal to pin 4 self-test output in the self-test connector. Turn the ignition switch ON (engine off) and read the trouble codes on the meter needle as previously described. A code 11 means that the EEC-IV sys-

tem is operating properly and no faults are detected by the computer.

NOTE: *This test will only detect "hard" failures that are present when the self-test is activated. For intermittent problems, remove the voltmeter clip from the self-test trigger terminal and wiggle the wiring harness. With the voltmeter still attached to the self-test output, watch for a needle deflection that signals an intermittent condition has occurred. The meter will deflect each time the fault is induced and a trouble code will be stored. Reconnect the self-test trigger terminal to the voltmeter to retrieve the code.*

## EEC-IV SYSTEM QUICK TEST

Correct test results for the quick test are dependent on the correct operation of related non-EEC components, such as ignition wires, battery, etc. It may be necessary to correct defects in these areas before the EEC-IV system will pass the quick test. Before connecting any test equipment to check the EEC system, make the following checks:

1. Check the air cleaner and intake ducts for leaks or restrictions. Replace the air cleaner if excessive amount of dust or dirt are found.

2. Check all engine vacuum hoses for proper routing according to the vacuum schematic on the underhood sticker.

Check for proper connections and repair any broken, cracked or pinched hoses or fittings.

## EEC IV Trouble Codes (1.6L)

| Code | Diagnosis |
|------|-----------|
| 11 | Normal operation (no codes stored) |
| 12 | Incorrect high idle rpm value |
| 13 | Incorrect curb idle rpm value |
| 15 | Read Only Memory (ROM) failure |
| 21 | Incorrect engine coolant temperature (ECT) sensor signal |
| 23 | Incorrect throttle position sensor (TPS) signal |
| 24 | Incorrect vane air temperature (VAT) sensor signal |
| 26 | Incorrect vane air flow (VAF) sensor signal |
| 41 | System always lean |
| 42 | System always rich |
| 67 | Neutral/Drive switch in Neutral |

NOTE: Incorrect rpm values could be high or low and an incorrect sensor signal could be caused by a defective sensor or a wiring harness problem. Use the trouble codes to isolate the circuit, then continue diagnosis to determine the exact cause of the problem.

3. Check the EEC system wiring harness connectors for tight fit, loose or detached terminals, corrosion, broken or frayed wires, short circuits to metal in the engine compartment or melted insulation exposing bare wire.

NOTE: *It may be necessary to disconnect or disassembly the connector to check for terminal damage or corrosion and perform some of the inspections. Note the location of each pin the connector before disassembly. When doing continuity checks to make sure there are no breaks in the wire, shake or wiggle the harness and connector during testing to check for looseness or intermittent contact.*

4. Check the control module, sensors and actuators for obvious physical damage.

5. Turn off all electrical loads then testing and make sure the doors are closed whenever reading are made. DO NOT disconnect any electrical connector with the key ON. Turn the key off to disconnect or reconnect the wiring harness to any sensor or the control unit.

6. Make sure he engine coolant and oil are at the proper level.

7. Check for leaks around the exhaust manifold, oxygen sensor and vacuum hoses connections with the engine idling at normal operating temperature.

8. Only after all the above checks have been performed should the voltmeter be connected to read the trouble codes. If not, the self-diagnosis system may indicate a failed component when all that is wring is a loose or broken connection.

## EEC-IV System – 2.3L HSC

The center of the EEC-IV system is a micro-processor called the electronic control assembly (ECA). The ECA receives data from a number of sensors and other electronic components (switches, relay, etc.). The ECA contains a specific calibration for optimizing emissions, fuel economy, and driveability. Based on information received and programmed into its memory, the ECA generates output signals to control various relay, solenoid, and other actuators.

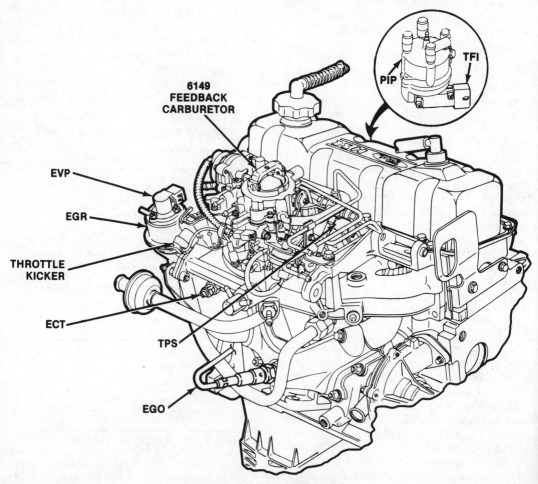

EEC-IV system—2.3L HSC engine

The ECA is mounted in the passenger compartment inside the dash on the steering column lateral shake brace.

The 2.3L HSC-EEC-IV system features electronic control of:

- Engine enrichment (feedback carburetor)
- Engine spark advance
- Exhaust gas recirculation (EGR)
- Curb idle speed
- Evaporative emissions purge (on/off)
- Engine diagnostic (self-test)
- A/C cutout for W.O.T. power
- Thermactor air
- Upshift light (MTX)

The 2.3L HSC-EEC-IV system can be divided into three subsystem:

- Fuel
- Air
- Electronic engine control

## FUEL SUBSYSTEM

The fuel subsystem consists of a mechanical fuel pump to deliver fuel from the fuel tank, a fuel filter to remove contaminants from the fuel, a 6149 feedback carburetor, and a feedback solenoid.

## AIR SUBSYSTEM

The air subsystem consists of an air cleaner, an air cleaner valve assembly, and the associated air tubes.

Air cleaner and air valve operation is similar to the operation on previous models.

This system uses a 90°F (32°C) bimetal with a new stainless valve that replaces the old style brass valve.

This system uses a blue 55°F (13°C) cold weather modulator (CWM).

## ELECTRONIC ENGINE CONTROL (EEC) SUBSYSTEM

The electronic engine control subsystem consists of the ECA and various sensors and actuators. The ECA reads inputs from various sensors to compute the required fuel flow necessary to achieve the desired air/fuel ratio. This is performed by the ECA controlling outputs to the duty cycle solenoid on the cowl. The duty cycle on-time determines the amount of fuel delivered to the engine by leaning the mixture with more air or by controlling the power valve circuit in the 6149 Holley feedback carburetor. The components which make up the 2.3L HSC-EEC-IV subsystem can be divided into three categories:

- Electronic control assembly (ECA)
- System inputs (sensors)
- System outputs (actuators)

## SYSTEM INPUTS

In order for the ECA to control engine operation properly, it must first receive specific information on various operating conditions. These include:

- Crankshaft position and speed
- Throttle plate position
- Engine coolant temperature
- Exhaust gas oxygen level
- A/C (on/off)
- Intake manifold vacuum/barometric pressure
- EGR valve position
- MT/AT load or no-load

These conditions are monitored by inputs to the system provided by the following:

- Profile ignition pick-up (PIP) (replaces the crank position sensor)
- Throttle position sensor (TPS) (plunger style)
- Engine coolant temperature sensor (ECT)
- Exhaust gas oxygen sensor (EGO)
- A/C clutch compressor signal (ACC)
- Manifold absolute pressure sensor (MAP)
- EGR valve position sensor (EVP)
- Self-test input (STI)

## SYSTEM OUTPUTS

When the ECA receives an input signal that indicates a change in one or more of the operating conditions, the change(s) must be evaluated to determine whether or not an output signal should be provided to control one of the following:

- Air/fuel ratio
- Spark timing
- Engine idle speed
- EGR
- Thermactor air/canister purge control
- A/C compressor on/off
- Engine cooling fan on/off
- MT gear selection (operator advised to shift to next highest gear)
- Self-test

These are controlled by system outputs applied to the following:

- Feedback control solenoid (FCS)
- TFI-IV ignition module
- Throttle kicker solenoid
- EGR solenoid (EGRV and EGRC)
- TAB and TAD (CANP vacuum teed to TAD)
- A/C and fan controller module
- Upshift light (MTX)
- Self-test output (STO)

## ENGINE OPERATING MODES

In order to effectively operate the various engine functions, three control modes have been programmed into the ECA. These are:

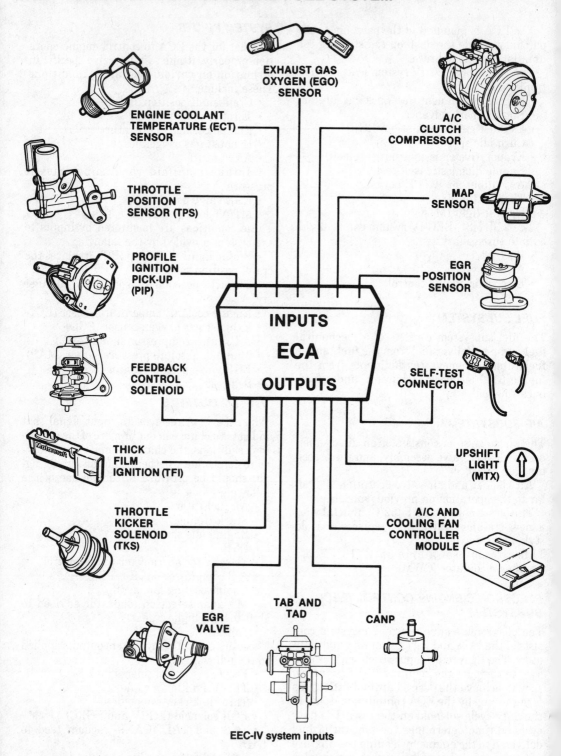

EEC-IV system inputs

- Normal engine operation
- Cold-or-hot engine operation
- Limited operating strategy (LOS)

In addition, fuel control operates in either an open loop mode (disregarding EGO sensor feedback) or a closed loop mode (using EGO sensor feedback).

Fuel control is in open loop mode when the engine is cold, during W.O.T. operation, or during LOS operation.

Fuel control enters closed loop operation within 80 seconds after start-up for most temperatures. The system remains in closed loop operation for part throttle and idle situations.

Normal engine operation conditions are divided into five separate modes:

- Crank mode
- Underspeed mode
- Closed throttle mode
- Part throttle mode
- Wide open throttle mode (W.O.T.)

Normal engine operation provides an optimum calibration for each of these modes. A mode evaluation circuit in the ECA determines which mode is present at any given time of engine operation and adjusts the calibration, if required.

### Crank mode

The crank mode is entered after initial engine power-up or after engine stall when the key is in START. A special operation program is used in the crank mode to aid engine starting. After engine start, one of the run modes is entered and normal engine operation is performed. If the engine stumbles during a run mode, the underspeed mode is entered to help it recover from the stumble, and to prevent it from stalling. A unique strategy is used in the underspeed mode in place of the normal engine run operation.

When the engine is cranked, fuel control is open loop operation the ECA sets engine timing at 10°–15° BTDC. The EGR solenoids are not energized, so the EGR valve is off. The canister purge solenoid is teed with the Thermactor air divert (TAD) solenoid, so, when the Thermactor air is upstream, the canister purge is off.

If the engine coolant is cold, the ECT sensor signal from the ECA causes the ECA to enrich the fuel to the engine through the feedback solenoid. In this operation, the ECT sensor is assisting the choke system to improve the cold start reaction and to provide good cold driveaway characteristics. At start-up, the TPS keeps the ECA informed on the position of the throttle plate.

### Underspeed Mode

Operation in the underspeed mode (under 600 rpm) is similar to that previously described for the crank mode. The system switches from the underspeed mode to the normal run mode at about 600 rpm. The underspeed mode is used to provide additional fuel enrichment and increased airflow to the engine to help it recover from a stumble.

### Closed Throttle Mode (Idle or Deceleration)

In the closed throttle mode, the air/fuel ratio is trimmed (by varying the duty cycle of the feedback solenoid to the carburetor) to obtain the desired mixture. To calculate what this output signal should be, the ECA evaluates signal inputs from the ECT sensor, MAP, EVP, PIP, TPS, and the EGO sensor. These sensors inform the ECA of the various conditions that must be evaluated in order for the ECA to determine the correct air/fuel ratio for the closed throttle condition present. Therefore, with the input from the EGO sensor fails to switch rich/lean, the ECA programming assumes the EGO sensor has cooled off, and the system goes to open loop fuel control. Ignition timing is also determined by the ECA, using these same inputs. The ECA has a series of tables programmed into the assembly at the factory. These tables provide the ECA with a reference of desired ignition timing for various operating conditions reflected by the sensor inputs.

The throttle kicker solenoid on/off is determined by the ECA as a function of rpm, ECT, A/C on or off, throttle mode, and time since start-up inputs. The EGR valve and the canister purge are off during a closed throttle condition. The signal from the TPS to the ECA indicates that the throttle plate is closed. The ECA then remove the energizing signal (if present) from the EGR solenoid.

### Part Throttle Mode (Cruise)

The air/fuel ratio and ignition timing are calculated in the same manner as previously described for the closed throttle mode. The fuel control system remains in closed loop during part throttle operation, as long as the EGO sensor keeps switching from rich to lean.

In part throttle operation, the throttle kicker is positioned to provide a dashpot function in the event that the throttle is close. Again, as in the closed throttle mode, the ECA makes this determination based on the inputs from the applicable sensors.

The TPS provides the throttle plate position signal to the ECA. With the throttle plate being in the partially open position, the ECA energizes the EGR control and vent solenoids. When the EGR solenoids are energized, the EGR flow rate is controlled by the EGR solenoids (EGRC and EGRV) by trapping, increasing, or venting vacuum to the EGR valve.

### Wide Open Throttle Mode (W.O.T.)

Control of the air/fuel ratio in the W.O.T. mode is the same as in part, or closed throttle situations, except that the fuel control switches to the open loop, and the feedback solenoid vacuum signal decreases to provide additional fuel enrichment. This vacuum decrease is applied as a result of the W.O.T. signal from the TPS to the ECA. This signal from the TPS also causes the ECA to remove the energizing signal from the EGR solenoids (if present).

Some spark advance is added in W.O.T. for improved performance. In addition, the A/C clutch and cooling fan are turned off to aid performance.

### Cold or Hot Engine Operation

This modified operation changes the normal engine operation output signals, as required, to adjust for uncommon operating conditions. These include a cold or an excessively hot engine.

### Limited Operation Strategy (LOS)

In this operation, the ECA assumes a passive condition, so the TFI and feedback solenoid allow the vehicle to "limp home" when an electronic malfunction occurs. The EGR is off, the Thermactor is bypassing, CANP is shut off, timing is locked at 10° BTDC, and the fuel control is maximum rich (no vacuum or air bleed). On this system, the vehicle will run with the ECA disconnected because the TFI module will fire at 10° MT, or 15° AT, BTDC and the carburetor will supply fuel to the engine.

## ENGINE OPERATION

### Cold Start-Up

*OPERATION AT FAST IDLE*

The driver turns the key to the ON position.

The crank timing is in synchronization with the PIP signal from the distributor.

The ECA outputs a signal to the throttle kicker, which provides an airflow path through the throttle plates, and produces an increased idle speed. The amount of rpm increase over base provided is dependent on the temperature of the choke at start. As the driver goes from closed throttle to part throttle (kickdown) and back, the choke will decrease rpm (airflow) to a level still above base. As the engine warms up, the idle speed will continue to step down until the base rpm is reached.

The amount of fuel delivered to the engine is controlled by the ECA. The amount of enrichment provided is dependent on engine coolant temperature and engine load. As the engine warms up, the amount of fuel enrichment is decreased.

EGR and canister purge are off until the vehicle is warm and in closed loop (40 seconds on a hot start).

Spark timing is controlled by the ECA, which outputs a signal to the TFI ignition module. The spark advance varies with rpm, engine load, coolant temperature, and EGR.

The bimetal sensor in the air cleaner is cold. Vacuum is applied to the air door motor. The motor has pulled the fresh air door close and opened the air cleaner to heated air from the exhaust manifold heat stove.

### Cold Driveaway

*LIGHT THROTTLE (PART THROTTLE)*

As engine coolant temperature increases and time since start increases, fuel enrichment provided by the ECA decreases.

The amount of extra airflow provided to overcome cold engine friction and to produce a high cam is decreased as engine temperature increases.

EGR and canister purge are off. The purge is not allowed on until approximately two minutes after engine coolant temperature reaches 130°F (55°C).

Spark advance is controlled by the ECA, which outputs a signal to the TFI ignition module.

The MT upshift light is enabled.

The bimetal in the air cleaner is still cold and vacuum is still applied to the air door motor. The fresh air door is closed and the air cleaner is opened to heated air.

### Warm-up Driveaway

*PARTLY WARM ENGINE/LIGHT THROTTLE ACCELERATION/ACCELERATION FROM A STOP ABOUT ONE MINUTE AFTER COLD DRIVEAWAY FROM 0°F (−18°C)*

Extra enrichment is provided as the vehicle is accelerated from a stop. The amount of fuel provided is controlled by the ECA and is based on engine coolant temperature and engine load.

The bimetal in the air cleaner has reached 90°F (32°C) and is starting to bleed vacuum off, causing the door to switch to fresh air. If ambient air is colder than 90°F (32°C), the door may modulate between positions. EGR and canister purge are off. The canister purge is still commanded off by the ECA.

Spark advance is controlled by the ECA, which outputs a 12 volt signal to the TFI ignition module on the distributor. The MT upshift light is enabled.

### Warm-Up Driveaway

*PARTLY WARM ENGINE/LIGHT THROTTLE ACCELERATION/ACCELERATION FROM A STOP ABOUT ONE MINUTE AFTER COLD DRIVEAWAY AT 30–40°F (−1 to +5°C)*

The engine coolant temperature has reached approximately 100°F (38°C) and conditions are such that the ECA starts to control the amount of fuel delivery based on the output of the EGO sensor. The engine is now operating in closed loop mode with the EGO sensor providing the required feedback information.

The EGR is on along with the canister purge. The amount of EGR is controlled by the sonic EGR valve. Canister purge is controlled by a purge shutoff valve teed to the Thermactor air divert (TAD) solenoid.

**55 WAYS TO IMPROVE FUEL ECONOMY**

# CHILTON'S
# FUEL ECONOMY
# & TUNE-UP TIPS

**Tune-up • Spark Plug Diagnosis • Emission Controls**

**Fuel System • Cooling System • Tires and Wheels**

**General Maintenance**

# CHILTON'S FUEL ECONOMY & TUNE-UP TIPS

Fuel economy is important to everyone, no matter what kind of vehicle you drive. The maintenance-minded motorist can save both money and fuel using these tips and the periodic maintenance and tune-up procedures in this Repair and Tune-Up Guide.

There are more than 130,000,000 cars and trucks registered for private use in the United States. Each travels an average of 10-12,000 miles per year, and, and in total they consume close to 70 billion gallons of fuel each year. This represents nearly ⅔ of the oil imported by the United States each year. The Federal government's goal is to reduce consumption 10% by 1985. A variety of methods are either already in use or under serious consideration, and they all affect you driving and the cars you will drive. In addition to "down-sizing", the auto industry is using or investigating the use of electronic fuel delivery, electronic engine controls and alternative engines for use in smaller and lighter vehicles, among other alternatives to meet the federally mandated Corporate Average Fuel Economy (CAFE) of 27.5 mpg by 1985. The government, for its part, is considering rationing, mandatory driving curtailments and tax increases on motor vehicle fuel in an effort to reduce consumption. The government's goal of a 10% reduction could be realized — and further government regulation avoided — if every private vehicle could use just 1 less gallon of fuel per week.

## How Much Can You Save?

Tests have proven that almost anyone can make at least a 10% reduction in fuel consumption through regular maintenance and tune-ups. When a major manufacturer of spark plugs sur-

## TUNE-UP

1. Check the cylinder compression to be sure the engine will really benefit from a tune-up and that it is capable of producing good fuel economy. A tune-up will be wasted on an engine in poor mechanical condition.

2. Replace spark plugs regularly. New spark plugs alone can increase fuel economy 3%.

3. Be sure the spark plugs are the correct type (heat range) for your vehicle. See the Tune-Up Specifications.

Heat range refers to the spark plug's ability to conduct heat away from the firing end. It must conduct the heat away in an even pattern to avoid becoming a source of pre-ignition, yet it must also operate hot enough to burn off conductive deposits that could cause misfiring.

The heat range is usually indicated by a number on the spark plug, part of the manufacturer's designation for each individual spark plug. The numbers in bold-face indicate the heat range in each manufacturer's identification system.

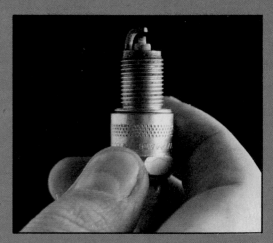

*Periodically, check the spark plugs to be sure they are firing efficiently. They are excellent indicators of the internal condition of your engine.*

| Manufacturer | Typical Designation |
|---|---|
| AC | R **45** TS |
| Bosch (old) | WA **145** T30 |
| Bosch (new) | HR **8** Y |
| Champion | RBL **15** Y |
| Fram/Autolite | 4**15** |
| Mopar | P-**62** PR |
| Motorcraft | BRF-**42** |
| NGK | BP **5** ES-15 |
| Nippondenso | W **16** EP |
| Prestolite | 14GR **5** 2A |

On AC, Bosch (new), Champion, Fram/Autolite, Mopar, Motorcraft and Prestolite, a higher number indicates a hotter plug. On Bosch (old), NGK and Nippondenso, a higher number indicates a colder plug.

4. Make sure the spark plugs are properly gapped. See the Tune-Up Specifications in this book.

5. Be sure the spark plugs are firing efficiently. The illustrations on the next 2 pages show you how to "read" the firing end of the spark plug.

6. Check the ignition timing and set it to specifications. Tests show that almost all cars have incorrect ignition timing by more than 2°.

veyed over 6,000 cars nationwide, they found that a tune-up, on cars that needed one, increased fuel economy over 11%. Replacing worn plugs alone, accounted for a 3% increase. The same test also revealed that 8 out of every 10 vehicles will have some maintenance deficiency that will directly affect fuel economy, emissions or performance. Most of this mileage-robbing neglect could be prevented with regular maintenance.

Modern engines require that all of the functioning systems operate properly for maximum efficiency. A malfunction anywhere wastes fuel. You can keep your vehicle running as efficiently and economically as possible, by being aware of your vehicle's operating and performance characteristics. If your vehicle suddenly develops performance or fuel economy problems it could be due to one or more of the following:

| PROBLEM | POSSIBLE CAUSE |
|---|---|
| Engine Idles Rough | Ignition timing, idle mixture, vacuum leak or something amiss in the emission control system. |
| Hesitates on Acceleration | Dirty carburetor or fuel filter, improper accelerator pump setting, ignition timing or fouled spark plugs. |
| Starts Hard or Fails to Start | Worn spark plugs, improperly set automatic choke, ice (or water) in fuel system. |
| Stalls Frequently | Automatic choke improperly adjusted and possible dirty air filter or fuel filter. |
| Performs Sluggishly | Worn spark plugs, dirty fuel or air filter, ignition timing or automatic choke out of adjustment. |

*Check spark plug wires on conventional point type ignition for cracks by bending them in a loop around your finger.*

*Be sure that spark plug wires leading to adjacent cylinders do not run too close together. (Photo courtesy Champion Spark Plug Co.)*

7. If your vehicle does not have electronic ignition, check the points, rotor and cap as specified.

8. Check the spark plug wires (used with conventional point-type ignitions) for cracks and burned or broken insulation by bending them in a loop around your finger. Cracked wires decrease fuel efficiency by failing to deliver full voltage to the spark plugs. One misfiring spark plug can cost you as much as 2 mpg.

9. Check the routing of the plug wires. Misfiring can be the result of spark plug leads to adjacent cylinders running parallel to each other and too close together. One wire tends to

pick up voltage from the other causing it to fire "out of time".

10. Check all electrical and ignition circuits for voltage drop and resistance.

11. Check the distributor mechanical and/or vacuum advance mechanisms for proper functioning. The vacuum advance can be checked by twisting the distributor plate in the opposite direction of rotation. It should spring back when released.

12. Check and adjust the valve clearance on engines with mechanical lifters. The clearance should be slightly loose rather than too tight.

# SPARK PLUG DIAGNOSIS

## Normal

APPEARANCE: This plug is typical of one operating normally. The insulator nose varies from a light tan to grayish color with slight electrode wear. The presence of slight deposits is normal on used plugs and will have no adverse effect on engine performance. The spark plug heat range is correct for the engine and the engine is running normally.

CAUSE: Properly running engine.

RECOMMENDATION: Before reinstalling this plug, the electrodes should be cleaned and filed square. Set the gap to specifications. If the plug has been in service for more than 10-12,000 miles, the entire set should probably be replaced with a fresh set of the same heat range.

## Oil Deposits

APPEARANCE: The firing end of the plug is covered with a wet, oily coating.

CAUSE: The problem is poor oil control. On high mileage engines, oil is leaking past the rings or valve guides into the combustion chamber. A common cause is also a plugged PCV valve, and a ruptured fuel pump diaphragm can also cause this condition. Oil fouled plugs such as these are often found in new or recently overhauled engines, before normal oil control is achieved, and can be cleaned and reinstalled.

RECOMMENDATION: A hotter spark plug may temporarily relieve the problem, but the engine is probably in need of work.

## Incorrect Heat Range

APPEARANCE: The effects of high temperature on a spark plug are indicated by clean white, often blistered insulator. This can also be accompanied by excessive wear of the electrode, and the absence of deposits.

CAUSE: Check for the correct spark plug heat range. A plug which is too hot for the engine can result in overheating. A car operated mostly at high speeds can require a colder plug. Also check ignition timing, cooling system level, fuel mixture and leaking intake manifold.

RECOMMENDATION: If all ignition and engine adjustments are known to be correct, and no other malfunction exists, install spark plugs one heat range colder.

## Carbon Deposits

APPEARANCE: Carbon fouling is easily identified by the presence of dry, soft, black, sooty deposits.

CAUSE: Changing the heat range can often lead to carbon fouling, as can prolonged slow, stop-and-start driving. If the heat range is correct, carbon fouling can be attributed to a rich fuel mixture, sticking choke, clogged air cleaner, worn breaker points, retarded timing or low compression. If only one or two plugs are carbon fouled, check for corroded or cracked wires on the affected plugs. Also look for cracks in the distributor cap between the towers of affected cylinders.

RECOMMENDATION: After the problem is corrected, these plugs can be cleaned and reinstalled if not worn severely.

## MMT Fouled

APPEARANCE: Spark plugs fouled by MMT (Methycyclopentadienyl Maganese Tricarbonyl) have reddish, rusty appearance on the insulator and side electrode.

CAUSE: MMT is an anti-knock additive in gasoline used to replace lead. During the combustion process, the MMT leaves a reddish deposit on the insulator and side electrode.

RECOMMENDATION: No engine malfunction is indicated and the deposits will not affect plug performance any more than lead deposits (see Ash Deposits). MMT fouled plugs can be cleaned, regapped and reinstalled.

## High Speed Glazing

APPEARANCE: Glazing appears as shiny coating on the plug, either yellow or tan in color.

CAUSE: During hard, fast acceleration, plug temperatures rise suddenly. Deposits from normal combustion have no chance to fluff-off; instead, they melt on the insulator forming an electrically conductive coating which causes misfiring.

RECOMMENDATION: Glazed plugs are not easily cleaned. They should be replaced with a fresh set of plugs of the correct heat range. If the condition recurs, using plugs with a heat range one step colder may cure the problem.

## Ash (Lead) Deposits

APPEARANCE: Ash deposits are characterized by light brown or white colored deposits crusted on the side or center electrodes. In some cases it may give the plug a rusty appearance.

CAUSE: Ash deposits are normally derived from oil or fuel additives burned during normal combustion. Normally they are harmless, though excessive amounts can cause misfiring. If deposits are excessive in short mileage, the valve guides may be worn.

RECOMMENDATION: Ash-fouled plugs can be cleaned, gapped and reinstalled.

## Detonation

APPEARANCE: Detonation is usually characterized by a broken plug insulator.

CAUSE: A portion of the fuel charge will begin to burn spontaneously, from the increased heat following ignition. The explosion that results applies extreme pressure to engine components, frequently damaging spark plugs and pistons.

Detonation can result by over-advanced ignition timing, inferior gasoline (low octane) lean air/fuel mixture, poor carburetion, engine lugging or an increase in compression ratio due to combustion chamber deposits or engine modification.

RECOMMENDATION: Replace the plugs after correcting the problem.

# EMISSION CONTROLS

13. Be aware of the general condition of the emission control system. It contributes to reduced pollution and should be serviced regularly to maintain efficient engine operation.

14. Check all vacuum lines for dried, cracked or brittle conditions. Something as simple as a leaking vacuum hose can cause poor performance and loss of economy.

15. Avoid tampering with the emission control system. Attempting to improve fuel econ-

# FUEL SYSTEM

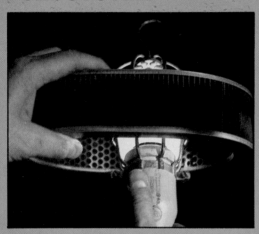

Check the air filter with a light behind it. If you can see light through the filter it can be reused.

Extremely clogged filters should be discarded and replaced with a new one.

18. Replace the air filter regularly. A dirty air filter richens the air/fuel mixture and can increase fuel consumption as much as 10%. Tests show that 1/3 of all vehicles have air filters in need of replacement.

19. Replace the fuel filter at least as often as recommended.

20. Set the idle speed and carburetor mixture to specifications.

21. Check the automatic choke. A sticking or malfunctioning choke wastes gas.

22. During the summer months, adjust the automatic choke for a leaner mixture which will produce faster engine warm-ups.

# COOLING SYSTEM

29. Be sure all accessory drive belts are in good condition. Check for cracks or wear.

30. Adjust all accessory drive belts to proper tension.

31. Check all hoses for swollen areas, worn spots, or loose clamps.

32. Check coolant level in the radiator or expansion tank.

33. Be sure the thermostat is operating properly. A stuck thermostat delays engine warm-up and a cold engine uses nearly twice as much fuel as a warm engine.

34. Drain and replace the engine coolant at least as often as recommended. Rust and scale

# TIRES & WHEELS

38. Check the tire pressure often with a pencil type gauge. Tests by a major tire manufacturer show that 90% of all vehicles have at least 1 tire improperly inflated. Better mileage can be achieved by over-inflating tires, but never exceed the maximum inflation pressure on the side of the tire.

39. If possible, install radial tires. Radial tires deliver as much as 1/2 mpg more than bias belted tires.

40. Avoid installing super-wide tires. They only create extra rolling resistance and decrease fuel mileage. Stick to the manufacturer's recommendations.

41. Have the wheels properly balanced.

omy by tampering with emission controls is more likely to worsen fuel economy than improve it. Emission control changes on modern engines are not readily reversible.

16. Clean (or replace) the EGR valve and lines as recommended.

17. Be sure that all vacuum lines and hoses are reconnected properly after working under the hood. An unconnected or misrouted vacuum line can wreak havoc with engine performance.

23. Check for fuel leaks at the carburetor, fuel pump, fuel lines and fuel tank. Be sure all lines and connections are tight.

24. Periodically check the tightness of the carburetor and intake manifold attaching nuts and bolts. These are a common place for vacuum leaks to occur.

25. Clean the carburetor periodically and lubricate the linkage.

26. The condition of the tailpipe can be an excellent indicator of proper engine combustion. After a long drive at highway speeds, the inside of the tailpipe should be a light grey in color. Black or soot on the insides indicates an overly rich mixture.

27. Check the fuel pump pressure. The fuel pump may be supplying more fuel than the engine needs.

28. Use the proper grade of gasoline for your engine. Don't try to compensate for knocking or "pinging" by advancing the ignition timing. This practice will only increase plug temperature and the chances of detonation or pre-ignition with relatively little performance gain.

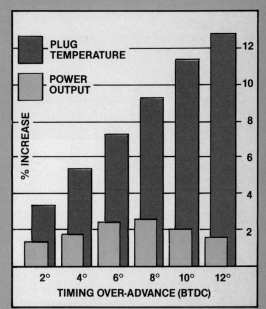

*Increasing ignition timing past the specified setting results in a drastic increase in spark plug temperature with increased chance of detonation or preignition. Performance increase is considerably less. (Photo courtesy Champion Spark Plug Co.)*

that form in the engine should be flushed out to allow the engine to operate at peak efficiency.

35. Clean the radiator of debris that can decrease cooling efficiency.

36. Install a flex-type or electric cooling fan, if you don't have a clutch type fan. Flex fans use curved plastic blades to push more air at low speeds when more cooling is needed; at high speeds the blades flatten out for less resistance. Electric fans only run when the engine temperature reaches a predetermined level.

37. Check the radiator cap for a worn or cracked gasket. If the cap does not seal properly, the cooling system will not function properly.

42. Be sure the front end is correctly aligned. A misaligned front end actually has wheels going in differed directions. The increased drag can reduce fuel economy by .3 mpg.

43. Correctly adjust the wheel bearings. Wheel bearings that are adjusted too tight increase rolling resistance.

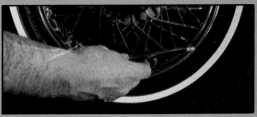

*Check tire pressures regularly with a reliable pocket type gauge. Be sure to check the pressure on a cold tire.*

# GENERAL MAINTENANCE

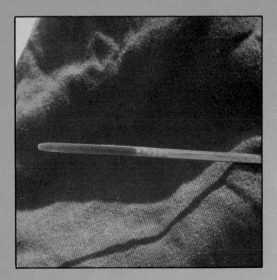

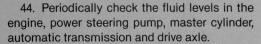

*Check the fluid levels (particularly engine oil) on a regular basis. Be sure to check the oil for grit, water or other contamination.*

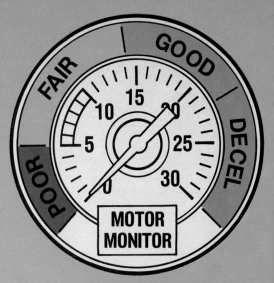

*A vacuum gauge is another excellent indicator of internal engine condition and can also be installed in the dash as a mileage indicator.*

44. Periodically check the fluid levels in the engine, power steering pump, master cylinder, automatic transmission and drive axle.

45. Change the oil at the recommended interval and change the filter at every oil change. Dirty oil is thick and causes extra friction between moving parts, cutting efficiency and increasing wear. A worn engine requires more frequent tune-ups and gets progressively worse fuel economy. In general, use the lightest viscosity oil for the driving conditions you will encounter.

46. Use the recommended viscosity fluids in the transmission and axle.

47. Be sure the battery is fully charged for fast starts. A slow starting engine wastes fuel.

48. Be sure battery terminals are clean and tight.

49. Check the battery electrolyte level and add distilled water if necessary.

50. Check the exhaust system for crushed pipes, blockages and leaks.

51. Adjust the brakes. Dragging brakes or brakes that are not releasing create increased drag on the engine.

52. Install a vacuum gauge or miles-per-gallon gauge. These gauges visually indicate engine vacuum in the intake manifold. High vacuum = good mileage and low vacuum = poorer mileage. The gauge can also be an excellent indicator of internal engine conditions.

53. Be sure the clutch is properly adjusted. A slipping clutch wastes fuel.

54. Check and periodically lubricate the heat control valve in the exhaust manifold. A sticking or inoperative valve prevents engine warm-up and wastes gas.

55. Keep accurate records to check fuel economy over a period of time. A sudden drop in fuel economy may signal a need for tune-up or other maintenance.

The upshift light for the MT is now working in first, second, third and fourth gear, and is locked out in fifth gear. Conditions needed to activate the light are approximately 2,000 engine rpm and 4 in.Hg manifold vacuum.

The bimetal in the air cleaner has reached 90°F (32°C) and is starting to bleed vacuum off, causing the door to switch to fresh air. If ambient air is colder than 90°F (32°C), the door may modulate between positions.

Spark advance is controlled by the ECA, which outputs a 12 volt signal to the TFI ignition module on the distributor.

## Acceleration at W.O.T.
### ENGINE HOT

W.O.T. condition is determined by the throttle position sensor.

Extra fuel enrichment is provided by the ECA, and the system goes to open loop fuel control out of feedback control.

Canister purge and EGR are off. Thermactor air is bypassed.

Extra spark advance is added with the amount being controlled by the ECA. The ECA outputs a 12 volt reference signal to the TFI ignition module to command the correct amount of advance.

If the A/C is on during acceleration, the ECA turns off the A/C compressor. This feature is called, W.O.T. A/C Shutoff. The A/C remains off for approximately three seconds after returning to part throttle, and will shut off again when a part throttle to W.O.T. transition occurs.

The upshift light for the MT will not operate until approximately 3,600 rpm is satisfied.

The bimetal sensor is warm and has bled vacuum from the air door motor. The motor has released the fresh air door to the OPEN position. Since no vacuum is available during W.O.T., the door will go to the fresh air mode after the delay valve bleeds trapped vacuum.

## Hot Curb Idle
### CLOSED THROTTLE

Fuel delivery is controlled by the ECA, which is operating in closed loop (feedback) mode. Feedback information is provided by the EGO sensor. Closed throttle for 300 seconds will cause re-entry to open loop enrichment.

The air inlet door on the bemetal sensor opens to fresh air, buy cannot maintain the 90°F (32°C) temperature, due to underhood temperatures.

Spark advance is controlled by the ECA.

If the A/C is on, the ECA commands the throttle kicker open for increased airflow to compensate for the extra load of the A/C compressor.

EGR and canister purge are off.

## Hot Engine Shutdown
### IGNITION OFF

The ECA is inoperative.
All ECA controlled outputs are off:
Canister purge
EGR
Spark
Fuel
Throttle kicker
Upshift light
Thermactor air

## Hot Cruise
### ENGINE HOT LIGHT THROTTLE (PART THROTTLE)

Fuel delivery is controlled by the ECA, which is operating in closed loop (feedback) mode. Feedback information is provided by the EGO sensor.

Spark advance is controlled by the ECA through the TFI ignition module on the distributor.

EGR and canister purge are on. The amount of EGR is controlled by the sonic EGR valve.

The Thermactor system is operating and is in the downstream mode.

The bimetal sensor is warm and is modulating vacuum to the air inlet door to maintain a 90°F (32°C) temperature.

## Deceleration
### COASTING DOWN AT CLOSED THROTTLE – ENGINE HOT

EGR and canister purge are off.

Bimetal sensor in the air cleaner is hot. Vacuum to the air motor has been bled off, releasing the fresh air door to the OPEN position.

The ECA calculates a duty cycle for the fuel solenoid based on EGO input.

Spark advance is controlled by the ECA, which outputs a signal to the TFI ignition module on the distributor.

Airflow provided by the throttle kicker is also controlled by an output from the ECA.

Thermactor air goes upstream on a MT on deceleration.

## TESTING

NOTE: *Testing the EEC-IV system requires special equipment and an expert knowledge of the system. Troubleshooting and servicing should be performed by a qualified personnel only.*

# Diesel FUEL SYSTEM

## Glow Plugs
### REMOVAL AND INSTALLATION

1. Disconnect battery ground cable from the battery, located in the luggage compartment.

2. Disconnect glow plug harness from the glow plugs.

3. Using a 12mm deep well socket, remove the glow plugs.

4. Install glow plugs, using a 12mm deep well socket. Tighten the glow plugs to 11–15 ft.lb.

5. Connect glow plug harness to the glow plugs. Tighten the nuts to 5–7 ft.lb.

6. Connect battery ground cable to the battery located in the luggage compartment.

7. Check the glow plug system operation.

## Injection Nozzles

### REMOVAL AND INSTALLATION

1. Disconnect and remove injection lines from injection pump and nozzles. Cap all lines and fittings using Protective Cap Set T84P-9395-A or equivalent.

2. Remove nuts attaching the fuel return line to the nozzles, and remove return line and seals.

3. Remove nozzles using a 27mm deep well socket.

3. Remove nozzles gaskets and washers from nozzle seat, using O-ring Pick Tool T71P-19703-C or equivalent.

5. Clean the outside of the nozzle assemblies using Nozzle Cleaning Kit, Rotunda model 14-0301 or equivalent, and a suitable solvent. Dry thoroughly.

6. Position new sealing gaskets in the nozzle seats.

NOTE: *Install gasket with red painted surface facing up.*

7. Position new copper washers in the nozzles bores.

8. Install nozzles and tighten to 44–51 ft.lb.

9. Position fuel return line on the nozzles, using new seals.

10. Install fuel return line retaining nuts and tighten to 10 ft.lb.

11. Install fuel lines on the injection pump and nozzles. Tighten capnuts to 18–22 ft.lb.

12. Air bleed fuel system.

13. Run engine and check for fuel leaks.

NOTE: *Other servicing of the diesel fuel system requires special tool and equipment. Servicing should be done by a mechanic experienced with diesels.*

## Fuel Cutoff Solenoid

### REMOVAL AND INSTALLATION

1. Disconnect battery ground cable from the battery, located in the luggage compartment.

2. Remove connector from the fuel cutoff solenoid.

3. Remove fuel cutoff solenoid and discard the O-ring.

4. Install fuel cutoff solenoid using a new O-ring. Tighten to 30–33 ft.lb.

5. Connect electrical connector.

6. Connect battery ground cable.

7. Run engine and check for fuel leaks.

## Injection Pump

### REMOVAL AND INSTALLATION

1. Disconnect battery ground cable from the battery. located in the luggage compartment.

2. Disconnect air inlet duct from the air cleaner and intake manifold. Install protective cap in intake manifold.

NOTE: *Cap is part of Protective Cap Set, T84P-9395-A.*

3. Remove rear timing belt cover and flywheel timing mark cover.

4. Remove rear timing belt.

5. Disconnect throttle cable and speed control cable, if so equipped.

6. Disconnect vacuum hoses at the altitude compensator and cold start diaphragm.

7. Disconnect fuel cutoff solenoid connector.

8. Disconnect fuel supply and fuel return hoses at injection pump.

9. Remove injection lines at the injection pump and nozzles. Cap all lines and fittings using Protective Cap Set T84P-9395-A or equivalent.

10. Rotate injection pump sprocket until timing marks are aligned. Install two M8 x 1.25 bolts in holes to hold the injection pump sprocket. Remove sprocket retaining nut.

11. Remove injection pump sprocket using Gear Puller T77F-4220-B1 and Adapter D80L-625-4 or equivalent, using two M8 x 1.25 bolts installed in the threaded holes in the sprocket.

12. Remove bolt attaching the injection pump to the pump front bracket.

13. Remove two nuts attaching the injection pump to the pump rear bracket and remove the pump.

14. Install injection pump in position on the pump bracket.

15. Install two nuts attaching the pump to the rear bracket and tighten to 23–34 ft.lb.

16. Install bolt attaching the pump to the front bracket and tighten to 12–16 ft.lb.

17. Install injection pump sprocket. Hold the sprocket in place using the procedure described in Step 10, Removal. Install the sprocket retaining nut and tighten to 51–58 ft.lb.

18. Remove protective caps and install the fuel lines at the injection pump and nozzles. Tighten the fuel line capnuts to 18–22 ft.lb.

19. Connect fuel supply and fuel return hoses at the injection pump.

20. Connect fuel cutoff solenoid connector.

21. Connect vacuum lines to the cold start diaphragm and altitude compensator.

22. Connect throttle cable and speed control cable, if so equipped.

23. Install and adjust the rear timing belt.

24. Remove protective cap and install the air inlet duct to the intake manifold and air cleaner.

25. Connect battery ground cable to battery.

26. Air bleed fuel system as outlined.

27. Check and adjust the injection pump timing.

28. Run engine and check for fuel leaks.

29. Check and adjust engine idle.

## Injection Timing

### ADJUSTMENT

NOTE: *Engine coolant temperature must be above 80°C (176°F) before the injection timing can be checked and/or adjusted.*

1. Disconnect the battery ground cable from the battery located in luggage compartment.

2. Remove the injection pump distributor head plug bolt and sealing washer.

3. Install Static Timing Gauge Adapter, Rotunda 14-0303 or equivalent with Metric Dial Indicator, so that indicator pointer is in contact with injection pump plunger.

4. Remove timing mark cover from transmission housing. Align timing mark (TDC) with pointer on the rear engine cover plate.

5. Rotate the crankshaft pulley slowly, counterclockwise until the dial indicator pointer stops moving (approximately 30–50° BTDC).

6. Adjust dial indicator to Zero.

NOTE: *Confirm that dial indicator pointer does not move from Zero by slightly rotating crankshaft left and right.*

7. Turn crankshaft clockwise until crankshaft timing mark aligns with indicator pin. Dial indicator should read 1.0mm ± 0.02mm. If reading is not within specification, adjust as follows:

    a. Loosen injection pump attaching bolt and nuts.

    b. Rotate the injection pump toward the engine to advance timing and away from the engine to retard timing. Rotate the injection pump until the dial indicator reads 1.0mm ± 0.02mm.

    c. Tighten the injection pump attaching nuts and bolt to 13–22 ft.lb.

    d. Repeat Steps 5,6, and 7 to check that timing is adjusted correctly.

8. Remove the dial indicator and adapter and install the injection pump distributor head plug and tighten to 10–14.5 ft.lb.

9. Connect the battery ground cable to the battery.

10. Run the engine, check and adjust idle rpm, if necessary. Check for fuel leaks.

### IDLE SPEED ADJUSTMENT

1. Place the transmission in Neutral.

2. Bring the engine up to normal operating temperature. Stop engine.

3. Remove the timing hole cover. Clean the flywheel surface and install reflective tape.

4. Idle speed is measured with manual transmission in Neutral.

5. Check curb idle speed, using Rotunda 99-0001 or equivalent. Curb idle speed is specified on the Vehicle Emissions Control Information decal (VECI). Adjust to specification by loosening the locknut on the idle speed bolt. Turn the idle speed adjusting bolt clockwise to increase, or counterclockwise to decrease engine idle speed. Tighten the locknut.

6. Place transmission in Neutral. Rev engine momentarily and recheck the curb idle RPM. Readjust if necessary.

7. Turn A/C On. Check the idle speed. Adjust to specification by loosening nut on the A/C throttle kicker and rotating screw.

## CENTRAL FUEL INJECTION – TEMPO AND TOPAZ

On the CFI system, the throttle body assembly meters fuel/air into the induction system of the 2.3L HSC engine.

The new low pressure CFI fuel system has only five major parts:

FUEL PUMP (Mounted in tank)

FUEL FILTER (R.F. Inner Fender Panel)

THROTTLE BODY ASSEMBLY (Mounts to Intake Manifold)

INJECTOR (Single Solenoid)

PRESSURE REGULATOR (Regulates fuel pressure at 14.5 psi)

There is no choke system and only one throttle valve is needed. So that a fast idle can be obtained during cold engine start-up and to provide normal (lower RPM) curb idle when the engine is at operating temperature, engineers added an Idle Speed Control (ISC) to do that important job. A small shaft extends or retracts on command from signals sent to it from the EEC-IV computer. An Idle Tracking Switch (ITS) is part of the ISC assembly. It is needed to signal the computer wherever the throttle lever has contacted the plunger thereby signaling the need for control of engine idle RPM.

## Throttle Position Sensor (TPS)

This non-adjustable sensor mounted to the throttle body and is interconnected to the throttle shaft. It sends an input signal to the EEC-IV computer in proportion to the amount of throttle plate opening (closed throttle, part throttle, and wide open throttle).

## Air Control

A single butterfly valve controls the flow of air into the intake manifold. It looks and operates similar to the throttle valve(s) used with carburetors.

Located just above the throttle plate is the electromechanical fuel injector which meters and also atomizes the fuel delivered to the engine.

An electrical control signal sent to the fuel injector from the EEC-IV computer causes the solenoid actuated fuel metering ball to move off its seat and allows fuel to flow as required by engine demands.

Injector flow opening is fixed. As a result, fuel flow to the engine is controlled by how long (the amount of time) the solenoid is energized (remains on) with the fuel metering ball off its seat.

## Fuel Pressure Regulator

Its location and design is such that supply line pressure drops are eliminated. Also, a second function of the pressure regulator is to maintain fuel supply pressure whenever the engine is not running (ignition key off). It acts as a downstream check valve and traps the fuel between itself and the fuel pump. By maintaining fuel pressure upon engine shutdown, fuel line vapor (vapor lock) does not develop.

## Fuel Charging Assembly

Two major components make up the fuel charging assembly. They are the Throttle Body and Main body. Fuel is sent through internal passages to the injector tip. Any excess fuel is returned to the pressure regulator and from there it is returned to the fuel tank at a reduced pressure of somewhere between 3 and 6 psi.

## Low Pressure Fuel Injector

Fuel flow into the air stream entering the cylinders is determined by the length of on-time the solenoid is energized. The longer on-time of the injector, the more fuel is permitted to flow into the intake system.

When the ball valve moves off its seat the small metering orifices are uncovered and a calibrated amount of fuel enters the intake manifold.

NOTE: *The injector air gap is not adjustable and the injector is only serviced as an assembly.*

### CHECKING FUEL PRESSURE

To check the fuel pressure, disconnect the Inertia Switch which is located at the right side of the trunk area. Now, crank the engine for 15 seconds to reduce system pressure before you remove the clips at each end of the fuel line between the fuel filter and the fuel inlet at the charging assembly.

NOTE: *Use extreme care to prevent combustion from fuel spillage.*

Install an accurate fuel pressure gauge between the fuel filter line and the throttle body assembly fuel inlet. You'll need a T-fitting to accomplish this fuel pressure gauge connection.

Reconnect the inertia switch, start the engine and check fuel pressure at idle. Throughout acceleration, you should have a stable pressure of 13.0 to 16.0 psi without any excessively high or low readings. To remove the pressure gauge, again disconnect the inertia switch, crank the engine for 15 seconds, then remove the gauge. Reinstall the original fuel line securely. Reconnect the inertia switch and start the engine. Check carefully for any fuel leakage.

### TESTING AND SERVICING

NOTE: *The CFI system is controlled by the EEC-IV system. Testing the system requires special equipment and an expert knowledge of the system. Troubleshooting and servicing should be performed by qualified personnel only.*

# FUEL TANK

### REMOVAL AND INSTALLATION

CAUTION: *Have the tank as empty as possible. No smoking or open flame while working on the fuel system.*

1. Disconnect the negative battery cable from the battery.
2. Raise the rear of the car and safely support it on jackstands.
3. Disconnect the gas fill and breather lines from the tank. Disconnect the fuel feed, return and breather lines from the front of the tank, plug these lines.
4. Remove the two mounting bolts at the top rear of the tank while supporting the tank on a piece of wood and a floor tank. Lower and remove the gas tank.
5. Installation is the reverse order of removal.

## Troubleshooting Basic Fuel System Problems

| Problem | Cause | Solution |
|---|---|---|
| Engine cranks, but won't start (or is hard to start) when cold | • Empty fuel tank<br>• Incorrect starting procedure<br>• Defective fuel pump<br>• No fuel in carburetor<br>• Clogged fuel filter<br>• Engine flooded<br>• Defective choke | • Check for fuel in tank<br>• Follow correct procedure<br>• Check pump output<br>• Check for fuel in the carburetor<br>• Replace fuel filter<br>• Wait 15 minutes; try again<br>• Check choke plate |
| Engine cranks, but is hard to start (or does not start) when hot— (presence of fuel is assumed) | • Defective choke | • Check choke plate |
| Rough idle or engine runs rough | • Dirt or moisture in fuel<br>• Clogged air filter<br>• Faulty fuel pump | • Replace fuel filter<br>• Replace air filter<br>• Check fuel pump output |
| Engine stalls or hesitates on acceleration | • Dirt or moisture in the fuel<br>• Dirty carburetor<br>• Defective fuel pump<br>• Incorrect float level, defective accelerator pump | • Replace fuel filter<br>• Clean the carburetor<br>• Check fuel pump output<br>• Check carburetor |
| Poor gas mileage | • Clogged air filter<br>• Dirty carburetor<br>• Defective choke, faulty carburetor adjustment | • Replace air filter<br>• Clean carburetor<br>• Check carburetor |
| Engine is flooded (won't start accompanied by smell of raw fuel) | • Improperly adjusted choke or carburetor | • Wait 15 minutes and try again, without pumping gas pedal<br>• If it won't start, check carburetor |

# Chassis Electrical

## UNDERSTANDING AND TROUBLESHOOTING ELECTRICAL SYSTEMS

Electrical problems generally fall into one of three areas:

1. The component that is not functioning is not receiving current.
2. The component itself is not functioning.
3. The component is not properly grounded.

Problems that fall into the first category are by far the most complicated. It is the current supply system to the component which contains all the switches, relays, fuses, etc.

The electrical system can be checked with a test light and a jumper wire. A test light is a device that looks like a pointed screwdriver with a wire attached to it. It has a light bulb in its handle. A jumper wire is a piece of insulated wire with an alligator clip attached to each end. To check the system you must follow the wiring diagram of the vehicle being worked on. A wiring diagram is a road map of the car's electrical system.

If a light bulb is not working, you must follow a systematic plan to determine which of the three causes is the villain.

1. Turn on the switch that controls the inoperable bulb.
2. Disconnect the power supply wire from the bulb.
3. Attach the ground wire on the test light to a good metal ground.
4. Touch the probe end of the test light to the end of the power supply wire that was disconnected from the bulb. If the bulb is receiving current, the test light will glow.

NOTE: *If the bulb is one which works only when the ignition key is turned on (turn signal), make sure the key is turned on.*

5. If the test light does not go on, then the problem is in the circuit between the battery and the bulb. As mentioned before, this includes all the switches, fuses, and relays in the system. Turn to the wiring diagram and find the bulb on the diagram. Follow the wire that runs back to the battery. The problem is an open circuit between the battery and the bulb. If the fuse is blown and, when replaced, immediately blows again, there is a short circuit in the system which must be located and repaired. If there is a switch in the system, bypass it with a jumper wire. This is done by connecting one end of the jumper wire to the power supply wire into the switch and the other end of the jumper wire to the wire coming out of the switch. Again, consult the wiring diagram. If the test light lights with the jumper wire installed, the switch or whatever was bypassed is defective.

NOTE: *Never substitute the jumper wire for the bulb, as the bulb is the component required to use the power from the source.*

6. If the bulb in the test light goes on, then the current is getting to the bulb that is not working in the car. This eliminates the first of the three possible causes. Connect the power supply wire and connect a jumper wire from the bulb to a good metal ground. Do this with the switch which controls the bulb turned on, and also the ignition switch turned on if it is required for the light to work. If the bulb works with the jumper wire installed, then it has a bad ground. This is usually caused by the metal area on which the bulb mounts to the car being coated with some type of foreign matter.

7. If neither test located the source of the trouble, then the light bulb itself is defective.

The above test procedure can be applied to any of the components of the chassis electrical system by substituting the component that is not working for the light bulb. Remember that for any electrical system to work, all connections must be clean and tight.

# HEATER

## Heater Core

### REMOVAL AND INSTALLATION

NOTE: *In some cases removal of the instrument panel may be necessary.*

#### Without A/C

1. Disconnect the negative battery cable.
2. Drain the coolant.
3. Disconnect the heater hoses from the core tubes at the firewall, inside the engine compartment. Plug the core tubes to prevent coolant spillage when the core is removed.
4. Open the glove compartment. Remove the glove compartment. Remove the glove compartment liner.
5. Remove the core access plate screws and remove the access plate.
6. Working under the hood, remove the two nuts attaching the heater assembly case to the dash panel.
7. Remove the core through the glove compartment opening.

8. Install the core through the glove compartment opening.
9. Working under the hood, install the two nuts attaching the heater assembly case to the dash panel.
10. Install the core access plate screws and install the access plate.
11. Install the glove compartment. Install the glove compartment liner.
12. Reconnect the heater hoses to the core tubes at the firewall, inside the engine compartment.
13. Refill the cooling system with coolant.
14. Reconnect the negative battery cable.

#### With A/C

1. Disconnect the negative battery cable and drain the cooling system.
2. Disconnect the heater hoses from the heater core.
3. Working inside the vehicle, remove the floor duct from the plenum (2 screws).
4. Remove the four screws attaching the heater core cover to the plenum, remove the cover and remove the heater core.

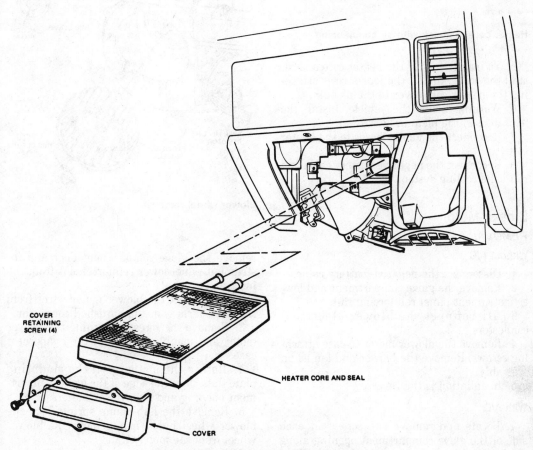

COVER RETAINING SCREW (4)

HEATER CORE AND SEAL

COVER

**Heater core removal; without air conditioning**

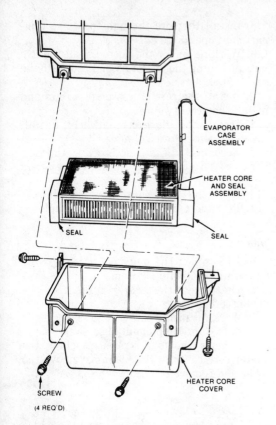

Heater core removal; with air conditioning

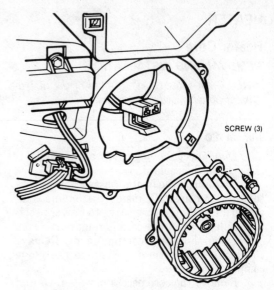

Blower motor and wheel removal

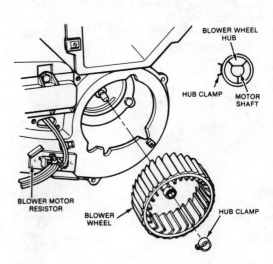

Blower wheel removal

5. To install: Install the heater core and install the cover. Install the four screws attaching the heater core cover to the plenum.

6. Working inside the vehicle, Install the floor duct to the plenum (2 screws).

7. Reconnect the heater hoses to the heater core.

8. Reconnect the negative battery cable and refill the cooling system.

## Blower Motor

### REMOVAL AND INSTALLATION

#### Without A/C

1. Disconnect the negative battery cable.

2. Remove the glove compartment and lower instrument panel reinforcing rail.

3. Disconnect the blower electrical connectors.

4. Remove the blower motor-to-case attaching screws. Remove the blower and fan as an assembly.

5. Installation is the reverse.

#### With A/C

1. Locate and remove two screws at each side of the glove compartment opening along the lower edge of the instrument panel. Then, remove the glove compartment door and instrument panel lower reinforcement from the instrument panel.

2. Disconnect the blower motor wires from the wire harness at the hardshell connector.

3. Remove the screws attaching the blower motor and mounting plate to the evaporator case.

4. Rotate the motor until the mounting plate flats clear the edge of the glove compartment opening and remove the motor.

5. Remove the hub clamp spring from the blower wheel hub. Then, remove the blower wheel from the motor shaft.

6. Installation is the reverse of removal.

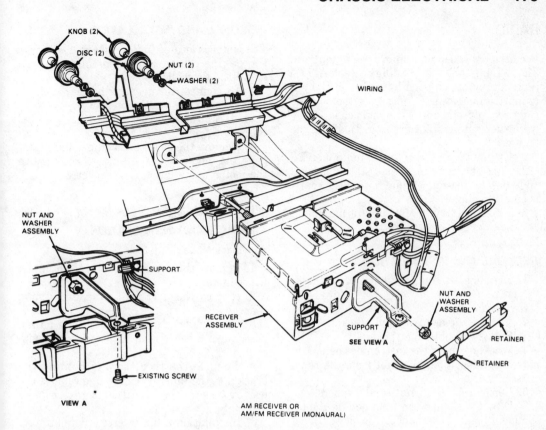

**VIEW A**

AM RECEIVER OR
AM/FM RECEIVER (MONAURAL)

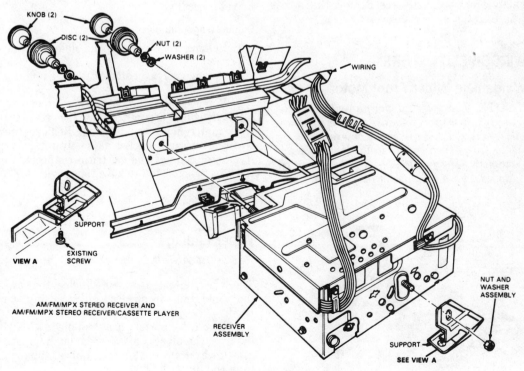

AM/FM/MPX STEREO RECEIVER AND
AM/FM/MPX STEREO RECEIVER/CASSETTE PLAYER

**Radio installation**

## RADIO

For best FM reception, adjust the antenna to 31″ (787mm) in height. Fading or weak AM reception may be adjusted by means of the antenna trimmer control. located either on the right rear of front side of the radio chassis. See the owner's manual for position. To adjust the trimmer:

1. Extend the antenna to maximum height.
2. Tune the radio to a weak station around 1600 KC. Adjust the volume so that the sound is barely audible.
3. Adjust the trimmer to obtain maximum volume.

### REMOVAL AND INSTALLATION

1. Disconnect the negative battery cable. NOTE: *Remove the A/C floor duct if so equipped.*
2. Remove the ash tray and bracket.
3. Pull the knobs from the shafts.
4. Working under the instrument panel, remove the support bracket nut from the radio chassis.
5. Remove the shaft nuts and washers.
6. Drop the radio down from behind the instrument panel. Disconnect the power lead, antenna, and speaker wires. Remove the radio.
7. Installation is the reverse.

## WINDSHIELD WIPERS

### Windshield Wiper Front Motor

NOTE: *The internal permanent magnets used in the wiper motor are a ceramic (glass-like) material. Care must be exercised in handling the motor to avoid damaging the magnets. The motor must not be struck or tapped with a hammer or other object.*

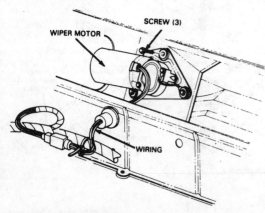

**Wiper motor installation**

### REMOVAL AND INSTALLATION

The motor is located in the right rear corner of the engine compartment, in the cowl area above the firewall.

1. Disconnect the negative battery cable.
2. Remove the plastic cowl cover.
3. Disconnect the motor electrical connector.
4. Remove the motor attaching bolts. Disengage the motor from the linkage and remove the motor. Installation is the reverse.

## Windshield Wiper Rear Motor
### REMOVAL AND INSTALLATION
#### Hatchback Models

1. Remove the wiper arm and blade from the wiper motor.
2. Remove the pivot shaft attaching nut and spacers.
3. Remove the liftgate inner trim panel. Disconnect the electrical connector to the wiper motor.
4. Remove the three screws holding the bracket to the inner door skin and remove the motor assembly, bracket and linkage assembly.
5. Installation is the reverse order of the removal procedure.

#### Station Wagon Models

1. Remove the wiper arm and blade from the wiper motor.
2. Remove the pivot shaft attaching nut and spacers.
3. Remove the screws attaching the license plate housing. Disconnect the license plate light and remove the housing. Remove the wiper motor and bracket assembly retaining screws, disconnect the electrical connector to the wiper motor and remove the motor.
4. Installation is the reverse order of the removal procedure.

## Wiper Linkage
### REMOVAL AND INSTALLATION

The wiper linkage is mounted below the cowl top panel and can be reached by raising the hood.

1. Remove the wiper arm and blade assembly from the pivot shaft. Pry the latch (on the arm) away from the shaft to unlock the arm from the pivot shaft.
2. Raise the hood and disconnect the negative battery cable.
3. Remove the clip and disconnect the linkage drive arm from the motor crank pin.

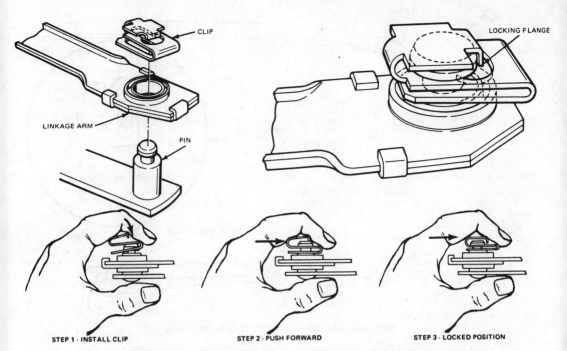

CLIP

LINKAGE ARM

PIN

LOCKING FLANGE

STEP 1 - INSTALL CLIP

STEP 2 - PUSH FORWARD

STEP 3 - LOCKED POSITION

**Removing and installing wiper linkage retaining clips**

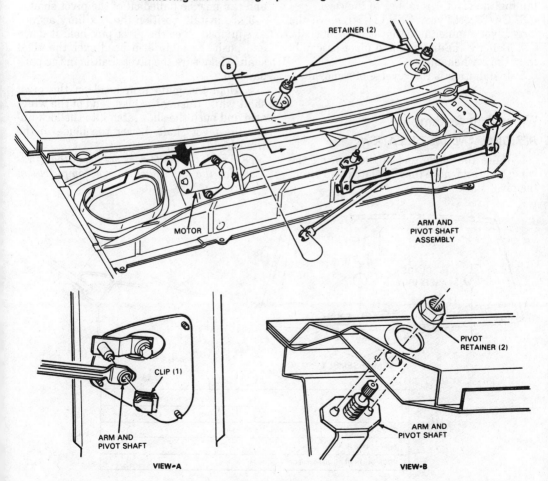

RETAINER (2)

B

A

MOTOR

ARM AND
PIVOT SHAFT
ASSEMBLY

CLIP (1)

ARM AND
PIVOT SHAFT

VIEW-A

PIVOT
RETAINER (2)

ARM AND
PIVOT SHAFT

VIEW-B

**Wiper linkage**

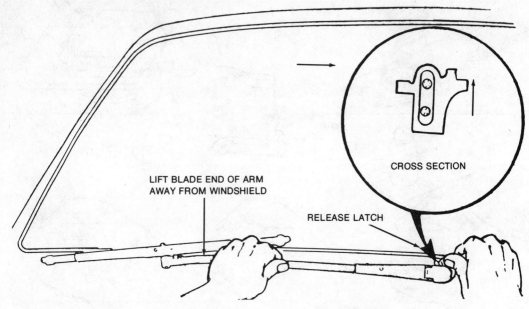

LIFT BLADE END OF ARM
AWAY FROM WINDSHIELD

CROSS SECTION

RELEASE LATCH

**Removing the wiper arm and blade assembly**

4. On Tempo/Topaz remove the screws retaining the pivot assemblies to the cowl.

6. On Escort/Lynx, EXP/LN-7 remove the large pivot retainer nuts from each pivot shaft.

7. Remove the linkage and pivot assembly from the cowl chamber.

8. Installation is the reverse of removal.

## Wiper Arm Assembly
### REMOVAL AND INSTALLATION

1. Raise the blade end of the arm off the windshield and move the slide latch away from the pivot shaft.

2. The wiper arm should not be unlocked and can now be pulled off of the pivot shaft.

3. To install, position the auxiliary arm (if so equipped) over the pivot pin, hold it down and push the main arm head over the pivot shaft. Make sure the pivot shaft is in the park position.

4. Hold the main arm head on the pivot shaft while raising the blade end of the wiper arm and push the slide latch into the lock under the pivot shaft. Lower the blade to the windshield.

NOTE: *If the blade does not touch the windshield, the slide latch is not completely in place.*

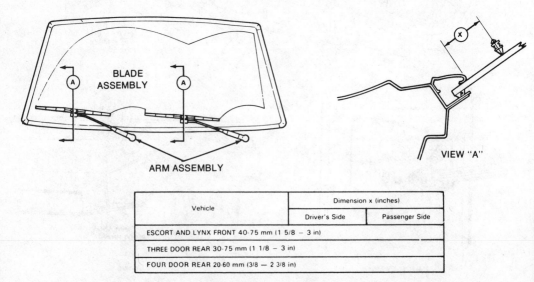

BLADE ASSEMBLY

ARM ASSEMBLY

VIEW "A"

| Vehicle | Dimension x (inches) | |
|---|---|---|
| | Driver's Side | Passenger Side |
| ESCORT AND LYNX FRONT 40-75 mm (1 5/8 — 3 in) | | |
| THREE DOOR REAR 30-75 mm (1 1/8 — 3 in) | | |
| FOUR DOOR REAR 20-60 mm (3/8 — 2 3/8 in) | | |

**Wiper arm adjustment**

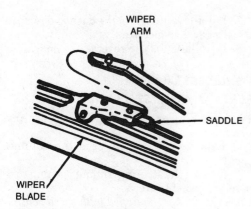

**Rear window wiper blade removal**

## Wiper Blade (Tridon® Type)
### REPLACEMENT

1. Pull up on the spring lock and pull the blade assembly from the pin.

2. To install, push the blade assembly onto the pin, so that the spring lock engages the pin.

## Wiper Element (Tridon®)
### REPLACEMENT

1. Locate a $\frac{7}{16}$" (11mm) long notch approximately 1" (25mm) from the end of the plastic backing strip, which is part of the rubber blade element assembly.

2. With the wiper blade removed from the arm place the blade assembly on a firm surface with the notched end of the backing strip visible.

3. Push down on one end of the wiper assembly until the blade is tightly bowed than grasp the tip of the backing strip firmly, pulling and twisting at the same time. The backing strip will then snap out of the retaining tab on the end of the wiper frame.

4. Lift the wiper blade assembly from the surface and slide the backing strip down the frame until the notch lines up with the next retaining tab then twist slightly and the backing strip will snap out. Follow this same procedure with the remaining tabs until the element is removed.

5. To install the blade element reverse the above procedure and make sure all six tabs are locked to the backing strip.

## Arm and Blade Adjustment

1. With the arm and blade assemblies removed from the pivot shafts turn on the wiper switch and allow the motor to move the pivot shaft three or four cycles, and then turn off the wiper switch. This will place the pivot shafts in the park position.

2. Install the arm and blade assemblies on the pivot shafts to the correct distance between the windshield lower molding or weatherstrip and the blade saddle centerline.

## INSTRUMENTS AND SWITCHES

### Headlight Switch
#### REMOVAL AND INSTALLATION

1. Disconnect the negative battery terminal.

2. Remove the left hand air vent control cable, and drop the cable and bracket down out of the way (cars without air conditioning only).

3. Remove the fuse panel bracket retaining screws and move the fuse panel assembly out of the way.

4. Pull the headlight knob out, to the on position.

5. Reach behind the dashboard and depress

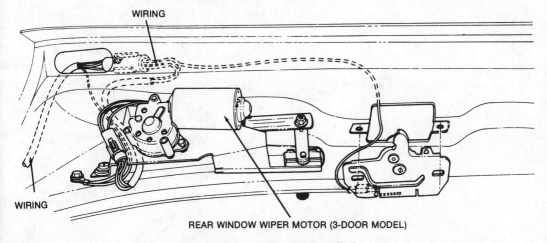

REAR WINDOW WIPER MOTOR (3-DOOR MODEL)

**Rear window wiper motor installation**

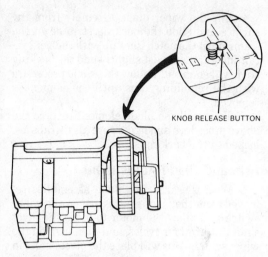

KNOB RELEASE BUTTON

**Headlight switch assembly**

the release button on the switch holding, while at the same time pulling the knob and shaft from the switch.

6. Remove the retaining nut from the dashboard.

7. Pull the switch from the dash and remove the electrical connections.

8. Installation is the reverse of removal.

## Instrument Cluster

### REMOVAL AND INSTALLATION

1. Disconnect the negative battery terminal.

2. Remove the bottom steering column cover.

3. Remove the steering column opening cover reinforcement screws.

NOTE: *On cars equipped with speed control disconnect the wires from the amplified assembly.*

4. Remove the steering column retaining screws from the steering column support bracket and lower the column.

5. Remove the column trim shrouds.

6. Disconnect all electrical connections from the column.

7. Remove the finish panel screws and the panel.

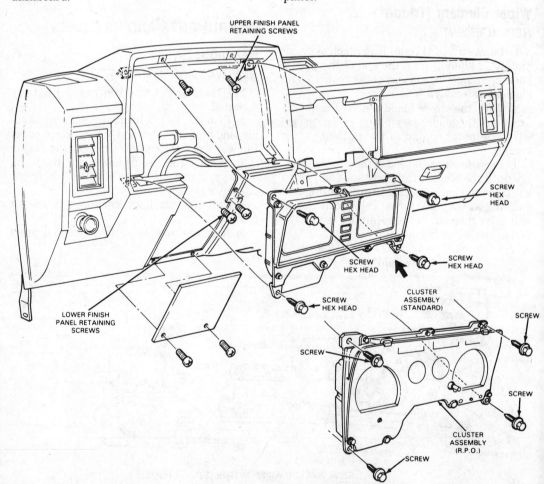

**Typical instrument cluster installation**

8. Remove the speedometer cable.

9. Remove the four cluster screws and remove the cluster.

10. Installation is the reverse of removal.

## Wiper Switch

NOTE: *The switch handle is an integral part of the switch and can not be removed separately. If there is any need for repairs to the wiper switch the multi-function switch must be replaced as a assembly.*

### REMOVAL

1. Disconnect the negative (ground) battery cable from the battery terminal.

2. Loosen the steering column attaching nuts enough to remove the upper trim shroud.

3. Remove the trim shrouds.

4. Disconnect the quick connect electrical connector.

5. Peel back the foam sight shield. Remove the two hex head screws holding the switch and remove the wash/wipe switch.

### INSTALLATION

1. Position the switch on the column and install the two hex head screws. Replace the foam sight shield over the switch.

2. Connect the quick connect electrical connector.

3. Install the upper and lower trim shrouds.

4. Tighten the steering column attaching nuts to 17–25 ft.lb. (23–33 Nm).

5. Connect the negative (ground) battery cable to the battery terminal.

6. Check the steering column for proper operation.

## Rear Wiper Switch

### REMOVAL

1. Remove the two or four cluster opening finish panel retaining screws and remove the finish panel by rocking the upper edge toward the driver.

2. Disconnect the wiring connector from the rear washer switch.

3. Remove the washer switch from the instrument panel. On the Sable models, the switch is attached to the instrument panel with two retaining screws.

### INSTALLATION

1. Install the cluster opening finish panel and the two or four retaining screws.

2. Connect the wiring connector.

3. Push the rear washer switch into the cluster finish panel until it snaps into place (on the Sable models, install the two retaining screws).

## Speedometer Cable

### REMOVAL AND INSTALLATION

1. Remove the instrument cluster.

2. Pull the speedometer cable from the casing. If the cable is broken, disconnect the casing from the transaxle and remove the broken piece from the transaxle end.

3. Lubricate the new cable with graphite lubricant. Feed the cable into the casing from the instrument panel end.

4. Attach the cable to the speedometer. Install the cluster.

# LIGHTING

## Headlights

Two rectangular dual sealed beam headlamps are used on all models up to 1985½. A dash mounted switch controls them and the steering column dimmer switch controls the high and low beams.

All models 1985½ and later are equipped with flush mount headlights. On these models the bulb may be replaced without removing the lens and body assembly.

### REMOVAL AND INSTALLATION

#### Sealed Beam Type — 1981–85½

1. Remove the headlamp door by removing the retaining screws. After the screws are removed, pull the door slightly forward (certain models have upper locking tabs which disengage by lifting out on the lower edge and pulling downward) and disconnect the parking light (if equipped). Remove the headlight door.

2. Remove the lamp retaining ring screws, pull the headlamp from the connector.

3. Installation is in the reverse order of removal.

#### Aerodynamic Type — 1985½ and later

CAUTION: *The replaceable Halogen headlamp bulb contains gas under pressure. The bulb may shatter if the glass envelope is scratched or the bulb is dropped. Handle the bulb carefully. Grasp the bulb ONLY by its plastic base. Avoid touching the glass envelope. Keep the bulb out of the reach of children.*

1. Check to see that the headlight switch is in the OFF position.

2. Raise the hood and locate the bulb installed in the rear of the headlight body.

3. Remove the electrical connector from the bulb by grasping the wires firmly and snapping the connector rearward.

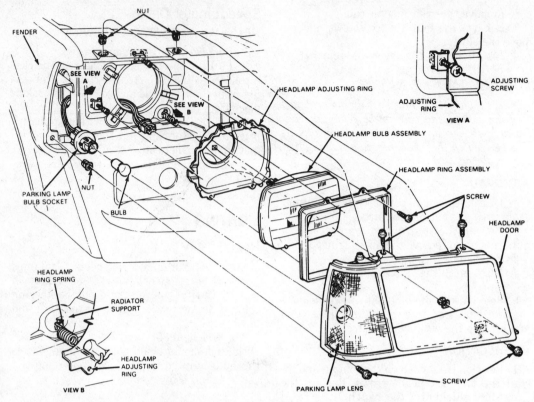

**Headlight replacement—sealed beam type headlights**

4. Remove the bulb retaining ring by rotating it counterclockwise (when viewed from the rear) about ⅛ of a turn, then slide the ring off the plastic base.

NOTE: *Keep the bulb retaining ring, it will be reused with the new bulb.*

5. Carefully remove the headlight bulb from its socket in the reflector by gently pulling it straight backward out of the socket. DO NOT rotate the bulb during removal.

**To install:**

6. With the flat side of the plastic base of the bulb facing upward, insert the glass envelope of the bulb into the socket. Turn the base slightly to the left or right, if necessary to align the grooves in the forward part of the plastic base with the corresponding locating tabs inside the socket. When the grooves are aligned, push the bulb firmly into the socket until the mounting flange on the base contacts the rear face of the socket.

7. Slip the bulb retaining ring over the rear of the plastic base against the mounting flange. Lock the ring into the socket by rotating the ring counterclockwise. A stop will be felt when the retaining ring is fully engaged.

8. Push the electrical connector into the rear of the plastic until it snaps and locks into position.

9. Turn the headlights on and check for proper operation.

## Front Turn Signal and Parking Lights

### REMOVAL AND INSTALLATION

**Escort/Lynx**

*1981–85*

1. Remove the screws that retain the headlamp door (bezel).

2. Pull the headlight door (bezel) forward

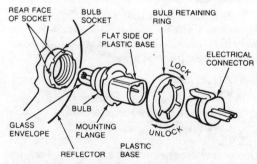

**Halogen bulb replacement—aerodynamic type headlights**

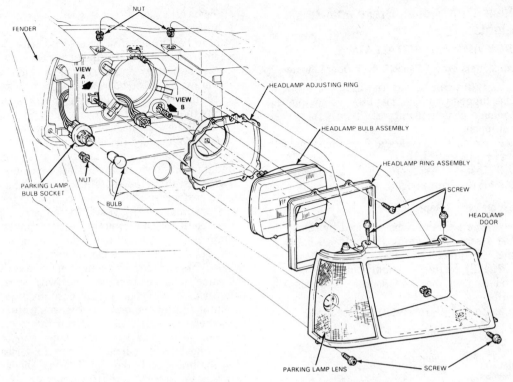

**Front turn signal and parking light—1981–85 Escort/Lynx**

and remove the parking light bulb socket from the light assembly.

3. To install, reverse the procedure.

### 1985½ AND LATER

1. Remove the 3 screws attaching the parking light to the headlight housing.

2. Hold the parking light with both hands and pull forward to release the hidden attachment.

3. From the side, remove the bulb socket and replace the bulb.

4. To install, reverse the procedure.

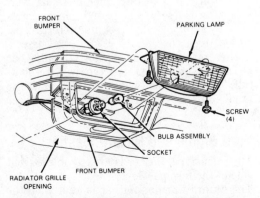

**Front turn signal and parking light—EXP/LN7**

### EXP/LN7

1. Remove the 2 parking light retaining screws and pull the light assembly forward.

2. Remove the bulb socket by twisting and remove the bulb.

3. To install, reverse the procedure.

### Tempo/Topaz

#### 1984–85

1. Remove the headlamp door.

2. Remove the 3 screws attaching the parking light and pull forward.

3. Remove the bulb socket by twisting and remove the bulb.

4. To install, reverse the procedure.

#### 1986 AND LATER

1. Remove the 2 screws retaining the parking light to the grille opening panel.

2. Hold the parking light with both hands and pull forward to release the hidden attachment.

3. Remove the bulb socket by twisting and replace the bulb.

4. To install, reverse the procedure.

## Rear Turn Signal, Brake and Parking Lights

### REMOVAL AND INSTALLATION

#### All Models except Escort/Lynx 4-Door Liftgate

1. Bulbs can be serviced from the inside of the luggage compartment by removing the luggage compartment rear trim panel, if so equipped.
2. Remove the socket(s) from the lamp body and replace the bulb(s).
3. Install the socket(s) in the lamp body and install the trim panel.

#### Escort/Lynx 4-Door Liftgate

1. The bulbs may be serviced by removing the 4 screws retaining the light assembly to the rear quarter opening.
2. Pull the light assembly out of the opening and remove the light socket to replace the bulb.
3. To install, reverse the procedure.

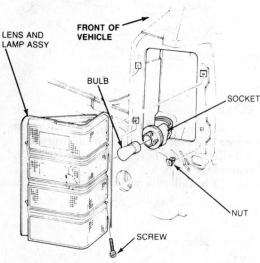

Rear turn signal and parking light—Escort/Lynx 4-door liftgate

## TRAILER WIRING

Wiring the car for towing is fairly easy. There are a number of good wiring kits available and these should be used, rather than trying to design your own. All trailers will need brake lights and turn signals as well as tail lights and side marker lights. Most states require extra marker lights for overly wide trailers. Also, most states have recently required back-up lights for trailers, and most trailer manufacturers have been building trailers with back-up lights for several years.

Additionally, some Class I, most Class II and just about all Class III trailers will have electric brakes.

Add to this number an accessories wire, to operate trailer internal equipment or to charge the trailer's battery, and you can have as many as seven wires in the harness.

Determine the equipment on your trailer and buy the wiring kit necessary. The kit will contain all the wires needed, plus a plug adapter set which included the female plug, mounted on the bumper or hitch, and the male plug, wired into, or plugged into the trailer harness.

When installing the kit, follow the manufacturer's instructions. The color coding of the wires is standard throughout the industry.

One point to note: some domestic vehicles, and most imported vehicles, have separate turn signals. On most domestic vehicles, the brake lights and rear turn signals operate with the same bulb. For those vehicles with separate turn signals, you can purchase an isolation unit so that the brake lights won't blink whenever the turn signals are operated, or, you can go to your local electronics supply house and buy four diodes to wire in series with the brake and turn signal bulbs. Diodes will isolate the brake and turn signals. The choice is yours. The isolation units are simple and quick to install, but far more expensive than the diodes. The diodes, however, require more work to install properly, since they require the cutting of each bulb's wire and soldering in place of the diode.

One final point, the best kits are those with a spring loaded cover on the vehicle mounted socket. This cover prevents dirt and moisture from corroding the terminals. Never let the vehicle socket hang loosely; always mount it securely to the bumper or hitch.

## CIRCUIT PROTECTION

### Circuit breakers

Circuit breakers operate when a circuit overload exceeds its rated amperage. Once operated, they automatically reset after a certain period of time.

There are two kinds of circuit breaker, as previously mentioned, one type will reset itself. The second will not reset itself until the problem in the circuit has been repaired.

### Turn Signal and Hazard Flasher

The turn signal flasher is located on the front side of the fuse panel.

The hazard warning flasher is located on the rear side of the fuse panel.

## Fuse Panel

The fuse panel is located below and to the left of the steering column.

Fuses are a one-time circuit protection. If a circuit is overloaded or shorts, the fuse will blow thus protecting the circuit. A fuse will continue to blow until the circuit is repaired.

## Fuse Link

The fuse link is a short length of special, Hypalon (high temperature) insulated wire, integral with the engine compartment wiring harness and should not be confused with standard wire. It is several wire gauges smaller than the circuit which it protects. Under no

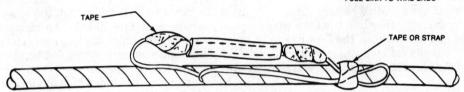

REMOVE EXISTING VINYL TUBE SHIELDING
REINSTALL OVER FUSE LINK BEFORE CRIMPING
FUSE LINK TO WIRE ENDS

TAPE

TAPE OR STRAP

TYPICAL REPAIR USING THE SPECIAL #17 GA. (9.00" LONG-YELLOW) FUSE LINK REQUIRED FOR THE AIR/COND. CIRCUITS

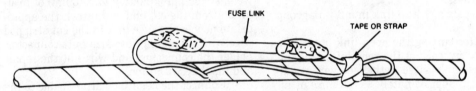

FUSE LINK

TAPE OR STRAP

TYPICAL REPAIR FOR ANY IN-LINE FUSE LINK USING THE SPECIFIED GAUGE FUSE LINK FOR THE SPECIFIC CIRCUIT

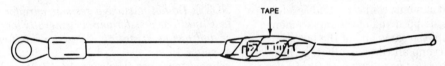

TAPE

TYPICAL REPAIR USING THE EYELET TERMINAL FUSE LINK OF THE SPECIFIED GAUGE FOR ATTACHMENT TO A CIRCUIT WIRE END

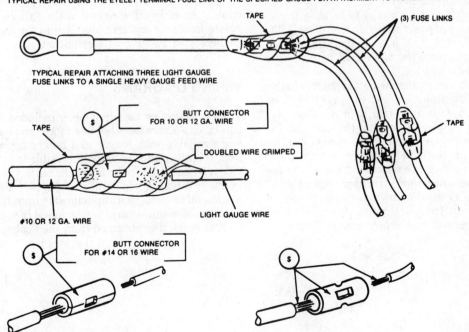

TAPE

(3) FUSE LINKS

TYPICAL REPAIR ATTACHING THREE LIGHT GAUGE FUSE LINKS TO A SINGLE HEAVY GAUGE FEED WIRE

TAPE

BUTT CONNECTOR FOR 10 OR 12 GA. WIRE

DOUBLED WIRE CRIMPED

TAPE

#10 OR 12 GA. WIRE

LIGHT GAUGE WIRE

BUTT CONNECTOR FOR #14 OR 16 WIRE

FUSIBLE LINK REPAIR PROCEDURE

**General fuse link repair procedures**

circumstances should a fuse link replacement repair be made using a length of standard wire cut from bulk stock or from another wiring harness.

To repair any blown fuse link use the following procedure:

1. Determine which circuit is damaged, its location and the cause of the open fuse link. If the damaged fuse link is one of three fed by a common No. 10 or 12 gauge feed wire, determine the specific affected circuit.

2. Disconnect the negative battery cable.

3. Cut the damaged fuse link from the wiring harness and discard it. If the fuse link is one of three circuits fed by a single feed wire, cut it out of the harness at each splice end and discard it.

4. Identify and procure the proper fuse link and butt connectors for attaching the fuse link to the harness.

5. To repair any fuse link in a 3-link group with one feed:

a. After cutting the open link out of the harness, cut each of the remaining undamaged fuse links close to the feed wire weld.

b. Strip approximately ½″ (13mm) of insulation from the detached ends of the two good fuse links, Then insert two wire ends into one end of a butt connector and carefully push one stripped end of the replacement fuse link into the same end of the butt connector and crimp all three firmly together.

NOTE: *Care must be taken when fitting the three fuse links into the butt connector as the internal diameter is a snug fit for three wires. Make sure to use a proper crimping tool. Pliers, side cutter, etc. will not apply the proper crimp to retain the wires and withstand a pull test.*

c. After crimping the butt connector to the three fuse links, cut the weld portion from the feed wire and strip approximately ½″ (13mm) of insulation from the cut end. Insert the stripped end into the open end of the butt connector and crimp very firmly.

d. To attach the remaining end of the replacement fuse link, strip approximately ½″ (13mm) of insulation from the wire end of the circuit from which the blown fuse link was removed, and firmly crimp a butt con-

nector or equivalent to the stripped wire. Then, insert the end of the replacement link into the other end of the butt connector and crimp firmly.

e. Using rosin core solder with a consistency of 60 percent tin and 40 percent lead, solder the connectors and the wires at the repairs and insulate with electrical tape.

6. To replace any fuse link on a single circuit in a harness, cut out the damaged portion, strip approximately ½″ (13mm) of insulation from the two wire ends and attach the appropriate replacement fuse link to the stripped wire ends with two proper size butt connectors. Solder the connectors and wires and insulate with tape.

7. To repair any fuse link which has an eyelet terminal on one end such as the charging circuit, cut off the open fuse link behind the weld, strip approximately ½″ (13mm) of insulation from the cut end and attach the appropriate new eyelet fuse link to the cut stripped wire with an appropriate size butt connector. Solder the connectors and wires at the repair and insulate with tape.

8. Connect the negative battery cable to the battery and test the system for proper operation.

NOTE: *Do not mistake a resistor wire for a fuse link. The resistor wire is generally longer and has print stating, "Resistor-don't cut or splice".*

When attaching a single No. 16, 17, 18 or 20 gauge fuse link to a heavy gauge wire, always double the stripped wire end of the fuse link before inserting and crimping it into the butt connector for positive wire retention.

## WIRING DIAGRAMS

Wiring Diagrams have not been included in this book. As cars have become more complex, and available with longer and longer option lists, it has become virtually impossible to provide a readable reproduction of the wiring diagrams in a reasonable number of pages. Information on ordering wiring diagrams from the automobile manufacturer can be found in your owners manual or obtained from the dealer.

# Troubleshooting Basic Turn Signal and Flasher Problems

Most problems in the turn signals or flasher system, can be reduced to defective flashers or bulbs, which are easily replaced. Occasionally, problems in the turn signals are traced to the switch in the steering column, which will require professional service.

F = Front    R = Rear    ● = Lights off    ○ = Lights on

| Problem | | Solution |
|---|---|---|
| Turn signals light, but do not flash | | • Replace the flasher |
| No turn signals light on either side | | • Check the fuse. Replace if defective.<br>• Check the flasher by substitution<br>• Check for open circuit, short circuit or poor ground |
| Both turn signals on one side don't work | | • Check for bad bulbs<br>• Check for bad ground in both housings |
| One turn signal light on one side doesn't work | | • Check and/or replace bulb<br>• Check for corrosion in socket. Clean contacts.<br>• Check for poor ground at socket |
| Turn signal flashes too fast or too slow | | • Check any bulb on the side flashing too fast. A heavy-duty bulb is probably installed in place of a regular bulb.<br>• Check the bulb flashing too slow. A standard bulb was probably installed in place of a heavy-duty bulb.<br>• Check for loose connections or corrosion at the bulb socket |
| Indicator lights don't work in either direction | | • Check if the turn signals are working<br>• Check the dash indicator lights<br>• Check the flasher by substitution |
| One indicator light doesn't light | | • On systems with 1 dash indicator: See if the lights work on the same side. Often the filaments have been reversed in systems combining stoplights with taillights and turn signals.<br>  Check the flasher by substitution<br>• On systems with 2 indicators: Check the bulbs on the same side<br>  Check the indicator light bulb<br>  Check the flasher by substitution |

## Troubleshooting the Heater

| Problem | Cause | Solution |
|---------|-------|----------|
| Blower motor will not turn at any speed | • Blown fuse<br>• Loose connection<br>• Defective ground<br>• Faulty switch<br>• Faulty motor<br>• Faulty resistor | • Replace fuse<br>• Inspect and tighten<br>• Clean and tighten<br>• Replace switch<br>• Replace motor<br>• Replace resistor |
| Blower motor turns at one speed only | • Faulty switch<br>• Faulty resistor | • Replace switch<br>• Replace resistor |
| Blower motor turns but does not circulate air | • Intake blocked<br>• Fan not secured to the motor shaft | • Clean intake<br>• Tighten security |
| Heater will not heat | • Coolant does not reach proper temperature<br>• Heater core blocked internally<br>• Heater core air-bound<br>• Blend-air door not in proper position | • Check and replace thermostat if necessary<br>• Flush or replace core if necessary<br>• Purge air from core<br>• Adjust cable |
| Heater will not defrost | • Control cable adjustment incorrect<br>• Defroster hose damaged | • Adjust control cable<br>• Replace defroster hose |

## Troubleshooting Basic Windshield Wiper Problems

| Problem | Cause | Solution |
|---------|-------|----------|
| **Electric Wipers** | | |
| Wipers do not operate—<br>Wiper motor heats up or hums | • Internal motor defect<br>• Bent or damaged linkage<br>• Arms improperly installed on linking pivots | • Replace motor<br>• Repair or replace linkage<br>• Position linkage in park and reinstall wiper arms |
| Wipers do not operate—<br>No current to motor | • Fuse or circuit breaker blown<br>• Loose, open or broken wiring<br>• Defective switch<br>• Defective or corroded terminals<br>• No ground circuit for motor or switch | • Replace fuse or circuit breaker<br>• Repair wiring and connections<br>• Replace switch<br>• Replace or clean terminals<br>• Repair ground circuits |
| Wipers do not operate—<br>Motor runs | • Linkage disconnected or broken | • Connect wiper linkage or replace broken linkage |
| **Vacuum Wipers** | | |
| Wipers do not operate | • Control switch or cable inoperative<br>• Loss of engine vacuum to wiper motor (broken hoses, low engine vacuum, defective vacuum/fuel pump)<br>• Linkage broken or disconnected<br>• Defective wiper motor | • Repair or replace switch or cable<br>• Check vacuum lines, engine vacuum and fuel pump<br><br><br><br>• Repair linkage<br>• Replace wiper motor |
| Wipers stop on engine acceleration | • Leaking vacuum hoses<br>• Dry windshield<br>• Oversize wiper blades<br><br>• Defective vacuum/fuel pump | • Repair or replace hoses<br>• Wet windshield with washers<br>• Replace with proper size wiper blades<br>• Replace pump |

# Troubleshooting Basic Dash Gauge Problems

| Problem | Cause | Solution |
|---|---|---|
| **Coolant Temperature Gauge** | | |
| Gauge reads erratically or not at all | • Loose or dirty connections<br>• Defective sending unit | • Clean/tighten connections<br>• Bi-metal gauge: remove the wire from the sending unit. Ground the wire for an instant. If the gauge registers, replace the sending unit. |
| | • Defective gauge | • Magnetic gauge: disconnect the wire at the sending unit. With ignition ON gauge should register COLD. Ground the wire; gauge should register HOT. |
| **Ammeter Gauge—Turn Headlights ON (do not start engine). Note reaction** | | |
| Ammeter shows charge<br>Ammeter shows discharge<br>Ammeter does not move | • Connections reversed on gauge<br>• Ammeter is OK<br>• Loose connections or faulty wiring<br>• Defective gauge | • Reinstall connections<br>• Nothing<br>• Check/correct wiring<br>• Replace gauge |
| **Oil Pressure Gauge** | | |
| Gauge does not register or is inaccurate | • On mechanical gauge, Bourdon tube may be bent or kinked | • Check tube for kinks or bends preventing oil from reaching the gauge |
| | • Low oil pressure | • Remove sending unit. Idle the engine briefly. If no oil flows from sending unit hole, problem is in engine. |
| | • Defective gauge | • Remove the wire from the sending unit and ground it for an instant with the ignition ON. A good gauge will go to the top of the scale. |
| | • Defective wiring | • Check the wiring to the gauge. If it's OK and the gauge doesn't register when grounded, replace the gauge. |
| | • Defective sending unit | • If the wiring is OK and the gauge functions when grounded, replace the sending unit |
| **All Gauges** | | |
| All gauges do not operate | • Blown fuse<br>• Defective instrument regulator | • Replace fuse<br>• Replace instrument voltage regulator |
| All gauges read low or erratically | • Defective or dirty instrument voltage regulator | • Clean contacts or replace |
| All gauges pegged | • Loss of ground between instrument voltage regulator and car<br>• Defective instrument regulator | • Check ground<br>• Replace regulator |
| **Warning Lights** | | |
| Light(s) do not come on when ignition is ON, but engine is not started | • Defective bulb<br>• Defective wire | • Replace bulb<br>• Check wire from light to sending unit |
| | • Defective sending unit | • Disconnect the wire from the sending unit and ground it. Replace the sending unit if the light comes on with the ignition ON. |
| Light comes on with engine running | • Problem in individual system<br>• Defective sending unit | • Check system<br>• Check sending unit (see above) |

## Troubleshooting Basic Lighting Problems

| Problem | Cause | Solution |
|---|---|---|
| **Lights** | | |
| One or more lights don't work, but others do | • Defective bulb(s)<br>• Blown fuse(s)<br>• Dirty fuse clips or light sockets<br>• Poor ground circuit | • Replace bulb(s)<br>• Replace fuse(s)<br>• Clean connections<br>• Run ground wire from light socket housing to car frame |
| Lights burn out quickly | • Incorrect voltage regulator setting or defective regulator<br>• Poor battery/alternator connections | • Replace voltage regulator<br><br>• Check battery/alternator connections |
| Lights go dim | • Low/discharged battery<br>• Alternator not charging<br><br>• Corroded sockets or connections<br><br>• Low voltage output | • Check battery<br>• Check drive belt tension; repair or replace alternator<br>• Clean bulb and socket contacts and connections<br>• Replace voltage regulator |
| Lights flicker | • Loose connection<br>• Poor ground<br><br>• Circuit breaker operating (short circuit) | • Tighten all connections<br>• Run ground wire from light housing to car frame<br>• Check connections and look for bare wires |
| Lights "flare"—Some flare is normal on acceleration—if excessive, see "Lights Burn Out Quickly" | • High voltage setting | • Replace voltage regulator |
| Lights glare—approaching drivers are blinded | • Lights adjusted too high<br>• Rear springs or shocks sagging<br>• Rear tires soft | • Have headlights aimed<br>• Check rear springs/shocks<br>• Check/correct rear tire pressure |
| **Turn Signals** | | |
| Turn signals don't work in either direction | • Blown fuse<br>• Defective flasher<br>• Loose connection | • Replace fuse<br>• Replace flasher<br>• Check/tighten all connections |
| Right (or left) turn signal only won't work | • Bulb burned out<br>• Right (or left) indicator bulb burned out<br>• Short circuit | • Replace bulb<br>• Check/replace indicator bulb<br><br>• Check/repair wiring |
| Flasher rate too slow or too fast | • Incorrect wattage bulb<br>• Incorrect flasher | • Flasher bulb<br>• Replace flasher (use a variable load flasher if you pull a trailer) |
| Indicator lights do not flash (burn steadily) | • Burned out bulb<br>• Defective flasher | • Replace bulb<br>• Replace flasher |
| Indicator lights do not light at all | • Burned out indicator bulb<br>• Defective flasher | • Replace indicator bulb<br>• Replace flasher |

## TRANSAXLE

Your car uses a front wheel drive transmission called a transaxle. The transaxle may either be manual or automatic.

A four or five speed fully synchronized manual transaxle is available, depending on year and model. An internally gated shift mechanism and a single rail shift linkage eliminate the need for periodic shift linkage adjustments. The MT is designed to use Type F or Dexron®II automatic transmission fluid as a lubricant. Never use gear oil (GL) in the place of Type F or Dexron®II.

The automatic transaxle (AT) is a 3-speed unit. A unique feature is a patented split path torque converter. The engine torque in second and third gears is divided, so that part of the engine torque is transmitted hydrokinetically through the torque converter, and part if transmitted mechanically by direct connection of the engine and transaxle. In the third gear, 93% of the torque is transmitted mechanically, making the AT highly efficient. Torque splitting is accomplished through a splitter gear set. A conventional compound gear set is also used.

Only one band is used in the AT. No periodic adjustments are required. No fluid changes are ever necessary in normal service. In service fluid additions or severe condition fluid changes may be made with Dexron®II or Dexron®II Series D fluid.

NOTE: *Refer to Chapter 1 for the Transaxle Identification Code Chart.*

## Halfshafts

The front wheel drive halfshafts are a one piece design. Constant velocity joint (CV) are used at each end. The left hand (driver's side) halfshaft is solid steel and is shorter than the right side halfshaft. The right hand (passenger's side) halfshaft is depending on year and model, constructed of tubular steel or solid construction. The automatic and manual transaxles use similar halfshafts.

The halfshafts can be replaced individually. The CV joint or boots can be cleaned or replaced. Individual parts of the CV joints are not available. The inboard and outboard joints differ in size. CV joint parts are fitted and should never be mixed or substituted with a part from another joint.

Inspect the boots periodically for cuts or splits. If a cut or split is found, inspect the joint, repack it with grease and install a new boot.

### REMOVAL

NOTE: *Special tools are required for removing, installing and servicing halfshafts. They are listed by descriptive name (Ford part number). Front Hub Installer Adapter (T81P1104A), Wheel Bolt Adapters (T81P1104B or T83P1104BH), CV Joint Separator (T81P3514A), Front Hub Installer/Remover (T81P1104C), Shipping Plug Tool (T81P1177B), Dust Deflector Installer CV Joint (T83P3425AH), Differential Rotator (T81P4026A).*

*It is necessary to have on hand new hub nuts and new lower control arm to steering knuckle attaching nuts and bolts. Once removed, these parts must not be reused. The torque holding ability is destroyed during removal.*

1. Loosen the front hub nut and the wheel lugs.
2. Jack up the front of the car and safely support it on jackstands.
3. Remove the tire and wheel assembly. Remove and discard the front hub nut. Save the washers.

NOTE: *Halfshaft removal and installation are the same for Manual and Automatic transaxles EXCEPT: The configuration of*

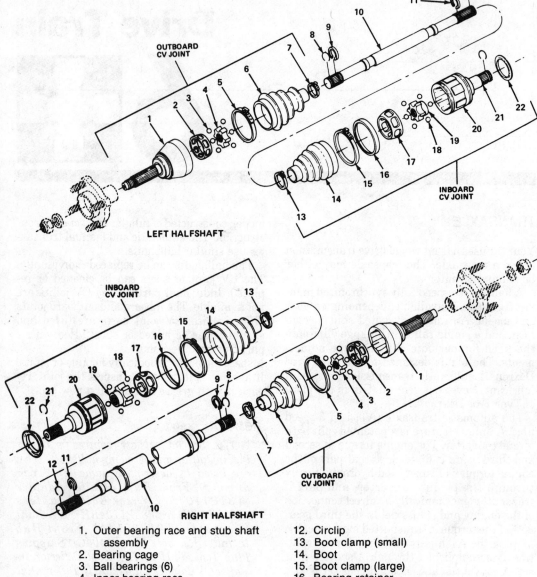

1. Outer bearing race and stub shaft
   assembly
2. Bearing cage
3. Ball bearings (6)
4. Inner bearing race
5. Boot clamp (large)
6. Boot
7. Boot clamp (small)
8. Circlip
9. Stop ring
10. Interconnecting shaft
11. Stop ring
12. Circlip
13. Boot clamp (small)
14. Boot
15. Boot clamp (large)
16. Bearing retainer
17. Bearing cage
18. Ball bearings (6)
19. Inner bearing race
20. Outer bearing race and stub shaft
    assembly
21. Circlip
22. Dust deflector

**Halfshafts exploded view—1981–85**

the AT (automatic transaxle) differential case requires that the right hand halfshaft assembly be removed first. The differential service tool T81P4026 (Differential Rotator) is then inserted to drive the left hand halfshaft from the transaxle. If only the left hand halfshaft is to be serviced, removed the right hand halfshaft from the transaxle side and support it with a length of wire. Drive the left hand halfshaft assembly from the transaxle.

4. Remove the bolt that retains the brake hose to the strut.

5. Remove the nut and bolt securing the lower ball joint and separate the joint from the steering knuckle by inserting a pry bar be-

HALFSHAFTS—DISASSEMBLED VIEW

OUTBOARD CV JOINT

LEFT HALFSHAFT ALL MODELS

INBOARD CV JOINT

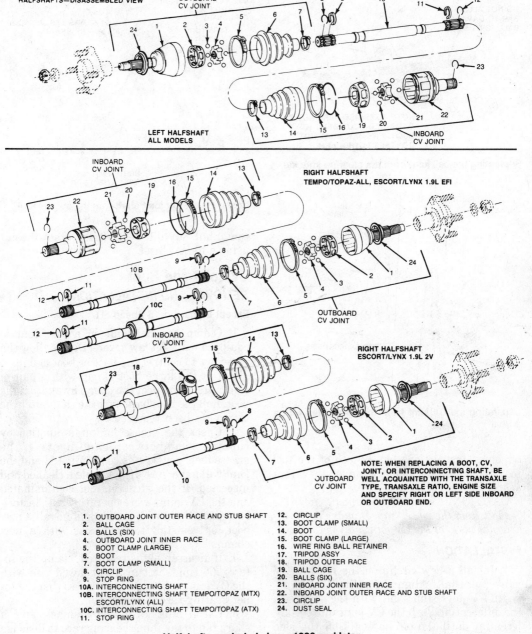

INBOARD CV JOINT

RIGHT HALFSHAFT
TEMPO/TOPAZ-ALL, ESCORT/LYNX 1.9L EFI

OUTBOARD CV JOINT

INBOARD CV JOINT

RIGHT HALFSHAFT
ESCORT/LYNX 1.9L 2V

OUTBOARD CV JOINT

NOTE: WHEN REPLACING A BOOT, CV, JOINT, OR INTERCONNECTING SHAFT, BE WELL ACQUAINTED WITH THE TRANSAXLE TYPE, TRANSAXLE RATIO, ENGINE SIZE AND SPECIFY RIGHT OR LEFT SIDE INBOARD OR OUTBOARD END.

| | |
|---|---|
| 1. OUTBOARD JOINT OUTER RACE AND STUB SHAFT | 12. CIRCLIP |
| 2. BALL CAGE | 13. BOOT CLAMP (SMALL) |
| 3. BALLS (SIX) | 14. BOOT |
| 4. OUTBOARD JOINT INNER RACE | 15. BOOT CLAMP (LARGE) |
| 5. BOOT CLAMP (LARGE) | 16. WIRE RING BALL RETAINER |
| 6. BOOT | 17. TRIPOD ASSY |
| 7. BOOT CLAMP (SMALL) | 18. TRIPOD OUTER RACE |
| 8. CIRCLIP | 19. BALL CAGE |
| 9. STOP RING | 20. BALLS (SIX) |
| 10A. INTERCONNECTING SHAFT | 21. INBOARD JOINT INNER RACE |
| 10B. INTERCONNECTING SHAFT TEMPO/TOPAZ (MTX) | 22. INBOARD JOINT OUTER RACE AND STUB SHAFT |
| ESCORT/LYNX (ALL) | 23. CIRCLIP |
| 10C. INTERCONNECTING SHAFT TEMPO/TOPAZ (ATX) | 24. DUST SEAL |
| 11. STOP RING | |

**Halfshafts exploded view—1986 and later**

tween the stabilizer and frame and pulling downward. Take care not to damage the ball joint boot.

NOTE: *The lower control arm ball joint fits into a pocket formed in a plastic disc rotor shield, on some models. The shield must be carefully bent back away from the ball joint while prying the ball joint out of the steering knuckle. Do not contact or pry on the lower control arm.*

6. Remove the halfshaft from the differen-

tial housing, using a pry bar. Position the pry bar between the case and the shaft and pry the joint away from the case. Do not damage the oil seal, the CV joint boot or the CV dust deflector. Install tool number T81P1177B (Shipping plug) to prevent fluid loss and differential side gear misalignment.

7. Support the end of the shaft with a piece of wire, suspending it from a chassis member.

8. Separate the shaft from the front hub using the special remover/installer tool and

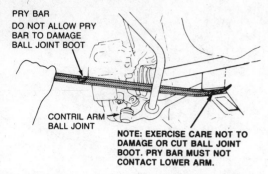

PRY BAR
DO NOT ALLOW PRY
BAR TO DAMAGE
BALL JOINT BOOT

CONTRIL ARM
BALL JOINT

NOTE: EXERCISE CARE NOT TO
DAMAGE OR CUT BALL JOINT
BOOT. PRY BAR MUST NOT
CONTACT LOWER ARM.

**Separating the ball joint from the steering knuckle**

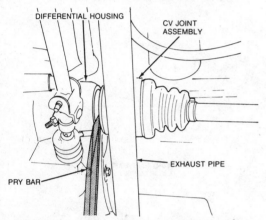

DIFFERENTIAL HOUSING

CV JOINT
ASSEMBLY

EXHAUST PIPE

PRY BAR

**Separating the CV joint from the differential with a prybar**

adapters. Instructions for the use of the tool may be found in Chapter 8 under the Front Wheel Bearing section.

CAUTION: *Never use a hammer to force the shaft from the wheel hub. Damage to the internal parts of the CV joint may occur.*

## INSTALLATION

1. Install a new circlip on the inboard CV joint stub shaft. Align the splines of the inboard CV joint stub shaft with the splines in the differential. Push the CV joint into the differential until the circlip seats on the side gear. Some force may be necessary to seat.

2. Carefully align the splines of the outboard CV joint stub shaft with the splines in the front wheel hub. Push the shaft into the hub as far as possible. Install the remover/installer tool and pull the CV stub shaft through the hub.

3. Connect the control arm to the steering knuckle and install a new mounting bolt and nut. Torque to 37–44 ft. lbs.

4. Connect the brake line to the strut.

5. Install the front hub washer and new hub nut. Install the tire and wheel assembly.

6. Lower the car to the ground. Tighten the

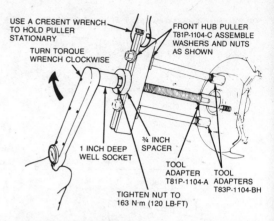

USE A CRESENT WRENCH
TO HOLD PULLER
STATIONARY

TURN TORQUE
WRENCH CLOCKWISE

FRONT HUB PULLER
T81P-1104-C ASSEMBLE
WASHERS AND NUTS
AS SHOWN

1 INCH DEEP
WELL SOCKET

¾ INCH
SPACER

TOOL
ADAPTER
T81P-1104-A

TOOL
ADAPTERS
T83P-1104-BH

TIGHTEN NUT TO
163 N·m (120 LB-FT)

**Installing the CV joint shaft with the special tool**

center hub nut to 180–200 ft. lbs. Stake the nut using a blunt chisel.

## CV Joint and Boot

### REMOVAL AND INSTALLATION

#### Except Inboard on 5 Speed MT

1. Clamp the halfshaft in a vise that is equipped with soft jaw covers. Do not allow the vise jaws to contact the boot or boot clamp.

2. Cut the large boot clamp with a pair of side cutters and peel the clamp away from the boot. Roll the boot back over the shaft after the clamp has been removed.

3. Check the grease for contamination by rubbing some between two fingers. If the grease feels gritty, it is contaminated and the joint will have to be disassembled, cleaned and inspected. If the grease is not contaminated and the CV joints were operating satisfactorily, repack them with grease and install a new boot, or reinstall the old boot with a new clamp.

4. If disassembly is required, clamp the interconnecting shaft in a soft jawed vise with the CV joint pointing downward so that the inner bearing race is exposed.

5. Use a brass drift and hammer, give a sharp tap to the inner bearing race to dislodge the internal snapring and separate the CV joint from the interconnecting shaft. Take care to secure the CV joint so that it does not drop on the ground after separation. Remove the clamp and boot from the shaft.

6. Remove and discard the snapring at the end of the interconnecting shaft. The stop ring, located just below the snapring should be removed and replaced only if damaged or worn.

7. Clean the interconnecting shaft splines and install a new snapring, and stop ring if removed. To install the snapring correctly, start one end in the groove and work the snapring over the shaft end and into the groove.

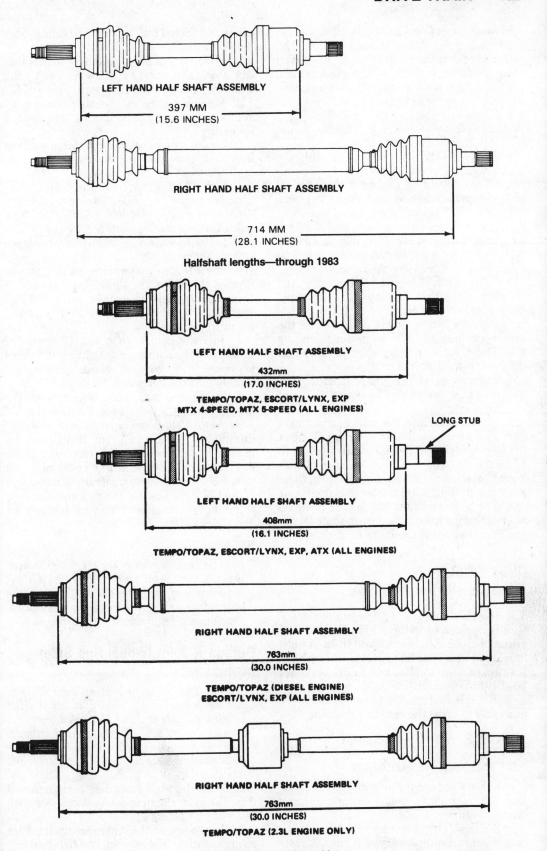

LEFT HAND HALF SHAFT ASSEMBLY

397 MM
(15.6 INCHES)

RIGHT HAND HALF SHAFT ASSEMBLY

714 MM
(28.1 INCHES)

Halfshaft lengths—through 1983

LEFT HAND HALF SHAFT ASSEMBLY

432mm
(17.0 INCHES)

TEMPO/TOPAZ, ESCORT/LYNX, EXP
MTX 4-SPEED, MTX 5-SPEED (ALL ENGINES)

LONG STUB

LEFT HAND HALF SHAFT ASSEMBLY

408mm
(16.1 INCHES)

TEMPO/TOPAZ, ESCORT/LYNX, EXP, ATX (ALL ENGINES)

RIGHT HAND HALF SHAFT ASSEMBLY

763mm
(30.0 INCHES)

TEMPO/TOPAZ (DIESEL ENGINE)
ESCORT/LYNX, EXP (ALL ENGINES)

RIGHT HAND HALF SHAFT ASSEMBLY

763mm
(30.0 INCHES)

TEMPO/TOPAZ (2.3L ENGINE ONLY)

Halfshaft lengths—1984 and later

8. Interconnecting shafts are different, depending on year and model application. The outboard end of the shaft is about ¼" (6mm) longer from the end of the boot groove to the shaft end than the inboard end. Take measurement to insure correct installation.

9. If removed, install a new boot. Make sure the boot is seated in the mounting groove and secure it in position with a new clamp.

10. Pack the CV joint and boot with the grease supplied in the joint or boot kit. The inboard joint should be packed with about 90 grams of grease; the boot with about 45 grams of grease. The outboard joint should be packed with about 45 grams of grease, and the boot with about 45 grams of grease. If grease from a replacement kit is not on hand, use only grease Ford Number E2FZ19590A or equivalent.

11. With the boot peeled back, position the CV joint on the shaft and tap into position using a plastic tipped hammer. The CV joint is fully seated when the snapring locks into the groove cut into the CV joint inner bearing race. Check for seating by attempting to pull the joint away from the shaft.

12. Remove all excess grease from the CV joint external surface and position the boot over the joint.

13. Before installing the boot clamp, make sure all air pressure that may have built up in the boot is removed. Pry up on the boot lip to allow the air to escape. Refer to the halfshaft length specifications and adjust the shaft to specs before tightening the boots clamps.

14. The large end clamp should be installed after making sure of the correct shaft length and that the boot is seated in its groove.

## DUST SHIELD
### REMOVAL AND INSTALLATION

The dust shield on the outside end of the CV joint is removed by using a light hammer and drift and tapping lightly around the seal until it becomes free. Install the dust shield with the flange facing outboard. Special Tools T83T3132A1 and T83P3425AH or equivalent (Spindle/Axle Tool and Dust Seal Installer) are necessary to drive the seal into position.

## Inboard CV-Joint — 5-Speed

### REMOVAL AND INSTALLATION

1. Remove the large clamp and roll the boot back over the shaft. Remove the wire ring bearing retainer.

2. Remove the outer race. Pull the inner race and bearing assembly out until it rests against the snapring. Use a pair of snapring

pliers and spread the stop ring and slide it back down the shaft.

3. Slide the inner bearing and race assembly down the shaft to allow access to the snapring. Remove the snapring.

4. Remove the inner race and bearing assembly. Remove the stop ring and boot if necessary.

5. Install a new boot and end clamp, fold the boot back, after cleaning the shaft splines. Install the stop ring in position.

NOTE: *The LH interconnecting shaft is the same end for end. The outboard or inboard CV joint may be installed at either end. The RH interconnecting shaft is different end for end. The tapered faces of the center balance faces outboard.*

6. Install a new snapring in the groove nearest the end of the shaft. Start one end of the snapring in the groove and word the snapring over the end of the shaft into the mounting groove.

7. Fill the boot with about 45 grams of grease and the outer race with about 90 grams of grease. Push the inner race and bearing assembly into the outer race by hand.

8. Install the wire ball retainer into the groove inside the outer race. Position the CV joint over the shaft and tap down with a plastic hammer until the snapring locks into the groove. Make sure the splines are aligned before hammering the joint into position.

9. Remove all excess grease from the outside of the CV joint. Position the boot and secure in retaining groove after removing trapped air and checking for proper length.

### SERVICE

NOTE: *Disassembly of the CV joints is necessary when the grease is contaminated. Contamination of the lubricant can damage the parts of the joint, an inspection is necessary to determine if replacement is required.*

## Outboard Joint (Wheel Hub Side)
### DISASSEMBLY

NOTE: *Two different bearing cage designs are used. One design uses four equal sized bearing cutouts and two elongated ones, the second design uses six equal sized cutouts. The step by step instructions will indicate the procedures necessary for the different designs.*

1. After the stub shaft has been removed from the axle, clamp in a soft jawed vise with the bearings facing up.

2. Press down on the inner race until it tiles enough to allow the removal of a ball bearing. If the bearing is tight, it might be necessary to

tap the inner race with a plastic faced hammer. Tap on the race, do not hit the cage.

3. When the cage is tilted, remove a ball. Repeat until all six balls have been removed. If the balls are tight, take a blunt edged pry bar and pry the balls from the cage. Be careful not to scratch or damage the inner race or cage.

4. Pivot the bearing cage and inner race 90° (straight up and down) to the center line of the outer race. Align the cage windows with the lands (grooves) in the outer race. When the windows are in alignment with the lands, lift the assembly from the outer race.

5. Separate the inner race from the cage.

• Six equal window type: rotate the inner race up and out of the cage.

• Two elongated window type: Pivot the inner race until it is straight up and down in the cage. Align one of the inner race bands with one of the elongated windows. Put the land through the elongated window and rotate the inner race up and lift out of the cage.

6. Wash all of the parts in safe solvent. Inspect the parts for wear. If the components of the CV joint are worn, a complete kit must be installed. Do not replace a joint merely because the parts appear polished. Shiny areas in the ball races and on the curves of the cage are normal. A CV joint should be replaced only if a component is cracked, broken, severely pitted or otherwise unserviceable.

### ASSEMBLY

1. Apply a light coating of grease on the inner and outer races. Install the inner race in the bearing cage by turning the inner race in the bearing cage by turning the inner race 90°. Position the land through the cage window and rotate into position.

2. Install the inner race and cage assembly into the outer race. Install the assembly in the vertical position and pivot into position. The counterbores in the inner race must be facing upwards.

3. Align the bearing cage and inner race with the outer race. Tilt the inner race and cage and install a ball bearing. Repeat until all six bearings are installed.

4. Pack the CV joint with 1/3 of the packet of grease. Use only the specified grease, Ford Part Number E2FZ19590A or the equivalent. Pack the grease into the joint by forcing it through the splined hole in the inner race.

## Inboard Joint (Transaxle Side)
### DISASSEMBLY

1. Remove the circlip from the end of the CV joint stub shaft. Inspect the dust deflector. If it is cracked or damaged it must be replaced. Refer to the section that appears later in this chapter.

2. Use a pair of side cutters to cut the ball retainer and discard it. The retainer is not required for assembly of the CV joint.

3. Gently tap the CV joint on the bench until the bearing assembly comes loose and can be removed by hand.

4. Remove the balls from the cage by prying them out. Take care not to scratch or damage the inner ball race or cage.

5. Rotate the inner race until the cage windows are aligned with the lands. Lift from cage through the wider side.

6. Clean all of the component parts in safe solvent and inspect for wear. If the components of the CV joint are worn, a complete kit must be installed. Do not replace a joint merely because the parts appear polished. Shiny areas in the ball races and on the curves of the cage are normal. A CV joint should be replaced only is a component is cracked, broken, severely pitted or otherwise unserviceable.

### ASSEMBLY

1. Install a new circlip on the stub shaft. Do not over expand or twist the clip.

2. If the dust deflector needs replacing, do so now. See the next section for instructions.

3. Install the inner bearing race into the bearing cage. Install the race through the larger end of the cage with the inner race hub facing the large end of the cage.

4. Align the bearing cage and inner race. Install the ball bearings. Press the bearings into position with the heel of your hand.

5. Pack the outer race with grease. Use only the specified grease, Ford Part Number D8RZ1950A or the equivalent.

6. Position the inner race and bearing assembly into the outer race. The assembly should be installed with the inner hub facing the outer race.

7. Push the inner race and bearing assembly into the outer race.

### DUST DEFLECTOR REPLACEMENT

NOTE: *The dust deflector should be replaced only if inspection determines it to be cracked, broken or deteriorated.*

Remove the old deflector. Soak the new dust deflector in a container of hot water and let it soak for five to ten minutes. Position the dust deflector over the sleeve with the ribbed side facing the CV joint. Tap the deflector into position with the Dust Deflector Installer (T81P3425A) and a hammer.

## MANUAL TRANSAXLE
### REMOVAL AND INSTALLATION
#### Escort/Lynx/EXP

1. Disconnect the negative battery terminal.

2. Remove the two transaxle to engine top mounting bolts.

3. Remove the clutch cable from the clutch release lever, after wedging a wooden block about 7" (178mm) long under the clutch pedal to hold it slightly beyond its normal position.

4. Raise the vehicle and support it on jackstands.

5. Remove the brake line routing clamps from the front wheels.

6. Remove the bolt that secures the lower control arm ball joint to the steering knuckle assembly, and pry the lower control arm away from the knuckle. When installing, a new nut and bolt must be used.

NOTE: *The plastic shield installed behind the rotor contains a molded pocket for the lower control arm ball joint. When removing the control arm from the knuckle, bend the shield toward the rotor to provide clearance.*

7. Pry the right inboard CV-joint from the transaxle, then remove the CV joint and halfshaft by pulling outward on the steering knuckle. Wire the CV-joint/halfshaft assembly in a level position to prevent it from expanding.

NOTE: *When the CV-joint is pulled out of the transaxle fluid will leak out. Install shipping plugs T81P-1177-B or the equivalent to prevent the dislocation of the of the differential side gears.*

8. Repeat the procedures and remove the left hand CV-joint/halfshaft from the transaxle.

9. Remove the stabilizer bar.

10. Disconnect the speedometer cable and back-up light.

11. Remove the (3) nuts from the starter mounting studs which hold the engine roll restrictor bracket.

12. Remove the roll restrictor and the starter stud bolts.

13. Remove the stiffener brace.

14. Remove the shift mechanism crossover spring.

15. Remove the shift mechanism stabilizer bar.

16. Remove the shift mechanism.

17. Place a transmission jack under the transaxle.

18. Remove the rear transmission mounts.

19. Remove the front transmission mounts.

20. Lower the transaxle support jack until it clears the rear mount and support the engine with a jack, under the oil pan.

21. Remove the four remaining engine to transaxle bolts.

22. Remove the transaxle.

NOTE: *The case may have sharp edges. Wear protective gloves when handling the transaxle.*

23. Installation is the reverse of removal.

NOTE: *When installing the CV-joint/halfshaft assemblies into the transaxle, install new circlips on the inner stub shaft, carefully install the assemblies into the transaxle to prevent damaging the oil seals, and insure that both joints are fully seated in the transaxle by lightly prying outward to confirm they are seated. If the circlips are not seated, the joints will move out of the transaxle.*

#### Tempo/Topaz

1. Wedge a wood block approximately 7" (178mm) long under the clutch pedal to hold the pedal up slightly beyond its normal position. Grasp the clutch cable and pull forward, disconnecting it from the clutch release shaft assembly. Remove the clutch casing from the rib on the top surface of the transaxle case.

2. Using a 13mm socket, remove the two top transaxle-to-engine mounting bolts. Using a 10mm socket, remove the air cleaner.

3. Raise and safely support the car. Remove the front stabilizer bar to control arm attaching nut and washer (driver side). Discard the attaching nut. Remove the two front stabilizer bar mounting brackets. Discard the bolts.

4. Using a 15mm socket, remove the nut and bolt that secures the lower control arm ball joint to the steering knuckle assembly. Discard the nut and bolt. Repeat this procedure on the opposite side.

5. Using a large pry bar, pry the lower control arm away from the knuckle.

CAUTION: *Exercise care not to damage or cut the ball joint boot. Pry bar must not contact the lower arm. Repeat this procedure on the opposite side.*

6. Using a large pry bar, pry the left inboard CV-joint assembly from the transaxle.

NOTE: *Lubricate will drain from the seal at this time. Install shipping plugs (T81P-1177-B or equivalent). Two plugs are required (one for each seal). Remove the inboard CV joint from the transaxle by grasping the left hand steering knuckle and swinging the knuckle and halfshaft outward from the transaxle.*

CAUTION: *Exercise care when using a pry*

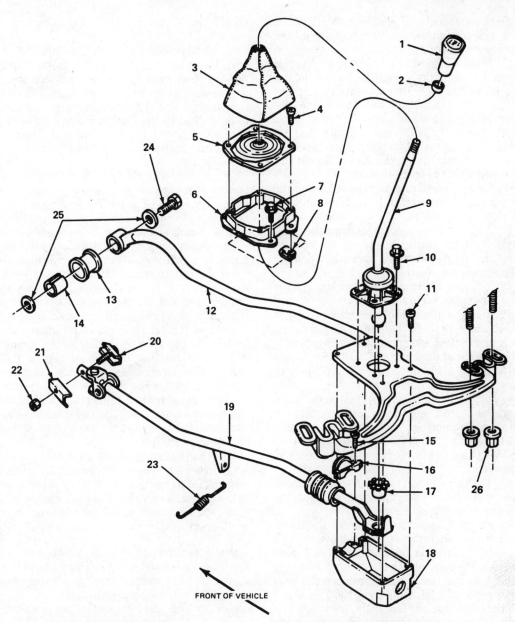

FRONT OF VEHICLE

1. Knob—gear shift lever
2. Nut—shift knob locking
3. Upper boot assembly—gear shift lever
4. Screw—tapping (4 required)
5. Lower boot assembly—gear shift lever
6. Boot retainer assembly—gear shift lever
7. Bolt—boot retainer (4 required)
8. Nut—spring (4 required)
9. Lever assembly—gearshift
10. Bolt—tapping (4 required)
11. Screw—tapping (4 required)
12. Support assembly (shift stabilizer bar)
13. Bushing—gear shift stabilizer bar

14. Sleeve—gear shift rod
15. Screw—tapping (2 required)
16. Cover—control selector
17. Bushing—anti tizz
18. Housing—control selector
19. Assembly—shift rod and clevis
20. Assembly—clamp
21. Clamp—gear shift lever (2 required)
22. Nut—clamp assembly
23. Retaining spring—gear shift tube
24. Bolt—stabilizer bar attaching
25. Washer—flat (2 required)
26. Assembly—nut/washer (4 required)

**Components of a typical manual shift linkage**

*bar to remove the CV joint assembly. If you're not careful, damage to the differential oil seal may result.*

7. If the CV-joint assembly cannot be pried from the transaxle, insert Differential Rotator Tool (T81P-4026-A or equivalent), through the left side and tap the joint out. Tool can be used from either side of transaxle.

8. Wire the halfshaft assembly in a near level position to prevent damage to the assembly during the remaining operations. Repeat this procedure on the opposite side.

9. Using a small prybar, remove the backup lamp switch connector from the transaxle back-up lamp switch.

10. Using a 15mm socket, remove the three nuts from the starter mounting studs which hold the engine roll restrictor bracket. Remove the engine roll restrictor.

11. Using a 13mm deep will socket, remove the three starter stud bolts.

12. Using a 10mm socket, remove the shift mechanism to shift shaft attaching nut and bolt and control selector indicator switch arm. Remove the shift shaft.

13. Using a 15mm socket, remove the shift mechanism stabilizer bar to transaxle attaching bolt. Remove the $\frac{7}{32}$" sheet metal screw and the control selector indicator switch and bracket assembly.

14. Using a 22mm ($\frac{7}{8}$") crows foot wrench, remove the speedometer cable from the transaxle.

15. Using a 13mm universal socket, remove the two stiffener brace attaching bolts from the oil pan to clutch housing.

16. Position a suitable jack under the transaxle. Using an 18mm socket, remove the two nuts that secure the left hand rear No. 4 insulator to the body bracket.

17. Using a 13mm socket, remove the bolts that secure the left hand front No. 1 insulator to the body bracket. Lower the transaxle jack until the transaxle clears the rear insulator. Support the engine with a screw jackstand under the oil pan. Use a 2 x 4 piece of wood on top of the screw jack.

18. Using a 13mm socket, remove the four engine to transaxle attaching bolts. One of these bolts holding the ground strap and wiring loom stand off bracket.

19. Remove the transaxle from the rear face of the engine and lower transaxle from the vehicle.

20. Install in reverse order. WARNING: THE TRANSAXLE CASE CASTING MAY HAVE SHARP EDGES. WEAR PROTECTIVE GLOVES WHEN HANDLING THE TRANSAXLE ASSEMBLY.

## CLUTCH

The transmission and clutch are employed to vary the relationship between engine speed and the speed of the wheels so that adequate engine power can be produced under all circumstances. The clutch allows engine torque to be applied to the transmission input shaft gradually, due to mechanical slippage. The car can, consequently, be started smoothly from a full stop.

The transmission changes the ratio between the rotating speeds of the engine and the wheels by the use of gears. The lower gears allow full engine power to be applied to the rear wheels during acceleration at low speeds.

The clutch driven plate is a thin disc, the center of which is splined to the transmission input shaft. Both sides of the disc are covered with a layer of material which is similar to brake lining and which is capable of allowing slippage without roughness or excessive noise.

The clutch cover is bolted to the engine flywheel and incorporates a diaphragm spring which provides the pressure to engage the clutch. The cover also houses the pressure plate. The driven disc is sandwiched between the pressure plate and the smooth surface of the flywheel when the clutch pedal is released, thus forcing it to turn at the same speed as the engine crankshaft.

The transmission contains a mainshaft which passes all the way through the transmission, from the clutch to the final drive gear in the transaxle. This shaft is separated at one point, so that front and rear portions can turn at different speeds.

Power is transmitted by a countershaft in the lower gears and reverse. The gears of the countershaft mesh with gears on the mainshaft, allowing power to be carried from one to the other. All the countershaft gears are integral with that shaft, while several of the mainshaft gears can either rotate independently of the shaft or be locked to it. Shifting from one gear to the next causes one of the gear to be freed from rotating with the shaft, and locks another to it. Gears are locked and unlocked by internal dog clutches which slide between the center of the gear and the shaft. The forward gears usually employ synchronizers: friction members which smoothly bring gear and shaft to the same speed before the toothed dog clutches are engaged.

The clutch is operating properly if:

1. It will stall the engine when released with the vehicle held stationary.

2. The shift lever can be moved freely be-

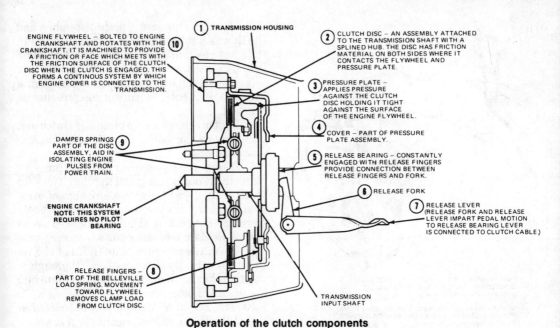

ENGINE FLYWHEEL – BOLTED TO ENGINE CRANKSHAFT AND ROTATES WITH THE CRANKSHAFT. IT IS MACHINED TO PROVIDE A FRICTION OR FACE WHICH MEETS WITH THE FRICTION SURFACE OF THE CLUTCH DISC WHEN THE CLUTCH IS ENGAGED. THIS FORMS A CONTINOUS SYSTEM BY WHICH ENGINE POWER IS CONNECTED TO THE TRANSMISSION.

① TRANSMISSION HOUSING

② CLUTCH DISC – AN ASSEMBLY ATTACHED TO THE TRANSMISSION SHAFT WITH A SPLINED HUB. THE DISC HAS FRICTION MATERIAL ON BOTH SIDES WHERE IT CONTACTS THE FLYWHEEL AND PRESSURE PLATE.

③ PRESSURE PLATE – APPLIES PRESSURE AGAINST THE CLUTCH DISC HOLDING IT TIGHT AGAINST THE SURFACE OF THE ENGINE FLYWHEEL.

④ COVER – PART OF PRESSURE PLATE ASSEMBLY.

⑨ DAMPER SPRINGS PART OF THE DISC ASSEMBLY. AID IN ISOLATING ENGINE PULSES FROM POWER TRAIN.

⑤ RELEASE BEARING – CONSTANTLY ENGAGED WITH RELEASE FINGERS PROVIDE CONNECTION BETWEEN RELEASE FINGERS AND FORK.

⑥ RELEASE FORK

⑦ RELEASE LEVER (RELEASE FORK AND RELEASE LEVER IMPART PEDAL MOTION TO RELEASE BEARING LEVER IS CONNECTED TO CLUTCH CABLE.)

ENGINE CRANKSHAFT NOTE: THIS SYSTEM REQUIRES NO PILOT BEARING

⑧ RELEASE FINGERS – PART OF THE BELLEVILLE LOAD SPRING. MOVEMENT TOWARD FLYWHEEL REMOVES CLAMP LOAD FROM CLUTCH DISC.

TRANSMISSION INPUT SHAFT

**Operation of the clutch components**

tween first and reverse gears when the vehicle is stationary and the clutch disengaged.

### FREE PLAY ADJUSTMENT

The free play in the clutch is adjusted by a built in mechanism that allows the clutch controls to be self-adjusted during normal operation.

The self-adjusting feature should be checked every 5000 miles. This is accomplished by insuring that the clutch pedal travels to the top of its upward position. Grasp the clutch pedal with your hand or put your foot under the clutch pedal. pull up on the pedal until it stops. Very little effort is required (about 10 lbs.). During the application of upward pressure, a click may be heard which means an adjustment was necessary and has been accomplished.

## Clutch Cable
### REMOVAL AND INSTALLATION

1. From under the hood, use a pair of pliers and grasp the extended tip of the clutch cable (on top of transaxle). Unhook the clutch cable from the clutch throwout bearing release lever.

2. From inside the car, remove the fresh air duct next to the clutch pedal (non-air conditioned cars). Remove the shield from the brake pedal support bracket. On Tempo/Topaz models remove the panel above the clutch pedal.

3. Lift up on the clutch pedal to release the adjusting pawl. Rotate the adjustment gear quadrant forward. Unhook the clutch cable from the gear quadrant. Swing the quadrant to the rear.

4. Pull the clutch cable out from between the clutch pedal and the gear quadrant and from the isolator on the gear quadrant.

5. From under the hood, pull the clutch cable through the firewall and remove it from the car.

6. From under the hood, insert the clutch cable through the firewall into the drivers compartment.

7. Push the clutch cable through the isolator on the pedal stop bracket and through the recess between the clutch pedal and the adjusting gear quadrant.

8. Lift the clutch pedal to release the pawl and rotate the gear quadrant forward. Hook the clutch cable to the gear quadrant.

9. Install the fresh air duct. Install the shield on the brake pedal support.

10. Secure the clutch pedal in the up position. Use a piece of wire, tape, etc.

11. From under the hood, hook the cable to the clutch throwout bearing release lever.

12. Unfasten the clutch pedal and adjust the clutch by operating the clutch pedal several times. Pull up on the pedal to make sure it is reaching the maximum upward position.

## Pressure Plate and Clutch Disc
### REMOVAL AND INSTALLATION

1. Remove the transaxle (refer to the previous Transaxle Removal and Installation sections).

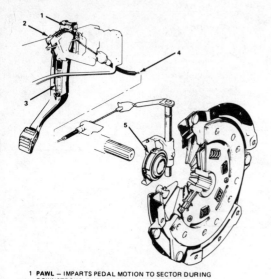

1 **PAWL** – IMPARTS PEDAL MOTION TO SECTOR DURING DOWNSTROKE. PAWL ENGAGES QUADRANT AT BEGINNING OF DOWNSTROKE.

2 **QUADRANT**–ACTUATES CABLE DURING PEDAL DOWN-STROKE FOLLOWING CABLE CORE AS CORE IS MOVED DURING DISC FACING WEAR.

3 **ADJUSTER SPRING** – KEEPS SECTOR IN FIRM CONTACT WITH CABLE. KEEPS RELEASE BEARING IN CONTACT WITH CLUTCH RELEASE FINGERS THROUGH CABLE LINKAGE WITH PEDAL IN UP POSITION.

4 **CABLE**

5 **RELEASE BEARING**

**Identification of the clutch parts**

2. Mark the pressure plate assembly and the flywheel so that they may be assembled in the same position if the original pressure plate is to be reused.

3. Loosen the attaching bolts one turn at a time, in sequence, until spring pressure is relieved.

4. Support the pressure plate and clutch disc and remove the bolts. Remove the pressure plate and disc.

5. Inspect the flywheel, clutch disc, pressure plate, throwout bearing and the clutch fork for wear. If the flywheel shows any sign of over-heating (blue discoloration), or if it is badly scored or grooved, it should be refaced or replaced. Replace any other parts that are worn.

6. Clean the pressure plate (if it is to be re-used) and the flywheel surfaces thoroughly. Position the clutch disc and pressure plate into the installed position.

NOTE: *The clutch disc must be assembled so that the flatter side is toward the flywheel.*

Align the match marks on the pressure plate and flywheel (when reusing the original pressure plate). Support the clutch disc and pressure plate with a dummy shaft or clutch aligning tool.

7. Install the pressure plate to flywheel

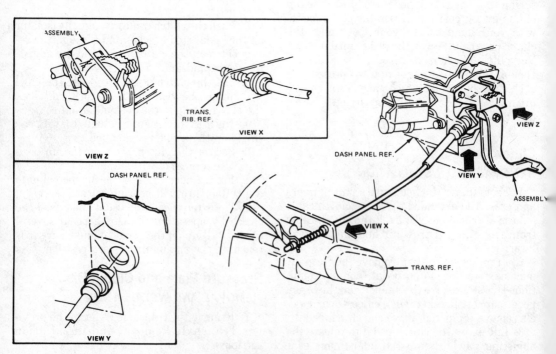

**Clutch cable installation**

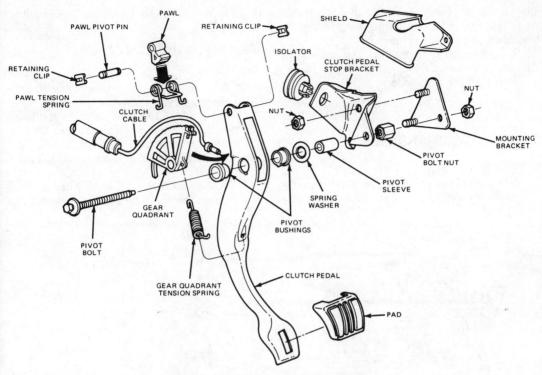

**Self-adjusting clutch pedal components**

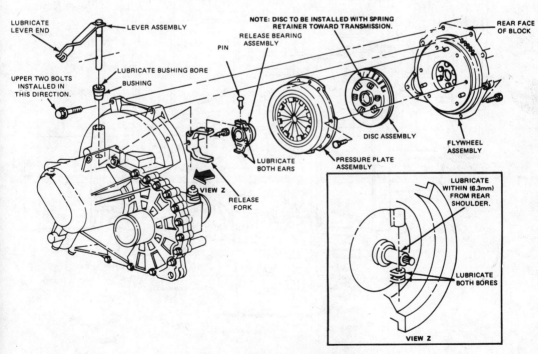

**Clutch installation (exploded view)**

bolts. Tighten them gradually in a criss-cross pattern. Remove the aligning tool. Mounting bolt torque is 12–24 ft.lb.

8. Lubricate the release bearing and install it on the throwout fork.

9. Install the transaxle.

## AUTOMATIC TRANSAXLE

NOTE: *On Tempo/Topaz models the 2.3L HSC engine and automatic transaxle must be removed together as a unit. Refer to the En-gine Removal and Installation Section in Chapter 3.*

### REMOVAL AND INSTALLATION
#### Escort/Lynx/EXP

1. Disconnect the negative battery cable from the battery.

2. From under the hood, remove the bolts that attach the air manage valve to the AT (automatic transaxle) valve body cover. Disconnect the wiring harness connector from the neutral safety switch.

3. Disconnect the throttle valve linkage and the manual control lever cable. Remove the

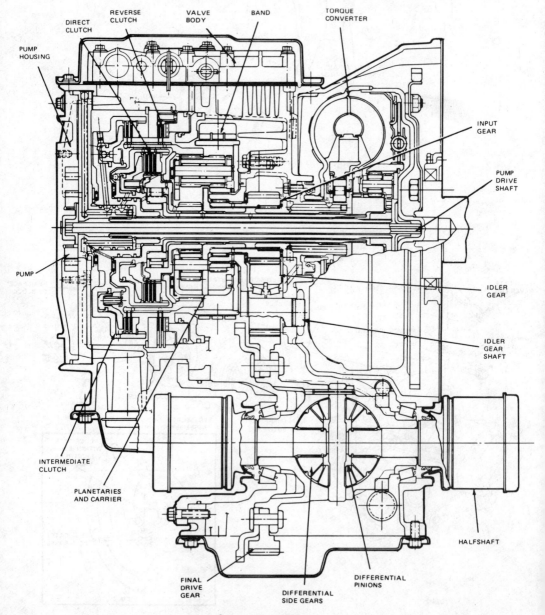

**Automatic transaxle**

two transaxle to engine upper attaching bolts. The bolts are located below and on either side of the distributor.

4. Loosen the front wheel lugs slightly. Jack up the front of the car and safely support it on jackstands. Remove the tire and wheel assemblies.

5. Drain the transmission fluid. Disconnect the brake hoses from the strut brackets on both sides. Remove the pinch bolts that secure the lower control arms to the steering knuckles. Separate the ball joint from the steering knuckle. Remove the stabilizer bar attaching bracket. Remove the nuts that retain the stabilizer to the control arms. Remove the stabilizer

bar. When removing the control arms from the steering knuckles, it will be necessary to bend the plastic shield slightly to gain ball joint clearance for removal.

6. Remove the tie rod ends from the steering knuckles. Use a special tie rod removing tool. Pry the right side halfshaft from the transaxle (see halfshaft removal section).

7. Remove the left side halfshaft from the transaxle. Support both right and left side halfshaft out of the way with wire.

8. Install sealing plugs or the equivalent into the transaxle halfshaft mounting holes.

9. Remove the starter support bracket. Disconnect the starter cable. Remove the starter

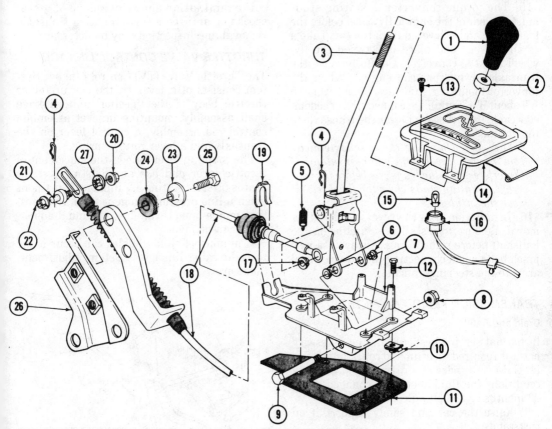

1. Knob assy., trans. gr. shift lever
2. Nut, trans. gr. shift lever ball lock
3. Lever & adaptor assy., trans. control selector
4. Pin, retaining
5. Spring, trans. park gear lockout rtn.
6. Bushing, trans. gear shift lever shaft
7. Housing, trans. control selector
8. Nut, M8-1.25 hex flg.
9. Bolt, M8 x 1.25 x 82.0 hex flg. pilot
10. Nut, M6-1.00 "U"
11. Seal, trans. control selector housing
12. Bolt, M6-1.00 x 25.0 hex flg. hd.
13. Screw, 4.2 x 13.0 hex wa. hd. tap.
14. Bezel assy., trans. control sel. dial

15. Bulb
16. Indicator bulb harness
17. Bushing, trans. gear shift lever cable
18. Cable & bracket assy.
19. Clip, hand brake cable spring lock
20. Nut & washer assy.
21. Stud, trans. gr. shift connecting rod adjusting
22. Bushing, trans. control shift rod clevis
23. Spacer, trans. control cable bracket
24. Insulator, trans. control cable bracket
25. Bolt, M10-1.5 x 20.0 hex flg. hd.
26. Retainer assy., trans. control cable bracket
27. Nut, 5/16-18 round push on

**Shift lever components, automatic transaxle**

mounting studs and the starter motor. Remove the transaxle support bracket.

10. Remove the lower cover from the transaxle. Turn the converter for access to the converter mounting nuts. Remove the nuts.

11. Remove the nuts that attach the left front insulator to the body bracket. Remove the bracket to body bolts and remove the bracket.

12. Remove the left rear insulator bracket attaching nut.

13. Disconnect the transmission cooler lines. Remove the bolts that attach the manual lever bracket to the transaxle case.

14. Position a floor jack with a wide saddle under the transaxle and remove the four remaining transaxle to engine attaching bolts.

15. The torque converter mounting studs must be clear of the engine flywheel before the transaxle can be lowered from the car. Take a small pry bar and place it between the flywheel and the convertor. Carefully move the transaxle away from the engine. When the convertor mounting studs are clear lower the AT about 3″ (76mm). Disconnect the speedometer cable from the AT. Lower the transaxle to the ground.

NOTE: *When moving the transaxle away from the engine watch the mount insulator. If it interferes with the transaxle before the converter mounting studs clear the flywheel, remove the insulator.*

16. Installation is in the reverse order of removal. Be sure to install new circlips on the halfshaft before reinstalling. Always use new pinch bolts when connecting the lower control arms to the steering knuckles.

### TRANSMISSION FLUID AND FILTER

**Drain and Refill**

In normal service it should not be necessary nor it it required to drain and refill the AT fluid. However, under severe operation or dusty conditions the fluid should be changed every 20 months or 20,000 miles.

1. Raise the car and safely support it on jackstands.

2. Place a suitable drain pan underneath the transaxle oil pan. Loosen the oil pan mounting bolts and allow the fluid to drain until it reaches the level of the pan flange. Remove the attaching bolts, leaving one end attached so that the pan will tip and the rest of the fluid will drain.

3. Remove the oil pan. Thoroughly clean the pan. Remove the old gasket. Make sure that the gasket mounting surfaces are clean.

4. Remove the transmission filter screen retaining bolt. Remove the screen.

5. Install a new filter screen and O-ring.

Place a new gasket on the pan and install the pan to the transmission.

6. Fill the transmission to the correct level. Remove the jackstands and lower the car to the ground.

### TRANSAXLE FLUID CONDITION

Pull the transmission dipstick out. Observe the color and odor of the transmission fluid. The color should be red not brown or black. An odor can sometimes indicate an overheating condition, clutch disc or band failure.

Wipe the dipstick with a clean white rag. Examine the stain on the rag for specks of solids (metal or dirt) and for signs of contaminates (antifreeze, gum or varnish condition).

If examination shows evidence of metal specks or antifreeze contamination transaxle removal and inspection may be necessary.

### THROTTLE VALVE CONTROL LINKAGE

The Throttle Valve (TV) Control Linkage System consists of a lever on the carburetor or throttle body of the injection unit, linkage shaft assembly, mounting bracket assembly, control rod assembly, a control lever on the transaxle and a lever return spring.

The coupling lever follows the movement of throttle lever and has an adjustment screw that is used for setting TV linkage adjustment when a line pressure gauge is used. If a pressure gauge is not available, a manual adjustment can be made.

A number of shift troubles can occur if the throttle valve linkage is not in adjustment. Some are:

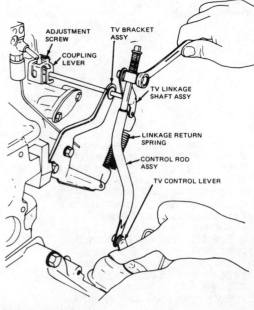

**TV rod adjustment**

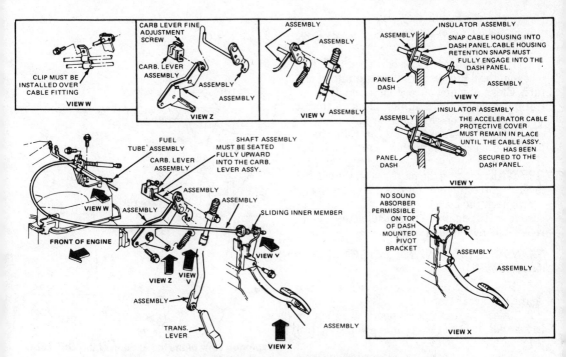

**Throttle linkage cable and components; automatic transaxle**

1. **Symptom:** Excessively early and/or soft upshift with or without slip-bump feel. No forced downshaft (kickdown) function at appropriate speeds.

**Cause:** TV control linkage is set too short.

**Remedy:** Adjust linkage.

2. **Symptom:** Extremely delayed or harsh upshafts and harsh idle engagement.

**Cause:** TV control linkage is set too long.

**Remedy:** Adjust linkage.

3. **Symptom:** Harsh idle engagement after the engine is warmed up. Shift clunk when throttle is backed off after full or heavy throttle acceleration. Harsh coasting downshifts (automatic 3–2, 2–1 shift in D range). Delayed upshift at light acceleration.

**Cause:** Interference due to hoses, wires, etc. prevents return of TV control rod or TV linkage shaft. Excessive friction caused by binding grommets prevents the TV control linkage to return to its proper location.

**Remedy:** Correct the interference area, check for bent or twisted rods, levers. or damaged grommets. Repair or replace whatever is necessary. Check and adjust linkage is necessary.

4. **Symptom:** Erratic/delayed upshifts, possibly no kickdown, harsh engagement.

**Cause:** Clamping bolt on trunnion at the upper end of the TV control rod is loose.

**Remedy:** Reset TV control linkage.

5. **Symptom:** No upshift and harsh engagements.

**Cause:** TV control rod is disconnected or the linkage return spring is broken or disconnected.

**Remedy:** Reconnect TV control rod, check and replace the connecting grommet if necessary, reconnect or replace the TV return spring.

### LINKAGE ADJUSTMENT

The TV control linkage is adjusted at the sliding trunnion block.

1. Adjust the curb idle speed to specification as shown on the under hood decal.

2. After the curb idle speed has been set, shut off the engine. Make sure the choke is completely opened. Check the carburetor throttle lever to make sure it is against the hot engine curb idle stop.

3. Set the coupling lever adjustment screw at its approximate midrange. Make sure the TV linkage shaft assembly is fully seated upward into the coupling lever.

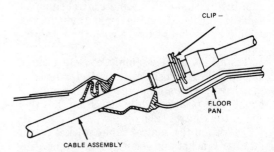

**Shift cable (ATX) installation through the floor pan**

CAUTION: *If adjustment of the linkage is necessary, allow the EGR valve to cool so you won't get burned.*

4. To adjust, loosen the bolt on the sliding block on the TV control rod a minimum of one turn. Clean any dirt or corrosion from the control rod, free-up the trunnion block so that it will slide freely on the control rod.

5. Rotate the transaxle TV control lever up using a finger and light force, to insure that the TV control lever is against its internal stop. With reducing the pressure on the control lever, tighten the bolt on the trunnion block.

6. Check the carburetor throttle lever to be sure it is still against the hot idle stop. If not, repeat the adjustment steps.

### TRANSMISSION CONTROL LEVER ADJUSTMENT

1. Position the selector lever in Drive against the rear stop.
2. Raise the car and support it safely on jackstands. Loosen the manual lever to control lever nut.
3. Move the transmission lever to the Drive position, second detent from the rearmost position. Tighten the attaching nut. Check the operation of the transmission in each selector position. Readjust if necessary. Lower the car.

### SHIFT LEVER CABLE REMOVAL AND INSTALLATION

1. Remove the shift knob, locknut, console, bezel assembly, control cable clip and cable retaining pin.
2. Disengage the rubber grommet from the floor pan by pushing it into the engine compartment. Raise the car and safely support it on jackstands.
3. Remove the retaining nut and control cable assembly from the transmission lever. Remove the control cable bracket bolts. Pull the cable through the floor.
4. To install the cable, feed the round end through the floor board. Press the rubber grommet into its mounting hole.
5. Position the control cable assembly in the selector lever housing and install the spring clip. Install the bushing and control cable assembly on the selector lever and housing assembly shaft and secure it with the retaining pin.

Install the bezel assembly, console, locknut and shift knob. Position the selector lever in the Drive position. The selector lever must be held in this position while attaching the other end of the control cable.
6. Position the control cable bracket on the retainer bracket and secure the tow mounting bolts.

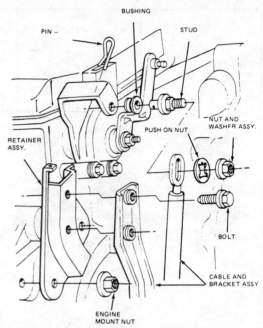

**Exploded view of the installation of the shift cable and bracket**

7. Shift the control lever into the second detent from full rearward (Drive position).
8. Place the cable end on the transmission lever stud. Align the flats on the stud with the slot in the cable. Make sure the transmission selector lever has not moved from the second detent position and tighten the retaining nut.
9. Lower the car to the ground. Check the operation of the transmission selector in all positions. Make sure the neutral safety switch is operating properly. (The engine should start only in Park or Neutral position).

### SELECTOR INDICATOR BULB REPLACEMENT

Remove the console and the four screws that mount the bezel. Lift the bezel assembly and disconnect the indicator bulb harness. Remove the indicator bulb. Install a new bulb and reverse the removal procedure.

### NEUTRAL SAFETY SWITCH

#### Removal and Installation

1. Disconnect the negative battery cable from the battery.
2. Remove the two hoses from the rear of the manage air valve. Remove all the vacuum hoses from the valve, label them for position before removal.
3. Remove the manage air valve supply hose band to intermediate shift control bracket attaching screw. Remove the air cleaner assembly.

4. Disconnect the neutral safety switch connector. Remove the two neutral safety switch retaining bolts and the neutral safety switch.

5. Installation is in the reverse order of removal.

**Adjustment**

When positioning the neutral safety switch a Number 43 drill (0.089″) is used to align the hole in the switch and mount before the mounting bolts are tightened.

## Troubleshooting the Manual Transmission

| Problem | Cause | Solution |
|---|---|---|
| Transmission shifts hard | • Clutch adjustment incorrect<br>• Clutch linkage or cable binding<br>• Shift rail binding | • Adjust clutch<br>• Lubricate or repair as necessary<br>• Check for mispositioned selector arm roll pin, loose cover bolts, worn shift rail bores, worn shift rail, distorted oil seal, or extension housing not aligned with case. Repair as necessary. |
| | • Internal bind in transmission caused by shift forks, selector plates, or synchronizer assemblies<br>• Clutch housing misalignment<br><br>• Incorrect lubricant<br>• Block rings and/or cone seats worn | • Remove, dissemble and inspect transmission. Replace worn or damaged components as necessary.<br>• Check runout at rear face of clutch housing<br>• Drain and refill transmission<br>• Blocking ring to gear clutch tooth face clearance must be 0.030 inch or greater. If clearance is correct it may still be necessary to inspect blocking rings and cone seats for excessive wear. Repair as necessary. |
| Gear clash when shifting from one gear to another | • Clutch adjustment incorrect<br>• Clutch linkage or cable binding<br>• Clutch housing misalignment<br><br>• Lubricant level low or incorrect lubricant<br><br>• Gearshift components, or synchronizer assemblies worn or damaged | • Adjust clutch<br>• Lubricate or repair as necessary<br>• Check runout at rear of clutch housing<br>• Drain and refill transmission and check for lubricant leaks if level was low. Repair as necessary.<br>• Remove, disassemble and inspect transmission. Replace worn or damaged components as necessary. |
| Transmission noisy | • Lubricant level low or incorrect lubricant<br><br>• Clutch housing-to-engine, or transmission-to-clutch housing bolts loose<br>• Dirt, chips, foreign material in transmission<br>• Gearshift mechanism, transmission gears, or bearing components worn or damaged<br>• Clutch housing misalignment | • Drain and refill transmission. If lubricant level was low, check for leaks and repair as necessary.<br>• Check and correct bolt torque as necessary<br>• Drain, flush, and refill transmission<br>• Remove, disassemble and inspect transmission. Replace worn or damaged components as necessary.<br>• Check runout at rear face of clutch housing |
| Jumps out of gear | • Clutch housing misalignment<br><br>• Gearshift lever loose<br><br>• Offset lever nylon insert worn or lever attaching nut loose | • Check runout at rear face of clutch housing<br>• Check lever for worn fork. Tighten loose attaching bolts.<br>• Remove gearshift lever and check for loose offset lever nut or worn insert. Repair or replace as necessary. |

## Troubleshooting the Manual Transmission (cont.)

| Problem | Cause | Solution |
|---|---|---|
| Jumps out of gear (cont.) | • Gearshift mechanism, shift forks, selector plates, interlock plate, selector arm, shift rail, detent plugs, springs or shift cover worn or damaged | • Remove, disassemble and inspect transmission cover assembly. Replace worn or damaged components as necessary. |
| | • Clutch shaft or roller bearings worn or damaged | • Replace clutch shaft or roller bearings as necessary |
| | • Gear teeth worn or tapered, synchronizer assemblies worn or damaged, excessive end play caused by worn thrust washers or output shaft gears | • Remove, disassemble, and inspect transmission. Replace worn or damaged components as necessary. |
| | • Pilot bushing worn | • Replace pilot bushing |
| Will not shift into one gear | • Gearshift selector plates, interlock plate, or selector arm, worn, damaged, or incorrectly assembled | • Remove, disassemble, and inspect transmission cover assembly. Repair or replace components as necessary. |
| | • Shift rail detent plunger worn, spring broken, or plug loose | • Tighten plug or replace worn or damaged components as necessary |
| | • Gearshift lever worn or damaged | • Replace gearshift lever |
| | • Synchronizer sleeves or hubs, damaged or worn | • Remove, disassemble and inspect transmission. Replace worn or damaged components. |
| Locked in one gear—cannot be shifted out | • Shift rail(s) worn or broken, shifter fork bent, setscrew loose, center detent plug missing or worn | • Inspect and replace worn or damaged parts |
| | • Broken gear teeth on countershaft gear, clutch shaft, or reverse idler gear | • Inspect and replace damaged part |
| | • Gearshift lever broken or worn, shift mechanism in cover incorrectly assembled or broken, worn damaged gear train components | • Disassemble transmission. Replace damaged parts or assemble correctly. |
| Transfer case difficult to shift or will not shift into desired range | • Vehicle speed too great to permit shifting | • Stop vehicle and shift into desired range. Or reduce speed to 3–4 km/h (2–3 mph) before attempting to shift. |
| | • If vehicle was operated for extended period in 4H mode on dry paved surface, driveline torque load may cause difficult shifting | • Stop vehicle, shift transmission to neutral, shift transfer case to 2H mode and operate vehicle in 2H on dry paved surfaces |
| | • Transfer case external shift linkage binding | • Lubricate or repair or replace linkage, or tighten loose components as necessary |
| | • Insufficient or incorrect lubricant | • Drain and refill to edge of fill hole with SAE 85W-90 gear lubricant only |
| | • Internal components binding, worn, or damaged | • Disassemble unit and replace worn or damaged components as necessary |
| Transfer case noisy in all drive modes | • Insufficient or incorrect lubricant | • Drain and refill to edge of fill hole with SAE 85W-90 gear lubricant only. Check for leaks and repair if necessary. Note: If unit is still noisy after drain and refill, disassembly and inspection may be required to locate source of noise. |

## Troubleshooting the Manual Transmission (cont.)

| Problem | Cause | Solution |
|---|---|---|
| Noisy in—or jumps out of four wheel drive low range | • Transfer case not completely engaged in 4L position<br><br>• Shift linkage loose or binding<br><br>• Shift fork cracked, inserts worn, or fork is binding on shift rail | • Stop vehicle, shift transfer case in Neutral, then shift back into 4L position<br>• Tighten, lubricate, or repair linkage as necessary<br>• Disassemble unit and repair as necessary |
| Lubricant leaking from output seals or from vent | • Transfer case overfilled<br>• Vent closed or restricted<br>• Output shaft seals damaged or installed incorrectly | • Drain to correct level<br>• Clear or replace vent if necessary<br>• Replace seals. Be sure seal lip faces interior of case when installed. Also be sure yoke seal surfaces are not scored or nicked. Remove scores, nicks with fine sandpaper or replace yoke(s) if necessary. |
| Abnormal tire wear | • Extended operation on dry hard surface (paved) roads in 4WD range | • Operate in 2WD on hard surface (paved) roads |

## Troubleshooting Basic Clutch Problems

| Problem | Cause |
|---|---|
| Excessive clutch noise | Throwout bearing noises are more audible at the lower end of pedal travel. The usual causes are:<br>• Riding the clutch<br>• Too little pedal free-play<br>• Lack of bearing lubrication<br>A bad clutch shaft pilot bearing will make a high pitched squeal, when the clutch is disengaged and the transmission is in gear or within the first 2″ of pedal travel. The bearing must be replaced.<br>Noise from the clutch linkage is a clicking or snapping that can be heard or felt as the pedal is moved completely up or down. This usually requires lubrication.<br>Transmitted engine noises are amplified by the clutch housing and heard in the passenger compartment. They are usually the result of insufficient pedal free-play and can be changed by manipulating the clutch pedal. |
| Clutch slips (the car does not move as it should when the clutch is engaged) | This is usually most noticeable when pulling away from a standing start. A severe test is to start the engine, apply the brakes, shift into high gear and SLOWLY release the clutch pedal. A healthy clutch will stall the engine. If it slips it may be due to:<br>• A worn pressure plate or clutch plate<br>• Oil soaked clutch plate<br>• Insufficient pedal free-play |
| Clutch drags or fails to release | The clutch disc and some transmission gears spin briefly after clutch disengagement. Under normal conditions in average temperatures, 3 seconds is maximum spin-time. Failure to release properly can be caused by:<br>• Too light transmission lubricant or low lubricant level<br>• Improperly adjusted clutch linkage |
| Low clutch life | Low clutch life is usually a result of poor driving habits or heavy duty use. Riding the clutch, pulling heavy loads, holding the car on a grade with the clutch instead of the brakes and rapid clutch engagement all contribute to low clutch life. |

## Troubleshooting Basic Automatic Transmission Problems

| Problem | Cause | Solution |
|---|---|---|
| Fluid leakage | • Defective pan gasket | • Replace gasket or tighten pan bolts |
| | • Loose filler tube | • Tighten tube nut |
| | • Loose extension housing to transmission case | • Tighten bolts |
| | • Converter housing area leakage | • Have transmission checked professionally |
| Fluid flows out the oil filler tube | • High fluid level | • Check and correct fluid level |
| | • Breather vent clogged | • Open breather vent |
| | • Clogged oil filter or screen | • Replace filter or clean screen (change fluid also) |
| | • Internal fluid leakage | • Have transmission checked professionally |
| Transmission overheats (this is usually accompanied by a strong burned odor to the fluid) | • Low fluid level | • Check and correct fluid level |
| | • Fluid cooler lines clogged | • Drain and refill transmission. If this doesn't cure the problem, have cooler lines cleared or replaced. |
| | • Heavy pulling or hauling with insufficient cooling | • Install a transmission oil cooler |
| | • Faulty oil pump, internal slippage | • Have transmission checked professionally |
| Buzzing or whining noise | • Low fluid level | • Check and correct fluid level |
| | • Defective torque converter, scored gears | • Have transmission checked professionally |
| No forward or reverse gears or slippage in one or more gears | • Low fluid level | • Check and correct fluid level |
| | • Defective vacuum or linkage controls, internal clutch or band failure | • Have unit checked professionally |
| Delayed or erratic shift | • Low fluid level | • Check and correct fluid level |
| | • Broken vacuum lines | • Repair or replace lines |
| | • Internal malfunction | • Have transmission checked professionally |

## Lockup Torque Converter Service Diagnosis

| Problem | Cause | Solution |
|---|---|---|
| No lockup | • Faulty oil pump | • Replace oil pump |
| | • Sticking governor valve | • Repair or replace as necessary |
| | • Valve body malfunction | • Repair or replace valve body or its internal components as necessary |
| | (a) Stuck switch valve | |
| | (b) Stuck lockup valve | |
| | (c) Stuck fail-safe valve | |
| | • Failed locking clutch | • Replace torque converter |
| | • Leaking turbine hub seal | • Replace torque converter |
| | • Faulty input shaft or seal ring | • Repair or replace as necessary |
| Will not unlock | • Sticking governor valve | • Repair or replace as necessary |
| | • Valve body malfunction | • Repair or replace valve body or its internal components as necessary |
| | (a) Stuck switch valve | |
| | (b) Stuck lockup valve | |
| | (c) Stuck fail-safe valve | |
| Stays locked up at too low a speed in direct | • Sticking governor valve | • Repair or replace as necessary |
| | • Valve body malfunction | • Repair or replace valve body or its internal components as necessary |
| | (a) Stuck switch valve | |
| | (b) Stuck lockup valve | |
| | (c) Stuck fail-safe valve | |

## Lockup Torque Converter Service Diagnosis

| Problem | Cause | Solution |
|---|---|---|
| Locks up or drags in low or second | • Faulty oil pump<br>• Valve body malfunction<br>  (a) Stuck switch valve<br>  (b) Stuck fail-safe valve | • Replace oil pump<br>• Repair or replace valve body or its internal components as necessary |
| Sluggish or stalls in reverse | • Faulty oil pump<br>• Plugged cooler, cooler lines or fittings<br>• Valve body malfunction<br>  (a) Stuck switch valve<br>  (b) Faulty input shaft or seal ring | • Replace oil pump as necessary<br>• Flush or replace cooler and flush lines and fittings<br>• Repair or replace valve body or its internal components as necessary |
| Loud chatter during lockup engagement (cold) | • Faulty torque converter<br>• Failed locking clutch<br>• Leaking turbine hub seal | • Replace torque converter<br>• Replace torque converter<br>• Replace torque converter |
| Vibration or shudder during lockup engagement | • Faulty oil pump<br><br>• Valve body malfunction<br><br><br>• Faulty torque converter<br>• Engine needs tune-up | • Repair or replace oil pump as necessary<br>• Repair or replace valve body or its internal components as necessary<br>• Replace torque converter<br>• Tune engine |
| Vibration after lockup engagement | • Faulty torque converter<br>• Exhaust system strikes underbody<br>• Engine needs tune-up<br>• Throttle linkage misadjusted | • Replace torque converter<br>• Align exhaust system<br>• Tune engine<br>• Adjust throttle linkage |
| Vibration when revved in neutral Overheating: oil blows out of dip stick tube or pump seal | • Torque converter out of balance<br>• Plugged cooler, cooler lines or fittings<br>• Stuck switch valve | • Replace torque converter<br>• Flush or replace cooler and flush lines and fittings<br>• Repair switch valve in valve body or replace valve body |
| Shudder after lockup engagement | • Faulty oil pump<br>• Plugged cooler, cooler lines or fittings<br>• Valve body malfunction<br><br><br>• Faulty torque converter<br>• Fail locking clutch<br>• Exhaust system strikes underbody<br>• Engine needs tune-up<br>• Throttle linkage misadjusted | • Replace oil pump<br>• Flush or replace cooler and flush lines and fittings<br>• Repair or replace valve body or its internal components as necessary<br>• Replace torque converter<br>• Replace torque converter<br>• Align exhaust system<br>• Tune engine<br>• Adjust throttle linkage |

## Transmission Fluid Indications

The appearance and odor of the transmission fluid can give valuable clues to the overall condition of the transmission. Always note the appearance of the fluid when you check the fluid level or change the fluid. Rub a small amount of fluid between your fingers to feel for grit and smell the fluid on the dipstick.

| If the fluid appears: | It indicates: |
|---|---|
| Clear and red colored | • Normal operation |
| Discolored (extremely dark red or brownish) or smells burned | • Band or clutch pack failure, usually caused by an overheated transmission. Hauling very heavy loads with insufficient power or failure to change the fluid, often result in overheating.<br>Do not confuse this appearance with newer fluids that have a darker red color and a strong odor (though not a burned odor). |
| Foamy or aerated (light in color and full of bubbles) | • The level is too high (gear train is churning oil)<br>• An internal air leak (air is mixing with the fluid). Have the transmission checked professionally. |
| Solid residue in the fluid | • Defective bands, clutch pack or bearings. Bits of band material or metal abrasives are clinging to the dipstick. Have the transmission checked professionally. |
| Varnish coating on the dipstick | • The transmission fluid is overheating |

## Troubleshooting Basic Steering and Suspension Problems

| Problem | Cause | Solution |
|---|---|---|
| Hard steering (steering wheel is hard to turn) | • Low or uneven tire pressure<br>• Loose power steering pump drive belt<br>• Low or incorrect power steering fluid<br>• Incorrect front end alignment<br>• Defective power steering pump<br>• Bent or poorly lubricated front end parts | • Inflate tires to correct pressure<br>• Adjust belt<br><br>• Add fluid as necessary<br><br>• Have front end alignment checked/adjusted<br>• Check pump<br>• Lubricate and/or replace defective parts |
| Loose steering (too much play in the steering wheel) | • Loose wheel bearings<br>• Loose or worn steering linkage<br>• Faulty shocks<br>• Worn ball joints | • Adjust wheel bearings<br>• Replace worn parts<br>• Replace shocks<br>• Replace ball joints |
| Car veers or wanders (car pulls to one side with hands off the steering wheel) | • Incorrect tire pressure<br>• Improper front end alignment<br><br>• Loose wheel bearings<br>• Loose or bent front end components<br>• Faulty shocks | • Inflate tires to correct pressure<br>• Have front end alignment checked/adjusted<br>• Adjust wheel bearings<br>• Replace worn components<br><br>• Replace shocks |
| Wheel oscillation or vibration transmitted through steering wheel | • Improper tire pressures<br>• Tires out of balance<br>• Loose wheel bearings<br>• Improper front end alignment<br><br>• Worn or bent front end components | • Inflate tires to correct pressure<br>• Have tires balanced<br>• Adjust wheel bearings<br>• Have front end alignment checked/adjusted<br>• Replace worn parts |
| Uneven tire wear | • Incorrect tire pressure<br>• Front end out of alignment<br><br>• Tires out of balance | • Inflate tires to correct pressure<br>• Have front end alignment checked/adjusted<br>• Have tires balanced |

# NOISE DIAGNOSIS

| The Noise Is | Most Probably Produced By |
|---|---|
| • Identical under Drive or Coast | • Road surface, tires or front wheel bearings |
| • Different depending on road surface | • Road surface or tires |
| • Lower as the car speed is lowered | • Tires |
| • Similar with car standing or moving | • Engine or transmission |
| • A vibration | • Unbalanced tires, rear wheel bearing, unbalanced driveshaft or worn U-joint |
| • A knock or click about every 2 tire revolutions | • Rear wheel bearing |
| • Most pronounced on turns | • Damaged differential gears |
| • A steady low-pitched whirring or scraping, starting at low speeds | • Damaged or worn pinion bearing |
| • A chattering vibration on turns | • Wrong differential lubricant or worn clutch plates (limited slip rear axle) |
| • Noticed only in Drive, Coast or Float conditions | • Worn ring gear and/or pinion gear |

# Suspension and Steering

## FRONT SUSPENSION

Your car has fully independent four-wheel suspension. Because wheel movements are controlled independently, the suspension provides exceptional road-hugging and ride comfort advantages.

Your car is equipped with a MacPherson strut front suspension. The strut acts upon a cast steering knuckle, which pivots on a ball joint mounted on a forged lower control arm. A stabilizer bar, which also acts as a locating link, is standard equipment. To maintain good directional stability, negative scrub radius is designed into the suspension geometry. This means that an imaginary line extended from the strut intersects the ground outside the tire patch. Caster and camber are present and non-adjustable. The front suspension fittings are "lubed-for-life"; no grease fittings are provided.

The front suspension fasteners for the lower arm, tie rod and shock struts require only one wrench for loosening and tightening making them easier to work on.

The front strut is attached to a shear type

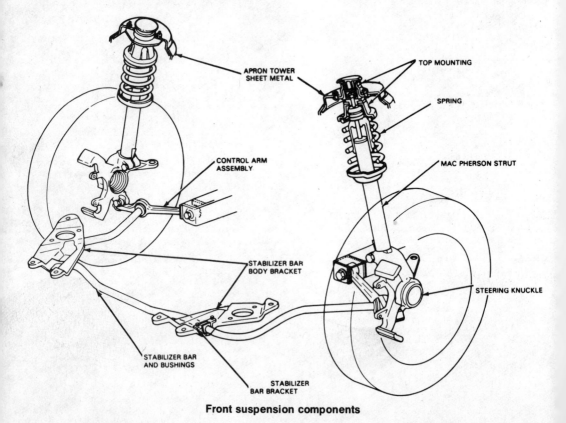

**Front suspension components**

upper mount to reduce engine, transaxle noise, vibration and harshness. The strut spring is contained between an offset lower spring seat fixed to the strut body and a rotating upper seat attached to the upper mount. The offset spring seat reduces friction in the strut to improve ride and decrease wear. The hydraulic damping (shock) system for the front strut has twin tubes with a single acting piston attached to the rod.

## Component Serviceability

The following components may be replaced individually or as components:
- Shock Absorber Struts (MacPherson)
- Strut Upper Mounts
- Coil Springs
- Ball Joints
- Lower Control Arm Bushing
- Forged Lower Control Arm
- Steering Knuckle
- Stabilizer Bar: The stabilizer bar is replaceable and contains the body mounting bushings. The stabilizer bar to lower arm insulator is replaceable as is the stabilizer bar to body bushing.

## MacPherson Strut and Coil Spring

### REMOVAL AND INSTALLATION

NOTE: *A coil spring compressor Ford Tool number T81P5310A for Escort/Lynx and EXP/LN-7 vehicles. DO NOT USE ON TEMPO/TOPAZ. Tempo/Topaz models require Rotunda 14-0259 or 86-0016 to compress the strut coil spring.*

1. Loosen the wheel lugs, raise the front of the car and safely support it on jackstands. Locate the jackstands under the frame jack pads, slightly behind the front wheels.
2. Remove the tire and wheel assembly.
3. Remove the brake line from the strut mounting bracket.
4. Place a floor jack or small hydraulic jack under the lower control arm. Raise the lower arm and strut as far as possible without raising the car.
5. Install the coil spring compressors. On Escort/Lynx/EXP/LN-7 models, place the top jaw of the compressors on the second coil from the top of the spring. Install the bottom jaw so that five coils will be gripped. Compress the spring evenly, from side to side, until there is about ⅛" (3mm) between any two spring coils. On Tempo/Topaz models, place the top jaw of the compressor on the fifth or sixth coil from the bottom. After the tool is installed, take a measurement from the bottom of the plate. Using the measurement as a reference, compress the spring a minimum of 3½" (89mm). The coil spring must be compressed evenly. Always oil the compressor tool threads.
6. A pinch bolt retains the strut to the steering knuckle. Remove the pinch bolt.
7. Loosen, but do not remove, the two top mount to strut tower nuts. Lower the jack supporting the lower control arm.
8. Use a pry bar and slightly spread the pinch bolt joint (knuckle to strut connection).
9. Place a piece of 2" x 4" wood, 7½" long, against the shoulder on the steering knuckle. Use a short pry bar between the wooden block and the lower spring seat to separate the strut from the knuckle.
10. Remove the two strut upper mounting nuts.
11. Remove the MacPherson strut, spring and top mount assembly from the car.
12. Place an 18mm deep socket that has an external hex drive top (Ford tool number D81P18045A1) over the strut shaft center nut. Insert a 6mm allen wrench into the shaft end. With the edge of the strut mount clamped in a vise, remove the top shaft mounting nut from the shaft while holding the allen wrench. Use vise grips, if necessary or a suitable extension to hold the allen wrench.

NOTE: *Make a wooden holding device the will clamp the strut barrel into the bench vise. (See illustration). Do not clamp directly onto the strut barrel, damage may occur.*

13. Clamp the strut into a bench vise. Remove the strut upper mount and the coil spring. If only the strut is to be serviced, do not

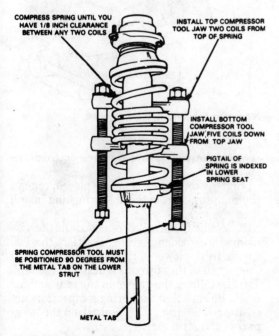

**COMPRESS SPRING UNTIL YOU HAVE 1/8 INCH CLEARANCE BETWEEN ANY TWO COILS**

**INSTALL TOP COMPRESSOR TOOL JAW TWO COILS FROM TOP OF SPRING**

**INSTALL BOTTOM COMPRESSOR TOOL JAW FIVE COILS DOWN FROM TOP JAW**

**PIGTAIL OF SPRING IS INDEXED IN LOWER SPRING SEAT**

**SPRING COMPRESSOR TOOL MUST BE POSITIONED 90 DEGREES FROM THE METAL TAB ON THE LOWER STRUT**

**METAL TAB**

**Typical coil spring compressor mounting**

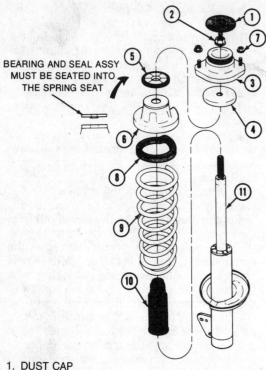

BEARING AND SEAL ASSY MUST BE SEATED INTO THE SPRING SEAT

1. DUST CAP
2. NUT AND WASHER
3. UPPER MOUNT
4. THRUST PLAGE
5. BEARING AND SEAL
6. SPRING SEAT
7. NUT
8. SPRING INSULATOR
9. SPRING
10. JOUNCE BUMPER, FRONT
11. SHOCK ABSORBER STRUT

**Typical strut upper mounting**

1. CUT STANDARD WOODEN 2 x 4 STOCK TO 7-1/2 INCH LENGTH
3. CUT BLOCK, THROUGH CENTER, INTO EQUAL HALVES
2. DRILL 1-5/8 INCH DIAMETER HOLE IN CENTER OF BLOCK
4. CHAMFER CORNERS 4 PLACES AS SHOWN
7-1/2"

**Strut holder construction**

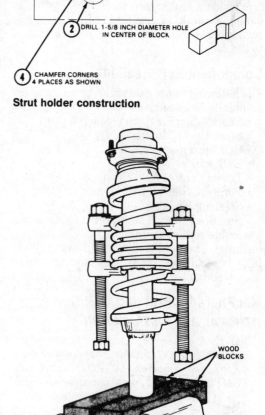

WOOD BLOCKS

**Mounting the strut in a bench vise**

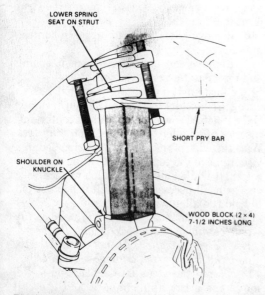

LOWER SPRING SEAT ON STRUT
SHORT PRY BAR
SHOULDER ON KNUCKLE
WOOD BLOCK (2 x 4) 7-1/2 INCHES LONG

**Block positioning**

remove the coil spring compressor from the spring.

14. If the coil spring is to be replaced, remove the compressor from the old spring and install it on the new.

15. Mount the strut (if removed) in the vise using the wooden fixture. Position the coil spring in the lower spring seat. Be sure that the pigtail of the spring is indexed in the seat. That is, follows the groove in the seat and fits flush. Be sure that the spring compressors are positioned 90° from the metal tab on the lower part of the strut.

16. Use a new nut and assembly the top

mount to the strut. Tighten the shaft nut to 48–62 ft.lb.

17. Install the assembled strut, spring and upper mount into the car. If you have installed a new coil spring, be sure it has been compressed enough.

18. Position the two top mounting studs through the holes in the tower and install two new mounting nuts. Do not tighten the nuts completely.

19. Install the bottom of the strut fully into the steering knuckle pinch joint.

20. Install a new pinch bolt and tighten it to 68–81 ft.lb. Tighten the tow upper mount nuts to 25–30 ft.lb.

21. Remove the coil spring compressor. Make sure the spring is fitting properly between the upper and lower seats.

22. Install the brake line to the strut bracket. Install the front tire and wheel assembly. Lower the car and tighten the lugs.

## Steering Knuckle

NOTE: *For illustrations refer to Chapter 8 under Wheel Bearings.*

### REMOVAL AND INSTALLATION

1. Loosen the wheel lugs, raise the front of the car and support safely on jackstand: Remove the tire and wheel assembly.

2. Remove the cotter pin from the tie rod end stud nut and remove the nut. Use a suitable removing tool and separate the tie rod end from the steering knuckle.

3. Remove the disc brake caliper, rotor and center hub as outlined in Chapter 8. Loosen, but do not remove the two top strut mounting nut.

4. Remove the lower control arm to steering knuckle pinch bolt, slightly spread the connection after the bolt has been removed.

5. Remove the strut to steering knuckle pinch bolt, slightly spread the connection after the bolt has been removed. Remove the driveaxle from the knuckle hub.

6. Remove the steering knuckle from the strut.

7. Remove the wheel bearings and rotor splash shield. Refer to Chapter 8.

8. Install the rotor splash shield and wheel bearings. Refer to Chapter 8.

9. Install the steering knuckle onto the strut. Install a new pinch bolt and tighten to 66–81 ft.lb.

10. Install the center hub onto the stub driveshaft as outlined in Chapter 8.

11. Install the lower control arm to the knuckle. Make sure the ball joint groove is aligned so the pinch bolt can slide through. In-

stall a new pinch bolt and tighten to 37–44 ft.lb.

12. Install the rotor and disc brake caliper (see Chapter 8). Position the tie rod end into the steering knuckle, install a new nut and tighten to 23–35 ft.lb. Align the cotter pin slot and install a new cotter pin.

13. Install the tire and wheel assembly. Lower the car and tighten the wheel lugs.

## Lower Control Arm and Ball Joint
### REMOVAL AND INSTALLATION

1. Jack up the front of the car and safely support it on jackstands.

2. Remove the nut connecting the stabilizer bar to the control arm. Pull off the large dished washer located behind the nut.

3. Remove the lower control arm inner pivot (frame mount) bolt and nut. Remove the pinch bolt from the ball joint to steering knuckle. It may be necessary to use a drift pin to drive out the pinch bolt. Spread the connection slightly after the bolt has been removed. Remove the lower control arm.

NOTE: *Be sure the steering wheel is in the unlocked position. DO NOT use a hammer to separate the ball joint from the steering knuckle.*

4. Installation is the reverse order of removal. When installing the ball joint into the steering knuckle, make sure the stud grooved is aligned so the pinch bolt to 37–44 ft.lb. When tightening the inner control arm mounting bolt/nut the torque should be 50–60 ft.lb. The stabilizer mounting nut is tightened to 75–80 ft.lb.

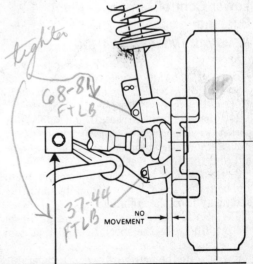

NOTE: AS WHEEL IS BEING MOVED IN AND OUT, OBSERVE THE LOWER END OF THE KNUCKLE AND THE LOWER CONTROL ARM. ANY MOVEMENT BETWEEN LOWER END OF THE KNUCKLE AND THE LOWER ARM INDICATES ABNORMAL BALL JOINT WEAR

**Checking the ball joint for excessive play**

## Stabilizer Bar and/or Bushings

### REMOVAL AND INSTALLATION

1. Raise the front of the car and safely support it on jackstands. The tire and wheel assembly may be removed for convenience.

2. Remove the stabilizer bar insulator mounting bracket bolts, end nuts and washers. Remove the bar assembly.

3. Carefully cut the center mounting insulators from the stabilizers.

NOTE: *A C-clamp type remover/installer tool is necessary to replace the control arm to stabilizer mounting bushings. The Ford part number of this tool is T81P5493A with T74P3044A1.*

4. Remove the control arm inner pivot nut and bolt. Pull the arm down from the inner mounting and away from the stabilizer bar (if still mounted on car).

5. Remove the old bar to control arm insulator bushing with the clamp type tool.

6. Use vegetable oil and saturate the new control arm bushing. Install the bushing with the clamp type tool. Coat the center stabilizer bar bushings with Ruglyde℠ or an equivalent lubricant. Slide the bushings into place. Install the inner control arm mounting. Tighten to 60–75 ft.lb.

7. Install the stabilizer bar using new insulator mounting bracket bolts. Tighten to 50–60 ft.lb. Install new end nuts with the old dished washers. Tighten to 75–80 ft.lb.

8. Install tire and wheel assembly if removed. Lower the car.

## Lower Control Arm Inner Pivot Bushing

### REMOVAL AND INSTALLATION

NOTE: *A special C-Clamp type removal/installation tool is required. See note under Stabilizer Bar for the Ford part number of this tool.*

1. Raise the front of the car and safely support it on jackstands.

2. Remove the stabilizer bar to control arm nut and the dished washer.

3. Remove the inner control arm pivot nut and bolt. Pull the arm down from its mounting and away from the stabilizer bar.

4. Carefully cut away the retaining lip of the bushing. Use the special clamp type tool and remove the bushing.

5. Saturate the new bushing with vegetable oil and install the bushing using the special tool.

6. Position the lower control arm over the stabilizer bar and install into the inner body

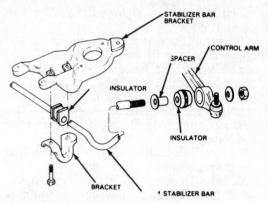

**Stabilizer and related part mountings**

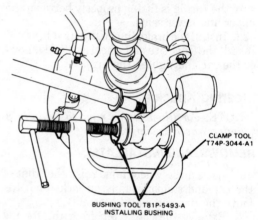

**Using a "C"-clamp bushing tool**

mounting using a new bolt and nut. Tighten the inner nut and bolt to 44–53 ft.lb. Tighten the stabilizer nut to 60–70 ft.lb. Be sure to install the dished washer ahead of the nut.

## Front End Alignment

### CASTER AND CAMBER

Caster and camber angles on your car are preset at the factory and cannot be adjusted in the field. Improper caster and camber can be corrected only through replacement of worn or bent parts.

### TOE ADJUSTMENT

Toe is the difference in distance between the front and the rear of the front wheels.

1. Loosen the slide off the small outer boot clamp so the boot will not twist during adjustment.

2. Loosen the locknuts on the outer tie rod ends.

3. Rotate both (right and left) tie rods in exactly equal amounts during adjustment. This will keep the steering wheel centered.

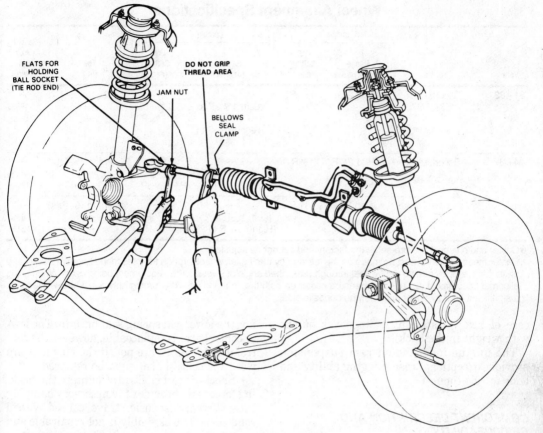

FLATS FOR
HOLDING
BALL SOCKET
(TIE ROD END)

DO NOT GRIP
THREAD AREA

JAM NUT

BELLOWS
SEAL
CLAMP

**Adjusting front end toe**

## Toe Adjustment

| Model | Normal | Minimum | Maximum |
|-------|--------|---------|---------|
| Escort/Lynx EXP | 0.10″ Out | 0.02″ In | 0.22″ Out |
| Tempo/Topaz | ⅛″ Out | 1/32″ In | 7/32″ Out |

4. Tighten the locknuts when the adjustment has been made. Install and tighten the boot clamps.

### FRONT SUSPENSION TIPS AND INSPECTION

• Maintain the correct tire pressures.
• Raise the front of the car and support on jackstands. Grasp the upper and lower edges of the tire. Apply up and downward movement to the tire and wheel. Check for looseness in the front ball joints. See previous ball joint inspection illustration. Inspect the various mounting bushings for wear. Tighten all loose nuts and bolts to specifications.
• Replace all worn parts found as soon as possible.

• Check the steering gear and assembly for looseness at its mountings. Check the tie rod ends for looseness.
• Check the shock absorbers. If any dampness from fluid leakage is observed, the shock should be replaced. Check the damping action of the shock by pushing up and down on each corner. If the damping effect is not uniform and smooth the shock should be suspect.

## REAR SUSPENSION

Your car features a strut type independent rear suspension. Each side has a shock absorber (strut), lower control (transverse) arm, tie rod, forged spindle and a coil spring mounted between the lower control arm and the body crossmember side rail or on the strut itself.

The lower control (transverse) arm and the tie rod provide lateral and longitudinal control. The shock strut counters backing forces and provides the necessry suspension damping. The coil is mounted on the lower control arm and acts as a metal to metal jounce stop in

## Wheel Alignment Specifications

| Year | Model | Caster Range (deg.)■▲ | Caster Pref. Setting (deg.) | Camber Range (deg.)■ | Camber Pref. Setting (deg.) | Toe (in.) | Steering Axis Inclin. (deg.) |
|---|---|---|---|---|---|---|---|
| '81–'83 | Escort, Lynx, EXP/LN7 | 9/16P to 2 1/16P | 1 5/16P | — | — | 1/32 to 7/32 | — |
| | | — | — | (Left) 1 13/32P to 2 29/32P | 2 5/32 P | — | 14 21/32 |
| | | — | — | (Right) 31/32P to 2 15/32P | 1 23/32P | — | 15 3/32 |
| '84–'87 | Escort, Lynx, EXP | 5/8P to 2 1/8P | 1 2/3P | — | — | 1/64 (in) to 7/32 (out) | — |
| | | | | (Left) 1 3/8P to 2 7/8P | 2 1/8P | — | 14 21/32 |
| | | | | (Right) 1 5/16P to 2 7/16P | 1 11/16P | — | 15 3/32 |
| | Tempo, Topaz | 9/16P to 2 1/16P | 1 5/16P | — | — | 1/32 (in) to 7/32 (out) | — |
| | | | | (Left) 1 1/8P to 2 5/8P | 1 7/8P | — | 14 5/8 |
| | | | | (Right) 1 11/16P to 2 3/16P | 1 1/2P | — | 15 1/8 |

■Caster and chamber are pre-set at the factory and cannot be adjusted
▲Caster measurements must be made on the left side by turning left wheel through the prescribed angle of sweep and on the right side by turning right wheel through prescribed angle of sweep for the equipment being used. When using alignment equipment designed to measure caster on both the right and left side, turning only one wheel will result in a significant error in caster angle for the opposite side.

case of heavy bottoming (going over bumps with weight in the back).

The unique independent rear suspension provides exceptional road hugging ability and adds to ride comfort.

### COMPONENT DESCRIPTION AND SERVICEABILITY

• Rear Coil Spring: Controls the suspension travel, provides ride height control and acts as a metal to metal jounce stop. The coil springs are replaceable, however the upper spring insulator must be replace at the same time.

• Lower Control (Transverse) Arm: Controls the side to side movement of each wheel and has the lower coil spring seat built in. The lower control arm is replaceable, however the control arm bushings are not. If the bushings are worn the control arm must be replaced.

• Shock Absorber Strut: Counters the braking forces and provides the necessary damping action to rear suspension travel caused by road conditions. The assembly is not repairable and must be replaced as a unit. The upper mounting may be serviced separately.

• Tie Rod: Controls the fore and aft wheel movement and holds the rear toe–in adjustment. The tie rod may be replaced as an assembly. Mounting bushings may be replaced separately , but new ones should be installed if the tie rod is replaced.

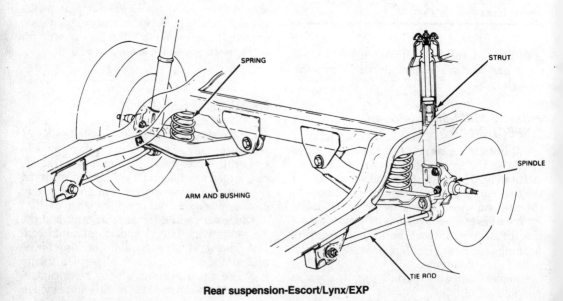

Rear suspension-Escort/Lynx/EXP

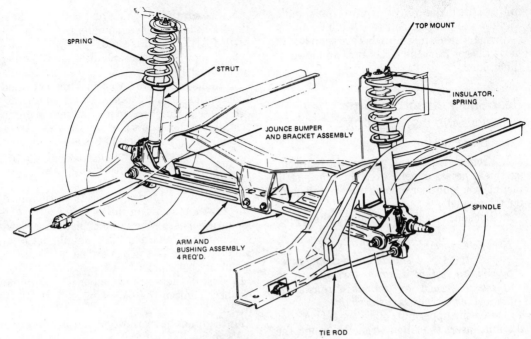

**Tempo/Topaz, rear suspension**

• Wheel Spindle: The one piece forged spindle attached to the lower arm, tie rod, shock strut and brake assembly. The rear wheel is mounted on the spindle. It may be replaced as a unit.

## Rear Coil Spring
### REMOVAL AND INSTALLATION
#### Escort/Lynx/EXP/LN-7

1. Jack up the rear of the car and safely support it on jackstands. The jackstand location should be on the frame pads slightly in front of the rear wheels.

2. Place a floor jack or small hydraulic jack under the rear control arm. Raise the control arm to its normal height with the jack, do not lift the car frame from the jackstands.

3. Remove the tire and wheel assembly. Remove the nut, bolt and washer that mounts the lower control arm to the wheel spindle.

4. Slowly lower the jack under the control arm. The coil spring will relax as the control arm is lowered. Lower the control arm until the spring can be removed.

5. Install a new upper spring insulator onto the top of the coil spring. Install the new spring on the control arm and slowly jack unto position. Be sure the spring is properly seated (indexed) in place on the control arm.

6. Jack up the control arm and position the top of the spring (insulator attached) into the body pocket.

7. Use a new attaching bolt, washers and

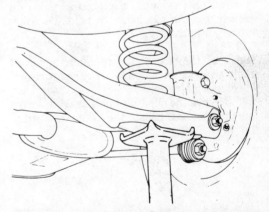

**Supporting the rear suspension on Escort/Lynx/EXP**

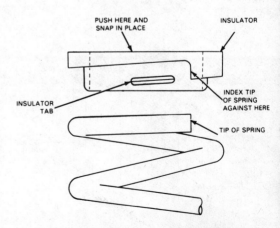

**Rear spring installation on the Escort/Lynx/EXP**

nut to attach the control arm to the spindle. Tighten the nut and bolt to 90–100 ft.lb.

8. Install the tire and wheel assembly. Remove the car from the jackstands and lower to the ground.

## Rear Shock Absorber Strut
### REMOVAL AND INSTALLATION
#### Excort/Lynx/EXP/LN-7

1. From inside the car, remove the rear compartment access panels (over the upper strut mount). On four door models remove the quarter trim panels.

2. Loosen, but do not remove the upper shock mounting nut.

NOTE: *A special 18mm deep socket is required, the socket should have a hex drive outer head so that it can be turned with an open-end wrench, as well as a ratchet. A 6mm Allen wrench is also required.*

To loosen the upper nut, place the socket over the nut, insert the Allen wrench through the center of the socket and into the upper strut rod. Hold the Allen wrench and loosen the nut by turning the socket with an open-end wrench. Use an extension to hold the Allen wrench, if necessary.
<32>

3. Jack up the rear of the car and support it safely on jackstands. Remove the rear tire and wheel assembly.

4. Remove the clip that holds the rear brake line to the shock. Locate the brake hose out of the way.

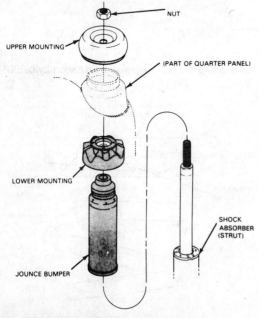

NUT

UPPER MOUNTING

(PART OF QUARTER PANEL)

LOWER MOUNTING

SHOCK ABSORBER (STRUT)

JOUNCE BUMPER

**Rear strut mounting on the Escort/Lynx/EXP**

5. Loosen the two nuts and bolts that hold the shock to the wheel spindle. DO NOT REMOVE THEM at this time.

6. Remove the upper mounting nut, washer and rubber insulator.

7. Remove the two lower nuts and bolts and remove the shock strut assembly from the car.

8. Extend the shock to its maximum length. Install the new (upper mount) lower washer and insulator assembly. Lubricate the insulator with a tire lubricant. Position the upper part of the shock shaft through the upper mount.

9. Slowly push upwards on the shock until the lower mounting holes align with the mounting holes in the spindle. Install new lower mounting bolts and nuts, buy do not completely tighten at this time. The heads of the mounting bolts must face the rear of the car.

10. Install the new top rubber insulator and washer. Tighten the mounting nuts to 60–70 ft.lb.

11. Tighten the two lower mounting nuts and bolts to 90–100 ft.lb.

12. Install the brake hose with the retaining clip. Put the tire and wheel assembly back on. Remove the jackstands and lower the car.

13. Reinstall the access or trim panels.

## Rear Strut, Upper Mount, Coil Spring
### REMOVAL AND INSTALLATION
#### Tempo/Topaz

1. Jack up the rear of the car and safely support it on jackstands. The jackstand location should be on the frame pads slightly in front of the rear wheels.

2. Open the trunk and loosen, but do not remove the two nuts retaining the upper strut mount to the body.

3. Remove the wheel and tire assembly. Raise the control arm slightly with a floor jack and support the arm on a jackstand. Do not jack the arm more than necessary. Just relieve the suspended position.

4. Remove the bolt that retains the brake hose to the strut. Position the hose out of the way of the strut removal.

5. Remove the jounce bumper retaining bolts and remove the bumper from the strut.

6. Disconnect the lower strut mounting from the spindle. Remove the two top mounting nuts. Remove the strut assembly from the car.

7. Refer to the Front Strut/Coil Spring service procedure proceeding this section for instructions on coil spring removal and replacement.

8. Install the strut assembly in the reverse order of removal. The lower mounting bolts are

tightened to 70–96 ft.lb. The upper to 25–30 ft.lb. Tighten the upper mounting nuts after the car is resting on the ground.

## Lower Control Arm

### REMOVAL AND INSTALLATION

#### Escort/Lynx/EXP/LN-7

1. Perform Steps 1–4 of the Coil Spring Removal Section.
2. After the spring and insulator have been removed. Take out the inner mounting bolt and nut. Remove the control arm.
3. Installation is in the reverse order of removal. Be sure that the coil is properly indexed (seated) when jacking into position.

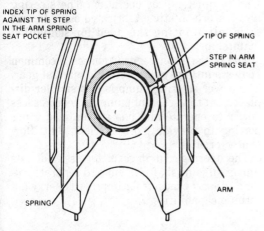

Indexing the rear coil spring on the Excort/Lynx/EXP

#### Tempo/Topaz

1. Raise and support the car on jackstands positioned ahead of the rear wheels on the body pads.
2. Remove the wheel and tire assembly.
3. Remove the control arm to spindle bolt and nut.
4. Remove the center mounting bolt and nut.
5. Remove the control arm.
6. Install in the reverse order.

## Tie Rod End

### REMOVAL AND INSTALLATION

#### Escort/Lynx/EXP/LN-7

1. Jack up the rear of the car and safely support it on jackstands. Remove the tire and wheel assembly.
2. At the front mounting bracket of the tie rod, take a sharp tool and scribe a vertical mark at the mounting bolt head center. This is so the tie rod can be mounted in the same position.

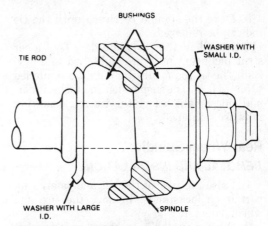

NOTE: WASHERS N801336 AND N801335 MUST BE INSTALLED IN THIS POSITION WITH DISH AWAY FROM BUSHINGS.

Typical tie rod installation

3. Remove the nut, washer and insulator that mount the rear of the tie rod to the wheel spindle.
4. Remove the front mounting nut and bolt that attach the tie rod to the front bracket. Remove the tie rod.
NOTE: *It may be necessary to separate the front body bracket slightly apart with a pry bar to remove the tie rod.*
5. Install new mounting bushings on the spindle end of the tie rod (reverse the removal order). Install the tie rod through the spindle and install the bushings, washer and nut. Tighten the nut to 65–75 ft.lb.
6. Use a floor jack or a small hydraulic jack and slowly raise the rear control arm to its curb height.
7. Line up the new front mounting bolt with the mark you scribed on the mounting bracket. Install the bolt and nut (bolt head facing inward). Tighten the nut and bolt to 90–100 ft.lb.

#### Tempo/Topaz

1. Raise and support the car on jackstands positioned ahead of the rear wheels on the body pads.
2. Loosen the two top strut mounting nuts, but do not remove them.
3. Position a jack under the rear suspension to relieve the suspended position.
4. Remove the wheel and tire assembly.
5. Remove the two upper mounting stud nuts.
6. Remove the nut that retains the tie rod to the rear spindle.
7. Remove the nut that retains the tie rod to the body.
8. Lower the rear suspension slightly until the upper strut mounting studs clear the body mounting holes.

9. Move the spindle rearward until the tie rod can be removed.

10. Install in the reverse order. The upper strut mounting nuts are tightened to 20–30 ft.lb. The tie rod mounting nuts are tightened to 52–74 ft.lb. The suspension should be at normal ride height before the tie rod mounting nuts are tightened.

## Rear Wheel Spindle
### REMOVAL AND INSTALLATION

1. Raise the rear of the car and safely support it on jackstands. Remove the tire and wheel assembly.

2. Disconnect the rear brake hose bracket from the strut mounting. Remove the rear brake drum, shoe assembly and brake backing plate. Refer to Chapter 8 for instructions on drum, shoe assembly and wheel cylinder removal. The backing plate is retained by four bolts, loosen and remove the bolts, and the backing plate.

3. Remove the tie rod to spindle retaining nut, washer and insulator. Remove the shock (strut) lower mounting nuts and bolts. Remove the nut and bolt retaining the lower control arm to the spindle. Remove the spindle.

4. Installation is in the reverse order of removal. Torque the mounting bolts and nuts.

Escort/Lynx/EXP/LN-7
Shock mount: 90–100 ft.lb.
Control arm: 90–100 ft.lb.
Tie rod: 65–75 ft.lb.
Tempo/Topaz
Spindle-to-Strut bolts: 70–96 ft.lb.
Tie rod nut: 52–74 ft.lb.
Control arm-to-Spindle nut: 60–86 ft.lb.

## Rear Suspension Inspection

Check the rear suspension at regular intervals for the following:

• Rear shock struts for leakage. A slight seepage is all right, heavy leakage requires that the shock be replaced.

• Check shock operation. Push up and down on a rear corner, if the car bounces and feels spongy the shock might need replacement.

• Inspect the condition of the various mounting bushings. If they show signs of deterioration or looseness they must be replaced.

• Condition of the tire tread. If it shows unusual wear the caster, camber or toe could be out.

## Rear End Alignment

Rear toe is adjustable but requires special equipment and procedures. If you suspect an alignment problem have it checked by a qualified repair shop. The alignment chart in this section is for factory setting reference.

## STEERING

Rack and pinion steering in either manual or power versions gives you car precise steering control. The manual rack and pinion gear is smaller and about seven and one half pounds lighten than that in any other Ford or Mercury small cars. The increased use of aluminum and the use of a one piece valve sleeve make this weight reduction possible.

Lightweight, sturdy bushings are used to mount the steering, these are long lasting and lend to quieter gear operation. The steering also features lifetime lubricated outer tie rod ends, eliminating the need for scheduled maintenance.

The power steering gear shares a common body mounting system with the manual gear. The power steering pump is of a smaller displacement than current pumps, it requires less power to operate and has streamlined inner porting to provide more efficient fluid flow characteristics.

The steering column geometry uses a double universal joint shaft system and separate column support brackets for improved energy absorbing capabilities.

## Steering Wheel
### REMOVAL AND INSTALLATION

1. Disconnect the negative (ground) battery cable from the battery.

2. Remove the steering wheel center hub cover (See illustration). Lift up on the outer edges, do not use a sharp tool or remove the screws from behind the steering wheel cross spoke. Loosen and remove the center mounting nut.

3. Remove the steering wheel with a crowfoot steering wheel puller. DO NOT USE a knock-off type puller it will cause damage to the collapsible steering column.

4. To reinstall the steering wheel, align the marks on the steering shaft and steering wheel. Place the wheel onto the shaft. Install a new center mounting nut. Tighten the nut to 30–40 ft.lb.

5. Install the center cover on the steering wheel. Connect the negative battery cable.

## Turn Signal (Combination Switch)

The turn signals, emergency (hazard) warning, horn, flash-to-pass and the headlight dimmer are all together on a combination switch.

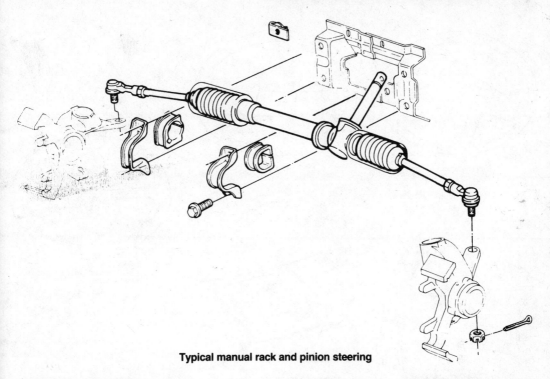

**Typical manual rack and pinion steering**

## REMOVAL AND INSTALLATION

1. Disconnect the negative (ground) cable from the battery.

2. Remove the steering column shroud by taking out the five mounting screws. Remove both halves of the shroud.

3. Remove the switch lever by using a twisting motion while pulling the lever straight out from the switch.

4. Peel back the foam cover to expose the switch.

5. Disconnect the two electrical connectors.

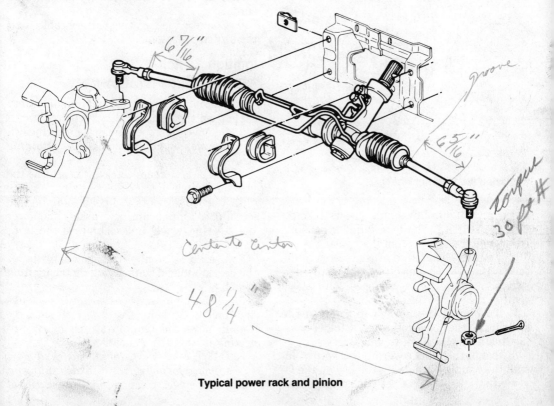

**Typical power rack and pinion**

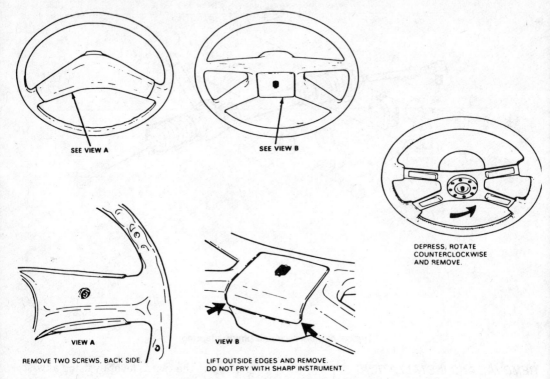

SEE VIEW A

SEE VIEW B

DEPRESS, ROTATE COUNTERCLOCKWISE AND REMOVE.

VIEW A

REMOVE TWO SCREWS, BACK SIDE.

VIEW B

LIFT OUTSIDE EDGES AND REMOVE. DO NOT PRY WITH SHARP INSTRUMENT.

**Typical wheel horn pad removal and installation**

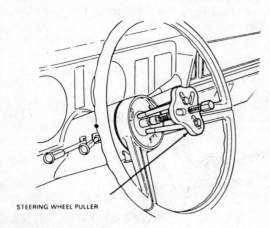

STEERING WHEEL PULLER

**Removing the steering wheel**

Remove the two self-tapping screws that attach the switch to the lock cylinder housing. Disengage the switch from the housing.

6. Transfer the ground brush located in the turn signal switch canceling cam to the new switch, if your car is equipped with speed control.

7. To install the new switch, align the switch with the holes in the lock cylinder housing. Install the two self-tapping screws.

8. Install the foam covering the switch. Install the handle by aligning the key on the lever with the keyway in the switch. Push the le-

ver into the switch until it is fully engaged.

9. Reconnect the two electrical connectors. Install the upper and lower steering column shrouds.

10. Connect the negative battery cable. Test the switch operation.

## Ignition Switch

### REMOVAL AND INSTALLATION

1. Disconnect the negative (ground) battery cable from the battery.

2. Remove the upper and lower steering column shrouds by taking out the five retaining screws.

3. Disconnect the electrical harness at the ignition switch.

4. Remove the nuts and bolts retaining the steering column mounting brackets and lower the steering wheel and column to the front seat.

5. Use an ⅛" (3mm) drill bit and drill out the break-off head bolts mounting the ignition switch.

6. Take a small screw extractor (Easy Out ) and remove the bolts.

7. Remove the ignition switch by disconnecting it from the actuator pin.

NOTE: *If reinstalling the old switch, it must be adjusted to the Lock or Run (depending on year and model) position. Slide the carrier of*

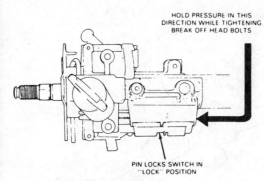

HOLD PRESSURE IN THIS DIRECTION WHILE TIGHTENING BREAK OFF HEAD BOLTS

PIN LOCKS SWITCH IN "LOCK" POSITION

**Typical ignition switch installation**

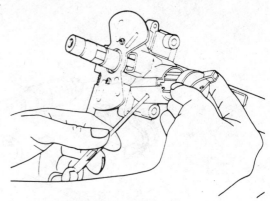

**Ignition lock assembly replacement**

*the switch to the required position and insert a $\frac{1}{16}$" (1.5mm) drill bit or pin through the switch housing into the carrier. This keeps the carrier from moving when the switch is connected to the actuator. It may be necessary to wiggle the carrier back and forth to line up the holes when installing the drill or pin. New switches come with a pin in place.*

8. When installing the ignition switch, rotate the key lock cylinder to the required position.

9. Install the ignition switch by connecting it to the actuator and loosely installing the two new mounting screws.

10. Move the switch up the steering column until it reaches the end of its elongated screw slots. Hold the switch in position, tighten the mounting screws until the heads bread off (special break-off bolts), or tighten to 15–25 ft.lb. if non-break off head bolts are used.

11. Remove the pin or drill bit that is locking the actuator carrier in position.

12. Raise the steering column and secure the mounting brackets.

13. Connect the wiring harness to the ignition switch. Install the upper and lower steering column shrouds.

14. Connect the negative battery cable.

15. Check the ignition for operation. Make sure the car will start in Neutral and Park, if equipped with automatic transaxle, but be sure it will not start in Drive or reverse. Make sure the steering (wheel) locks when the key switch is in the LOCK position.

## Ignition Lock Cylinder Assembly

### REMOVAL AND INSTALLATION

1. Disconnect the negative (ground) battery cable from the battery.

2. Remove the steering column lower shroud on Escort/Lynx/EXP/LN-7. On Tempo/Topaz models, remove the two trim halves by removing the five attaching screws. On models with tilt wheel, remove the upper extension shroud by unsnapping from a retain-

ing clip that is located at the nine o'clock position.

3. Disconnect the warning buzzer electrical connector. Turn the key cylinder to the Run position.

4. Take a ⅛" (3mm) diameter pin or small punch and push on the cylinder retaining pin. The pin is visible through a hole in the mounting surrounding the key cylinder. As you push on the pin pull out on the lock cylinder.

5. To reinstall the switch, make sure it is in the **RUN** position. Push in on the retaining pin and insert the cylinder into the casting. Be sure it is fully seated and aligned with the interlocking washer. Turn the key cylinder to the **OFF** position. When the lock cylinder is turned to the **OFF** position, the retaining pin locks the cylinder into the casting.

6. Rotate the lock cylinder through the different positions to make sure it is working freely.

7. Connect the wire to the buzzer, mount the shrouds and/or trim panels, connect the battery cable and test the operation of the lock cylinder.

## Manual Rack and Pinion Steering

If your car is equipped with manual steering, it is of the rack and pinion type. The gear input shaft is connected to the steering shaft by a double U-joint. A pinion gear, machined on the input shaft, engages the rack. The rotation of the input shaft pinion causes the rack to move laterally. The rack has tow tie rods whose ends are connected to the front wheels. When the rack moves so do the front wheel knuckles. Toe adjustment is made by turning the outer tie rod ends in or out equally as required.

### REMOVAL AND INSTALLATION

1. Disconnect the negative battery cable from the battery. Jack up the front of the car and support it safely on jackstands.

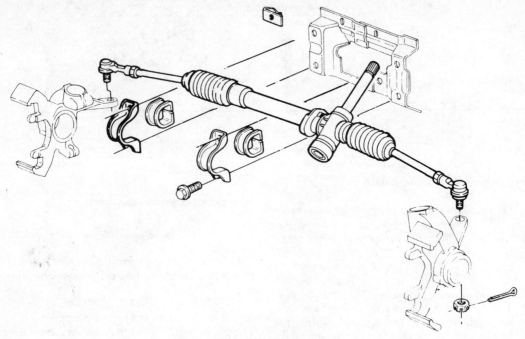

**Manual steering gear replacement**

2. Turn the ignition switch to the **On/Run** position. Remove the lower access (kick) panel from below the steering wheel.

3. Remove the intermediate shaft bolts at the gear input shaft and at the steering column shaft.

4. Spread the slots of the clamp to loosen the intermediate shaft at both ends. The next steps must be performed before the intermediate shaft and gear input shaft can be separated.

5. Turn the steering wheel full left so the tie rod will clear the shift linkage. Separate the outer tie rod ends from the steering knuckle by using a tie rod end remover.

6. Remove the left tie rod end from the tie rod (wheel must be at full left position). Disconnect the speedometer cable from the transmission if the car is equipped with an automatic transaxle. Disconnect the secondary air tube at the check valve. Disconnect the exhaust pipe from the exhaust manifold and wire it out of the way to allow enough room to remove the steering gear.

7. Remove the exhaust hanger bracket from below the steering gear. Remove the steering gear mounting brackets and rubber mounting insulators.

8. Have someone help by holding the gear from the inside of the car. Separate the intermediate shaft from the input shaft.

9. Make sure the gear is still in the full left turn position. Rotate the gear forward and down to clear the input shaft through the opening. Move the gear to the right to clear the

splash panel and other linkage that interferes with the removal. Lower the gear and remove from under the car.

10. Installation is in the reverse order of removal. Have the toe adjustment checked after installing a new rack and pinion assembly.

## Integral Power Rack and Pinion Steering

A rotary design control valve uses relative rotational motion of the input shaft and valve sleeve to direct fluid flow. When the steering wheel is turned, resistance of the wheels and the weight of the car cause a torsion bar to twist. The twisting causes the valve to move in the sleeve and aligns fluid passages for right/left and straight ahead position. The pressure forces on the valve and helps move the rack to assist in the turning effort. The piston is attached directly to the rack. The housing tube functions as the power cylinder. The hydraulic areas of the gear assembly are always filled with fluid. The mechanical gears are filled with grease making periodic lubrication unnecessary. The fluid and grease act as a cushion to absorb road shock.

### REMOVAL AND INSTALLATION

Removal and installation is basically the same as the manual rack and pinion steering. However, the pressure and return lines must be disconnected at the intermediate connectors

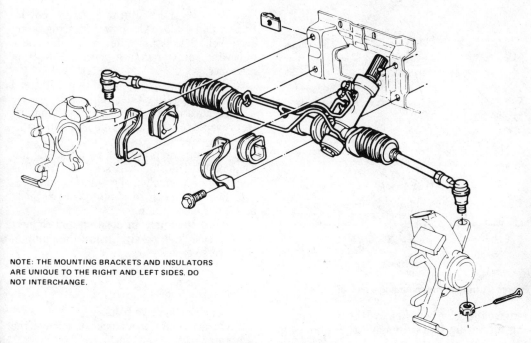

NOTE: THE MOUNTING BRACKETS AND INSULATORS
ARE UNIQUE TO THE RIGHT AND LEFT SIDES. DO
NOT INTERCHANGE.

**Power steering gear replacement**

and drained of fluid. It is necessary to remove
the pressure switch from the pressure line.

## Tie Rod Ends
### REMOVAL AND INSTALLATION

1. Remove and discard the cotter pin and
nut from the worn tie rod end stud.
2. Disconnect the tie rod end from the steering knuckle with an appropriate puller.
3. Hold the end with a wrench and loosen
the jam nut.
4. Measure the depth of the tie rod end and
count the number of turns as you unscrew it.
5. Clean the tie rod threads. Screw in the
new end the same number of turns as the one
removed. Check depth measurement. Complete installation in the reverse order of removal. Have the toe setting checked and
adjusted.

## Power Steering Pump
### REMOVAL AND INSTALLATION
**Escort/Lynx/EXP/LN-7**

1. Remove the air cleaner, air pump and
belt. Remove the reservoir extension and plug
the hole with a clean rag.
   NOTE: *On 1986 and later vehicles equipped
with a remote reservoir, remove the reservoir
supply hose at the pump, drain the fluid, and
plug the cap opening at the pump to prevent
dirt from entering.*

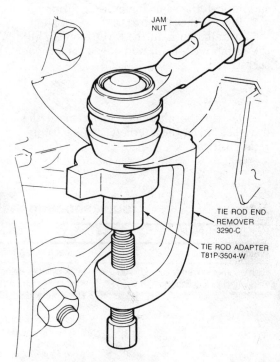

**Tie rod end replacement**

2. From under the car, loosen the pump adjusting bolt. Remove the pump to bracket
mounting bolt and disconnect the fluid return
line. Be prepared to catch any spilled fluid in a
suitable container.
3. From above, loosen the adjusting bolt and

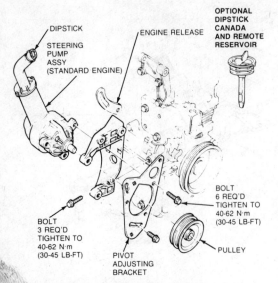

DIPSTICK

STEERING PUMP ASSY (STANDARD ENGINE)

ENGINE RELEASE

OPTIONAL DIPSTICK CANADA AND REMOTE RESERVOIR

BOLT 6 REQ'D TIGHTEN TO 40-62 N·m (30-45 LB-FT)

BOLT 3 REQ'D TIGHTEN TO 40-62 N·m (30-45 LB-FT)

PIVOT ADJUSTING BRACKET

PULLEY

**Power steering pump mounting—typical**

remove the drive belt. Remove the two remaining mounting bolts. Remove the adjusting bolts.

4. Remove the pump by passing the pulley end through the adjusting bracket opening.

5. Remove the pressure hose from the pump.

6. Installation is in the reverse order. Fill the pump with fluid and check for proper operation.

**Tempo/Topaz**

1. Loosen the alternator and remove the drive belt. Pivot the alternator to its most upright position.

2. Remove the radiator overflow bottle. Loosen and remove the power steering pump drive belt. Mark the pulley and pump drive hub with paint or grease pencil for location reference.

3. Remove the pulley retaining bolts and the two pulleys from the pump shaft.

4. Remove the return line from the pump. Be prepared to catch any spilled fluid in a suitable container.

5. Back off the pressure line attaching nut completely. The line will separate from the pump connection when the pump is removed.

6. Remove the three pump mounting bolts and remove the pump.

7. Place the pump in position and connect the pressure line loosely, Install the pump in the reverse order.

**Diesel Engine Models**

1. Remove the drive belts.

2. On air conditioned models, remove the alternator.

3. Remove both braces from the support bracket on air conditioned models.

4. Disconnect the power steering fluid lines and drain the fluid into a suitable container.

5. Remove the four bracket mounting bolts and remove the pump and bracket assembly.

6. The pulley must be remove before the pump can be separated from the mounting bracket. Tool T65P3A733C or equivalent is required to remove and install the drive pulley.

7. Install the pump and mounting bracket in the reverse order of removal.

## Troubleshooting the Steering Column

| Problem | Cause | Solution |
|---|---|---|
| Will not lock | • Lockbolt spring broken or defective | • Replace lock bolt spring |
| High effort (required to turn ignition key and lock cylinder) | • Lock cylinder defective | • Replace lock cylinder |
| | • Ignition switch defective | • Replace ignition switch |
| | • Rack preload spring broken or deformed | • Replace preload spring |
| | • Burr on lock sector, lock rack, housing, support or remote rod coupling | • Remove burr |
| | • Bent sector shaft | • Replace shaft |
| | • Defective lock rack | • Replace lock rack |
| | • Remote rod bent, deformed | • Replace rod |
| | • Ignition switch mounting bracket bent | • Straighten or replace |
| | • Distorted coupling slot in lock rack (tilt column) | • Replace lock rack |
| Will stick in "start" | • Remote rod deformed | • Straighten or replace |
| | • Ignition switch mounting bracket bent | • Straighten or replace |

## Troubleshooting the Steering Column (cont.)

| Problem | Cause | Solution |
|---|---|---|
| Key cannot be removed in "off-lock" | • Ignition switch is not adjusted correctly<br>• Defective lock cylinder | • Adjust switch<br>• Replace lock cylinder |
| Lock cylinder can be removed without depressing retainer | • Lock cylinder with defective retainer<br>• Burr over retainer slot in housing cover or on cylinder retainer | • Replace lock cylinder<br><br>• Remove burr |
| High effort on lock cylinder between "off" and "off-lock" | • Distorted lock rack<br>• Burr on tang of shift gate (automatic column)<br>• Gearshift linkage not adjusted | • Replace lock rack<br>• Remove burr<br><br>• Adjust linkage |
| Noise in column | • One click when in "off-lock" position and the steering wheel is moved (all except automatic column)<br>• Coupling bolts not tightened<br>• Lack of grease on bearings or bearing surfaces<br>• Upper shaft bearing worn or broken<br>• Lower shaft bearing worn or broken<br>• Column not correctly aligned<br>• Coupling pulled apart<br>• Broken coupling lower joint<br><br>• Steering shaft snap ring not seated<br><br>• Shroud loose on shift bowl. Housing loose on jacket—will be noticed with ignition in "off-lock" and when torque is applied to steering wheel. | • Normal—lock bolt is seating<br><br><br><br>• Tighten pinch bolts<br>• Lubricate with chassis grease<br><br>• Replace bearing assembly<br><br>• Replace bearing. Check shaft and replace if scored.<br>• Align column<br>• Replace coupling<br>• Repair or replace joint and align column<br>• Replace ring. Check for proper seating in groove.<br>• Position shroud over lugs on shift bowl. Tighten mounting screws. |
| High steering shaft effort | • Column misaligned<br>• Defective upper or lower bearing<br>• Tight steering shaft universal joint<br>• Flash on I.D. of shift tube at plastic joint (tilt column only)<br>• Upper or lower bearing seized | • Align column<br>• Replace as required<br>• Repair or replace<br>• Replace shift tube<br><br>• Replace bearings |
| Lash in mounted column assembly | • Column mounting bracket bolts loose<br>• Broken weld nuts on column jacket<br>• Column capsule bracket sheared<br>• Column bracket to column jacket mounting bolts loose<br>• Loose lock shoes in housing (tilt column only)<br>• Loose pivot pins (tilt column only)<br>• Loose lock shoe pin (tilt column only)<br>• Loose support screws (tilt column only) | • Tighten bolts<br><br>• Replace column jacket<br>• Replace bracket assembly<br>• Tighten to specified torque<br><br>• Replace shoes<br><br>• Replace pivot pins and support<br>• Replace pin and housing<br><br>• Tighten screws |
| Housing loose (tilt column only) | • Excessive clearance between holes in support or housing and pivot pin diameters<br>• Housing support-screws loose | • Replace pivot pins and support<br><br>• Tighten screws |
| Steering wheel loose—every other tilt position (tilt column only) | • Loose fit between lock shoe and lock shoe pivot pin | • Replace lock shoes and pivot pin |

## Troubleshooting the Steering Column

| Problem | Cause | Solution |
|---|---|---|
| Steering column not locking in any tilt position (tilt column only) | • Lock shoe seized on pivot pin<br>• Lock shoe grooves have burrs or are filled with foreign material<br>• Lock shoe springs weak or broken | • Replace lock shoes and pin<br>• Clean or replace lock shoes<br><br>• Replace springs |
| Noise when tilting column (tilt column only) | • Upper tilt bumpers worn<br>• Tilt spring rubbing in housing | • Replace tilt bumper<br>• Lubricate with chassis grease |
| One click when in "off-lock" position and the steering wheel is moved | • Seating of lock bolt | • None. Click is normal characteristic sound produced by lock bolt as it seats. |
| High shift effort (automatic and tilt column only) | • Column not correctly aligned<br>• Lower bearing not aligned correctly<br>• Lack of grease on seal or lower bearing areas | • Align column<br>• Assemble correctly<br>• Lubricate with chassis grease |
| Improper transmission shifting—automatic and tilt column only | • Sheared shift tube joint<br>• Improper transmission gearshift linkage adjustment<br>• Loose lower shift lever | • Replace shift tube<br>• Adjust linkage<br><br>• Replace shift tube |

## Troubleshooting the Ignition Switch

| Problem | Cause | Solution |
|---|---|---|
| Ignition switch electrically inoperative | • Loose or defective switch connector<br>• Feed wire open (fusible link)<br>• Defective ignition switch | • Tighten or replace connector<br><br>• Repair or replace<br>• Replace ignition switch |
| Engine will not crank | • Ignition switch not adjusted properly | • Adjust switch |
| Ignition switch wil not actuate mechanically | • Defective ignition switch<br>• Defective lock sector<br>• Defective remote rod | • Replace switch<br>• Replace lock sector<br>• Replace remote rod |
| Ignition switch cannot be adjusted correctly | • Remote rod deformed | • Repair, straighten or replace |

## Troubleshooting the Turn Signal Switch

| Problem | Cause | Solution |
|---|---|---|
| Turn signal will not cancel | • Loose switch mounting screws<br>• Switch or anchor bosses broken<br>• Broken, missing or out of position detent, or cancelling spring | • Tighten screws<br>• Replace switch<br>• Reposition springs or replace switch as required |
| Turn signal difficult to operate | • Turn signal lever loose<br>• Switch yoke broken or distorted<br>• Loose or misplaced springs<br><br>• Foreign parts and/or materials in switch<br>• Switch mounted loosely | • Tighten mounting screws<br>• Replace switch<br>• Reposition springs or replace switch<br>• Remove foreign parts and/or material<br>• Tighten mounting screws |
| Turn signal will not indicate lane change | • Broken lane change pressure pad or spring hanger<br>• Broken, missing or misplaced lane change spring<br>• Jammed wires | • Replace switch<br><br>• Replace or reposition as required<br>• Loosen mounting screws, reposition wires and retighten screws |

## Troubleshooting the Turn Signal Switch (cont.)

| Problem | Cause | Solution |
|---|---|---|
| Turn signal will not stay in turn position | • Foreign material or loose parts impeding movement of switch yoke<br>• Defective switch | • Remove material and/or parts<br><br><br>• Replace switch |
| Hazard switch cannot be pulled out | • Foreign material between hazard support cancelling leg and yoke | • Remove foreign material. No foreign material impeding function of hazard switch—replace turn signal switch. |
| No turn signal lights | • Inoperative turn signal flasher<br>• Defective or blown fuse<br>• Loose chassis to column harness connector<br>• Disconnect column to chassis connector. Connect new switch to chassis and operate switch by hand.<br>If vehicle lights now operate normally, signal switch is inoperative<br>• If vehicle lights do not operate, check chassis wiring for opens, grounds, etc. | • Replace turn signal flasher<br>• Replace fuse<br>• Connect securely<br><br>• Replace signal switch<br><br><br><br><br><br>• Repair chassis wiring as required |
| Instrument panel turn indicator lights on but not flashing | • Burned out or damaged front or rear turn signal bulb<br>• If vehicle lights do not operate, check light sockets for high resistance connections, the chassis wiring for opens, grounds, etc.<br>• Inoperative flasher<br>• Loose chassis to column harness connection<br>• Inoperative turn signal switch<br>• To determine if turn signal switch is defective, substitute new switch into circuit and operate switch by hand. If the vehicle's lights operate normally, signal switch is inoperative. | • Replace bulb<br><br>• Repair chassis wiring as required<br><br><br><br><br>• Replace flasher<br>• Connect securely<br><br>• Replace turn signal switch<br>• Replace turn signal switch |
| Stop light not on when turn indicated | • Loose column to chassis connection<br>• Disconnect column to chassis connector. Connect new switch into system without removing old. Operate switch by hand. If brake lights work with switch in the turn position, signal switch is defective.<br>• If brake lights do not work, check connector to stop light sockets for grounds, opens, etc. | • Connect securely<br><br>• Replace signal switch<br><br><br><br><br><br><br>• Repair connector to stop light circuits using service manual as guide |
| Turn indicator panel lights not flashing | • Burned out bulbs<br>• High resistance to ground at bulb socket<br>• Opens, ground in wiring harness from front turn signal bulb socket to indicator lights | • Replace bulbs<br>• Replace socket<br><br>• Locate and repair as required |
| Turn signal lights flash very slowly | • High resistance ground at light sockets<br>• Incorrect capacity turn signal flasher or bulb | • Repair high resistance grounds at light sockets<br>• Replace turn signal flasher or bulb |

## Troubleshooting the Turn Signal Switch (cont.)

| Problem | Cause | Solution |
|---|---|---|
| Turn signal lights flash very slowly (cont.) | • If flashing rate is still extremely slow, check chassis wiring harness from the connector to light sockets for high resistance | • Locate and repair as required |
| | • Loose chassis to column harness connection | • Connect securely |
| | • Disconnect column to chassis connector. Connect new switch into system without removing old. Operate switch by hand. If flashing occurs at normal rate, the signal switch is defective. | • Replace turn signal switch |
| Hazard signal lights will not flash— turn signal functions normally | • Blow fuse | • Replace fuse |
| | • Inoperative hazard warning flasher | • Replace hazard warning flasher in fuse panel |
| | • Loose chassis-to-column harness connection | • Conect securely |
| | • Disconnect column to chassis connector. Connect new switch into system without removing old. Depress the hazard warning lights. If they now work normally, turn signal switch is defective. | • Replace turn signal switch |
| | • If lights do not flash, check wiring harness "K" lead for open between hazard flasher and connector. If open, fuse block is defective | • Repair or replace brown wire or connector as required |

## Troubleshooting the Manual Steering Gear

| Problem | Cause | Solution |
|---|---|---|
| Hard or erratic steering | • Incorrect tire pressure | • Inflate tires to recommended pressures |
| | • Insufficient or incorrect lubrication | • Lubricate as required (refer to Maintenance Section) |
| | • Suspension, or steering linkage parts damaged or misaligned | • Repair or replace parts as necessary |
| | • Improper front wheel alignment | • Adjust incorrect wheel alignment angles |
| | • Incorrect steering gear adjustment | • Adjust steering gear |
| | • Sagging springs | • Replace springs |
| Play or looseness in steering | • Steering wheel loose | • Inspect shaft spines and repair as necessary. Tighten attaching nut and stake in place. |
| | • Steering linkage or attaching parts loose or worn | • Tighten, adjust, or replace faulty components |
| | • Pitman arm loose | • Inspect shaft splines and repair as necessary. Tighten attaching nut and stake in place |
| | • Steering gear attaching bolts loose | • Tighten bolts |
| | • Loose or worn wheel bearings | • Adjust or replace bearings |
| | • Steering gear adjustment incorrect or parts badly worn | • Adjust gear or replace defective parts |
| Wheel shimmy or tramp | • Improper tire pressure | • Inflate tires to recommended pressures |
| | • Wheels, tires, or brake rotors out-of-balance or out-of-round | • Inspect and replace or balance parts |
| | • Inoperative, worn, or loose shock absorbers or mounting parts | • Repair or replace shocks or mountings |

## Troubleshooting the Manual Steering Gear (cont.)

| Problem | Cause | Solution |
|---|---|---|
| Wheel shimmy or tramp (cont.) | • Loose or worn steering or suspension parts | • Tighten or replace as necessary |
| | • Loose or worn wheel bearings | • Adjust or replace bearings |
| | • Incorrect steering gear adjustments | • Adjust steering gear |
| | • Incorrect front wheel alignment | • Correct front wheel alignment |
| Tire wear | • Improper tire pressure | • Inflate tires to recommended pressures |
| | • Failure to rotate tires | • Rotate tires |
| | • Brakes grabbing | • Adjust or repair brakes |
| | • Incorrect front wheel alignment | • Align incorrect angles |
| | • Broken or damaged steering and suspension parts | • Repair or replace defective parts |
| | • Wheel runout | • Replace faulty wheel |
| | • Excessive speed on turns | • Make driver aware of conditions |
| Vehicle leads to one side | • Improper tire pressures | • Inflate tires to recommended pressures |
| | • Front tires with uneven tread depth, wear pattern, or different cord design (i.e., one bias ply and one belted or radial tire on front wheels) | • Install tires of same cord construction and reasonably even tread depth, design, and wear pattern |
| | • Incorrect front wheel alignment | • Align incorrect angles |
| | • Brakes dragging | • Adjust or repair brakes |
| | • Pulling due to uneven tire construction | • Replace faulty tire |

## Troubleshooting the Power Steering Gear

| Problem | Cause | Solution |
|---|---|---|
| Hissing noise in steering gear | • There is some noise in all power steering systems. One of the most common is a hissing sound most evident at standstill parking. There is no relationship between this noise and performance of the steering. Hiss may be expected when steering wheel is at end of travel or when slowly turning at standstill. | • Slight hiss is normal and in no way affects steering. Do not replace valve unless hiss is extremely objectionable. A replacement valve will also exhibit slight noise and is not always a cure. Investigate clearance around flexible coupling rivets. Be sure steering shaft and gear are aligned so flexible coupling rotates in a flat plane and is not distorted as shaft rotates. Any metal-to-metal contacts through flexible coupling will transmit valve hiss into passenger compartment through the steering column. |
| Rattle or chuckle noise in steering gear | • Gear loose on frame | • Check gear-to-frame mounting screws. Tighten screws to 88 N·m (65 foot pounds) torque. |
| | • Steering linkage looseness | • Check linkage pivot points for wear. Replace if necessary. |
| | • Pressure hose touching other parts of car | • Adjust hose position. Do not bend tubing by hand. |
| | • Loose pitman shaft over center adjustment | • Adjust to specifications |
| | NOTE: A slight rattle may occur on turns because of increased clearance off the "high point." This is normal and clearance must not be reduced below specified limits to eliminate this slight rattle. | |

## Troubleshooting the Power Steering Gear (cont.)

| Problem | Cause | Solution |
|---|---|---|
| Rattle or chuckle noise in steering gear | • Loose pitman arm | • Tighten pitman arm nut to specifications |
| Squawk noise in steering gear when turning or recovering from a turn | • Damper O-ring on valve spool cut | • Replace damper O-ring |
| Poor return of steering wheel to center | • Tires not properly inflated<br>• Lack of lubrication in linkage and ball joints<br>• Lower coupling flange rubbing against steering gear adjuster plug<br>• Steering gear to column misalignment<br>• Improper front wheel alignment<br>• Steering linkage binding<br>• Ball joints binding<br>• Steering wheel rubbing against housing<br>• Tight or frozen steering shaft bearings<br>• Sticking or plugged valve spool<br>• Steering gear adjustments over specifications<br>• Kink in return hose | • Inflate to specified pressure<br>• Lube linkage and ball joints<br>• Loosen pinch bolt and assemble properly<br>• Align steering column<br>• Check and adjust as necessary<br>• Replace pivots<br>• Replace ball joints<br>• Align housing<br>• Replace bearings<br>• Remove and clean or replace valve<br>• Check adjustment with gear out of car. Adjust as required.<br>• Replace hose |
| Car leads to one side or the other (keep in mind road condition and wind. Test car in both directions on flat road) | • Front end misaligned<br>• Unbalanced steering gear valve<br>NOTE: If this is cause, steering effort will be very light in direction of lead and normal or heavier in opposite direction | • Adjust to specifications<br>• Replace valve |
| Momentary increase in effort when turning wheel fast to right or left | • Low oil level<br>• Pump belt slipping<br>• High internal leakage | • Add power steering fluid as required<br>• Tighten or replace belt<br>• Check pump pressure. (See pressure test) |
| Steering wheel surges or jerks when turning with engine running especially during parking | • Low oil level<br>• Loose pump belt<br>• Steering linkage hitting engine oil pan at full turn<br>• Insufficient pump pressure<br>• Pump flow control valve sticking | • Fill as required<br>• Adjust tension to specification<br>• Correct clearance<br>• Check pump pressure. (See pressure test). Replace relief valve if defective.<br>• Inspect for varnish or damage, replace if necessary |
| Excessive wheel kickback or loose steering | • Air in system<br>• Steering gear loose on frame<br>• Steering linkage joints worn enough to be loose<br>• Worn poppet valve<br>• Loose thrust bearing preload adjustment<br>• Excessive overcenter lash | • Add oil to pump reservoir and bleed by operating steering. Check hose connectors for proper torque and adjust as required.<br>• Tighten attaching screws to specified torque<br>• Replace loose pivots<br>• Replace poppet valve<br>• Adjust to specification with gear out of vehicle<br>• Adjust to specification with gear out of car |
| Hard steering or lack of assist | • Loose pump belt<br>• Low oil level | • Adjust belt tension to specifiction<br>• Fill to proper level. If excessively |

## Troubleshooting the Power Steering Gear (cont.)

| Problem | Cause | Solution |
|---|---|---|
| Hard steering or lack of assist | NOTE: Low oil level will also result in excessive pump noise | low, check all lines and joints for evidence of external leakage. Tighten loose connectors. |
| | • Steering gear to column misalignment | • Align steering column |
| | • Lower coupling flange rubbing against steering gear adjuster plug | • Loosen pinch bolt and assemble properly |
| | • Tires not properly inflated | • Inflate to recommended pressure |
| Foamy milky power steering fluid, low fluid level and possible low pressure | • Air in the fluid, and loss of fluid due to internal pump leakage causing overflow | • Check for leak and correct. Bleed system. Extremely cold temperatures will cause system aeriation should the oil level be low. If oil level is correct and pump still foams, remove pump from vehicle and separate reservoir from housing. Check welsh plug and housing for cracks. If plug is loose or housing is cracked, replace housing. |
| Low pressure due to steering pump | • Flow control valve stuck or inoperative | • Remove burrs or dirt or replace. Flush system. |
| | • Pressure plate not flat against cam ring | • Correct |
| Low pressure due to steering gear | • Pressure loss in cylinder due to worn piston ring or badly worn housing bore | • Remove gear from car for disassembly and inspection of ring and housing bore |
| | • Leakage at valve rings, valve body-to-worm seal | • Remove gear from car for disassembly and replace seals |

## Troubleshooting the Power Steering Pump

| Problem | Cause | Solution |
|---|---|---|
| Chirp noise in steering pump | • Loose belt | • Adjust belt tension to specification |
| Belt squeal (particularly noticeable at full wheel travel and stand still parking) | • Loose belt | • Adjust belt tension to specification |
| Growl noise in steering pump | • Excessive back pressure in hoses or steering gear caused by restriction | • Locate restriction and correct. Replace part if necessary. |
| Growl noise in steering pump (particularly noticeable at stand still parking) | • Scored pressure plates, thrust plate or rotor | • Replace parts and flush system |
| | • Extreme wear of cam ring | • Replace parts |
| Groan noise in steering pump | • Low oil level | • Fill reservoir to proper level |
| | • Air in the oil. Poor pressure hose connection. | • Tighten connector to specified torque. Bleed system by operating steering from right to left—full turn. |
| Rattle noise in steering pump | • Vanes not installed properly | • Install properly |
| | • Vanes sticking in rotor slots | • Free up by removing burrs, varnish, or dirt |
| Swish noise in steering pump | • Defective flow control valve | • Replace part |
| Whine noise in steering pump | • Pump shaft bearing scored | • Replace housing and shaft. Flush system. |

## Troubleshooting the Power Steering Pump (cont.)

| Problem | Cause | Solution |
|---------|-------|----------|
| Hard steering or lack of assist | • Loose pump belt<br>• Low oil level in reservoir<br>**NOTE:** Low oil level will also result in excessive pump noise<br><br>• Steering gear to column misalignment<br>• Lower coupling flange rubbing against steering gear adjuster plug<br>• Tires not properly inflated | • Adjust belt tension to specification<br>• Fill to proper level. If excessively low, check all lines and joints for evidence of external leakage. Tighten loose connectors.<br>• Align steering column<br>• Loosen pinch bolt and assemble properly<br><br>• Inflate to recommended pressure |
| Foaming milky power steering fluid, low fluid level and possible low pressure | • Air in the fluid, and loss of fluid due to internal pump leakage causing overflow | • Check for leaks and correct. Bleed system. Extremely cold temperatures will cause system aeriation should the oil level be low. If oil level is correct and pump still foams, remove pump from vehicle and separate reservoir from body. Check welsh plug and body for cracks. If plug is loose or body is cracked, replace body. |
| Low pump pressure | • Flow control valve stuck or inoperative<br>• Pressure plate not flat against cam ring | • Remove burrs or dirt or replace. Flush system.<br>• Correct |
| Momentary increase in effort when turning wheel fast to right or left | • Low oil level in pump<br><br>• Pump belt slipping<br>• High internal leakage | • Add power steering fluid as required<br>• Tighten or replace belt<br>• Check pump pressure. (See pressure test) |
| Steering wheel surges or jerks when turning with engine running especially during parking | • Low oil level<br>• Loose pump belt<br>• Steering linkage hitting engine oil pan at full turn<br>• Insufficient pump pressure | • Fill as required<br>• Adjust tension to specification<br>• Correct clearance<br><br>• Check pump pressure. (See pressure test). Replace flow control valve if defective. |
| Steering wheel surges or jerks when turning with engine running especially during parking (cont.) | • Sticking flow control valve | • Inspect for varnish or damage, replace if necessary |
| Excessive wheel kickback or loose steering | • Air in system | • Add oil to pump reservoir and bleed by operating steering. Check hose connectors for proper torque and adjust as required. |
| Low pump pressure | • Extreme wear of cam ring<br>• Scored pressure plate, thrust plate, or rotor<br>• Vanes not installed properly<br>• Vanes sticking in rotor slots<br><br>• Cracked or broken thrust or pressure plate | • Replace parts. Flush system.<br>• Replace parts. Flush system.<br><br>• Install properly<br>• Freeup by removing burrs, varnish, or dirt<br>• Replace part |

## BRAKE SYSTEM

### Understanding the Brakes Hydraulic System

*BASIC OPERATING PRINCIPLES*

Hydraulic systems are used to actuate the brakes of all modern automobiles. The system transports the power required to force the frictional surfaces of the braking system together from the pedal to the individual brake units at each wheel. A hydraulic system is used for two reasons. First, fluid under pressure can be carried to all parts of an automobile by small hoses, some of which are flexible, without taking up a significant amount of room or posing routing problems. Second, a great mechanical advantage can be given to the brake pedal end of the system, and the foot pressure required to actuate the brakes can be reduced by making surface area of the master cylinder pistons smaller than that of any of the pistons in the wheel cylinders or calipers.

The master cylinder consists of a double reservoir and piston assembly as well as other springs, fittings etc. Double (dual) master cylinders are designed to separate two wheels from the others. Your car's braking system is separated diagonally. That is, the right front and left rear use one reservoir and the left front and right rear use the other.

Steel lines carry the brake fluid to a point on the car's frame near each wheel. A flexible hose usually carries the fluid to the disc caliper or wheel cylinder. The flexible line allows for suspension and steering movements.

The rear wheel cylinders contain two pistons each, one at either end, which push outward in opposite directions. The front disc brake calipers contain one piston each.

All pistons employ some type of seal, usually make of rubber, to minimize fluid leakage. A rubber dust boot seals the outer end of the cylinder against dust and dirt. The boot fits around the outer end of the piston on disc brake calipers, and around the brake actuating rod on wheel cylinders.

The hydraulic system operates as follows: When at rest, the entire system, from the piston(s) in the master cylinder to those in the wheel cylinders or calipers, is full of brake fluid. Upon application of the brake pedal, fluid trapped in front of the master cylinder piston(s) is forced through the lines to the wheel cylinders. Here, it forces the pistons outward, in the case of drum brakes, and inward toward the disc, in the case of disc brakes. The motion of the pistons is opposed by return springs mounted outside the cylinders in drum brakes, and by internal springs or spring seal, in disc brakes.

Upon release of the brake pedal, a spring located inside the master cylinder immediately return the master cylinder pistons to the normal position. The pistons contain check valves and the master cylinder has compensating ports drilled in it. These are uncovered as the pistons reach their normal position. The piston check valves allow fluid to flow toward the wheel cylinders or calipers as the pistons withdraw. Then, as the return springs force the brake pads or shoes into the released position, the excess fluid reservoir through the compensating ports. It is during the time the pedal is in the released position that any fluid that has leaked out of the system will be replaced from the reservoirs through the compensating ports.

The dual master cylinder has two pistons, located one behind the other. The primary piston is actuated directly by mechanical linkage from the brake pedal. The secondary piston is actuated by fluid trapped between the two pistons. If a leak develops in front of the secondary piston, it moves forward until it bottoms against the front of the master cylinder. The fluid trapped between the piston will operate one side of the diagonal system. If the other side of the system develops a leak, the primary piston will move forward until direct contact with the secondary piston takes place, and it will force the secondary piston to actuate the other side of the diagonal system. In either case the brake pedal drops closer to the floor board and less braking power is available.

The brake system uses a switch to warn the driver when only half of the brake system is operational. This switch is located in a valve body which is mounted on the firewall or the frame below the master cylinder. A hydraulic piston receives pressure from both circuits, each circuit's pressure being applied to one end of the piston. When the pressures are in balance, the piston remains stationary. When one circuit has a leak, however, the greater pressure in the circuit during application of the brakes will push the piston to one side, closing the switch and activating the brake warning light.

In disc brake system, this valve body contains a metering valve and, in some cases, a proportioning valve or valves, The metering valve keeps pressure from traveling to the disc brakes on the front wheels until the brake shoes on the rear wheels have contacted the drums, ensuring that the front brakes will never be used alone. The proportioning valve controls the pressure to the rear brakes to avoid rear wheel lock-up during very hard braking.

Warning lights may be tested by depressing the brake pedal and holding it while opening one of the wheel cylinder bleeder screws. If this does not cause the light to go on, substitute a new lamp, make continuity checks, and finally, replace the switch as necessary.

The hydraulic system may be checked for leaks by applying pressure to the pedal gradually and steadily. If the pedal sinks very slowly to the floor, the system has a leak. This is not to be confused with a springy or spongy feel due to the compression of air within the lines. If the system leaks, there will be a gradual change in the position of the pedal with a constant pressure.

Check for leaks along all lines and at wheel cylinders or calipers. If no external leaks are apparent, the problem is inside the master cylinder.

## Disc Brakes
### BASIC OPERATING PRINCIPLES

Instead of the traditional expanding brakes that press outward against a circular drum,

disc brake systems utilize a disc (rotor) with brake pads positioned on either side of it. Braking effect is achieved in a manner similar to the way you would squeeze a spinning phonograph record between your fingers. The disc (rotor) is a casting with cooling fins between the two braking surfaces. This enables air to circulate between the braking surfaces making them less sensitive to heat buildup and more resistant to fade. Dirt and water do not affect braking action since contaminants are thrown off by the centrifugal action of the rotor or scraped off by the pads. Also, the equal clamping action of the two brake pads tends to ensure uniform, straight line stops. Disc brakes are inherently self-adjusting.

Your car uses a pin slider front wheel caliper. The brake pad on the inside of the brake rotor is moved in contact with the rotor by hydraulic pressure. The caliper, which is not held in a fixed position, moves slightly, bringing the outside brake pad into contact with the disc rotor.

## Drum Brakes (Rear)
### BASIC OPERATING PRINCIPLES

Drum brakes employ two brake shoes mounted on a stationary backing plate. These shoes are positioned inside a circular drum which rotates with the wheel assembly. The shoes are held in place by springs. This allows them to slide toward the drums (when they are applied) while keeping the linings and drums in alignment. The shoes are actuated by a wheel cylinder which is mounted at the top of the backing plate. When the brakes are applied, hydraulic pressure forces the wheel cylinder's actuating links outward. Since these links bear directly against the top of the brake shoes, the tops of the shoes are then forced against the inner side of the drum. This action forces the bottoms of the two shoes to contact the brake drum by rotating the entire assembly slightly (know as servo action). When pressure within the wheel cylinder is relaxed, return springs pull the shoes back away from the drum.

The rear drum brakes on your car are designed to self-adjust themselves during application. Motion causes both shoes to rotate very slightly with the drum, rocking an adjusting lever, thereby causing rotation of the adjusting screw or lever.

## Power Brake Boosters

Power brakes operate just as standard brake systems except in the actuation of the master cylinder pistons. A vacuum diaphragm is located on the front of the master cylinder and assists the driver in applying the brakes, reducing both the effort and travel he must put into moving the brake pedal.

The vacuum diaphragm housing is connected to the intake manifold by a vacuum hose. A check valve is placed at the point where the hose enters the diaphragm housing, so that during periods of low manifold vacuum brake assist vacuum will not be lost.

Depressing the brake pedal closes off the vacuum sources and allows atmospheric pressure to enter on one side of the diaphragm. This causes the master cylinder pistons to move and apply the brakes. When the brake pedal is released, vacuum is applied to both sides of the diaphragm, and return springs return the diaphragm and master cylinder pistons to the released position. If the vacuum fails, the brake pedal rod will butt against the end of the master cylinder actuating rod, and direct mechanical application will occur as the pedal is depressed.

The hydraulic and mechanical problems that apply to conventional brake systems also apply to power brakes, and should be checked for if the tests below do not reveal the problem. **Test for a system vacuum leak as described below:**

1. Operate the engine at idle without touching the brake pedal for at least one minute.

2. Turn off the engine, and wait one minute.

3. Test for the presence of assist vacuum by depressing the brake pedal and releasing it several times. Light application will produce less and less pedal travel, if vacuum was present. If there is no vacuum, air is leaking into the system somewhere. **Test for system operation as follows:**

1. Pump the brake pedal (with engine off) until the supply vacuum is entirely gone.

2. Put a light, steady pressure on the pedal.

3. Start the engine, and operate it at idle. If the system is operating, the brake pedal should fall toward the floor if constant pressure is maintained on the pedal.

Power brake systems may be tested for hydraulic leaks just as ordinary systems are tested.

## Brake Adjustment
### FRONT DISC BRAKES

Front disc brakes require no adjustment. Hydraulic pressure maintains the proper pad-to-disc contact at all times.

### REAR DRUM BRAKES

The rear drum brakes, on your car, are self-adjusting. The only adjustment necessary should be an initial one after new brake shoes have been installed or some type of service work has been done on the rear brake system.

NOTE: *After any brake service, obtain a firm brake pedal before moving the car. Adjusted brakes must not drag. The wheel must turn freely. Be sure the parking brake cables are not too tightly adjusted.*

*A special brake shoe gauge is necessary, if your car is equipped with 8" (203mm) brakes, for making an accurate adjustment after installing new brake shoes. The special gauge measures both the drum diameter and the brake shoe setting.*

Since no adjustment is necessary except when service work is done on the rear brakes, we will assume that the car is jacked up and

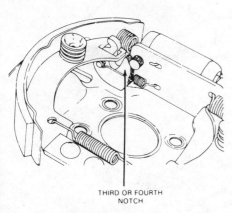

SET QUADRANT ON THIRD OR FOURTH
NOTCH PRIOR TO ASSEMBLY

THIRD OR FOURTH
NOTCH

180 mm (7-INCH) REAR BRAKE

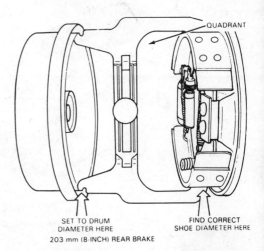

QUADRANT

SET TO DRUM
DIAMETER HERE

FIND CORRECT
SHOE DIAMETER HERE

203 mm (8-INCH) REAR BRAKE

**Rear brake shoe adjustment**

safely supported by jackstands, and that the rear drums have been removed. (If not, refer to the appropriate sections of this Chapter for the procedures necessary).

### Cars Equipped with 7″ (178mm) Brakes

Pivot the adjuster quadrant (see illustration) until the third or fourth notch from the outer end of the quadrant meshes with the knurled pin on the adjuster strut. Install the hub and drum.

### Cars Equipped with 8″ (203mm) Brakes

Measure and set the special brake gauge to the inside diameter of the brake drum. Lift the adjuster lever from the starwheel teeth. Turn the starwheel until the brake shoes are adjusted out to the shoe setting fingers of the brake gauge. Install the hub and drum.

NOTE: *Complete the adjustment (7″ or 8″ brakes) by applying the brakes several times. After the brakes have been properly adjusted, check their operation by making several stops from varying forward speeds.*

### Adjustment for Brake Drum Removal

If the brake drum will not come off for brake servicing, pry the rubber plug from the backing plate inspection hole and use the following procedure:

On 7″ (178mm) brakes: Insert a thin blade screwdriver through the hole until it contacts the adjuster assembly pivot. Apply side pressure to the pivot point allowing the adjuster quadrant to ratchet and back off the brake adjustment.

On 8″ (203mm) brakes: Remove the brake line to axle retention bracket. This will allow sufficient room for the use of a thin screwdriver and brake adjusting tool. Push the adjuster lever away from the adjuster wheel with the screwdriver and release adjustment with the brake tool.

## Master Cylinder

The fluid reservoir of the master cylinder has a large and small compartment. The larger serves the right front and left rear brakes, while the smaller serves the left front and right rear brakes.

Always be sure that the fluid level of the reservoirs is within ¼″ (6mm) of the top. Use only DOT 3 approved brake fluid.

### *REMOVAL AND INSTALLATION*

#### Models without Power Brakes

1. Disconnect the negative (ground) battery cable from the battery.

2. From under the dash panel, disconnect

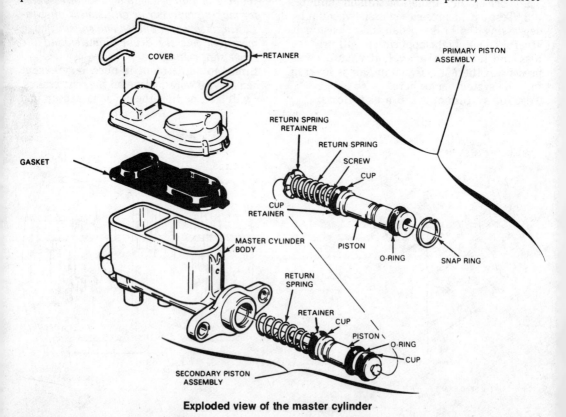

**Exploded view of the master cylinder**

the wires to the stoplight switch. Remove the spring clip that retains the stoplight switch and the master cylinder pushrod to the brake pedal.

3. Slide the stoplight switch off the brake pedal pin. Remove the switch.

4. From under the hood, loosen the two retaining nuts mounting the master cylinder to the firewall. Disconnect the brake lines from the master cylinder.

5. Slide the master cylinder pushrod, washers and bushings from the brake pedal pin.

NOTE: *Models with speed control have an adapter instead of a washer on the brake pedal mounting pin.*

6. Remove the cylinder mounting nuts. Lift the cylinder out and away from the firewall.

CAUTION: *Take care not to spill any brake fluid on the painted surfaces of your car. If you spill any on you car, flush off with water as soon as possible. Brake fluid will act like a paint remover.*

**To install:**

1. Insert the master cylinder pushrod through the opening in the firewall. Place the cylinder mounting flange over the studs on the firewall and loosely install the mounting nuts.

2. Coat the nylon pushrod mounting bushing with oil. Install the washer, pushrod and bushing on the brake pedal shaft. (Speed control models use a snap-on adapter instead of a washer).

3. Position the stoplight switch on the brake pedal pin. Install the nylon bushing and washer and secure with the spring pin.

4. Connect the wires to the stoplight switch.

5. Connect the brake lines to the master cylinder, but do not tighten them completely.

6. Secure the cylinder mounting nuts. Fill the master cylinder to within ¼" (6mm) of the top. Slowly pump the brake pedal to help evacuate the air in the master cylinder.

NOTE: *Cover the brake line connections (at the master cylinder) with a rag to prevent brake fluid spray.*

7. Tighten the brake lines at the master cylinder. Add brake fluid if necessary.

8. Connect the negative battery cable. Bleed the entire brake system. Centralize the pressure differential valve (refer to the following sections).

9. Check for hydraulic leads. Road test the car.

### Power Brake Models

1. Disconnect the brake lines from the master cylinder.

2. Remove the two nuts that mount the master cylinder to the brake booster.

3. Pull the master cylinder forward and away from the booster.

CAUTION: *Brake fluid acts like a paint remover. If you spill any on the finish of your car, flush it off with water.*

**To install:**

1. Slip the master cylinder base over the pushrod at the poser brake booster. Align the mounting flange and place over the mounting studs on the booster. Loosely secure with the two mounting nuts.

2. Connect the brake lines to the master cylinder. Tighten the mounting nuts. Tighten brake lines.

3. Fill the master cylinder to within ¼" (6mm) of the top. Bleed the brake system. Centralize the pressure differential valve (refer to the following sections). Check for system leaks. Road test the car.

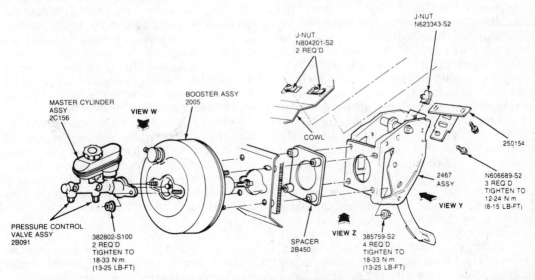

**Power booster and master cylinder assembly**

## *MASTER CYLINDER OVERHAUL*

Referring to the exploded view of the dual master cylinder components, disassemble the unit as follows: Clean the exterior of the cylinder and remove the filler cover and diaphragm. Any brake fluid remaining in the cylinder should be poured out and discarded. Remove the secondary piston stop bolt from the bottom of the cylinder and remove the bleed screw, if required. With the primary piston depressed, remove the snapring from its retaining groove at the rear of the cylinder bore. Withdraw the pushrod and the primary piston assembly from the bore.

Remove the secondary piston assembly. If the piston does not come out easily, apply air pressure carefully through the secondary outlet port to assist in piston removal.

NOTE: *Do not remove the outlet tube seats, outlet check valves and outlet check valve springs from the cylinder body unless they are damaged.*

All components should be cleaned in clean isopropyl alcohol or clean brake fluid and inspected for chipping, excessive wear and damage. Check to ensure that all recesses, openings and passageways are clear and free of foreign matter. Dirt and cleaning solvent may be removed by using compressed air. After cleaning, keep all parts on a clean surface. Inspect the cylinder bore for etching, pitting, scoring or rusting. Since honing is not recommended for aluminum master cylinders, deep scratches or pitting will require master cylinder replacement.

During the assembly operation, be sure to use all parts supplied with the master cylinder repair kit. With the exception of the master cylinder body, submerge all parts in extra heavy duty brake fluid. Carefully insert the complete secondary piston and return spring assembly into the cylinder bore and install the primary piston assembly into the bore. With the primary piston depressed, install the snapring into its groove in the cylinder bore. Install the pushrod, boot and retainer (if equipped), then install the pushrod assembly into the primary piston. Be sure that the retainer is properly seated and is holding the pushrod securely. Position the inner end of the pushrod boot (if equipped) in the master cylinder body retaining groove. Install the secondary piston stop bolt and O-ring at the bottom of the master cylinder body. Install the bleed screw (if equipped) and position the gasket on the master cylinder filler cover. Be sure that the gasket is securely seated. Reinstall the master cylinder and fill the brake fluid. Install the cover and secure with the retainer. Bleed the brake system and road test the car.

## Vacuum Booster

### *REMOVAL AND INSTALLATION*

1. Working from inside the car, beneath the instrument panel, remove the booster pushrod from the brake pedal.
2. Disconnect the stop light switch wires and remove the switch from the brake pedal. Use care not to damage the switch during removal.
3. Raise the hood and remove the master cylinder from the booster.
4. Remove the manifold vacuum hose from the booster.
5. Remove the booster to firewall attaching bolts and remove the booster from the car.
6. Reverse above procedure to reinstall.

### *TESTING THE POWER BRAKE BOOSTER*

The power brake booster depends on vacuum produced by the engine for proper operation.

If you suspect problems in the power brake system, check the following:

1. Inspect all hoses and hose connections. All unused vacuum connectors should be sealed. Hoses and connections should be tightly secured and in good condition. The hoses should be pliable with no holes or cracks and no collapsed areas.
2. Inspect the check valve which is located in line between the intake manifold and booster. Disconnect the hose on the intake manifold side of the valve. Attempt to blow through the valve. If air passes through the valve, it is defective and must be replaced.
3. Check the level of brake fluid in the master cylinder. If the level is low, check the system for fluid leaks.
4. Idle the engine briefly and then shut it off. Pump the brake pedal several times to exhaust all of the vacuum stored in the booster. Keep the brake pedal depressed and start the engine. The brake pedal should drop slightly, if vacuum is present after the engine is started less pressure should be necessary on the brake pedal. If no drop, or action is felt the power brake booster should be suspect.
5. With the parking brake applied and the wheels blocked, start the engine and allow to idle in Neutral (Park if automatic). Disconnect the vacuum line to the check valve on the intake manifold side. If vacuum is felt, connect the hose and repeat Step 4. Once again, if no action is felt on the brake pedal, suspect the booster.
6. Operate the engine at a fast idle for about ten seconds, shut off the engine. Allow the car to sit for about ten minutes. Depress the brake pedal with moderate force (about 20 pounds). The pedal should feel about the same as when

the engine was running. If the brake pedal feels hard (no power assist) suspect the power booster.

## Brake Control Valve
### REPLACEMENT

The brake control valve is located to the left and below the master cylinder and mounted to the shock (strut) tower by a removable bracket. Use the proper size flare wrench and disconnect the brake lines to the valve. Disconnect the warning switch wire. Remove the bolt(s) retaining the valve to the mount and remove the valve. Installation is in the reverse order of removal. Bleed the brake system after installing the new valve.

## Pressure Differential Valve

If a loss of brake fluid occurs on either side of the diagonally split system when the brakes are applied, a piston mounted in the valve moves off center allowing the brakes on the non-leaking side of the split system to operate. When the piston moves off center a brake warning switch, located in the center of the valve body, will turn on a dash mounted warning light indicating brake problems.

After repairs are made on the brake system and the system bled, the warning switch will reset itself when you pump the brake pedal and the dash light will turn off.

## Proportioning Valve

The dual proportioning valve, located between the rear brake system inlet and outlet port, controls the rear brake system hydraulic pressure. When the brakes are applied, the dual proportioning valve reduces pressure to the rear wheels and provides balanced braking.

## TROUBLESHOOTING THE PROPORTIONING VALVE

If the rear brakes lock-up during light brake application or do not lock-up under heavy braking the problem could be with the dual proportioning valve.
1. Check tires and tire pressures.
2. Check the brake linings for thickness, and for contamination by fluid, grease etc.
3. Check the brake system hoses, steel lines, calipers and wheel cylinders for leaks.
4. If none of the proceeding checks have uncovered any problems, suspect the proportioning valve.
NOTE: *Take the car to a qualified service center and ask them to do a pressure test on the valve. If a pressure test is not possible, replace the control valve.*

## Bleeding the Brake System

It is necessary to bleed the brake system of air whenever a hydraulic component, of the system, has been rebuilt or replaced, or if the brakes feel spongy during application.

Your car has a diagonally split brake system. Each side of this system must be bled as an individual system. **Bleed the right rear brake, left front brake, left rear brake and right front brake. Always start with the longest line from the master cylinder first.**

CAUTION: *When bleeding the system(s) never allow the master cylinder to run completely out of brake fluid. Always use DOT 3 heavy duty brake fluid or the equivalent. Never reuse brake fluid that has been drained from the system or that has been allowed to stand in an opened container for an extended period of time. If your car is equipped with*

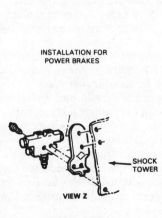

INSTALLATION FOR POWER BRAKES

SHOCK TOWER

VIEW Z

PROPORTIONING VALVE

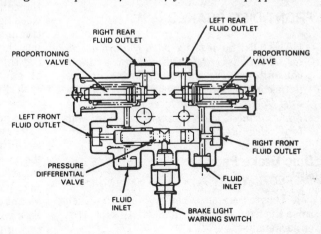

RIGHT REAR FLUID OUTLET

LEFT REAR FLUID OUTLET

PROPORTIONING VALVE

PROPORTIONING VALVE

LEFT FRONT FLUID OUTLET

RIGHT FRONT FLUID OUTLET

PRESSURE DIFFERENTIAL VALVE

FLUID INLET

FLUID INLET

BRAKE LIGHT WARNING SWITCH

**Combination brake valve**

power brakes, remove the reserve vacuum stored in the booster by pumping the brake pedal several times before bleeding the brakes.

1. Clean all of the dirt away from the master cylinder filler cap.

2. Raise and support the car on jackstands. Make sure your car is safely supported and it is raised evenly front and back.

3. Starting with the right rear wheel cylinder. Remove the dust cover from the bleeder screw. Place the proper size box wrench over the bleeder fitting and attach a piece of rubber tubing (about three feet long and snug fitting) over the end of the fitting.

4. Submerge the free end of the rubber tube into a container half filled with clean brake fluid.

5. Have a friend pump up the brake pedal and then push down to apply the brakes while you loosen the bleeder screw. When the pedal reaches the bottom of its travel close the bleeder fitting before your friend release the brake pedal.

6. Repeat Step 5 until air bubbles cease to appear in the container in which the tubing is submerged. Tighten the fitting, remove the rubber tubing and replace the dust cover.

7. Repeat Steps 3 through 6 to the left front wheel, then to the left rear and right front.

NOTE: *Refill the master cylinder after each wheel cylinder or caliper is bled. Be sure the master cylinder top gasket is mounted correctly and the brake fluid level is within ¼" (6mm) of the top.*

8. After bleeding the brakes, pump the brake pedal several times, this ensures proper seating of the rear linings and the front caliper pistons.

## FRONT DISC BRAKES

CAUTION: *Some brake pads contain asbestos, which has been determined to be a cancer causing agent. Never clean the brake surfaces with compressed air! Avoid inhaling any dust from any brake surface! When cleaning brake surfaces, use a commercially available brake cleaning fluid.*

### Disc Brake Pads
#### INSPECTION

1. Loosen the front wheel lugs slightly, then raise the front of the car and safely support it on jackstands.

2. Remove the front wheel and tire assemblies.

3. The cut out in the top of the front brake

caliper allows visual inspection of the disc brake pad. If the lining is worn to within ⅛" (3mm) of the metal disc shoe (check local inspection requirements) replace all four pads (both sides).

4. While you are inspecting the brake pads, visually inspect the caliper for hydraulic fluid leaks. If a leak is visible the caliper will have to be rebuilt or replaced.

### PAD REMOVAL AND INSTALLATION

1. Loosen the front wheel lugs slightly, then raise the front of the car and safely support it on jackstands.

2. Remove the front wheel and tire assemblies.

3. Remove the master cylinder cap. Siphon off some fluid from each reservoir until they are half full. Replace the cap.

4. Remove the anti-rattle spring from the bottom of the caliper by pushing up on the center until the tabs are free of the mounting holes.

5. Back out the Torx® headed caliper locating pins. DO NOT REMOVE THEM ALL THE WAY. If removed, the pins are difficult to install and require new guide bushings.

6. Lift the caliper assembly from the knuckle, anchor plate and rotor.

7. Remove the outer and inner disc brake pads. The outer pad has two clips that fit into the bosses on the outer edge of the caliper. The inner pad uses a three point clip that fits inside the caliper piston.

8. Suspend the caliper, with wire, inside the fender housing.

CAUTION: *Do not suspend in such a way to put stress on the brake hose.*

9. Use a 4" (102mm) C-clamp and a block of 2¾"x 1" (70mm x 25mm) piece of wood to seat the caliper piston back in its bore. Place the wood against the face of the piston, attach the clamp and slowly close it pushing the piston into the caliper. Extra care must be taken during this procedure to prevent damage to the aluminum piston.

NOTE: *The piston must be fully seated in its bore to provide clearance for the caliper with the new pads to fit over the disc rotor.*

10. Install the inner brake pad with the mounting clips onto the caliper piston. Install the outer pad, make sure the slips are properly seated on the caliper bosses.

11. Unwire the caliper from the fender well. Mount the caliper over the rotor and fasten the Torx® headed pins. Reinstall the anti-rattle spring making sure it is firmly located in the mounting holes.

12. Refill the master cylinder to correct levels.

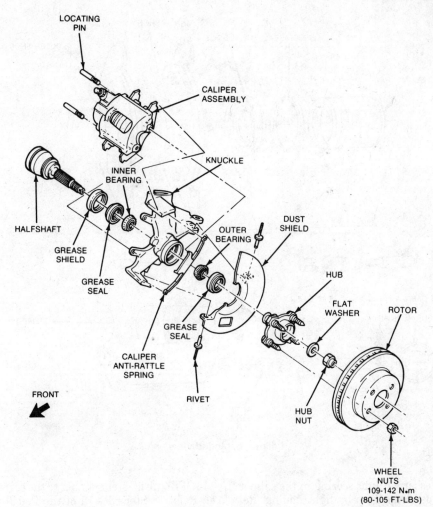

LOCATING
PIN

CALIPER
ASSEMBLY

KNUCKLE

INNER
BEARING

HALFSHAFT

GREASE
SHIELD

GREASE
SEAL

CALIPER
ANTI-RATTLE
SPRING

OUTER
BEARING

DUST
SHIELD

GREASE
SEAL

HUB

FLAT
WASHER

ROTOR

HUB
NUT

RIVET

FRONT

WHEEL
NUTS
109-142 N•m
(80-105 FT-LBS)

**Disc brake components**

13. Pump the brakes several times to position the new pads.

14. Install the wheels and tighten the lugs snugly.

15. Lower the car from the jackstands. Tighten the lug nuts to 80–105 ft.lb.

16. Road test the car.

## Brake Caliper

### OVERHAUL

1. Follow Steps 1–3 of the Pad Removal and Installation procedure.

2. Disconnect the hydraulic brake hose from the caliper. To disconnect the hose, loosen the tube fitting at the frame bracket. Remove the horseshoe clip from between the hose and bracket. Remove the hollow bolt fastening the hose to the caliper and remove the hose. Do not loosen the two gaskets used in mounting the brake hose to the caliper.

3. Follow Steps 4–7 of the Pad Removal and Installation procedures.

4. The next step requires a controllable air source. If you have one fine, if not take the caliper(s) to your local gas station and ask them to do Step 5 for you.

5. Place a folded cloth, shop rag, etc. over the caliper piston. Apply air pressure through the brake line fitting hole with a rubber tipped air blow gun. The air pressure will force the caliper piston from its bore. If the piston is seized, tap lightly on the caliper with a plastic hammer while applying air pressure.

CAUTION: *Apply air pressure slowly. Pressure can built up inside the caliper and the piston may come out with considerable force.*

6. Remove the dust boot and piston seal from the caliper. Clean all parts with alcohol or clean brake fluid. Blow out the passage ways in the caliper. Check the condition of the caliper bore and piston. If they are pitted or scored or show excessive wear, replacement

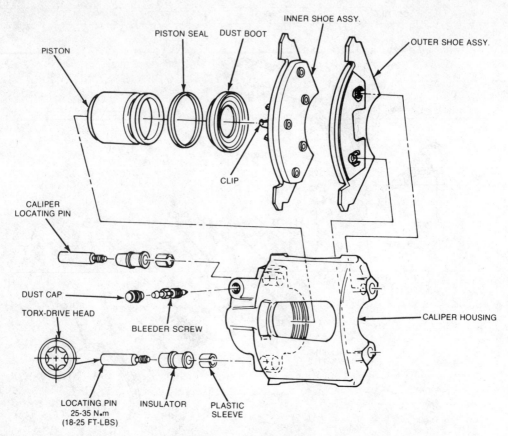

PISTON

PISTON SEAL    DUST BOOT

INNER SHOE ASSY.

OUTER SHOE ASSY.

CLIP

CALIPER LOCATING PIN

DUST CAP

TORX-DRIVE HEAD

BLEEDER SCREW

LOCATING PIN 25-35 N•m (18-25 FT-LBS)    INSULATOR    PLASTIC SLEEVE

CALIPER HOUSING

**Caliper, exploded view**

will be necessary. Slight scoring in the caliper bore may be cleaned up by light honing. Replace the piston if it is scored.

7. Apply a coating of brake fluid to the new caliper piston seal and caliper bore. Some rebuilding kits provide a lubricant for this purpose. Install the seal in the caliper bore, make sure it is not twisted and is firmly seated in the groove.

8. Install the new dust seal in the caliper mounting groove, be sure it is mounted firmly.

9. Coat the piston with clean brake fluid or the special lubricant and install it in the caliper bore, make sure it is firmly seated in the bottom of the caliper bore. Spread the dust boot over the piston and seat in the piston groove.

10. Install the brake pads as outlined in the previous section.

11. Install the caliper over the rotor. Mount the caliper as described in the previous section.

12. Install the bake hose to the caliper. Be sure to use a new gasket on each side of the hose fitting. Position and install the upper end of the hose, remember to put the horseshoe clip in place, take care not to twist the hose.

13. Bleed the brake system and centralize the brake warning switch.

14. Fill the master cylinder to the correct level. Refer to Steps 12–15 of the Pad Removal and Installation for the remaining procedures.

## Front Brake Disc (Rotor)
### REMOVAL AND INSTALLATION

1. Follow Steps 1–6 of the Pad Removal and Installation omitting Step 3 (it is not necessary to siphon off any brake fluid).

2. Suspend the caliper with a piece of wire from the fender support, do not put any stress on the brake hose.

3. Pull the rotor outward from the wheel hub.

4. Installation is in the reverse order of removal.

## Front Wheel Bearings

The bearing design relies on component stack up and deformation/torque at assembly to determine bearing setting. The bearings, therefore, cannot be adjusted after assembly.

The front bearings are located in the front suspension knuckle, not in the rotor or wheel hub. Two inner and one outer seal protect the bearings (the seal closer to the CV-joint is a shield) on models through 1983.1984 and later models use bearings of a cartridge design and are pregreased and sealed, and require no scheduled maintenance. The wheel hub is installed with a close slip fit through the wheel bearings and an interference fit over the splines of the halfshaft's constant velocity stub shaft. A flat washer and a staked hub nut maintain the correct endplay and prevent the wheel bearing inner races from spinning on the wheel hub.

### REMOVAL

NOTE: *The wheel hub and knuckle must be removed for bearing replacement or servicing. A special puller is required to remove and install the hub. (Ford Part Number T81P-1104-A, T81P-1104-C and adapters T81P-1104-B or T83P-1104-AH). The adaptors screw over the lugs and attach to the puller, which uses a long screw attached to the end of the stub shaft to pull off or install the hub.*

1. Remove wheel cover and slightly loosen the lugs.

2. Remove the hub retaining nut and washer. The nut is crimped staked to the shaft. Use a socket and sufficient torque to overcome the locking force of the crimp.

3. Raise the front of the car and support safely with jackstands. Remove the tire and wheel assembly.

4. Remove the brake caliper and disc rotor. Refer to the proceeding sections in this Chapter for the necessary procedures.

5. Disconnect the lower control arm and tie rod from the steering knuckle. Loosen tow top strut mounting nuts, but do not remove them. Install the hub remover/installer tool and remove the hub. If the outer bearing is seized on the hub remove it with a puller.

6. Remove the front suspension knuckle.

7. On models through 1983, after the front knuckle is removed, pull out the inner grease shield, the inner seal and bearing.

8. Remove the outer grease seal and bearing.

9. If you hope to reuse the bearings, clean them in a safe solvent. After cleaning the bearings and races, carefully inspect them for damage, pitting, heat coloring etc. If damage etc. has occurred, replace all components (bearings, cups and seals). Always replace the seals with new ones. Always use a new hub nut whenever the old one has been removed.

10. If new bearings are to be used, remove the inner and outer races from the knuckle. A three jawed puller on a slide hammer will do the job.

11. Clean the interior bore of the knuckle.

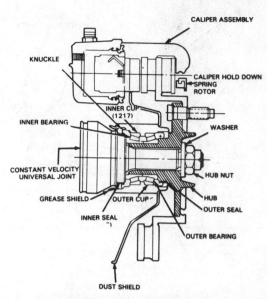

**Cross section of the front wheel bearings—through 1982**

12. On 1984 and later models, remove the snapring that retains the bearing in the steering knuckle.

13. Position the knuckle, outboard side up under a hydraulic press with appropriate adapters in place, and press the bearing from the knuckle.

14. Clean the interior bore of the knuckle.

### INSTALLATION

1. On models through 1983, install the new bearing cups using a suitable driver. Be sure the cups are fully seated in the knuckle bore.

2. Pack the wheel bearings with multi-purpose lubricant (Ford part number C1AZ-19590-B or the equivalent). If a bearing packer is not available, place a large portion of grease into the palm of your hand and slide the edge of the roller cage through the grease with your other hand. Work as much grease as you can between the bearing rollers.

3. Put a sufficient amount of grease between the bearing cups in the center of the knuckle. Apply a thin film of grease on the bearing cups.

4. Place the outer bearing and new grease seal into the knuckle. Place a thin film of grease on all three lips of the new outer seal.

5. Turn the knuckle over and install the inner bearing and seal. Once again, apply a thin film of grease to the three lips of the seal.

6. Install the inner grease shield. A small block of wood may be used to tap the seal into the knuckle bore.

7. Keep the knuckle in the vertical position or the inner bearing will fall out. Start the wheel hub into the outer knuckle bore and

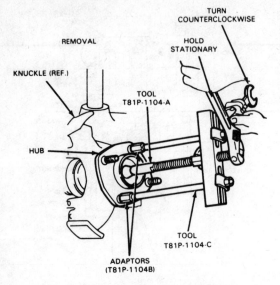

REMOVE HUB FROM CONSTANT VELOCITY
UNIVERSAL JOINT SPLINED STUB SHAFT AS SHOWN

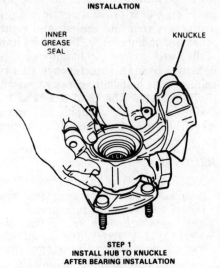

**STEP 1**
**INSTALL HUB TO KNUCKLE**
**AFTER BEARING INSTALLATION**

KNUCKLE MUST BE POSITIONED
AS SHOWN AND HUB MUST BE INSERTED
THROUGH BEARINGS USING HAND PRESSURE ONLY

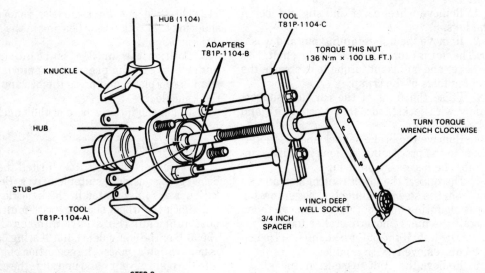

**STEP 2**
**INSTALL HUB TO CONSTANT**
**VELOCITY UNIVERSAL JOINT**
**SPLINED STUB SHAFT**

TIGHTEN TOOL NUT TO 150 N·m (110 lb-ft)
USING TORQUE WRENCH TO SEAT HUB

**Using the front stub shaft remover/installer tool**

push the hub as far as possible through the outer and inner bearings by hand.

NOTE: *Prior to installing the hub, make sure it is clean and free from burrs. Use crocus cloth to polish the hub is necessary. It is important to use only hand pressure when installing the hub, make sure the hub is through both the outer and inner bearings.*

8. With the hub as fully seated as possible through the bearings, position the hub and knuckle to the front strut. Refer to Chapter 7 for instructions on attaching the strut and knuckle.

9. On 1984 and later models, position the knuckle. outboard side down on the appropriate adapter and press in the new bearing. Be sure the bearing is fully seated. Install a new retainer snapring.

10. Install the hub using tool T83T-1104-AH3 and press. Check that the hub rotates freely.

11. Lubricate the stub shaft splines with a thin film of SAE 20 motor oil. Use hand pressure only and insert the splines into the knuckle and hub as far as possible.

NOTE: *Do not allow the hub to back out of*

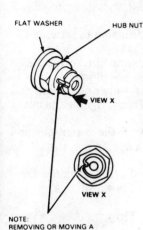

FLAT WASHER    HUB NUT

TIGHTEN NUT TO 240-270 N·m 180 200 LB-FT AFTER HUB IS SEATED USING SPECIAL HUB INSTALLER TOOL T81P-1104-A. DO NOT USE IMPACT WRENCH FOR REMOVAL OR INSTALLATION OF HUB NUT. AFTER NUT IS TORQUED, DEFORM NUT COLLAR **INTO** SLOT OF DRIVESHAFT USING TOOL AS INDICATED THIS FIGURE. THE NUT MUST NOT SPLIT OR CRACK WHEN STAKED. IF NUT IS SPLIT OR CRACKED AFTER STAKING, IT MUST BE REMOVED AND REPLACED WITH NEW, UNUSED NUT.

VIEW X

NOTE:
REMOVING OR MOVING A HUB NUT AFTER STAKING REQUIRES **THE NUT BE REPLACED WITH A NEW NUT.**

THE STAKING TOOL CAN BE FABRICATED FROM AN EXISTED HARDENED CHISEL. THE CORRECT RADIUS ON THE CHISEL TIP WILL PREVENT IMPROPER STAKING. **DO NOT ATTEMPT TO STAKE WITH A SHARP EDGED TOOL.**

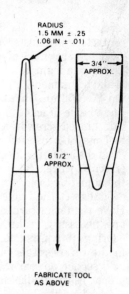

RADIUS 1.5 MM ± .25 (.06 IN ± .01)

3/4" APPROX.

6 1/2" APPROX.

FABRICATE TOOL AS ABOVE

**How to stake the front wheel retainer nut**

*the bearings while installing the stub shaft, otherwise it will be necessary to start all over from Step 7.*

12. Complete the installation of the suspension parts as described in Chapter 7.

13. Install the hub remover/installer tool and tighten the center adapter to 120 foot pounds, this ensures the hub is fully seated.

14. Remove the installer tool and install the hub washer and nut. Tighten the hub nut finger tight.

15. Install the disc rotor, caliper etc. in reverse order of removal. Refer to the proceeding sections of this Chapter, if necessary, for procedures.

16. Install the tire and wheel assembly and snug the wheel lugs.

17. Lower the car to the ground, set the parking brake and block the wheels.

18. Tighten the wheel lugs to 80–105 ft.lb.

19. Tighten the center hub nut to 180–200 ft.lb. DO NOT USE A POWER WRENCH TO TIGHTEN THE HUB NUT.

20. Stake the hub nut using a rounded, dull chisel. DO NOT USE A SHARP CHISEL.

## REAR BRAKES

CAUTION: *Some brake pads contain asbestos, which has been determined to be a cancer causing agent. Never clean the brake surfaces with compressed air! Avoid inhaling any dust from any brake surface! When cleaning brake surfaces, use a commercially available brake cleaning fluid.*

The rear brakes used on your car are of the non-servo leading/trailing shoe design. This means that the leading shoe does the majority of the braking when the car is going forward and the trailing shoe does the majority of the braking when the car is backing up.

The brakes are self-adjusting. The only time any adjustment should be necessary is during servicing of brake shoe replacement. Depending on the model of your car, either 7″ (178mm) or 8″ (203mm) brakes are used.

### BRAKE SHOE INSPECTION

Two access holes, covered by a rubber plug, are provided in the brake backing plate. By removing the plugs the brake lining thickness and condition can be inspected.

## Rear Brake Drum
### REMOVAL AND INSTALLATION (ALL MODELS)

1. Remove the wheel cover, loosen the lugs, jack up the rear end of your car and safely support it on jackstands.

2. Remove the wheel lugs and the tire and wheel assembly.

3. Remove the center grease car from the brake drum hub. Remove the cotter pin, nut retainer, spindle nut, and keyed flat washer.

4. Make sure the parking brake is completely released. Slide the brake drum off of the spindle. Be careful not to drop the outer bearing. Make sure that you keep the drum straight and not drag the inner grease seal across the spindle threads.

NOTE: *If the hub and drum assembly will not slide off of the spindle, the brake shoe adjustment will have to be backed off.*

**On 7″ (178mm) brakes:** Insert a thin blade

screwdriver in to the inspection slot until it contacts the adjuster assembly pivot. Apply side pressure on the pivot point to allow the adjuster quadrant to ratchet and release the brake adjustment.

**On 8″ (203mm) brakes:** Remove the brake line to axle bracket to gain enough room so a thin bladed screwdriver and brake adjusting tool may be inserted in the inspection slot. Push the adjusting lever away from the adjuster screw wheel. Back off the starwheel with the adjusting tool.

5. Inspect the brake drum for scoring, etc. Have the drum turned if necessary. Perform any necessary brake work. Pack the wheel bearings if required. Reinstall the brake drum in the reverse order of removal. Consult the next section on rear wheel bearing service for proper bearing adjustment when reinstalling the brake drum.

## Rear Wheel Bearings

### REMOVAL, PACKING, INSTALLATION AND ADJUSTMENT

The rear wheel bearings are located in the brake drum hub. The inner wheel bearing is protected by a grease seal. A washer and spindle nut retain the hub/drum assembly and control the bearing endplay.

1. Complete Steps 1–4 in the proceeding Drum Removal section.

2. The outer bearing will be loose when the drum is removed and may be lifted out by hand. The inner bearing is retained by a grease seal. To remove the inner bearing, insert a wooden dowel or soft drift through the hub from the outer bearing side and carefully drive out the inner bearing and grease seal.

3. Clean the bearings, cups and hubs with a suitable solvent. Inspect the bearings and cups for damage or heat discoloring. Replace as a set if necessary. Always install a new grease seal.

4. If new bearings are to be used, use a three jawed slidehammer puller to remove the cups from the drum hub. Install the new bearing cups using a suitable driver. Make sure they are fully seated in the hub.

5. Pack the bearings with a multi-purpose grease. (See the front wheel bearing section for packing instructions).

6. Coat the cups with a thin film of grease. Install the inner bearing and grease seal.

7. Coat the bearing surfaces of the spindle with a thin film of grease. Slowly and carefully slide the drum and hub over the spindle and brake shoes. Install the outer bearing over the spindle and into the hub.

8. Install the keyed flat washer and adjusting nut on the spindle.

9. Tighten the adjusting nut to between 17–25 ft.lb.

10. Back off the adjusting nut ½ turn. Then retighten it to between 10–15 in.lb.

11. Position the nut retainer on the nut and install the cotter pin. Do not tighten the nut to install the cotter pin.

12. Spread the ends of the cotter pin and bend then around the nut retainer. Install the center grease cap.

13. Install the tire and wheel assembly. Lower the car and tighten the wheel lugs.

## Rear Brake Shoes Tips

After any brake service work, obtain a firm brake pedal before moving the car. Adjusted brakes must not put a drag on the wheel, the wheel must turn freely.

The rear brakes are self-adjusting and require adjustment only after new shoes have been installed or service work has been done which required the disassembly of the brake shoes.

When adjusting the rear brake shoes, make sure the parking brakes cables are not adjusted too tightly.

After the brakes have been installed and adjusted, check the operation of the brakes by making several stops from varying speeds. Readjust if necessary.

### REMOVAL AND INSTALLATION

#### 7″ (178mm) Rear Brakes

1. Perform Steps 1–4 of the Brake Drum Removal section.

2. Remove the holddown pins and springs by pushing down on and rotating the outer washer 90°. It may be necessary to hold the back of the pin (behind the backing plate) while pressing down and turning the washer.

3. After the holddown pins and spring have been removed from both brake shoes, remove both shoes and the adjuster assembly by lifting up and away from the bottom anchor plate and shoe guide. Take care not to damage the wheel cylinder boots when removing the shoes from the wheel cylinder.

4. Remove the parking brake cable from the brake lever to allow the removal of the shoes and adjuster assembly.

5. Remove the lower shoe to shoe spring by rotating the leading brake shoe to release the spring tension. Do not pry the spring from the shoe.

6. Remove the adjuster strut from the trailing shoe by pulling the strut away from the shoe and twisting it downward toward yourself

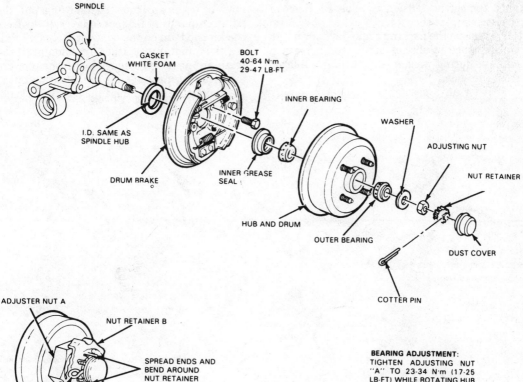

SPINDLE

GASKET
WHITE FOAM

BOLT
40-64 N·m
29-47 LB-FT

INNER BEARING

WASHER

ADJUSTING NUT

NUT RETAINER

I.D. SAME AS
SPINDLE HUB

DRUM BRAKE

INNER GREASE
SEAL

HUB AND DRUM

OUTER BEARING

DUST COVER

COTTER PIN

ADJUSTER NUT A

NUT RETAINER B

SPREAD ENDS AND
BEND AROUND
NUT RETAINER

COTTER PIN C

**BEARING ADJUSTMENT:**
TIGHTEN ADJUSTING NUT
"A" TO 23-34 N·m (17-25
LB-FT) WHILE ROTATING HUB
AND DRUM ASSEMBLY.
BACK OFF ADJUSTING NUT
APPROXIMATELY 100
DEGREES. POSITION NUT RE-
TAINER "B" OVER AD-
JUSTING NUT SO SLOTS ARE
IN LINE WITH COTTER PIN
HOLE WITHOUT ROTATING
ADJUSTING NUT. INSTALL
COTTER PIN.

NOTE: THE SPINDLE HAS A
PREVAILING TORQUE
FEATURE THAT PREVENTS
ADJUSTING THE NUT BY
HAND.

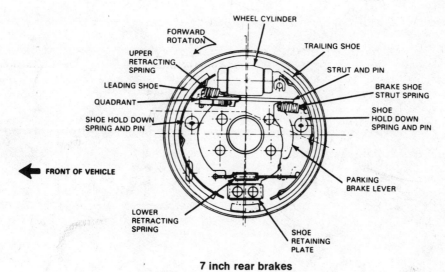

WHEEL CYLINDER

FORWARD
ROTATION

TRAILING SHOE

UPPER
RETRACTING
SPRING

STRUT AND PIN

LEADING SHOE

BRAKE SHOE
STRUT SPRING

QUADRANT

SHOE
HOLD DOWN
SPRING AND PIN

SHOE HOLD DOWN
SPRING AND PIN

FRONT OF VEHICLE

PARKING
BRAKE LEVER

LOWER
RETRACTING
SPRING

SHOE
RETAINING
PLATE

**7 inch rear brakes**

until the spring tension is released. Remove the spring from the slot.

7. Remove the parking brake lever from the trailing shoe by disconnecting the horseshoe clip and spring washer and pulling the lever from the shoe.

8. If for any reason the adjuster assembly must be taken apart, do the following: pull the adjuster quadrant (U-shaped lever) away from the knurled pin on the adjuster strut by rotating the quadrant in either direction until the teeth are no longer engaged with the pin. Remove the spring and slide the quadrant out of the slot on the end of the adjuster strut. Do not

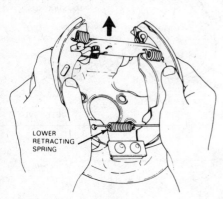

**STEP 1**

a. Remove holddown springs and pins.

b. Lift assembly off backing plate.

c. Disengage parking brake cable.

d. Remove lower retracting spring.

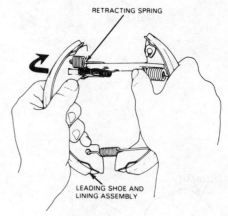

**STEP 2**

Remove leading shoe retracting spring by rotating shoe as shown to release spring tension. Do not pry spring off shoe.

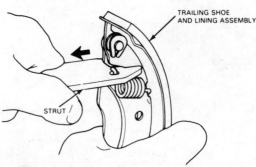

**STEP 3a**

Remove strut to trailing shoe and lining assembly by pulling strut away from shoe and...

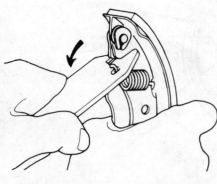

**STEP 3b**

...twisting strut downward

**STEP 3c**

...toward technician until spring tension is released. Remove spring from slots.

**Removing the 7 inch rear brake shoes**

put too much stress on the spring during disassembly.

**To install:**

1. Clean the brake backing (mounting) plate with a soft paint brush or vacuum cleaner.

CAUTION: *Never inhale the dust from the brake linings. Asbestos dust when inhaled can be injurious to your health. Use a vacuum cleaner. Do not blow off the dust with air pressure.*

2. Apply a thin film of high temperature grease at the points on the backing plate where the brake shoes make contact.

3. Apply a thin film of multi-purpose grease to the adjuster strut at the point between the quadrant and strut.

4. If the adjuster has been disassembled, install the quadrant mounting pin into the slot on the adjuster strut and install the adjuster spring.

5. Assemble the parking brake lever to the trailing shoe. Install the spring washer and a new horseshoe clip, squeeze the clip with pliers until the lever is secured on the shoe.

6. Install the adjuster strut attaching spring on to the trailing shoe. Attach the adjusting strut by fastening the spring in the slot and pivoting the strut into position. This will tension the spring. Make sure the end of the spring where the hook is parallel to the center line of the spring coils is hooked into the web of the brake shoe. The installed spring should be flat against the web and parallel to the adjuster strut.

7. Install the shoe to shoe spring with the longest hook attached to the trailing shoe.

8. Install the leading shoe to adjuster strut spring by installing the spring to both parts and pivoting the leading shoe over the quadrant and into position, this will tension the spring.

9. Place the shoes and adjuster assembly onto the backing plate. Spread the shoes slightly and position them into the wheel cylinder piston inserts and anchor plate. Take care not to damage the wheel cylinder boots.

10. Attach the parking brake cable to the parking brake lever.

**REMOVAL PROCEDURE**

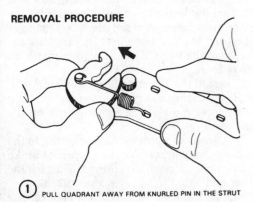

① PULL QUADRANT AWAY FROM KNURLED PIN IN THE STRUT

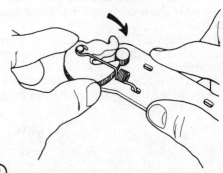

② ROTATE QUADRANT UNTIL TEETH ARE NO LONGER MESHED WITH PIN.

**INSTALLATION PROCEDURE**

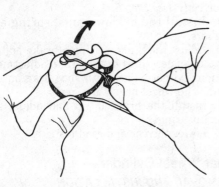

③ REMOVE THE SPRING AND SLIDE QUADRANT OUT OF STRUT — BE CAREFUL NOT TO OVERSTRESS SPRING.

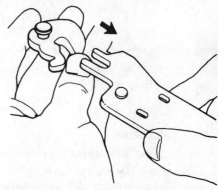

INSTALL ADJUSTER QUADRANT PIN INTO SLOT IN STRUT. TURN ASSEMBLY OVER AND INSTALL SPRING.

**7 inch brakes; quadrant removal and installation**

11. Install the holddown pins, springs, and washers.

12. Adjust the brakes as described in the proceeding brake adjustment section.

13. Install the rear drums and adjust the bearings as described in the previous section.

### 8″ (203mm) Rear Brakes

1. Perform Steps 1–4 of the Brake Drum Removal section.

2. Remove the holddown pins and springs by pushing down on and rotating the outer washer 90°. It may be necessary to hold the back of the pin (behind the backing plate) while pressing down and turning the washer.

3. After the holddown pins and springs have been removed, remove both shoes and the adjuster assembly by lifting up and away from the anchor plate and wheel cylinder. Take care not to damage the wheel cylinder boots or bend the adjusting lever.

4. Disconnect the parking brake cable from the parking brake lever.

5. Remove the lower shoe to shoe spring and the upper spring attaching the adjusting lever to the brake shoe. This will separate the brake shoes and disengage the adjuster.

6. Spread the horseshoe clip and remove the parking brake lever from the trailing shoe.

**To install:**

1. Clean the brake backing (mounting) plate with a soft paint brush or vacuum cleaner.

CAUTION: *Never inhale the dust from the brake linings. Asbestos dust when inhaled*

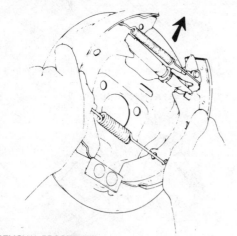

REMOVAL PROCEDURE

1. REMOVE BRAKE SHOE HOLDDOWN SPRINGS AND PINS

2. LIFT ASSEMBLY OFF THE BACKING PLATE.

3. REMOVE PARKING BRAKE CABLE FROM THE PARKING BRAKE.

4. REMOVE RETRACTING SPRINGS AND ADJUSTING LEVEL.

**8 inch brakes; removal**

*can be injurious to your health. Use a vacuum cleaner. Do not blow off the dust with air pressure.*

2. Apply a thin film of high temperature grease at the points on the backing plate where the brake shoes make contact.

3. Apply a thin film of multi-purpose grease to the threads of the adjuster screw and to the socket end of the adjuster. Turn the adjuster screw into the socket and then back off from bottom a number of threads.

4. Install the parking brake lever on the trailing shoe. Use a new horseshoe clip. Be sure to pull the spring washer in position. Connect the parking brake cable to the parking brake lever.

5. Attach the lower retracting spring between the two brake shoes and install the shoes on the backing plate. It will be necessary to spread the shoes apart to mount them on the anchor plate and wheel cylinder.

6. Install the adjuster screw assembly between the slot in the leading shoe and the slots in the trailing shoe and parking brake lever. Lengthen the screw if necessary. The adjuster socket blades are marked **L** for left side or **R** for right side and fit onto the trailing shoe and the parking brake lever (slots provided). The letter must face up toward the wheel cylinder when the blade is installed. This permits the deeper of the two slots to fit onto the parking brake lever.

7. Install the adjusting lever, also marked **L** or **R**, by sliding the groove over the parking brake lever pin slot and into a groove on the starwheel.

8. Attach the upper retracting spring to the leading shoe anchor hole. Use a pair of brake spring pliers, stretch the spring and attach the other end onto the adjuster lever notch.

NOTE: *If the adjuster lever does not contact the starwheel after installing the spring, make sure that the adjuster socket is installed correctly. (see Step 6).*

9. Install the holddown pins, spring and washers.

10. Adjust the brakes, using a brake adjusting tool as described in the brake adjustment section. Do not adjust with shoe drag on the drum. The wheel must turn freely.

11. Install the brake drum and adjust the wheel bearings.

12. Lower the car and road test.

## Rear Wheel Cylinder

### REMOVAL AND INSTALLATION

1. Remove the rear wheel, brake drum and brake shoes as described in the proceeding sections.

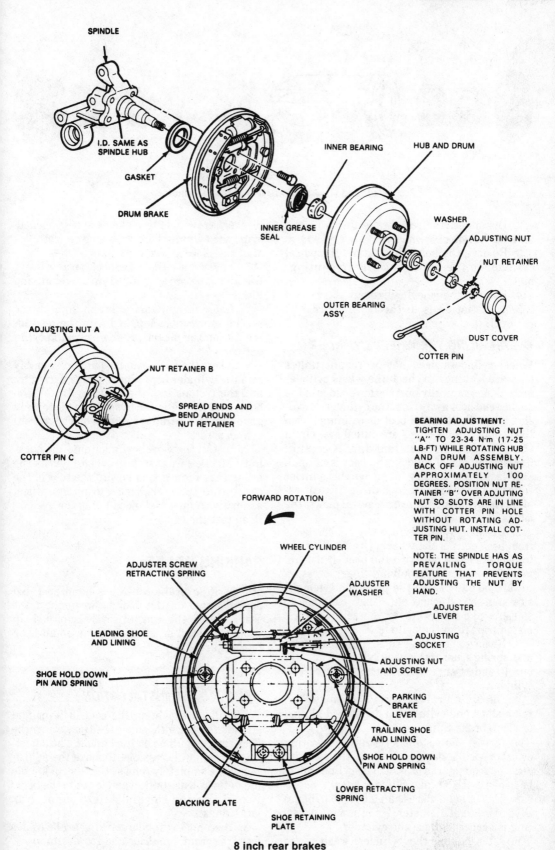

SPINDLE

I.D. SAME AS
SPINDLE HUB

GASKET

DRUM BRAKE

INNER GREASE
SEAL

INNER BEARING

HUB AND DRUM

WASHER

ADJUSTING NUT

NUT RETAINER

OUTER BEARING
ASSY

DUST COVER

COTTER PIN

ADJUSTING NUT A

NUT RETAINER B

SPREAD ENDS AND
BEND AROUND
NUT RETAINER

COTTER PIN C

**BEARING ADJUSTMENT:**
TIGHTEN ADJUSTING NUT
"A" TO 23-34 N·m (17-25
LB-FT) WHILE ROTATING HUB
AND DRUM ASSEMBLY.
BACK OFF ADJUSTING NUT
APPROXIMATELY 100
DEGREES. POSITION NUT RE-
TAINER "B" OVER ADJUTING
NUT SO SLOTS ARE IN LINE
WITH COTTER PIN HOLE
WITHOUT ROTATING AD-
JUSTING HUT. INSTALL COT-
TER PIN.

NOTE: THE SPINDLE HAS AS
PREVAILING TORQUE
FEATURE THAT PREVENTS
ADJUSTING THE NUT BY
HAND.

FORWARD ROTATION

WHEEL CYLINDER

ADJUSTER SCREW
RETRACTING SPRING

ADJUSTER
WASHER

ADJUSTER
LEVER

ADJUSTING
SOCKET

ADJUSTING NUT
AND SCREW

PARKING
BRAKE
LEVER

LEADING SHOE
AND LINING

SHOE HOLD DOWN
PIN AND SPRING

TRAILING SHOE
AND LINING

SHOE HOLD DOWN
PIN AND SPRING

LOWER RETRACTING
SPRING

BACKING PLATE

SHOE RETAINING
PLATE

**8 inch rear brakes**

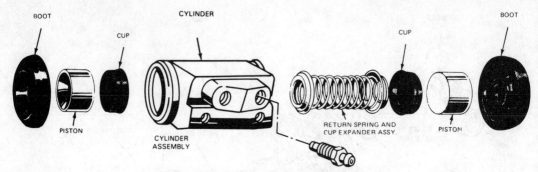

BOOT  CYLINDER  BOOT

CUP  CUP

PISTON  PISTON

CYLINDER
ASSEMBLY

RETURN SPRING AND
CUP EXPANDER ASSY.

**Exploded view of a rear wheel brake cylinder**

2. Disconnect the rear brake line from the back of the wheel cylinder.

3. Remove the bolts that attach the wheel cylinder to the brake backing (mounting) plate.

4. Remove the wheel cylinder.

5. Installation is in the reverse order of removal.

### OVERHAULING THE WHEEL CYLINDER

Wheel cylinders need not be rebuilt unless they are leaking. To check the wheel cylinder for leakage, carefully pull the lower edge of the rubber end boot away from the cylinder. Excessive brake fluid in the boot or running out of the boot, when the edges are pulled away from the cylinder, denotes leakage. A certain (slight) amount of fluid in the boot is normal.

1. It is not necessary to remove the cylinder from the brake backing (mounting) plate to rebuild the cylinder, however removal makes the job easier.

2. Disengage and remove the rubber boots from both ends of the wheel cylinder. The piston should come out with the boot. If not, remove the piston by applying finger pressure inward on one piston, the piston on the opposite end should come out. Take care not to splash brake fluid all over yourself when the piston pops from the cylinder.

3. Remove the rubber cups, center expander and spring from the wheel cylinder. Remove the bleeder screw from the back of the cylinder.

4. Discard all rubber boots and cups. Wash the pistons and cylinder in denatured alcohol or clean brake fluid.

5. Inspect the pistons for scratches, scoring or other visible damage. Inspect the cylinder bore for score marks or rust. The cylinder may be honed (with a brake cylinder hone) if necessary. Do not hone more than 0.003″ (0.076mm) beyond original diameter. If the scoring or pitting is deeper, replace the cylinder.

6. After honing the cylinder, wash again with alcohol or clean brake fluid. Check the bleeder screw hole to make sure it is opened. Wipe the cylinder bore with a clean cloth. Install the bleeder screw.

7. Never reuse the old rubber parts. Always use all of the parts supplied in the rebuilding kit.

8. Apply a light coat of brake fluid, or the special lubricant if supplied with the rebuilding kit, on the pistons, rubber cups and cylinder bore.

9. Insert the spring and expander assembly into the cylinder bore. Put the cups, facing in, and the pistons into the cylinder. Install the boots and fit the outer lips into the retaining grooves on the outer edges of the wheel cylinder.

10. Install the wheel cylinder onto the backing plate. Be sure that the inlet port (where the brake hose connects) is toward the rear of the car. Install the brake shoes, drum and wheel assembly. Adjust and bleed the brake system. Road test the car.

## PARKING BRAKE

The parking brake control is hand operated and mounted on the floor between the front seats. When the control lever is pulled up (from the floor) an attached cable applies the rear brakes.

### Cable

#### REMOVAL AND INSTALLATION

1. Pull up slowly on the control lever and stop at the seventh notch position, count the clicks as you pull up on the handle. The adjusting nut is now accessible. Remove the adjusting nut. Completely release the control handle (push the release button and lower to the floor.

2. Raise the car and safely support on jackstands.

3. Disconnect the rear parking brake cables from the front equalizer and rod assembly.

4. If the front equalizer and rod assembly is

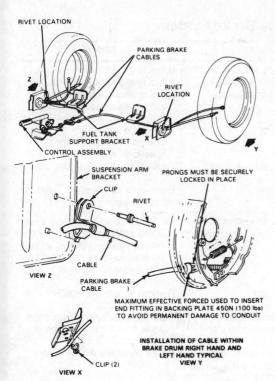

RIVET LOCATION

PARKING BRAKE CABLES

RIVET LOCATION

FUEL TANK SUPPORT BRACKET

CONTROL ASSEMBLY

VIEW Z

SUSPENSION ARM BRACKET

CLIP

RIVET

PRONGS MUST BE SECURELY LOCKED IN PLACE

CABLE

PARKING BRAKE CABLE

MAXIMUM EFFECTIVE FORCED USED TO INSERT END FITTING IN BACKING PLATE 450N (100 lbs) TO AVOID PERMANENT DAMAGE TO CONDUIT

INSTALLATION OF CABLE WITHIN BRAKE DRUM RIGHT HAND AND LEFT HAND TYPICAL VIEW Y

CLIP (2)

VIEW X

**Parking brake cable installation**

to be replaced, drill out the rivets that hold the cable guide to the floor pan. Remove the equalizer and rod assembly from the parking brake control lever and withdraw it through the floor pan.

5. To install the front equalizer and rod assembly, feed the adjusting rod end of the assembly through the floor pan and into the parking control lever clevis. Attach the cable guide to the floor pan using new pop rivets. Borrow a pop rivet gun from a friend.

6. If the rear parking brake cable is to be replaced, first disconnect from the front equalizer and rod assembly. Remove the hairpin clip that holds the cable to the floor pan tunnel bracket.

7. Remove the wire retainer that hold the cable to the fuel tank mounting bracket. Remove the cable from the retaining clip.

8. Remove the rear tire and wheel assemblies and the brake drums.

9. Disconnect the parking brake cable from the trailing shoe parking brake levers. Depress the cable prongs that hold the cable in the backing plate hole. Remove the cable through the holes.

10. Installation is in the reverse order of removal.

11. Adjust the parking brake cable as per instructions in the next section.

### CABLE ADJUSTMENT

1. If a new cable has been installed, the parking brake lever control should be in the seventh notch and the adjusting nut run down to the approximate position it was removed from. Release the hand brake and pump the brake pedal several times. If you car has power brakes, start the engine and allow it to idle when pumping the brakes. Shut off the engine.

2. Place the control lever in the twelfth notch, two notches before complete application. Tighten the adjusting nut until the rear brakes have a slight drag when the parking brake control lever is completely released. Repeat the parts of this step as necessary.

3. Loosen the adjusting nut until there is no rear brake drag when the control lever is completely released.

4. Lower the car and test the parking brake application.

## Brake Specifications
All Specifications in inches

| Years | Model | Brake Disc | | | Brake Drum | | Wheel Cyl. or Caliper Bore | |
| | | Original Thickness | Minimum Thickness | Maximum Run-out | Orig. Inside Dia. | Maximum Machine O/S | Front | Rear |
|---|---|---|---|---|---|---|---|---|
| '81–'87 | All w/7" rear brake | .945 | .882 | .002 | 7.090 | 7.149 | 2.362 | .811 |
| | w/8" rear brake | .945 | .882 | .002 | 8.000 | 8.060 | 2.362 | .811 ① |

① Tempo/Topaz: .875 in.

## Troubleshooting the Brake System

| Problem | Cause | Solution |
|---|---|---|
| Low brake pedal (excessive pedal travel required for braking action.) | • Excessive clearance between rear linings and drums caused by inoperative automatic adjusters | • Make 10 to 15 alternate forward and reverse brake stops to adjust brakes. If brake pedal does not come up, repair or replace adjuster parts as necessary. |
| | • Worn rear brakelining | • Inspect and replace lining if worn beyond minimum thickness specification |
| | • Bent, distorted brakeshoes, front or rear | • Replace brakeshoes in axle sets |
| | • Air in hydraulic system | • Remove air from system. Refer to Brake Bleeding. |
| Low brake pedal (pedal may go to floor with steady pressure applied.) | • Fluid leak in hydraulic system | • Fill master cylinder to fill line; have helper apply brakes and check calipers, wheel cylinders, differential valve tubes, hoses and fittings for leaks. Repair or replace as necessary. |
| | • Air in hydraulic system | • Remove air from system. Refer to Brake Bleeding. |
| | • Incorrect or non-recommended brake fluid (fluid evaporates at below normal temp). | • Flush hydraulic system with clean brake fluid. Refill with correct-type fluid. |
| | • Master cylinder piston seals worn, or master cylinder bore is scored, worn or corroded | • Repair or replace master cylinder |
| Low brake pedal (pedal goes to floor on first application—o.k. on subsequent applications.) | • Disc brake pads sticking on abutment surfaces of anchor plate. Caused by a build-up of dirt, rust, or corrosion on abutment surfaces | • Clean abutment surfaces |
| Fading brake pedal (pedal height decreases with steady pressure applied.) | • Fluid leak in hydraulic system | • Fill master cylinder reservoirs to fill mark, have helper apply brakes, check calipers, wheel cylinders, differential valve, tubes, hoses, and fittings for fluid leaks. Repair or replace parts as necessary. |
| | • Master cylinder piston seals worn, or master cylinder bore is scored, worn or corroded | • Repair or replace master cylinder |
| Decreasing brake pedal travel (pedal travel required for braking action decreases and may be accompanied by a hard pedal.) | • Caliper or wheel cylinder pistons sticking or seized | • Repair or replace the calipers, or wheel cylinders |
| | • Master cylinder compensator ports blocked (preventing fluid return to reservoirs) or pistons sticking or seized in master cylinder bore | • Repair or replace the master cylinder |
| | • Power brake unit binding internally | • Test unit according to the following procedure: (a) Shift transmission into neutral and start engine (b) Increase engine speed to 1500 rpm, close throttle and fully depress brake pedal (c) Slow release brake pedal and stop engine (d) Have helper remove vacuum check valve and hose from power unit. Observe for backward movement of brake pedal. (e) If the pedal moves backward, the power unit has an internal bind—replace power unit |

# CHILTON'S
# AUTO BODY
# REPAIR TIPS

**Tools and Materials • Step-by-Step Illustrated Procedures**
**How To Repair Dents, Scratches and Rust Holes**
**Spray Painting and Refinishing Tips**

With a little practice, basic body repair procedures can be mastered by any do-it-yourself mechanic. The step-by-step repairs shown here can be applied to almost any type of auto body repair.

# TOOLS & MATERIALS

You may already have basic tools, such as hammers and electric drills. Other tools unique to body repair — body hammers, grinding attachments, sanding blocks, dent puller, half-round plastic file and plastic spreaders — are relatively inexpensive and can be obtained wherever auto parts or auto body repair parts are sold. Portable air compressors and paint spray guns can be purchased or rented.

## Auto Body Repair Kits

The best and most often used products are available to the do-it-yourselfer in kit form, from major manufacturers of auto body repair products. The same manufacturers also merchandise the individual products for use by pros.

Kits are available to make a wide variety of repairs, including holes, dents and scratches and fiberglass, and offer the advantage of buying the materials you'll need for the job. There is little waste or chance of materials going bad from not being used. Many kits may also contain basic body-working tools such as body files, sanding blocks and spreaders. Check the contents of the kit before buying your tools.

# BODY REPAIR TIPS

## Safety

Many of the products associated with auto body repair and refinishing contain toxic chemicals. Read all labels before opening containers and store them in a safe place and manner.

• Wear eye protection (safety goggles) when using power tools or when performing any operation that involves

the removal of any type of material.

• Wear lung protection (disposable mask or respirator) when grinding, sanding or painting.

## Sanding

**1** Sand off paint before using a dent puller. When using a non-adhesive sanding disc, cover the back of the disc with an overlapping layer or two of masking tape and trim the edges. The disc will last considerably longer.

**2** Use the circular motion of the sanding disc to grind *into* the edge of the repair. Grinding or sanding away from the jagged edge will only tear the sandpaper.

**3** Use the palm of your hand flat on the panel to detect high and low spots. Do not use your fingertips. Slide your hand slowly back and forth.

# WORKING WITH BODY FILLER

## Mixing The Filler

**C** leanliness and proper mixing and application are extremely important. Use a clean piece of plastic or glass or a disposable artist's palette to mix body filler.

**1** Allow plenty of time and follow directions. No useful purpose will be served by adding more hardener to make it cure (set-up) faster. Less hardener means more curing time, but the mixture dries harder; more hardener means less curing time but a softer mixture.

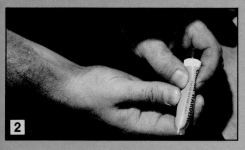

**2**

**2** Both the hardener and the filler should be thoroughly kneaded or stirred before mixing. Hardener should be a solid paste and dispense like thin toothpaste. Body filler should be smooth, and free of lumps or thick spots.

Getting the proper amount of hardener in the filler is the trickiest part of preparing the filler. Use the same amount of hardener in cold or warm weather. For contour filler (thick coats), a bead of hardener twice the diameter of the filler is about right. There's about a 15% margin on either side, but, if in doubt use less hardener.

**2**

**2**

**3** Mix the body filler and hardener by wiping across the mixing surface, picking the mixture up and wiping it again. Colder weather requires longer mixing times. Do not mix in a circular motion; this will trap air bubbles which will become holes in the cured filler.

**3**

## Applying The Filler

**1** For best results, filler should not be applied over ¼″ thick.

Apply the filler in several coats. Build it up to above the level of the repair surface so that it can be sanded or grated down.

The first coat of filler must be pressed on with a firm wiping motion.

Apply the filler in one direction only. Working the filler back and forth will either pull it off the metal or trap air bubbles.

# REPAIRING DENTS

**B** efore you start, take a few minutes to study the damaged area. Try to visualize the shape of the panel before it was damaged. If the damage is on the left fender, look at the right fender and use it as a guide. If there is access to the panel from behind, you can reshape it with a body hammer. If not, you'll have to use a dent puller. Go slowly and work the metal a little at a time. Get the panel as straight as possible before applying filler.

**1** This dent is typical of one that can be pulled out or hammered out from behind. Remove the headlight cover, headlight assembly and turn signal housing.

**2** Drill a series of holes 1/2 the size of the end of the dent puller along the stress line. Make some trial pulls and assess the results. If necessary, drill more holes and try again. Do not hurry.

**3** If possible, use a body hammer and block to shape the metal back to its original contours. Get the metal back as close to its original shape as possible. Don't depend on body filler to fill dents.

**4** Using an 80-grit grinding disc on an electric drill, grind the paint from the surrounding area down to bare metal. Use a new grinding pad to prevent heat buildup that will warp metal.

**5** The area should look like this when you're finished grinding. Knock the drill holes in and tape over small openings to keep plastic filler out.

**6** Mix the body filler (see Body Repair Tips). Spread the body filler evenly over the entire area (see Body Repair Tips). Be sure to cover the area completely.

**7** Let the body filler dry until the surface can just be scratched with your fingernail. Knock the high spots from the body filler with a body file ("Cheesegrater"). Check frequently with the palm of your hand for high and low spots.

**8** Check to be sure that trim pieces that will be installed later will fit exactly. Sand the area with 40-grit paper.

**9** If you wind up with low spots, you may have to apply another layer of filler.

**10** Knock the high spots off with 40-grit paper. When you are satisfied with the contours of the repair, apply a thin coat of filler to cover pin holes and scratches.

**11** Block sand the area with 40-grit paper to a smooth finish. Pay particular attention to body lines and ridges that must be well-defined.

**12** Sand the area with 400 paper and then finish with a scuff pad. The finished repair is ready for priming and painting (see Painting Tips).

Materials and photos courtesy of Ritt Jones Auto Body, Prospect Park, PA.

# REPAIRING RUST HOLES

There are many ways to repair rust holes. The fiberglass cloth kit shown here is one of the most cost efficient for the owner because it provides a strong repair that resists cracking and moisture and is relatively easy to use. It can be used on large and small holes (with or without backing) and can be applied over contoured areas. Remember, however, that short of replacing an entire panel, no repair is a guarantee that the rust will not return.

**1** Remove any trim that will be in the way. Clean away all loose debris. Cut away all the rusted metal. But be sure to leave enough metal to retain the contour or body shape.

**2** Grind away all traces of rust with a 24-grit grinding disc. Be sure to grind back 3-4 inches from the edge of the hole down to bare metal and be sure all traces of paint, primer and rust are removed.

**3** Block sand the area with 80 or 100 grit sandpaper to get a clear, shiny surface and feathered paint edge. Tap the edges of the hole inward with a ball peen hammer.

**4** If you are going to use release film, cut a piece about 2-3″ larger than the area you have sanded. Place the film over the repair and mark the sanded area on the film. Avoid any unnecessary wrinkling of the film.

**5** Cut 2 pieces of fiberglass matte to match the shape of the repair. One piece should be about 1″ smaller than the sanded area and the second piece should be 1″ smaller than the first. Mix enough filler and hardener to saturate the fiberglass material (see Body Repair Tips).

**6** Lay the release sheet on a flat surface and spread an even layer of filler, large enough to cover the repair. Lay the smaller piece of fiberglass cloth in the center of the sheet and spread another layer of filler over the fiberglass cloth. Repeat the operation for the larger piece of cloth.

**7** Place the repair material over the repair area, with the release film facing outward. Use a spreader and work from the center outward to smooth the material, following the body contours. Be sure to remove all air bubbles.

**8** Wait until the repair has dried tack-free and peel off the release sheet. The ideal working temperature is 60°-90° F. Cooler or warmer temperatures or high humidity may require additional curing time. Wait longer, if in doubt.

**9** Sand and feather-edge the entire area. The initial sanding can be done with a sanding disc on an electric drill if care is used. Finish the sanding with a block sander. Low spots can be filled with body filler; this may require several applications.

**10** When the filler can just be scratched with a fingernail, knock the high spots down with a body file and smooth the entire area with 80-grit. Feather the filled areas into the surrounding areas.

**11** When the area is sanded smooth, mix some topcoat and hardener and apply it directly with a spreader. This will give a smooth finish and prevent the glass matte from showing through the paint.

**12** Block sand the topcoat smooth with finishing sandpaper (200 grit), and 400 grit. The repair is ready for masking, priming and painting (see Painting Tips).

Materials and photos courtesy Marson Corporation, Chelsea, Massachusetts

# PAINTING TIPS

## Preparation

**1** SANDING — Use a 400 or 600 grit wet or dry sandpaper. Wet-sand the area with a 1/4 sheet of sandpaper soaked in clean water. Keep the paper wet while sanding. Sand the area until the repaired area tapers into the original finish.

**2** CLEANING — Wash the area to be painted thoroughly with water and a clean rag. Rinse it thoroughly and wipe the surface dry until you're sure it's completely free of dirt, dust, fingerprints, wax, detergent or other foreign matter.

**3** MASKING — Protect any areas you don't want to overspray by covering them with masking tape and newspaper. Be careful not get fingerprints on the area to be painted.

**4** PRIMING — All exposed metal should be primed before painting. Primer protects the metal and provides an excellent surface for paint adhesion. When the primer is dry, wet-sand the area again with 600 grit wet-sandpaper. Clean the area again after sanding.

## Painting Techniques

**P**aint applied from either a spray gun or a spray can (for small areas) will provide good results. Experiment on an old piece of metal to get the right combination before you begin painting.

**SPRAYING VISCOSITY (SPRAY GUN ONLY)** — Paint should be thinned to spraying viscosity according to the directions on the can. Use only the recommended thinner or reducer and the same amount of reduction regardless of temperature.

**AIR PRESSURE (SPRAY GUN ONLY)** — This is extremely important. Be sure you are using the proper recommended pressure.

**TEMPERATURE** — The surface to be painted should be approximately the same temperature as the surrounding air. Applying warm paint to a cold surface, or vice versa, will completely upset the paint characteristics.

**THICKNESS** — Spray with smooth strokes. In general, the thicker the coat of paint, the longer the drying time. Apply several thin coats about 30 seconds apart. The paint should remain wet long enough to flow out and no longer; heavier coats will only produce sags or wrinkles. Spray a light (fog) coat, followed by heavier color coats.

**DISTANCE** — The ideal spraying distance is 8"-12" from the gun or can to the surface. Shorter distances will produce ripples, while greater distances will result in orange peel, dry film and poor color match and loss of material due to overspray.

**OVERLAPPING** — The gun or can should be kept at right angles to the surface at all times. Work to a wet edge at an even speed, using a 50% overlap and direct the center of the spray at the lower or nearest edge of the previous stroke.

**RUBBING OUT (BLENDING) FRESH PAINT** — Let the paint dry thoroughly. Runs or imperfections can be sanded out, primed and repainted.

Don't be in too big a hurry to remove the masking. This only produces paint ridges. When the finish has dried for at least a week, apply a small amount of fine grade rubbing compound with a clean, wet cloth. Use lots of water and blend the new paint with the surrounding area.

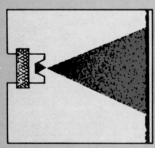

**WRONG**

*Thin coat. Stroke too fast, not enough overlap, gun too far away.*

**CORRECT**

*Medium coat. Proper distance, good stroke, proper overlap.*

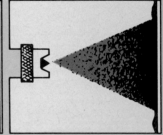

**WRONG**

*Heavy coat. Stroke too slow, too much overlap, gun too close.*

## Troubleshooting the Brake System (cont.)

| Problem | Cause | Solution |
|---|---|---|
| Spongy brake pedal (pedal has abnormally soft, springy, spongy feel when depressed.) | • Air in hydraulic system<br><br>• Brakeshoes bent or distorted<br>• Brakelining not yet seated with drums and rotors<br>• Rear drum brakes not properly adjusted | • Remove air from system. Refer to Brake Bleeding.<br>• Replace brakeshoes<br>• Burnish brakes<br><br>• Adjust brakes |
| Hard brake pedal (excessive pedal pressure required to stop vehicle. May be accompanied by brake fade.) | • Loose or leaking power brake unit vacuum hose<br>• Incorrect or poor quality brakelining<br>• Bent, broken, distorted brakeshoes<br>• Calipers binding or dragging on mounting pins. Rear brakeshoes dragging on support plate.<br><br><br><br><br><br><br><br>• Caliper, wheel cylinder, or master cylinder pistons sticking or seized<br>• Power brake unit vacuum check valve malfunction<br><br><br><br><br><br><br><br><br><br><br>• Power brake unit has internal bind<br><br><br><br><br><br><br><br><br><br><br><br><br><br><br><br>• Master cylinder compensator ports (at bottom of reservoirs) blocked by dirt, scale, rust, or have small burrs (blocked ports prevent fluid return to reservoirs).<br>• Brake hoses, tubes, fittings clogged or restricted<br><br>• Brake fluid contaminated with improper fluids (motor oil, transmission fluid, causing rubber components to swell and stick in bores<br>• Low engine vacuum | • Tighten connections or replace leaking hose<br>• Replace with lining in axle sets<br><br>• Replace brakeshoes<br>• Replace mounting pins and bushings. Clean rust or burrs from rear brake support plate ledges and lubricate ledges with molydisulfide grease.<br>**NOTE:** If ledges are deeply grooved or scored, do not attempt to sand or grind them smooth—replace support plate.<br>• Repair or replace parts as necessary<br><br>• Test valve according to the following procedure:<br>(a) Start engine, increase engine speed to 1500 rpm, close throttle and immediately stop engine<br>(b) Wait at least 90 seconds then depress brake pedal<br>(c) If brakes are not vacuum assisted for 2 or more applications, check valve is faulty<br>• Test unit according to the following procedure:<br>(a) With engine stopped, apply brakes several times to exhaust all vacuum in system<br>(b) Shift transmission into neutral, depress brake pedal and start engine<br>(c) If pedal height decreases with foot pressure and less pressure is required to hold pedal in applied position, power unit vacuum system is operating normally. Test power unit. If power unit exhibits a bind condition, replace the power unit.<br>• Repair or replace master cylinder<br>**CAUTION:** Do not attempt to clean blocked ports with wire, pencils, or similar implements. Use compressed air only.<br>• Use compressed air to check or unclog parts. Replace any damaged parts.<br>• Replace all rubber components, combination valve and hoses. Flush entire brake system with DOT 3 brake fluid or equivalent.<br><br>• Adjust or repair engine |

## Troubleshooting the Brake System (cont.)

| Problem | Cause | Solution |
|---|---|---|
| Grabbing brakes (severe reaction to brake pedal pressure.) | • Brakelining(s) contaminated by grease or brake fluid | • Determine and correct cause of contamination and replace brakeshoes in axle sets |
| | • Parking brake cables incorrectly adjusted or seized | • Adjust cables. Replace seized cables. |
| | • Incorrect brakelining or lining loose on brakeshoes | • Replace brakeshoes in axle sets |
| | • Caliper anchor plate bolts loose | • Tighten bolts |
| | • Rear brakeshoes binding on support plate ledges | • Clean and lubricate ledges. Replace support plate(s) if ledges are deeply grooved. Do not attempt to smooth ledges by grinding. |
| | • Incorrect or missing power brake reaction disc | • Install correct disc |
| | • Rear brake support plates loose | • Tighten mounting bolts |
| Dragging brakes (slow or incomplete release of brakes) | • Brake pedal binding at pivot | • Loosen and lubricate |
| | • Power brake unit has internal bind | • Inspect for internal bind. Replace unit if internal bind exists. |
| | • Parking brake cables incorrrectly adjusted or seized | • Adjust cables. Replace seized cables. |
| | • Rear brakeshoe return springs weak or broken | • Replace return springs. Replace brakeshoe if necessary in axle sets. |
| | • Automatic adjusters malfunctioning | • Repair or replace adjuster parts as required |
| | • Caliper, wheel cylinder or master cylinder pistons sticking or seized | • Repair or replace parts as necessary |
| | • Master cylinder compensating ports blocked (fluid does not return to reservoirs). | • Use compressed air to clear ports. Do not use wire, pencils, or similar objects to open blocked ports. |
| Vehicle moves to one side when brakes are applied | • Incorrect front tire pressure | • Inflate to recommended cold (reduced load) inflation pressure |
| | • Worn or damaged wheel bearings | • Replace worn or damaged bearings |
| | • Brakelining on one side contaminated | • Determine and correct cause of contamination and replace brakelining in axle sets |
| | • Brakeshoes on one side bent, distorted, or lining loose on shoe | • Replace brakeshoes in axle sets |
| | • Support plate bent or loose on one side | • Tighten or replace support plate |
| | • Brakelining not yet seated with drums or rotors | • Burnish brakelining |
| | • Caliper anchor plate loose on one side | • Tighten anchor plate bolts |
| | • Caliper piston sticking or seized | • Repair or replace caliper |
| | • Brakelinings water soaked | • Drive vehicle with brakes lightly applied to dry linings |
| | • Loose suspension component attaching or mounting bolts | • Tighten suspension bolts. Replace worn suspension components. |
| | • Brake combination valve failure | • Replace combination valve |
| Chatter or shudder when brakes are applied (pedal pulsation and roughness may also occur.) | • Brakeshoes distorted, bent, contaminated, or worn | • Replace brakeshoes in axle sets |
| | • Caliper anchor plate or support plate loose | • Tighten mounting bolts |
| | • Excessive thickness variation of rotor(s) | • Refinish or replace rotors in axle sets |
| Noisy brakes (squealing, clicking, scraping sound when brakes are applied.) | • Bent, broken, distorted brakeshoes | • Replace brakeshoes in axle sets |
| | • Excessive rust on outer edge of rotor braking surface | • Remove rust |

## Troubleshooting the Brake System (cont.)

| Problem | Cause | Solution |
|---|---|---|
| Noisy brakes (squealing, clicking, scraping sound when brakes are applied.) (cont.) | • Brakelining worn out—shoes contacting drum of rotor | • Replace brakeshoes and lining in axle sets. Refinish or replace drums or rotors. |
| | • Broken or loose holdown or return springs | • Replace parts as necessary |
| | • Rough or dry drum brake support plate ledges | • Lubricate support plate ledges |
| | • Cracked, grooved, or scored rotor(s) or drum(s) | • Replace rotor(s) or drum(s). Replace brakeshoes and lining in axle sets if necessary. |
| | • Incorrect brakelining and/or shoes (front or rear). | • Install specified shoe and lining assemblies |
| Pulsating brake pedal | • Out of round drums or excessive lateral runout in disc brake rotor(s) | • Refinish or replace drums, re-index rotors or replace |

# Body and Trim

# 9

## EXTERIOR

## Doors

### REMOVAL

1. Remove the trim panel, watershield, and all usable outside mouldings and clips (if the door is to be replaced).
2. Remove all usable window and door latch components from the door (if the door is to be replaced).
3. Support the door.
4. Remove the door hinge attaching bolts from the door and remove the door.

### INSTALLATION

1. Drill holes, as necessary, for attaching outside moulding.
2. Position the door hinges and partially tighten the bolts.
3. Install the latch mechanism, window mechanism, glass and glass weatherstripping. Adjust the window mechanism.
4. Install the exterior trim, watershield, and the interior trim.

### ADJUSTMENTS

#### Door Alignment

The door hinges provide sufficient adjustment to correct most door misalignment conditions.

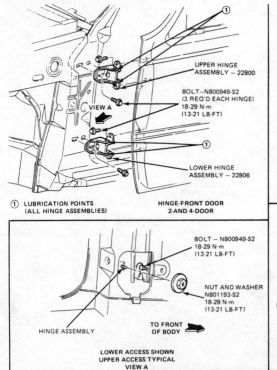

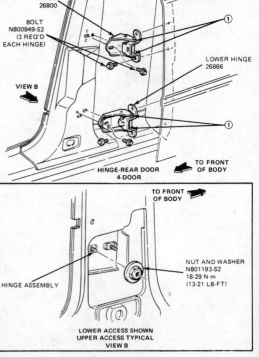

**Door hinge assembly—Tempo/Topaz**

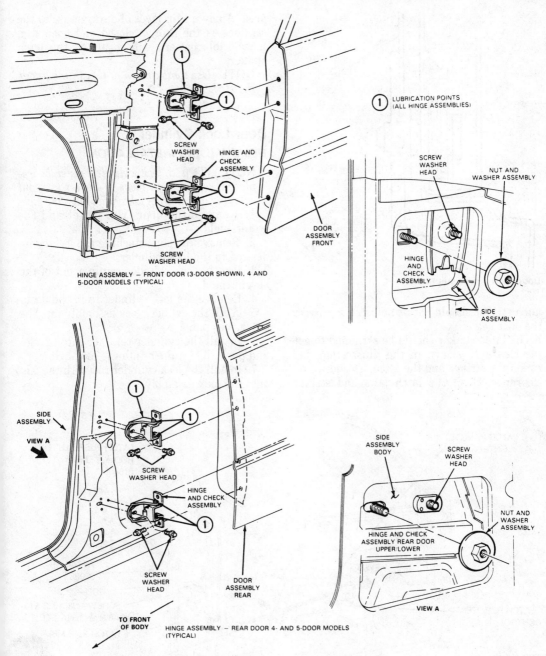

LUBRICATION POINTS
(ALL HINGE ASSEMBLIES)

SCREW
WASHER
HEAD

HINGE AND
CHECK
ASSEMBLY

SCREW
WASHER HEAD

DOOR
ASSEMBLY
FRONT

HINGE ASSEMBLY — FRONT DOOR (3-DOOR SHOWN), 4 AND
5-DOOR MODELS (TYPICAL)

SCREW
WASHER
HEAD

NUT AND
WASHER ASSEMBLY

HINGE
AND
CHECK
ASSEMBLY

SIDE
ASSEMBLY

SIDE
ASSEMBLY

VIEW A

SCREW
WASHER HEAD

HINGE
AND CHECK
ASSEMBLY

SCREW
WASHER
HEAD

DOOR
ASSEMBLY
REAR

TO FRONT
OF BODY

HINGE ASSEMBLY — REAR DOOR 4- AND 5-DOOR MODELS
(TYPICAL)

SIDE
ASSEMBLY
BODY

SCREW
WASHER
HEAD

NUT AND
WASHER
ASSEMBLY

HINGE AND CHECK
ASSEMBLY REAR DOOR
UPPER/LOWER

VIEW A

**Door hinge assembly—Escort/Lynx, EXP/LN7**

The holes of the hinge and/or the hinge attaching points are enlarged or elongated to provide for hinge and door alignment.

NOTE: *DO NOT cover up a poor alignment with a latch striker adjustment.*

### SIDE DOOR ADJUSTMENT

1. Refer to the illustration to determine which hinge screws must be loosened to move the door in the desired direction.

2. Loosen the hinge screws just enough to permit movement of the door with a padded pry bar.

3. Move the door the distance estimated to be necessary for a correct fit. Tighten the hinge bolts and check the door fit to be sure there is no bind or interference with the adjacent panel.

### DOOR LATCH STRIKER ADJUSTMENT

The door latch striker pin can be adjusted laterally and vertically as well as for and aft. The

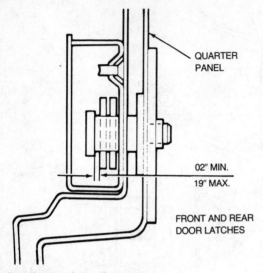

QUARTER
PANEL

02" MIN.
19" MAX.

FRONT AND REAR
DOOR LATCHES

**Door latch striker adjustment**

latch striker should not be adjusted to correct the door sag.

The latch striker should be shimmed to get the clearance shown in the illustration, between the striker and the latch. To check this clearance, clean the latch jaws and striker

area. Apply a thin layer of dark grease to the striker. As the door is closed and opened, a measurable pattern will result on the latch striker.

NOTE: *Use a maximum of two shims under the striker.*

## Door Lock Cylinder

### REMOVAL AND INSTALLATION

NOTE: *When a lock cylinder must be replaced, replace both locks in the set to avoid carrying an extra key which fits only one lock.*

1. Remove the door trim panel and the watershield.

2. Remove the clip attaching the lock cylinder rod to the lock cylinder.

3. Pry the lock cylinder retainer out of the slot in the door.

4. Remove the lock cylinder from the door.

5. Work the cylinder lock assembly into the outer door panel.

6. Install the cylinder retainer into its slot and push the retainer onto the lock cylinder.

7. Install the lock cylinder rod with the clip onto the lock assembly.

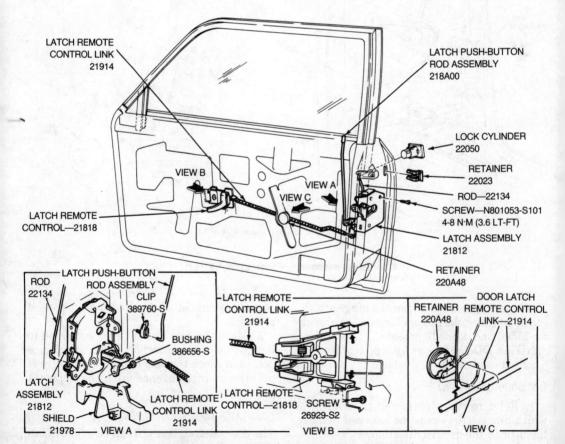

LATCH REMOTE
CONTROL LINK
21914

LATCH PUSH-BUTTON
ROD ASSEMBLY
218A00

LOCK CYLINDER
22050

RETAINER
22023

ROD—22134

SCREW—N801053-S101
4-8 N·M (3.6 LT-FT)

LATCH ASSEMBLY
21812

RETAINER
220A48

VIEW B

VIEW A

VIEW C

LATCH REMOTE
CONTROL—21818

ROD
22134

LATCH PUSH-BUTTON
ROD ASSEMBLY
CLIP
389760-S

BUSHING
386656-S

LATCH
ASSEMBLY
21812

SHIELD
21978 — VIEW A

LATCH REMOTE
CONTROL LINK
21914

LATCH REMOTE
CONTROL LINK
21914

LATCH REMOTE
CONTROL—21818

SCREW
26929-S2

VIEW B

DOOR LATCH
RETAINER    REMOTE CONTROL
220A48      LINK—21914

VIEW C

**Door latch and lock mechanism—Escort/Lynx, EXP/LN7**

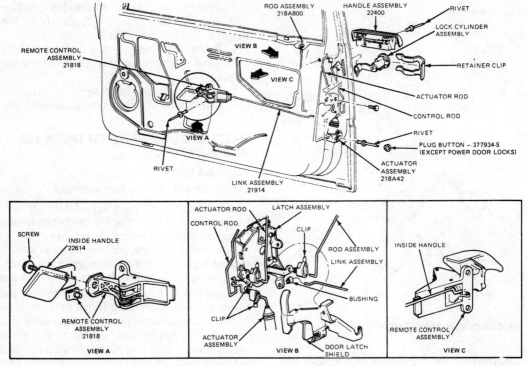

**Door latch and lock mechanism—Tempo/Topaz**

8. Lock and unlock the door to check the lock cylinder operation.

9. Install the watershield and door trim panel.

## Hood

### REMOVAL AND INSTALLATION

1. Open the hood and prop in the open position.

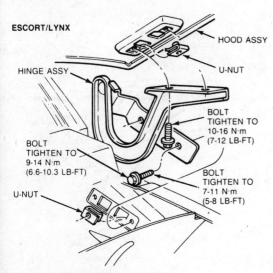

**Hood hinge assembly—Escort/Lynx**

2. Cover the cowl area to prevent damage to the paint.

3. With the aid of a helper to hold the hood, remove the hinge bolts to the hood and remove the hood from the vehicle.

4. Installation is the reverse of removal. Torque the hinge-to-hood bolts to 12–19 ft. lbs. Close the hood, check the alignment and adjust as necessary.

### ALIGNMENT

The hood can be adjusted for and aft and side to side by loosening the hood-to-hinge attaching bolts and reposition the hood. To raise or lower the hood, loosen the hinge hood on body attaching bolts and raise or lower the hinge as necessary.

The hood lock can be moved from side-to-side and up and down and laterally to obtain a snug hood fit by loosening the lock attaching screws and moving as necessary.

## Hatchback, Liftgate or Trunk Lid

### REMOVAL AND INSTALLATION

#### Hatchback

1. Open the hatchback assembly.

2. Remove the weatherstripping along the top of the hatchback opening and remove the headlining covering attaching screw.

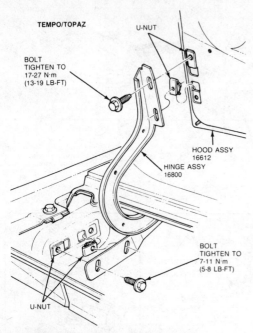

**Hood hinge assembly—Tempo/Topaz**

3. Support the hatchback in an open position and remove the support cylinder from the hatchback.

4. Remove the hinge to roof frame attaching screw and washer assembly, then remove the hatchback.

5. Installation is the reverse of removal. Check and perform alignment as necessary.

**Liftgate**

1. Open the liftgate assembly.

2. Remove the weatherstripping along the top of the liftgate opening and remove the headlining covering attaching screw.

3. Support the liftgate in an open position and remove the support cylinder from the liftgate.

4. Remove the hinge to roof frame attaching screw and washer assembly, then remove the liftgate.

5. Installation is the reverse of removal. Check and perform alignment as necessary.

## HATCHBACK, LIFTGATE OR TRUNK LID ALIGNMENT

### Hatchback Hinge

*Escort/Lynx, EXP/LN-7 – 3-Door Hatchback*

The hatchback can be adjusted fore and aft, and side to side by loosening the hinge to roof frame attaching screw at each hinge.

To adjust the hinge, pull down on the weatherstrip across the entire top edge of the hatchback opening. Carefully loosen and pull down the headlining to expose the access holes to the hinge screws. Adjust the hinge as necessary. Seal the hinge after adjustment with clear silicone sealer. Apply trim cement to the sheet metal flange, and install the headlining and smooth out any wrinkles. Install the weatherstrip.

The hatchback can be adjusted in and out by shimming the hinge at the header roof frame.

The hatchback should be adjusted for an even and parallel fit with the hatchback opening and shrouding panels.

### Liftgate hinge

*ESCORT/LYNX – 4-DOOR LIFTGATE*

On the 4-door liftgate models the liftgate can be adjusted up and down and side to side by loosening the header roof frame attaching

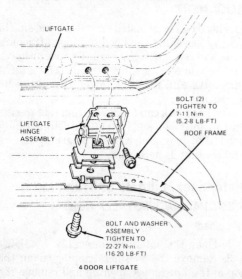

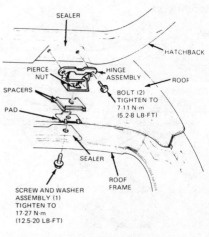

**Hatchback and liftgate hinge assembly—Escort/Lynx, EXP/LN7**

screw and washer assembly. The liftgate can be adjusted in and out by shimmering the hinges at the header roof frame.

The liftgate should be adjusted for an even parallel fit with the liftgate opening and surrounding panels.

To adjust a hinge, or hinges, remove the weatherstrip and pull down the headliner to gain access to the hinge attachment(s). Adjust the hinge(s) as necessary. Seal the hinge after adjustment with clear silicone sealer. Apply trim cement to the sheet metal flange, and install the headlining and smooth out any wrinkles. Install the weatherstrip.

### Trunk Lid

*Tempo/Topaz*

The trunk lid can be shifted fore and aft on all models and from side to side. The up and down adjustment is made by loosening the hinge to door attaching screws and raising or lowering the door.

The trunk lid should be adjusted for an even and parallel fit with the lid opening. The door should also be adjusted up and down for a flush fit with the surrounding panels. Care should be taken not to distort or mar the trunk lid or surrounding body panels.

## Windshield and Rear Window Glass
### REMOVAL AND INSTALLATION

The Ford FWD models use a Butyl/Urethane type sealed windshield and rear window which requires the use of special tools for removal and installation. It is advised that if the windshield needs replacement the vehicle be taken to a professional glass shop.

## INTERIOR

## Front Door Panels
### REMOVAL AND INSTALLATION

**Escort/Lynx, EXP/LN-7**

1. Remove the window regulator handle retaining screw and handle.
2. Remove the door handle pull cup.
3. Remove the retaining screws from the armrest assembly. Remove the armrest. On vehicles with power door locks, disconnect the wiring connector.
4. Remove the trim panel retaining screws from the bottom of the map compartment, if so equipped.
5. Remove the retaining set screw from the remote control mirror bezel, if so equipped.
6. With a push pin tool, putty knife or similar flat tool, pry the trim panel retaining push pins from the door interior panel.

NOTE: *Do not use the trim panel to pull the push pins from the door inner panel holes.*

7. If the trim panel is to be replaced, transfer the trim panel retaining push pins to the new panel assembly. Replace any bent, broken or missing push pins.

NOTE: *If the watershield has been removed, be sure to position it correctly before installing the trim panel.*

8. Be sure that the armrest retaining clips are properly positioned on the door inner panel. If they have been dislodged, they must be installed before installing the watershield.

9. Position the trim panel to the door inner panel. Route the remote control outside mirror cable through the bezel, if so equipped.

10. Position the trim panel to the door inner panel and locate the push pins in the countersunk holes. Firmly push the trim panel at the push pin locations to set each push pin.

11. Install the set screw from the remote control outside mirror bezel, if so equipped.

12. Install the trim panel retaining screws at the bottom of the map pocket, if so equipped.

13. On vehicles with power door locks, connect the wiring connector. Position the armrest to the trim panel and install the retaining screws.

14. Install the door handle pull cup.

15. Install the window regulator handle.

**Tempo/Topaz**

1. Remove the window regulator handle retaining screw and remove the handle.

2. Remove the retaining screw from the armrest recess and around the edge of the door panel.

3. Remove the retaining set screw from the remote control mirror bezel. Remove the bezel, if so equipped.

4. Remove the door handle pull cap, if so equipped.

5. With a push pin tool, putty knife or similar flat tool, pry the trim panel retaining push pins from the door interior panel.

NOTE: *Do not use the trim panel to pull the push pins from the door inner panel holes.*

6. If the trim panel is to be replaced, transfer the trim panel retaining push pins to the new panel assembly. Replace any bent, broken or missing push pins.

NOTE: *If the watershield has been removed, be sure to position it correctly before installing the trim panel.*

7. Be sure that the armrest retaining clips are properly positioned on the door inner panel. If they have been dislodged, they must be installed before installing the watershield.

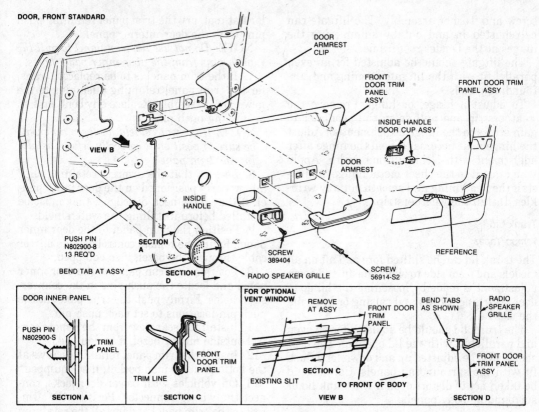

DOOR, FRONT STANDARD

Escort/Lynx door panel removal—typical

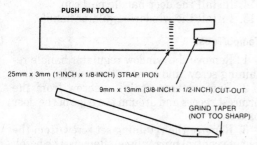

Push pin removal tool construction

8. Position the trim panel to the door inner panel. Route the remote control outside mirror cable through the bezel, if so eqiuipped.

9. Position the trim panel to the door inner panel and locate the push pins in the counter-sunk holes. Firmly push the trim panel at the push pin locations to set each push pin.

10. Install the set screw from the remote control outside mirror bezel, if so equipped.

11. Install the trim panel retaining screws.

12. Install the door handle pull cup.

13. Install the window regulator handle.

## Door Glass

### REMOVAL

1. Remove the door trim panel and watershield.

2. Remove the 2 rivets attaching the glass to the run and bracket assembly.

NOTE: *Prior to the removing center pins from the rivet, it is recommended that a suitable block support be inserted between the door outer panel and the glass bracket to stabilize the glass during the rivet removal. Remove the center pin from each rivet with a drift punch. Then, using a ¼" diameter drill carefully drill out the remainder of each rivet as damage to the plastic glass retainer and spacer could result.*

3. Remove the glass.

4. Remove the drillings and pins from the bottom of the door.

### INSTALLATION

1. Snap the plastic retainer and spacer into the two glass retainer holes. Make certain that the metal washer in the retainer assembly is on the outboard side of the glass.

2. Insert the glass into the door.

3. Position the door glass to the door glass bracket and align the glass and glass bracket retaining holes

4. Install the retaining rivets.

5. Raise the glass to the full UP position.

6. Install the rear glass run retainer and rear glass run.

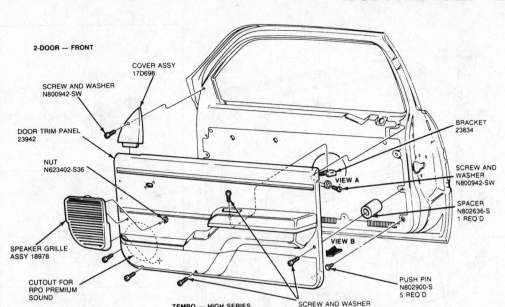

2-DOOR — FRONT

COVER ASSY
17D698

SCREW AND WASHER
N800942-SW

DOOR TRIM PANEL
23942

NUT
N623402-S36

SPEAKER GRILLE
ASSY 18978

CUTOUT FOR
RPO PREMIUM
SOUND

BRACKET
23834

SCREW AND
WASHER
N800942-SW

VIEW A

SPACER
N802636-S
1 REQ'D

VIEW B

PUSH PIN
N802900-S
5 REQ'D

TEMPO — HIGH SERIES
TOPAZ — LOW AND HIGH SERIES

SCREW AND WASHER
ASSY N800943-SW

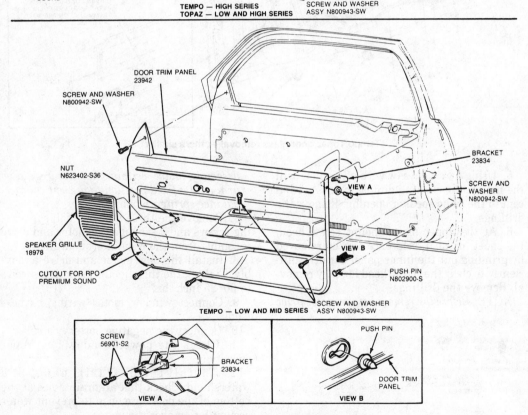

DOOR TRIM PANEL
23942

SCREW AND WASHER
N800942-SW

NUT
N623402-S36

SPEAKER GRILLE
18978

CUTOUT FOR RPO
PREMIUM SOUND

BRACKET
23834

SCREW AND
WASHER
N800942-SW

VIEW A

VIEW B

PUSH PIN
N802900-S

TEMPO — LOW AND MID SERIES

SCREW AND WASHER
ASSY N800943-SW

SCREW
56901-S2

BRACKET
23834

VIEW A

PUSH PIN

DOOR TRIM
PANEL

VIEW B

**Tempo/Topaz door panel removal—typical**

7. Check the operation of the window.
8. Install the trim panel and watershield.

## Electric Window Motor
### *REMOVAL AND INSTALLATION*
#### Front — 4-Door

1. Raise the window to the full up position, if possible. If the glass cannot be raised and is partially down or in the full down position, it must be supported so that it will not fall into the door well during motor removal.

2. Disconnect the negative battery cable.

3. Remove the door trim panel and watershield.

4. Disconnect the electric window motor wire from the wire harness connector and move the motor away from the area to be drilled.

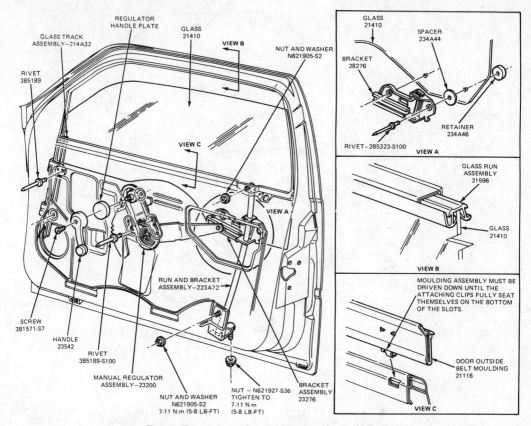

**Tempo/Topaz door glass removal—others similar**

5. Using a ¾" hole saw with a ¼" pilot, drill the hole at the existing dimple (point A) adjacent to the radio speaker opening. Remove the drillings.

6. At the upper motor mount screw head, the sheet metal interference can be removed by grinding out the inner panel surface sufficiently to clear the screw head for easy removal. Remove the drillings.

NOTE: *Before the removal of the motor drive assembly, make certain that the regulator arm is in a fixed position to prevent counterbalance spring unwind.*

7. Remove the three window motor mounting screws and disengage the motor and drive assembly from the regulator quadrant gear.

8. Install the new motor and drive assembly. Tighten the three motor mounting screws to 50–85 inch lbs.

9. Connect window motor wiring harness leads.

10. Connect the negative battery cable.

11. Check the power window for proper operation.

12. Install the door trim panel and watershield. Check that all drain holes at the bottom of the doors are open to prevent water accumulation over the motor.

**Rear — 4-Door**

1. Raise the window to the full up position, if possible. If the glass cannot be raised and is partially down or in the full down position, it must be supported so that it will not fall into the door well during motor removal.

2. Disconnect the negative battery cable.

3. Remove the door trim panel and watershield.

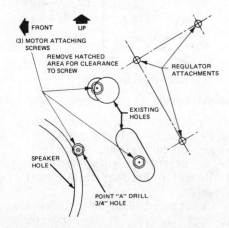

**Front door window motor template—4-door**

4. Disconnect the electric window motor wire from the wire harness connector and move the motor away from the area to be drilled.

5. Using a ¾" hole saw with a ¼" pilot, drill three holes in the door inner panel at the three existing dimples to gain access to the three motor and drive attaching screws. Remove the drillings.

NOTE: *Before the removal of the motor drive assembly, make certain that the regulator arm is in a fixed position to prevent counterbalance spring unwind.*

7. Remove the three window motor mounting screws and disengage the motor and drive assembly from the regulator quadrant gear.

8. Install the new motor and drive assembly. Tighten the three motor mounting screws to 50–85 inch lbs.

9. Connect window motor wiring harness leads.

10. Connect the negative battery cable.

11. Check the power window for proper operation.

12. Install the door trim panel and watershield. Check that all drain holes at the bottom of the doors are open to prevent water accumulation over the motor.

### Front — 2-Door

1. Raise the window to the full up position, if possible. If the glass cannot be raised and is partially down or in the full down position, it must be supported so that it will not fall into the door well during motor removal.

2. Disconnect the negative battery cable.

3. Remove the door trim panel and watershield.

4. Disconnect the electric window motor wire from the wire harness connector and move the motor away from the area to be drilled.

5. Using a ¾" hole saw with a ¼" pilot, drill the hole at point **A** and point **B** dimples. Remove the drillings.

NOTE: *Before the removal of the motor drive assembly, make certain that the regulator arm is in a fixed position to prevent counterbalance spring unwind.*

6. Remove the three window motor mounting screws and disengage the motor and drive assembly from the regulator quadrant gear.

7. Install the new motor and drive assembly. Tighten the three motor mounting screws to 50–85 inch lbs.

8. Connect window motor wiring harness leads.

9. Connect the negative battery cable.

10. Check the power window for proper operation.

11. Install the door trim panel and watershield. Check that all drain holes at the bottom of the doors are open to prevent water accumulation over the motor.

## Power Seat Motor and Cables
### REMOVAL AND INSTALLATION

NOTE: *It is recommended that when a cable is to be replaced, the power seat motor should be removed in order to ease the replacement of the defective cable.*

1. Disconnect the negative battery cable.

2. Remove the seat assembly from the vehicle.

3. Remove the motor retaining bolts from the seat mounting.

4. Disconnect the housings and the cables from the motor.

5. Remove the motor assembly from its mounting.

6. Installation is the reverse of the removal procedure.

## Headliner
### REMOVAL AND INSTALLATION

Headlining removal and installation procedures generally apply to all trim levels. If one or more of the steps do not apply to a particular trim level, proceed to the next step.

Before removing the headlining on the Escort/Lynx, EXP/LN-7, the hatchback or liftgate weatherstrip, door weatherstrip, and the quarter window glass and the weatherstrip assemblies must be removed. When installing the headlining, start at the hatchback, or the liftgate and move toward the front of the vehicle.

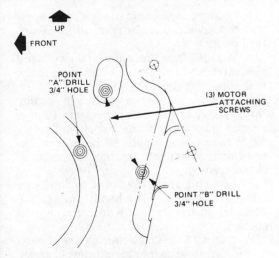

UP

FRONT

POINT "A" DRILL 3/4" HOLE

(3) MOTOR ATTACHING SCREWS

POINT "B" DRILL 3/4" HOLE

**Front door window motor template—2-door**

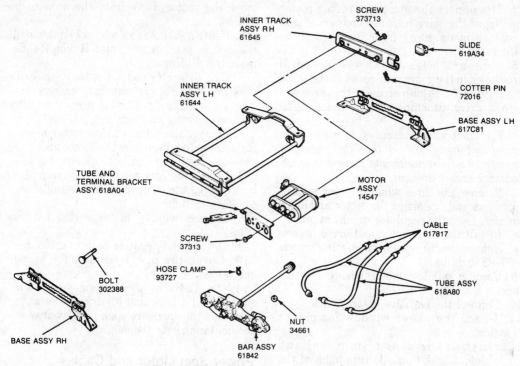

**Power seat motor assembly—Tempo/Topaz**

If the vehicle is equipped with assist handles, they must be removed during the replacement procedure.

### Escort/Lynx, EXP/LN-7

*3-DOOR, 2-DOOR HATCHBACK*

1. Remove the right and left sun visors and the visor center clips.

NOTE: *If the vehicle is equipped with illuminated sun visors, disconnect the electrical leads.*

2. Remove the header garnish moulding.

3. Remove the windshield side garnish mouldings.

4. Remove the dome light.

5. Remove the roof rail assist handles and coat hooks.

6. Remove the roof rail weatherstrip assemblies.

7. Detach the liftgate gas cylinders at body opening.

8. Detach the ground wire for the heated rear window, if so equipped.

9. Remove the folding rear seat assembly including the luggage cover.

10. Remove the quarter window and weatherstrip assemblies.

11. Remove the headlining.

12. **To install:**Unpackage the new headlining and lay it out on a flat surface. Mark and trim the new headlining using the old one as a pattern.

13. Trim the listings, pockets, on the new headlining to the approximate length of the old one. Remove the support rods from the old headlining and install them in the same relative rod positions of the new headliner. The roof headlining support rods are color coded at each end. When ordering new rods, be sure to note the color at each end of the rod.

14. Position the headliner in the vehicle, connect the bows.

15. Starting at the rear window area, apply trim cement and align the rear bow to the vertical position.

16. Working from the center to the outboard side, stretch and cement the headliner to the rear window opening flange.

17. Apply cement to the windshield opening flange, door opening weatherstrip flange, quarter glass and hatchback opening flanges. Align the bows and pull the headlining forward and cement into position at the windshield opening.

18. Working from the front to the rear, stretch and cement the headlining to the door(s), quarter window and hatchback opening.

19. Trim all excess material, leaving approximately ½" to wrap into the pinchweld areas.

20. Apply cement to the pinchweld areas.

**2-Door Hatchback**

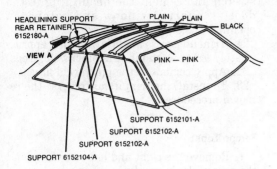

**4-Door Wagon**

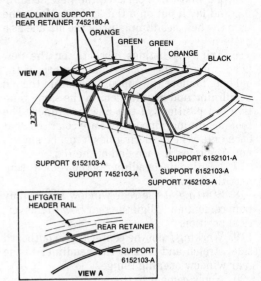

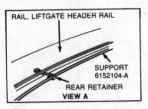

**Headliner support rods—Escort/Lynx, EXP/LN7**

21. To install the trim items, reverse the removal procedures.

*4-DOOR HATCHBACK, 4-DOOR WAGON*

1. Remove the right and left sun visors and the visor center clips.

NOTE: *If the vehicle is equipped with illuminated sun visors, disconnect the electrical leads.*

2. Remove the header garnish moulding.
3. Remove the windshield side garnish mouldings.
4. Remove the dome light.

5. Remove the roof rail assist handles and coat hooks.
6. Remove the roof rail weatherstrip assemblies.
7. Detach the liftgate gas cylinders at body opening.
8. Remove the folding seat assembly.
9. Remove the luggage compartment cover.
10. Remove the center body pillar trim panels.
11. Remove the lower back trim panel.
12. Remove the quarter trim panels.
13. Remove the side window assemblies and seats.

**4-Door Hatchback**

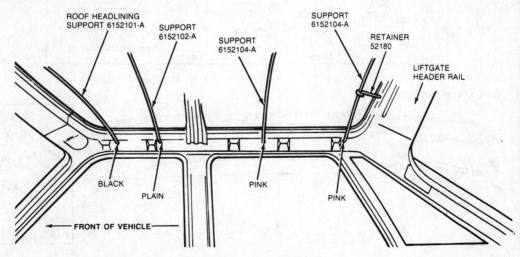

**Headliner support rods—Escort/Lynx**

14. Remove the headlining.

15. **To install:**Unpackage the new headlining and lay it out on a flat surface. Mark and trim the new headlining using the old one as a pattern.

16. Trim the listings, pockets, on the new headlining to the approximate length of the old one. Remove the support rods from the old headlining and install them in the same relative rod positions of the new headliner. The roof headlining support rods are color coded at each end. When ordering new rods, be sure to note the color at each end of the rod.

17. Position the headliner in the vehicle, connect the bows.

18. Starting at the rear window area, apply trim cement and align the rear bow to the vertical position.

19. Working from the center to the outboard side, stretch and cement the headliner to the rear window opening flange.

20. Apply cement to the windshield opening flange, door opening weatherstrip flange, quarter glass and hatchback opening flanges. Align the bows and pull the headlining forward and cement into position at the windshield opening.

18. Working from the front to the rear, stretch and cement the headlining to the door(s), quarter window and hatchback opening.

21. Trim all excess material, leaving approximately ½″ to wrap into the pinchweld areas.

22. Apply cement to the pinchweld areas.

23. To install the trim items, reverse the removal procedures.

**Tempo/Topaz**

1. Remove the right and left sun visors and the center retaining clips.

NOTE: *If the vehicle is equipped with illuminated sun visors, disconnect the electrical leads.*

2. Remove the upper and side windshield mouldings, rear window upper mouldings and roof side rail mouldings.

3. Remove the dome lamp assembly.

4. Remove the roof rail assist handles and coat hooks.

5. Shift the headlining all the way to one side allowing it to be removed and bend the opposite side flap inboard to remove.

NOTE: *On vehicles equipped with a sunroof,*

**Except 2.0L Diesel Engine**

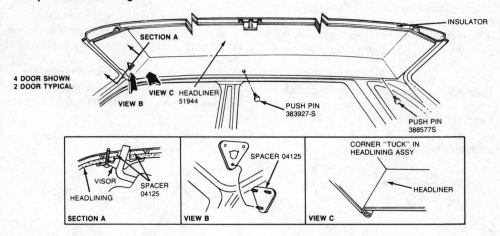

**2.0L Diesel Engine**

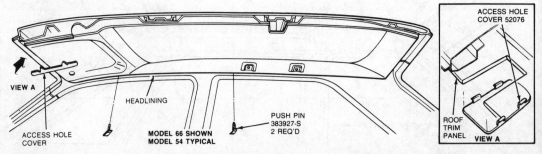

Tempo/Topaz headliner assembly—typical

*remove the headliner retainer before removing the headliner.*

6. Remove the headliner through the passenger door on the 2-door models and through either rear door on the 4-door models.

7. **To install:**Pre-fold the replacement headliner along the score lines on the flat surface prior to installing it in the vehicle (side flaps should overlap the front and rear panels).

8. Install the headliner through the passenger door on the 2-door models and through either rear door on the 4-door models.

9. Position the headliner so the visors, dome light and roof rail assist handle holes line up properly.

10. Insert one side of the into place, then bend the opposite side flap into position.

11. Install the dome light.

12. Install the right and left sun visors and the center retaining clips.

13. Install the coat hooks and roof rail assist handles.

14. Install the upper and side windshield mouldings and roof side rail mouldings.

15. Install the headliner retainer on vehicles equipped with a sunroof.

## How to Remove Stains from Fabric Interior

For rest results, spots and stains should be removed as soon as possible. Never use gasoline, lacquer thinner, acetone, nail polish remover or bleach. Use a 3′ x 3″ piece of cheesecloth. Squeeze most of the liquid from the fabric and wipe the stained fabric from the outside of the stain toward the center with a lifting motion. Turn the cheesecloth as soon as one side becomes soiled. When using water to remove a stain, be sure to wash the entire section after the spot has been removed to avoid water stains. Encrusted spots can be broken up with a dull knife and vacuumed before removing the stain.

| Type of Stain | How to Remove It |
|---|---|
| Surface spots | Brush the spots out with a small hand brush or use a commercial preparation such as K2R to lift the stain. |
| Mildew | Clean around the mildew with warm suds. Rinse in cold water and soak the mildew area in a solution of 1 part table salt and 2 parts water. Wash with upholstery cleaner. |
| Water stains | Water stains in fabric materials can be removed with a solution made from 1 cup of table salt dissolved in 1 quart of water. Vigorously scrub the solution into the stain and rinse with clear water. Water stains in nylon or other synthetic fabrics should be removed with a commercial type spot remover. |
| Chewing gum, tar, crayons, shoe polish (greasy stains) | Do not use a cleaner that will soften gum or tar. Harden the deposit with an ice cube and scrape away as much as possible with a dull knife. Moisten the remainder with cleaning fluid and scrub clean. |
| Ice cream, candy | Most candy has a sugar base and can be removed with a cloth wrung out in warm water. Oily candy, after cleaning with warm water, should be cleaned with upholstery cleaner. Rinse with warm water and clean the remainder with cleaning fluid. |
| Wine, alcohol, egg, milk, soft drink (non-greasy stains) | Do not use soap. Scrub the stain with a cloth wrung out in warm water. Remove the remainder with cleaning fluid. |
| Grease, oil, lipstick, butter and related stains | Use a spot remover to avoid leaving a ring. Work from the outisde of the stain to the center and dry with a clean cloth when the spot is gone. |
| Headliners (cloth) | Mix a solution of warm water and foam upholstery cleaner to give thick suds. Use only foam—liquid may streak or spot. Clean the entire headliner in one operation using a circular motion with a natural sponge. |
| Headliner (vinyl) | Use a vinyl cleaner with a sponge and wipe clean with a dry cloth. |
| Seats and door panels | Mix 1 pint upholstery cleaner in 1 gallon of water. Do not soak the fabric around the buttons. |
| Leather or vinyl fabric | Use a multi-purpose cleaner full strength and a stiff brush. Let stand 2 minutes and scrub thoroughly. Wipe with a clean, soft rag. |
| Nylon or synthetic fabrics | For normal stains, use the same procedures you would for washing cloth upholstery. If the fabric is extremely dirty, use a multi-purpose cleaner full strength with a stiff scrub brush. Scrub thoroughly in all directions and wipe with a cotton towel or soft rag. |

# Mechanic's Data

## General Conversion Table

| Multiply By | To Convert | To | |
|---|---|---|---|
| **LENGTH** | | | |
| 2.54 | Inches | Centimeters | .3937 |
| 25.4 | Inches | Millimeters | .03937 |
| 30.48 | Feet | Centimeters | .0328 |
| .304 | Feet | Meters | 3.28 |
| .914 | Yards | Meters | 1.094 |
| 1.609 | Miles | Kilometers | .621 |
| **VOLUME** | | | |
| .473 | Pints | Liters | 2.11 |
| .946 | Quarts | Liters | 1.06 |
| 3.785 | Gallons | Liters | .264 |
| .016 | Cubic inches | Liters | 61.02 |
| 16.39 | Cubic inches | Cubic cms. | .061 |
| 28.3 | Cubic feet | Liters | .0353 |
| **MASS (Weight)** | | | |
| 28.35 | Ounces | Grams | .035 |
| .4536 | Pounds | Kilograms | 2.20 |
| — | To obtain | From | Multiply by |

| Multiply By | To Convert | To | |
|---|---|---|---|
| **AREA** | | | |
| .645 | Square inches | Square cms. | .155 |
| .836 | Square yds. | Square meters | 1.196 |
| **FORCE** | | | |
| 4.448 | Pounds | Newtons | .225 |
| .138 | Ft./lbs. | Kilogram/meters | 7.23 |
| 1.36 | Ft./lbs. | Newton-meters | .737 |
| .112 | In./lbs. | Newton-meters | 8.844 |
| **PRESSURE** | | | |
| .068 | Psi | Atmospheres | 14.7 |
| 6.89 | Psi | Kilopascals | .145 |
| **OTHER** | | | |
| 1.104 | Horsepower (DIN) | Horsepower (SAE) | .9861 |
| .746 | Horsepower (SAE) | Kilowatts (KW) | 1.34 |
| 1.60 | Mph | Km/h | .625 |
| .425 | Mpg | Km/1 | 2.35 |
| — | To obtain | From | Multiply by |

## Tap Drill Sizes

### National Coarse or U.S.S.

| Screw & Tap Size | Threads Per Inch | Use Drill Number |
|---|---|---|
| No. 5 | 40 | 39 |
| No. 6 | 32 | 36 |
| No. 8 | 32 | 29 |
| No. 10 | 24 | 25 |
| No. 12 | 24 | 17 |
| 1/4 | 20 | 8 |
| 5/16 | 18 | F |
| 3/8 | 16 | 5/16 |
| 7/16 | 14 | U |
| 1/2 | 13 | 27/64 |
| 9/16 | 12 | 31/64 |
| 5/8 | 11 | 17/32 |
| 3/4 | 10 | 21/32 |
| 7/8 | 9 | 49/64 |

### National Coarse or U.S.S.

| Screw & Tap Size | Threads Per Inch | Use Drill Number |
|---|---|---|
| 1 | 8 | 7/8 |
| 1 1/8 | 7 | 63/64 |
| 1 1/4 | 7 | 1 7/64 |
| 1 1/2 | 6 | 1 11/32 |

### National Fine or S.A.E.

| Screw & Tap Size | Threads Per Inch | Use Drill Number |
|---|---|---|
| No. 5 | 44 | 37 |
| No. 6 | 40 | 33 |
| No. 8 | 36 | 29 |
| No. 10 | 32 | 21 |

### National Fine or S.A.E.

| Screw & Tap Size | Threads Per Inch | Use Drill Number |
|---|---|---|
| No. 12 | 28 | 15 |
| 1/4 | 28 | 3 |
| 6/16 | 24 | 1 |
| 3/8 | 24 | Q |
| 7/16 | 20 | W |
| 1/2 | 20 | 29/64 |
| 9/16 | 18 | 33/64 |
| 5/8 | 18 | 37/64 |
| 3/4 | 16 | 11/16 |
| 7/8 | 14 | 13/16 |
| 1 1/8 | 12 | 1 3/64 |
| 1 1/4 | 12 | 1 11/64 |
| 1 1/2 | 12 | 1 27/64 |

**AIR/FUEL RATIO**: The ratio of air to gasoline by weight in the fuel mixture drawn into the engine.

**AIR INJECTION**: One method of reducing harmful exhaust emissions by injecting air into each of the exhaust ports of an engine. The fresh air entering the hot exhaust manifold causes any remaining fuel to be burned before it can exit the tailpipe.

**ALTERNATOR**: A device used for converting mechanical energy into electrical energy.

**AMMETER**: An instrument, calibrated in amperes, used to measure the flow of an electrical current in a circuit. Ammeters are always connected in series with the circuit being tested.

**AMPERE**: The rate of flow of electrical current present when one volt of electrical pressure is applied against one ohm of electrical resistance.

**ANALOG COMPUTER**: Any microprocessor that uses similar (analogous) electrical signals to make its calculations.

**ARMATURE**: A laminated, soft iron core wrapped by a wire that converts electrical energy to mechanical energy as in a motor or relay. When rotated in a magnetic field, it changes mechanical energy into electrical energy as in a generator.

**ATMOSPHERIC PRESSURE**: The pressure on the Earth's surface caused by the weight of the air in the atmosphere. At sea level, this pressure is 14.7 psi at 32°F (101 kPa at 0°C).

**ATOMIZATION**: The breaking down of a liquid into a fine mist that can be suspended in air.

**AXIAL PLAY**: Movement parallel to a shaft or bearing bore.

**BACKFIRE**: The sudden combustion of gases in the intake or exhaust system that results in a loud explosion.

**BACKLASH**: The clearance or play between two parts, such as meshed gears.

**BACKPRESSURE**: Restrictions in the exhaust system that slow the exit of exhaust gases from the combustion chamber.

**BAKELITE**: A heat resistant, plastic insulator material commonly used in printed circuit boards and transistorized components.

**BALL BEARING**: A bearing made up of hardened inner and outer races between which hardened steel ball roll.

**BALLAST RESISTOR**: A resistor in the primary ignition circuit that lowers voltage after the engine is started to reduce wear on ignition components.

**BEARING**: A friction reducing, supportive device usually located between a stationary part and a moving part.

**BIMETAL TEMPERATURE SENSOR**: Any sensor or switch made of two dissimilar types of metal that bend when heated or cooled due to the different expansion rates of the alloys. These types of sensors usually function as an on/off switch.

**BLOWBY**: Combustion gases, composed of water vapor and unburned fuel, that leak past the piston rings into the crankcase during normal engine operation. These gases are removed by the PCV system to prevent the buildup of harmful acids in the crankcase.

**BRAKE PAD**: A brake shoe and lining assembly used with disc brakes.

**BRAKE SHOE**: The backing for the brake lining. The term is, however, usually applied to the assembly of the brake backing and lining.

**BUSHING**: A liner, usually removable, for a bearing; an anti-friction liner used in place of a bearing.

**BYPASS**: System used to bypass ballast resistor during engine cranking to increase voltage supplied to the coil.

**CALIPER**: A hydraulically activated device in a disc brake system, which is mounted straddling the brake rotor (disc). The caliper contains at least one piston and two brake pads. Hydraulic pressure on the piston(s) forces the pads against the rotor.

**CAMSHAFT**: A shaft in the engine on which are the lobes (cams) which operate the valves. The camshaft is driven by the crankshaft, via a belt, chain or gears, at one half the crankshaft speed.

**CAPACITOR**: A device which stores an electrical charge.

**CARBON MONOXIDE (CO)**: a colorless, odorless gas given off as a normal byproduct of combustion. It is poisonous and extremely dangerous in confined areas, building up slowly to toxic levels without warning if adequate ventilation is not available.

**CARBURETOR**: A device, usually mounted on the intake manifold of an engine, which mixes the air and fuel in the proper proportion to allow even combustion.

**CATALYTIC CONVERTER**: A device installed in the exhaust system, like a muffler, that converts harmful byproducts of combustion into carbon dioxide and water vapor by means of a heat-producing chemical reaction.

**CENTRIFUGAL ADVANCE**: A mechanical method of advancing the spark timing by using flyweights in the distributor that react to centrifugal force generated by the distributor shaft rotation.

**CHECK VALVE**: Any one-way valve installed to permit the flow of air, fuel or vacuum in one direction only.

**CHOKE**: A device, usually a moveable valve, placed in the intake path of a carburetor to restrict the flow of air.

**CIRCUIT**: Any unbroken path through which an electrical current can flow. Also used to describe fuel flow in some instances.

**CIRCUIT BREAKER**: A switch which protects an electrical circuit from overload by opening the circuit when the current flow exceeds a predetermined level. Some circuit breakers must be reset manually, while other reset automatically

**COIL (IGNITION)**: A transformer in the ignition circuit which steps of the voltage provided to the spark plugs.

**COMBINATION MANIFOLD**: An assembly which includes both the intake and exhaust manifolds in one casting.

**COMBINATION VALVE**: A device used in some fuel systems that routes fuel vapors to a charcoal storage canister instead of venting them into the atmosphere. The valve relieves fuel tank pressure and allows fresh air into the tank as fuel level drops to prevent a vapor lock situation.

**COMPRESSION RATIO**: The comparison of the total volume of the cylinder and combustion chamber with the piston at BDC and the piston at TDC.

**CONDENSER**: 1. An electrical device which acts to store an electrical charge, preventing voltage surges.
2. A radiator-like device in the air conditioning system in which refrigerant gas condenses into a liquid, giving off heat.

**CONDUCTOR**: Any material through which an electrical current can be transmitted easily.

**CONTINUITY**: Continuous or complete circuit. Can be checked with an ohmmeter.

**COUNTERSHAFT**: An intermediate shaft which is rotated by a mainshaft and transmits, in turn, that rotation to a working part.

**CRANKCASE**: The lower part of an engine in which the crankshaft and related parts operate.

**CRANKSHAFT**: The main driving shaft of an engine which receives reciprocating motion from the pistons and converts it to rotary motion.

**CYLINDER**: In an engine, the round hole in the engine block in which the piston(s) ride.

**CYLINDER BLOCK**: The main structural member of an engine in which is found the cylinders, crankshaft and other principal parts.

**CYLINDER HEAD**: The detachable portion of the engine, fastened, usually, to the top of the cylinder block, containing all or most of the combustion chambers. On overhead valve engines, it contains the valves and their operating parts. On overhead cam engines, it contains the camshaft as well.

**DEAD CENTER**: The extreme top or bottom of the piston stroke.

**DETONATION**: An unwanted explosion of the air fuel mixture in the combustion chamber caused by excess heat and compression, advanced timing, or an overly lean mixture. Also referred to as "ping".

**DIAPHRAGM**: A thin, flexible wall separating two cavities, such as in a vacuum advance unit.

**DIESELING**: A condition in which hot spots in the combustion chamber cause the engine to run on after the key is turned off.

**DIFFERENTIAL**: A geared assembly which allows the transmission of motion between drive axles, giving one axle the ability to turn faster than the other.

**DIODE**: An electrical device that will allow current to flow in one direction only.

**DISC BRAKE**: A hydraulic braking assembly consisting of a brake disc, or rotor, mounted on an axle, and a caliper assembly containing, usually two brake pads which are activated by hydraulic pressure. The pads are forced against the sides of the disc, creating friction which slows the vehicle.

**DISTRIBUTOR**: A mechanically driven device on an engine which is responsible for electrically firing the spark plug at a predetermined point of the piston stroke.

**DOWEL PIN**: A pin, inserted in mating holes in two different parts allowing those parts to maintain a fixed relationship.

**DRUM BRAKE**: A braking system which consists of two brake shoes and one or two wheel cylinders, mounted on a fixed backing plate, and a brake drum, mounted on an axle, which revolves around the assembly. Hydraulic action applied to the wheel cylinders forces the shoes outward against the drum, creating friction and slowing the vehicle.

**DWELL**: The rate, measured in degrees of shaft rotation, at which an electrical circuit cycles on and off.

**ELECTRONIC CONTROL UNIT (ECU)**: Ignition module, module, amplifier or igniter. See Module for definition.

**ELECTRONIC IGNITION**: A system in which the timing and firing of the spark plugs is controlled by an electronic control unit, usually called a module. These systems have not points or condenser.

**ENDPLAY**: The measured amount of axial movement in a shaft.

**ENGINE**: A device that converts heat into mechanical energy.

**EXHAUST MANIFOLD**: A set of cast passages or pipes which conduct exhaust gases from the engine.

**FEELER GAUGE**: A blade, usually metal, of precisely predetermined thickness, used to measure the clearance between two parts. These blades usually are available in sets of assorted thicknesses.

**F-Head**: An engine configuration in which the intake valves are in the cylinder head, while the camshaft and exhaust valves are located in the cylinder block. The camshaft operates the intake valves via lifters and pushrods, while it operates the exhaust valves directly.

**FIRING ORDER**: The order in which combustion occurs in the cylinders of an engine. Also the order in which spark is distributed to the plugs by the distributor.

**FLATHEAD**: An engine configuration in which the camshaft and all the valves are located in the cylinder block.

**FLOODING**: The presence of too much fuel in the intake manifold and combustion chamber which prevents the air/fuel mixture from firing, thereby causing a no-start situation.

**FLYWHEEL**: A disc shaped part bolted to the rear end of the crankshaft. Around the outer perimeter is affixed the ring gear. The starter drive engages the ring gear, turning the flywheel, which rotates the crankshaft, imparting the initial starting motion to the engine.

**FOOT POUND (ft.lb. or sometimes, ft. lbs.)**: The amount of energy or work needed to raise an item weighing one pound, a distance of one foot.

**FUSE**: A protective device in a circuit which prevents circuit overload by breaking the circuit when a specific amperage is present. The device is constructed around a strip or wire of a lower amperage rating than the circuit it is designed to protect. When an amperage higher than that stamped on the fuse is present in the circuit, the strip or wire melts, opening the circuit.

**GEAR RATIO**: The ratio between the number of teeth on meshing gears.

**GENERATOR**: A device which converts mechanical energy into electrical energy.

**HEAT RANGE**: The measure of a spark plug's ability to dissipate heat from its firing end. The higher the heat range, the hotter the plug fires.

**HUB**: The center part of a wheel or gear.

**HYDROCARBON (HC)**: Any chemical compound made up of hydrogen and carbon. A major pollutant formed by the engine as a byproduct of combustion.

**HYDROMETER**: An instrument used to measure the specific gravity of a solution.

**INCH POUND (in.lb. or sometimes, in. lbs.)**: One twelfth of a foot pound.

**INDUCTION**: A means of transferring electrical energy in the form of a magnetic field. Principle used in the ignition coil to increase voltage.

**INJECTION PUMP**: A device, usually mechanically operated, which meters and delivers fuel under pressure to the fuel injector.

**INJECTOR**: A device which receives metered fuel under relatively low pressure and is activated to inject the fuel into the engine under relatively high pressure at a predetermined time.

**INPUT SHAFT**: The shaft to which torque is applied, usually carrying the driving gear or gears.

**INTAKE MANIFOLD**: A casting of passages or pipes used to conduct air or a fuel/air mixture to the cylinders.

**JOURNAL**: The bearing surface within which a shaft operates.

**KEY**: A small block usually fitted in a notch between a shaft and a hub to prevent slippage of the two parts.

**MANIFOLD**: A casting of passages or set of pipes which connect the cylinders to an inlet or outlet source.

**MANIFOLD VACUUM**: Low pressure in an engine intake manifold formed just below the throttle plates. Manifold vacuum is highest at idle and drops under acceleration.

**MASTER CYLINDER**: The primary fluid pressurizing device in a hydraulic system. In automotive use, it is found in brake and hydraulic clutch systems and is pedal activated, either directly or, in a power brake system, through the power booster.

**MODULE**: Electronic control unit, amplifier or igniter of solid state or integrated design which controls the current flow in the ignition primary circuit based on input from the pickup coil. When the module opens the primary circuit, the high secondary voltage is induced in the coil.

**NEEDLE BEARING**: A bearing which consists of a number (usually a large number) of long, thin rollers.

**OHM**: ($\Omega$) The unit used to measure the resistance of conductor to electrical flow. One ohm is the amount of resistance that limits current flow to one ampere in a circuit with one volt of pressure.

**OHMMETER**: An instrument used for measuring the resistance, in ohms, in an electrical circuit.

**OUTPUT SHAFT**: The shaft which transmits torque from a device, such as a transmission.

**OVERDRIVE**: A gear assembly which produces more shaft revolutions than that transmitted to it.

**OVERHEAD CAMSHAFT (OHC)**: An engine configuration in which the camshaft is mounted on top of the cylinder head and operates the valve either directly or by means of rocker arms.

**OVERHEAD VALVE (OHV)**: An engine configuration in which all of the valves are located in the cylinder head and the camshaft is located in the cylinder block. The camshaft operates the valves via lifters and pushrods.

**OXIDES OF NITROGEN (NOx)**: Chemical compounds of nitrogen produced as a byproduct of combustion. They combine with hydrocarbons to produce smog.

**OXYGEN SENSOR**: Used with the feedback system to sense the presence of oxygen in the exhaust gas and signal the computer which can reference the voltage signal to an air/fuel ratio.

**PINION**: The smaller of two meshing gears.

**PISTON RING**: An open ended ring which fits into a groove on the outer diameter of the piston. Its chief function is to form a seal between the piston and cylinder wall. Most automotive pistons have three rings: two for compression sealing; one for oil sealing.

**PRELOAD**: A predetermined load placed on a bearing during assembly or by adjustment.

**PRIMARY CIRCUIT**: Is the low voltage side of the ignition system which consists of the ignition switch, ballast resistor or resistance wire, bypass, coil, electronic control unit and pick-up coil as well as the connecting wires and harnesses.

**PRESS FIT**: The mating of two parts under pressure, due to the inner diameter of one being smaller than the outer diameter of the other, or vice versa; an interference fit.

**RACE**: The surface on the inner or outer ring of a bearing on which the balls, needles or rollers move.

**REGULATOR**: A device which maintains the amperage and/or voltage levels of a circuit at predetermined values.

**RELAY**: A switch which automatically opens and/or closes a circuit.

**RESISTANCE**: The opposition to the flow of current through a circuit or electrical device, and is measured in ohms. Resistance is equal to the voltage divided by the amperage.

**RESISTOR**: A device, usually made of wire, which offers a preset amount of resistance in an electrical circuit.

**RING GEAR**: The name given to a ring-shaped gear attached to a differential case, or affixed to a flywheel or as part a planetary gear set.

**ROLLER BEARING**: A bearing made up of hardened inner and outer races between which hardened steel rollers move.

**ROTOR**: 1. The disc-shaped part of a disc brake assembly, upon which the brake pads bear; also called, brake disc.
2. The device mounted atop the distributor shaft, which passes current to the distributor cap tower contacts.

**SECONDARY CIRCUIT**: The high voltage side of the ignition system, usually above 20,000 volts. The secondary includes the ignition coil, coil wire, distributor cap and rotor, spark plug wires and spark plugs.

**SENDING UNIT**: A mechanical, electrical, hydraulic or electromagnetic device which transmits information to a gauge.

**SENSOR**: Any device designed to measure engine operating conditions or ambient pressures and temperatures. Usually electronic in nature and designed to send a voltage signal to an on-board computer, some sensors may operate as a simple on/off switch or they may provide a variable voltage signal (like a potentiometer) as conditions or measured parameters change.

**SHIM**: Spacers of precise, predetermined thickness used between parts to establish a proper working relationship.

**SLAVE CYLINDER**: In automotive use, a device in the hydraulic clutch system which is activated by hydraulic force, disengaging the clutch.

**SOLENOID**: A coil used to produce a magnetic field, the effect of which is produce work.

**SPARK PLUG**: A device screwed into the combustion chamber of a spark ignition engine. The basic construction is a conductive core inside of a ceramic insulator, mounted in an outer conductive base. An electrical charge from the spark plug wire travels along the conductive core and jumps a preset air gap to a grounding point or points at the end of the conductive base. The resultant spark ignites the fuel/air mixture in the combustion chamber.

**SPLINES**: Ridges machined or cast onto the outer diameter of a shaft or inner diameter of a bore to enable parts to mate without rotation.

**TACHOMETER**: A device used to measure the rotary speed of an engine, shaft, gear, etc., usually in rotations per minute.

**THERMOSTAT**: A valve, located in the cooling system of an engine, which is closed when cold and opens gradually in response to engine heating, controlling the temperature of the coolant and rate of coolant flow.

**TOP DEAD CENTER (TDC)**: The point at which the piston reaches the top of its travel on the compression stroke.

**TORQUE**: The twisting force applied to an object.

**TORQUE CONVERTER**: A turbine used to transmit power from a driving member to a driven member via hydraulic action, providing changes in drive ratio and torque. In automotive use, it links the driveplate at the rear of the engine to the automatic transmission.

**TRANSDUCER**: A device used to change a force into an electrical signal.

**TRANSISTOR**: A semi-conductor component which can be actuated by a small voltage to perform an electrical switching function.

**TUNE-UP**: A regular maintenance function, usually associated with the replacement and adjustment of parts and components in the electrical and fuel systems of a vehicle for the purpose of attaining optimum performance.

**TURBOCHARGER**: An exhaust driven pump which compresses intake air and forces it into the combustion chambers at higher than atmospheric pressures. The increased air pressure allows more fuel to be burned and results in increased horsepower being produced.

**VACUUM ADVANCE**: A device which advances the ignition timing in response to increased engine vacuum.

**VACUUM GAUGE**: An instrument used to measure the presence of vacuum in a chamber.

**VALVE**: A device which control the pressure, direction of flow or rate of flow of a liquid or gas.

**VALVE CLEARANCE**: The measured gap between the end of the valve stem and the rocker arm, cam lobe or follower that activates the valve.

**VISCOSITY**: The rating of a liquid's internal resistance to flow.

**VOLTMETER**: An instrument used for measuring electrical force in units called volts. Voltmeters are always connected parallel with the circuit being tested.

**WHEEL CYLINDER**: Found in the automotive drum brake assembly, it is a device, actuated by hydraulic pressure, which, through internal pistons, pushes the brake shoes outward against the drums.

# ABBREVIATIONS AND SYMBOLS

A: Ampere

AC: Alternating current

A/C: Air conditioning

A-h: Ampere hour

AT: Automatic transmission

ATDC: After top dead center

$\mu$A: Microampere

bbl: Barrel

BDC: Bottom dead center

bhp: Brake horsepower

BTDC: Before top dead center

BTU: British thermal unit

C: Celsius (Centigrade)

CCA: Cold cranking amps

cd: Candela

$cm^2$: Square centimeter

$cm^3$, cc: Cubic centimeter

CO: Carbon monoxide

$CO_2$: Carbon dioxide

cu.in., $in^3$: Cubic inch

CV: Constant velocity

Cyl.: Cylinder

DC: Direct current

ECM: Electronic control module

EFE: Early fuel evaporation

EFI: Electronic fuel injection

EGR: Exhaust gas recirculation

Exh.: Exhaust

F: Fahrenheit

F: Farad

pF: Picofarad

$\mu$F: Microfarad

FI: Fuel injection

ft.lb., ft. lb., ft. lbs.: foot pound(s)

gal: Gallon

g: Gram

HC: Hydrocarbon

HEI: High energy ignition

HO: High output

hp: Horsepower

Hyd.: Hydraulic

Hz: Hertz

ID: Inside diameter

in.lb.; in. lb.; in. lbs: inch pound(s)

Int.: Intake

K: Kelvin

kg: Kilogram

kHz: Kilohertz

km: Kilometer

km/h: Kilometers per hour

k$\Omega$: Kilohm

kPa: Kilopascal

kV: Kilovolt

kW: Kilowatt

l: Liter

l/s: Liters per second

m: Meter

mA: Milliampere

mg: Milligram

mHz: Megahertz

mm: Millimeter

mm$^2$: Square millimeter

m$^3$: Cubic meter

M$\Omega$: Megohm

m/s: Meters per second

MT: Manual transmission

mV: Millivolt

$\mu$m: Micrometer

N: Newton

N-m: Newton meter

NOx: Nitrous oxide

OD: Outside diameter

OHC: Over head camshaft

OHV: Over head valve

$\Omega$: Ohm

PCV: Positive crankcase ventilation

psi: Pounds per square inch

pts: Pints

qts: Quarts

rpm: Rotations per minute

rps: Rotations per second

R-12: A refrigerant gas (Freon)

SAE: Society of Automotive Engineers

SO$_2$: Sulfur dioxide

T: Ton

t: Megagram

TBI: Throttle Body Injection

TPS: Throttle Position Sensor

V: 1. Volt; 2. Venturi

$\mu$V: Microvolt

W: Watt

$\infty$: Infinity

$<$: Less than

$>$: Greater than

# Index

# Chilton's Repair & Tune-Up Guides

## The Complete line covers domestic cars, imports, trucks, vans, RV's and 4-wheel drive vehicles.

| RTUG Title | Part No. |
|---|---|
| **AMC 1975-82** | 7199 |
| Covers all U.S. and Canadian models | |
| **Aspen/Volare 1976-80** | 6637 |
| Covers all U.S. and Canadian models | |
| **Audi 1970-73** | 5902 |
| Covers all U.S. and Canadian models. | |
| **Audi 4000/5000 1978-81** | 7028 |
| Covers all U.S. and Canadian models including turbocharged and diesel engines | |
| **Barracuda/Challenger 1965-72** | 5807 |
| Covers all U.S. and Canadian models | |
| **Blazer/Jimmy 1969-82** | 6931 |
| Covers all U.S. and Canadian 2- and 4-wheel drive models, including diesel engines | |
| **BMW 1970-82** | 6844 |
| Covers U.S. and Canadian models | |
| **Buick/Olds/Pontiac 1975-85** | 7308 |
| Covers all U.S. and Canadian full size rear wheel drive models | |
| **Cadillac 1967-84** | 7462 |
| Covers all U.S. and Canadian rear wheel drive models | |
| **Camaro 1967-81** | 6735 |
| Covers all U.S. and Canadian models | |
| **Camaro 1982-85** | 7317 |
| Covers all U.S. and Canadian models | |
| **Capri 1970-77** | 6695 |
| Covers all U.S. and Canadian models | |
| **Caravan/Voyager 1984-85** | 7482 |
| Covers all U.S. and Canadian models | |
| **Century/Regal 1975-85** | 7307 |
| Covers all U.S. and Canadian rear wheel drive models, including turbocharged engines | |
| **Champ/Arrow/Sapporo 1978-83** | 7041 |
| Covers all U.S. and Canadian models | |
| **Chevette/1000 1976-86** | 6836 |
| Covers all U.S. and Canadian models | |
| **Chevrolet 1968-85** | 7135 |
| Covers all U.S. and Canadian models | |
| **Chevrolet 1968-79 Spanish** | 7082 |
| **Chevrolet/GMC Pick-Ups 1970-82 Spanish** | 7468 |
| **Chevrolet/GMC Pick-Ups and Suburban 1970-86** | 6936 |
| Covers all U.S. and Canadian 1/2, 3/4 and 1 ton models, including 4-wheel drive and diesel engines | |
| **Chevrolet LUV 1972-81** | 6815 |
| Covers all U.S. and Canadian models | |
| **Chevrolet Mid-Size 1964-86** | 6840 |
| Covers all U.S. and Canadian models of 1964-77 Chevelle, Malibu and Malibu SS; 1974-77 Laguna; 1978-85 Malibu; 1970-86 Monte Carlo; 1964-84 El Camino, including diesel engines | |
| **Chevrolet Nova 1986** | 7658 |
| Covers all U.S. and Canadian models | |
| **Chevy/GMC Vans 1967-84** | 6930 |
| Covers all U.S. and Canadian models of 1/2, 3/4, and 1 ton vans, cutaways, and motor home chassis, including diesel engines | |
| **Chevy S-10 Blazer/GMC S-15 Jimmy 1982-85** | 7383 |
| Covers all U.S. and Canadian models | |
| **Chevy S-10/GMC S-15 Pick-Ups 1982-85** | 7310 |
| Covers all U.S. and Canadian models | |
| **Chevy II/Nova 1962-79** | 6841 |
| Covers all U.S. and Canadian models | |
| **Chrysler K- and E-Car 1981-85** | 7163 |
| Covers all U.S. and Canadian front wheel drive models | |
| **Colt/Challenger/Vista/Conquest 1971-85** | 7037 |
| Covers all U.S. and Canadian models | |
| **Corolla/Carina/Tercel/Starlet 1970-85** | 7036 |
| Covers all U.S. and Canadian models | |
| **Corona/Cressida/Crown/Mk.II/Camry/Van 1970-84** | 7044 |
| Covers all U.S. and Canadian models | |
| **Corvair 1960-69** | 6691 |
| Covers all U.S. and Canadian models | |
| **Corvette 1953-62** | 6576 |
| Covers all U.S. and Canadian models | |
| **Corvette 1963-84** | 6843 |
| Covers all U.S. and Canadian models | |
| **Cutlass 1970-85** | 6933 |
| Covers all U.S. and Canadian models | |
| **Dart/Demon 1968-76** | 6324 |
| Covers all U.S. and Canadian models | |
| **Datsun 1961-72** | 5790 |
| Covers all U.S. and Canadian models of Nissan Patrol; 1500, 1600 and 2000 sports cars; Pick-Ups; 410, 411, 510, 1200 and 240Z | |
| **Datsun 1973-80 Spanish** | 7083 |
| **Datsun/Nissan F-10, 310, Stanza, Pulsar 1977-86** | 7196 |
| Covers all U.S. and Canadian models | |
| **Datsun/Nissan Pick-Ups 1970-84** | 6816 |
| Covers all U.S. and Canadian models | |
| **Datsun/Nissan Z & ZX 1970-86** | 6932 |
| Covers all U.S. and Canadian models | |
| **Datsun/Nissan 1200, 210, Sentra 1973-86** | 7197 |
| Covers all U.S. and Canadian models | |
| **Datsun/Nissan 200SX, 510, 610, 710, 810, Maxima 1973-84** | 7170 |
| Covers all U.S. and Canadian models | |
| **Dodge 1968-77** | 6554 |
| Covers all U.S. and Canadian models | |
| **Dodge Charger 1967-70** | 6486 |
| Covers all U.S. and Canadian models | |
| **Dodge/Plymouth Trucks 1967-84** | 7459 |
| Covers all 1/2, 3/4, and 1 ton 2- and 4-wheel drive U.S. and Canadian models, including diesel engines | |
| **Dodge/Plymouth Vans 1967-84** | 6934 |
| Covers all 1/2, 3/4, and 1 ton U.S. and Canadian models of vans, cutaways and motor home chassis | |
| **D-50/Arrow Pick-Up 1979-81** | 7032 |
| Covers all U.S. and Canadian models | |
| **Fairlane/Torino 1962-75** | 6320 |
| Covers all U.S. and Canadian models | |
| **Fairmont/Zephyr 1978-83** | 6965 |
| Covers all U.S. and Canadian models | |
| **Fiat 1969-81** | 7042 |
| Covers all U.S. and Canadian models | |
| **Fiesta 1978-80** | 6846 |
| Covers all U.S. and Canadian models | |
| **Firebird 1967-81** | 5996 |
| Covers all U.S. and Canadian models | |
| **Firebird 1982-85** | 7345 |
| Covers all U.S. and Canadian models | |
| **Ford 1968-79 Spanish** | 7084 |
| **Ford Bronco 1966-83** | 7140 |
| Covers all U.S. and Canadian models | |
| **Ford Bronco II 1984** | 7408 |
| Covers all U.S. and Canadian models | |
| **Ford Courier 1972-82** | 6983 |
| Covers all U.S. and Canadian models | |
| **Ford/Mercury Front Wheel Drive 1981-85** | 7055 |
| Covers all U.S. and Canadian models Escort, EXP, Tempo, Lynx, LN-7 and Topaz | |
| **Ford/Mercury/Lincoln 1968-85** | 6842 |
| Covers all U.S. and Canadian models of FORD Country Sedan, Country Squire, Crown Victoria, Custom, Custom 500, Galaxie 500, LTD through 1982, Ranch Wagon, and XL; MERCURY Colony Park, Commuter, Marquis through 1982, Gran Marquis, Monterey and Park Lane; LINCOLN Continental and Towne Car | |
| **Ford/Mercury/Lincoln Mid-Size 1971-85** | 6696 |
| Covers all U.S. and Canadian models of FORD Elite, 1983-85 LTD, 1977-79 LTD II, Ranchero, Torino, Gran Torino, 1977-85 Thunderbird; MERCURY 1972-85 Cougar, | |

continued on next page

| RTUG Title | Part No. |
|---|---|
| 1983-85 Marquis, Montego, 1980-85 XR-7; LINCOLN 1982-85 Continental, 1984-85 Mark VII, 1978-80 Versailles | |
| **Ford Pick-Ups 1965-86** | 6913 |
| Covers all 1/2, 3/4 and 1 ton, 2- and 4-wheel drive U.S. and Canadian pick-up, chassis cab and camper models, including diesel engines | |
| **Ford Pick-Ups 1965-82 Spanish** | 7469 |
| **Ford Ranger 1983-84** | 7338 |
| Covers all U.S. and Canadian models | |
| **Ford Vans 1961-86** | 6849 |
| Covers all U.S. and Canadian 1/2, 3/4 and 1 ton van and cutaway chassis models, including diesel engines | |
| **GM A-Body 1982-85** | 7309 |
| Covers all front wheel drive U.S. and Canadian models of BUICK Century, CHEVROLET Celebrity, OLDSMOBILE Cutlass Ciera and PONTIAC 6000 | |
| **GM C-Body 1985** | 7587 |
| Covers all front wheel drive U.S. and Canadian models of BUICK Electra Park Avenue and Electra T-Type, CADILLAC Fleetwood and deVille, OLDSMOBILE 98 Regency and Regency Brougham | |
| **GM J-Car 1982-85** | 7059 |
| Covers all U.S. and Canadian models of BUICK Skyhawk, CHEVROLET Cavalier, CADILLAC Cimarron, OLDSMOBILE Firenza and PONTIAC 2000 and Sunbird | |
| **GM N-Body 1985-86** | 7657 |
| Covers all U.S. and Canadian models of front wheel drive BUICK Somerset and Skylark, OLDSMOBILE Calais, and PONTIAC Grand Am | |
| **GM X-Body 1980-85** | 7049 |
| Covers all U.S. and Canadian models of BUICK Skylark, CHEVROLET Citation, OLDSMOBILE Omega and PONTIAC Phoenix | |
| **GM Subcompact 1971-80** | 6935 |
| Covers all U.S. and Canadian models of BUICK Skyhawk (1975-80), CHEVROLET Vega and Monza, OLDSMOBILE Starfire, and PONTIAC Astre and 1975-80 Sunbird | |
| **Granada/Monarch 1975-82** | 6937 |
| Covers all U.S. and Canadian models | |
| **Honda 1973-84** | 6980 |
| Covers all U.S. and Canadian models | |
| **International Scout 1967-73** | 5912 |
| Covers all U.S. and Canadian models | |
| **Jeep 1945-87** | 6817 |
| Covers all U.S. and Canadian CJ-2A, CJ-3A, CJ-3B, CJ-5, CJ-6, CJ-7, Scrambler and Wrangler models | |
| **Jeep Wagoneer, Commando, Cherokee, Truck 1957-86** | 6739 |
| Covers all U.S. and Canadian models of Wagoneer, Cherokee, Grand Wagoneer, Jeepster, Jeepster Commando, J-100, J-200, J-300, J-10, J20, FC-150 and FC-170 | |
| **Laser/Daytona 1984-85** | 7563 |
| Covers all U.S. and Canadian models | |
| **Maverick/Comet 1970-77** | 6634 |
| Covers all U.S. and Canadian models | |
| **Mazda 1971-84** | 6981 |
| Covers all U.S. and Canadian models of RX-2, RX-3, RX-4, 808, 1300, 1600, Cosmo, GLC and 626 | |
| **Mazda Pick-Ups 1972-86** | 7659 |
| Covers all U.S. and Canadian models | |
| **Mercedes-Benz 1959-70** | 6065 |
| **Mereceds-Benz 1968-73** | 5907 |
| Covers all U.S. and Canadian models | |

| RTUG Title | Part No. |
|---|---|
| **Mercedes-Benz 1974-84** | 6809 |
| Covers all U.S. and Canadian models | |
| **Mitsubishi, Cordia, Tredia, Starion, Galant 1983-85** | 7583 |
| Covers all U.S. and Canadian models | |
| **MG 1961-81** | 6780 |
| Covers all U.S. and Canadian models | |
| **Mustang/Capri/Merkur 1979-85** | 6963 |
| Covers all U.S. and Canadian models | |
| **Mustang/Cougar 1965-73** | 6542 |
| Covers all U.S. and Canadian models | |
| **Mustang II 1974-78** | 6812 |
| Covers all U.S. and Canadian models | |
| **Omni/Horizon/Rampage 1978-84** | 6845 |
| Covers all U.S. and Canadian models of DODGE omni, Miser, 024, Charger 2.2; PLYMOUTH Horizon, Miser, TC3, TC3 Tourismo; Rampage | |
| **Opel 1971-75** | 6575 |
| Covers all U.S. and Canadian models | |
| **Peugeot 1970-74** | 5982 |
| Covers all U.S. and Canadian models | |
| **Pinto/Bobcat 1971-80** | 7027 |
| Covers all U.S. and Canadian models | |
| **Plymouth 1968-76** | 6552 |
| Covers all U.S. and Canadian models | |
| **Pontiac Fiero 1984-85** | 7571 |
| Covers all U.S. and Canadian models | |
| **Pontiac Mid-Size 1974-83** | 7346 |
| Covers all U.S. and Canadian models of Ventura, Grand Am, LeMans, Grand LeMans, GTO, Phoenix, and Grand Prix | |
| **Porsche 924/928 1976-81** | 7048 |
| Covers all U.S. and Canadian models | |
| **Renault 1975-85** | 7165 |
| Covers all U.S. and Canadian models | |
| **Roadrunner/Satellite/Belvedere/GTX 1968-73** | 5821 |
| Covers all U.S. and Canadian models | |
| **RX-7 1979-81** | 7031 |
| Covers all U.S. and Canadian models | |
| **SAAB 99 1969-75** | 5988 |
| Covers all U.S. and Canadian models | |
| **SAAB 900 1979-85** | 7572 |
| Covers all U.S. and Canadian models | |
| **Snowmobiles 1976-80** | 6978 |
| Covers Arctic Cat, John Deere, Kawasaki, Polaris, Ski-Doo and Yamaha | |
| **Subaru 1970-84** | 6982 |
| Covers all U.S. and Canadian models | |
| **Tempest/GTO/LeMans 1968-73** | 5905 |
| Covers all U.S. and Canadian models | |
| **Toyota 1966-70** | 5795 |
| Covers all U.S. and Canadian models of Corona, MkII, Corolla, Crown, Land Cruiser, Stout and Hi-Lux | |
| **Toyota 1970-79 Spanish** | 7467 |
| **Toyota Celica/Supra 1971-85** | 7043 |
| Covers all U.S. and Canadian models | |
| **Toyota Trucks 1970-85** | 7035 |
| Covers all U.S. and Canadian models of pick-ups, Land Cruiser and 4Runner | |
| **Valiant/Duster 1968-76** | 6326 |
| Covers all U.S. and Canadian models | |
| **Volvo 1956-69** | 6529 |
| Covers all U.S. and Canadian models | |
| **Volvo 1970-83** | 7040 |
| Covers all U.S. and Canadian models | |
| **VW Front Wheel Drive 1974-85** | 6962 |
| Covers all U.S. and Canadian models | |
| **VW 1949-71** | 5796 |
| Covers all U.S. and Canadian models | |
| **VW 1970-79 Spanish** | 7081 |
| **VW 1970-81** | 6837 |
| Covers all U.S. and Canadian Beetles, Karmann Ghia, Fastback, Squareback, Vans, 411 and 412 | |

Chilton's Repair & Tune-Up Guides are available at your local retailer or by mailing a check or money order for **$13.95** plus **$3.25** to cover postage and handling to:

**Chilton Book Company
Dept. DM
Radnor, PA 19089**

NOTE: When ordering be sure to include your name & address, book part No. & title.